# Bending Adversity

# Bending Adversity

*Japan and the Art of Survival*

## DAVID PILLING

THE PENGUIN PRESS

NEW YORK

2014

THE PENGUIN PRESS
Published by the Penguin Group
Penguin Group (USA) LLC
375 Hudson Street
New York, New York 10014

USA · Canada · UK · Ireland · Australia
New Zealand · India · South Africa · China

penguin.com
A Penguin Random House Company

Published by The Penguin Press, a member of Penguin Group (USA) LLC, 2014

First published in Great Britain by Allen Lane, an imprint of Penguin Books Ltd.

Photograph credits appear on pages ix – x.

ISBN 9781594205842

Printed in the United States of America
1   3   5   7   9   10   8   6   4   2

*To Ingrid, Dylan and Travis*

*And to my Mum and Dad*

*With love and gratitude*

# Contents

# List of Illustrations

# List of Maps

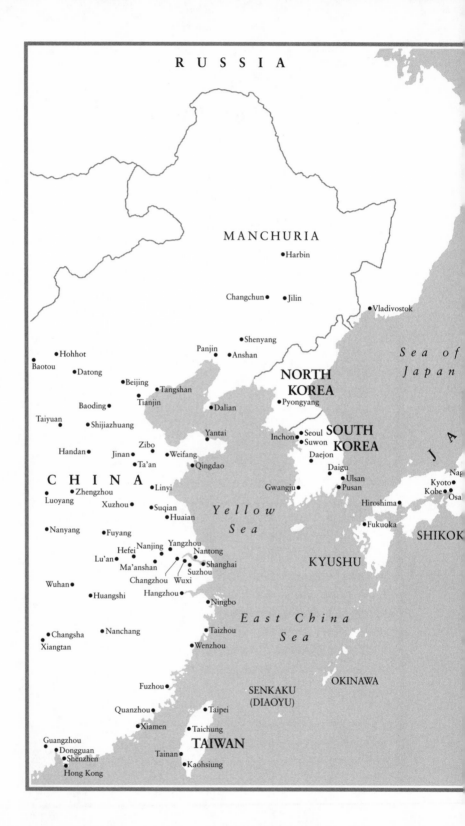

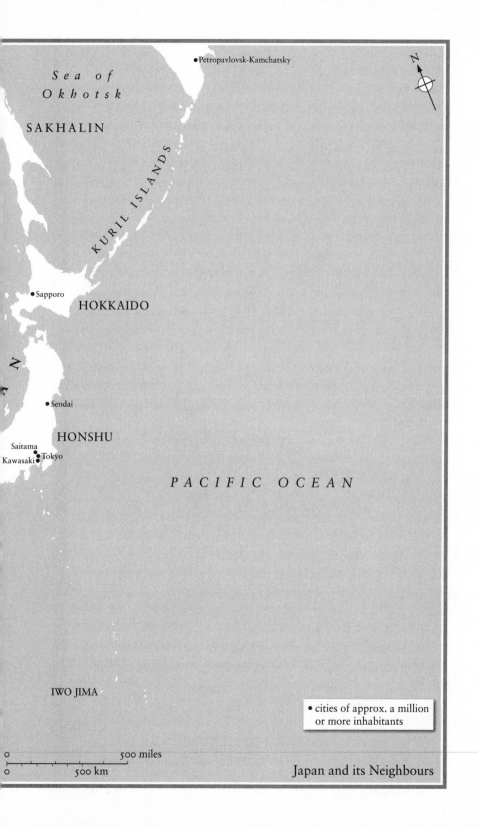

Sea of
Okhotsk

SAKHALIN

• Petropavlovsk-Kamchatsky

KURIL ISLANDS

• Sapporo

HOKKAIDO

• Sendai

HONSHU

Saitama
Kawasaki • Tokyo

PACIFIC OCEAN

IWO JIMA

• cities of approx. a million
or more inhabitants

0 ——————————— 500 miles

0 ——————————— 500 km

Japan and its Neighbours

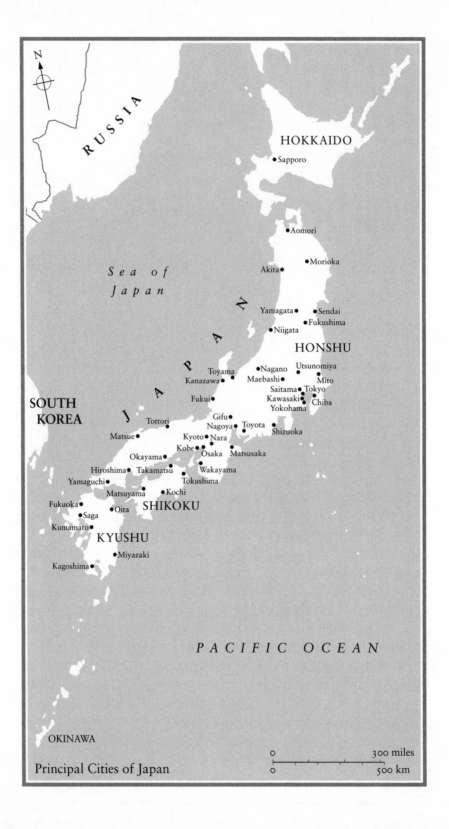

N

RUSSIA

*Sea of Japan*

HOKKAIDO

• Sapporo

• Aomori

Akita • • Morioka

Yamagata • • Sendai
• Fukushima
• Niigata

HONSHU

SOUTH
KOREA

J A P A N

Toyama •
Kanazawa •

Fukui •

Nagano •
Maebashi •

Utsunomiya •

• Mito
Saitama • Tokyo •
Kawasaki • • Chiba
Yokohama •

Tottori •

Gifu •
Nagoya • • Toyota
Kyoto • Nara •
Kobe • • Matsusaka
Osaka •

Shizuoka •

Matsue •

Okayama •

Hiroshima • Takamatsu •
Yamaguchi •
Matsuyama •

Fukuoka •
• Saga
• Oita
Kumamoto •

KYUSHU

Kagoshima •

• Miyazaki

Wakayama •
Tokushima •

Kochi •

SHIKOKU

PACIFIC OCEAN

OKINAWA

Principal Cities of Japan

0                    300 miles
0                    500 km

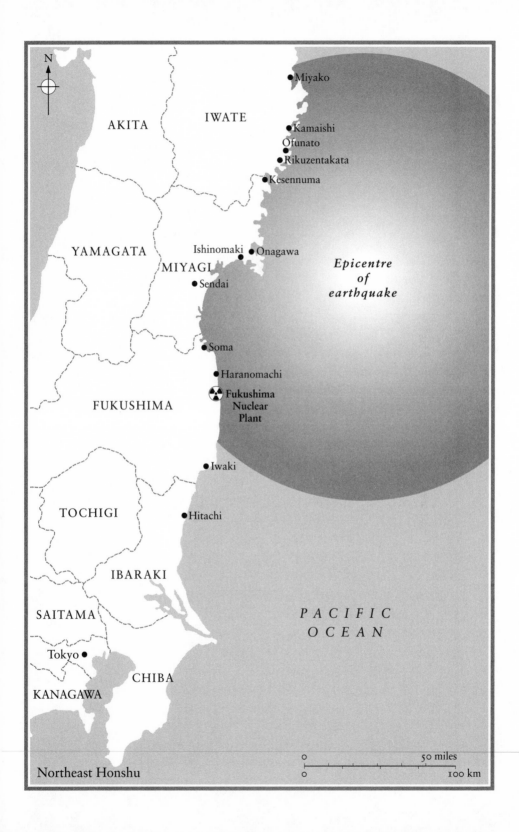

N

Miyako

AKITA

IWATE

Kamaishi
Ofunato
Rikuzentakata

Kesennuma

YAMAGATA

Ishinomaki ● Onagawa

MIYAGI

● Sendai

*Epicentre*
*of*
*earthquake*

● Soma

● Haranomachi

Fukushima
Nuclear
Plant

FUKUSHIMA

● Iwaki

● Hitachi

TOCHIGI

IBARAKI

SAITAMA

*PACIFIC*
*OCEAN*

Tokyo ●

CHIBA

KANAGAWA

Northeast Honshu

0          50 miles

0          100 km

*We are lost and we don't know which way we should go. But this is a very natural thing, a very healthy thing.*

Haruki Murakami,
Tokyo, January 2003

# Foreword

All books come from somewhere. This one was swept into existence by a giant wave. For me, the catalyst for writing about Japan was the earthquake and tsunami of March 2011. I had lived in Japan as a foreign correspondent from 2001 to 2008, and had often thought about writing a book back then. But the daily pressures of news reporting and my own lack of urgency ensured that the idea of a book remained just that – an idea. I left Japan at the end of 2008 and went on to other things. When the earthquake struck on 11 March 2011, I flew to Japan to cover the disaster both in the immediate aftermath and over the ensuing months. The scale and horror of the catastrophe, and the way the Japanese sought to confront it, provided impetus for an idea that had lain dormant in my mind for several years. My aim was to create a portrait of a stubbornly resistant nation with a history of overcoming successive waves of adversity from would-be Mongolian invasions to repeated natural disasters. The portrait would be rooted in my own seven years' experience of reporting and living in the country during a time of economic slowdown and loss of national confidence, but one told, as far as possible, through the voices of Japanese people themselves. It would largely be a portrait of contemporary Japan, a country that, in spite of its obvious difficulties, is changing and adapting in ways that are often invisible to the outside world. But it would also be a depiction rooted in its historical context, since events in the present are rarely fully comprehensible without reference to the past. That is certainly true of Japan, where history and tradition are ubiquitous, peeping from behind the endless concrete of what can seem one of the most relentlessly modern urban landscapes on earth.

This, then, is not a book *about* the tsunami. The scope is much broader. But the 'triple disaster' of earthquake, tsunami and nuclear meltdown provided a starting point for an enquiry into how Japanese institutions and, just as important, Japanese people, have dealt with adversity. As the crisis unfolded, there were many failings as well as much to admire, but the tragedy reminded us of what we should not have forgotten: the extraordinary resilience of a people who live in one of the most naturally unstable regions on earth. In Hong Kong, where I now live, in the disaster's aftermath, many marvelled at the television images of orderly lines outside shops and in evacuation centres; they admired the quiet dignity of survivors; and they shook their heads in wonderment at the near-absence of crime. A country supposedly on its knees after two decades of stagnation had shown itself stronger than many had given it credit for. It highlighted what Pico Iyer, an author and long-time resident, called 'the self-possession and community-mindedness that are so striking in Japan; suddenly, the country that had seemed to insist on its difference from the rest of the world could be seen in its more human, compassionate and brave dimensions'.[1]

The disaster revealed, too, if only for an instant, Japan's continuing relevance to the world. Even most Japanese were unaware that the northeast of their country, where the tsunami hit, produced anything other than rice, fish and sake. Though hardly Japan's industrial heartland, the northeastern Tohoku region turned out to be a vital link in the global supply chain. One factory alone produced 40 per cent of the world's micro-controllers, the 'little brains' that run power steering in cars and the images on flat-screen televisions. After the tsunami destroyed the plant that makes them, halfway round the world in Louisiana, General Motors was forced to suspend vehicle production. Likewise, because of electricity shortages after the Fukushima nuclear crisis, Japan – already the world's biggest importer of liquefied natural gas – stepped up its purchases of LNG, oil and subsequently coal, becoming an important swing factor in global energy demand.

What the Japanese call 'Japan bashing' stems partly from the country's continued importance to the global economy. No one bothers much to bash Switzerland, which also grew at approximately 1 per cent a year in the 1990s, thus suffering, by the Japanese yardstick, its own 'lost decade'. But Switzerland, though an important financial centre, is a smallish economy. Japan has shrunk in relative terms, but still accounts for 8 per cent of global output against 3.4 per cent for Britain and 20 per cent for the US. Japan is the world's biggest creditor nation, not its biggest debtor as is sometimes supposed. It has the second highest foreign exchange reserves and by 2012 was again vying with China to be the biggest holder of US debt. The tsunami briefly reminded people of these neglected facts. It was ironic that, just when Japan was truly in the midst of crisis, some people should be reminded of how important it still was.

Of course, the crisis also revealed much weakness. Many argued that the tsunami, which destroyed factories, roads and other infrastructure worth an astonishing 10 per cent of GDP, would be the final nail in Japan's economic coffin. If nothing else, it would accelerate what was already the slow exodus of manufacturing to China and other cheaper production bases. Even worse than Japan's economic vulnerability was evidence of a rotten body politic. The crisis at Fukushima exposed an official culture riddled with paternalism, complacency and deceit. The risks of a nuclear catastrophe in the most seismically unstable country on earth ought to have been foreseeable, as should the vulnerability of plants so close to a tsunami-prone coastline. Bureaucrats, politicians and nuclear plant operators were blinded by their faith in Japanese technology and organization. In other ways too, the Japanese state was shown to be unprepared. Some old people's homes had inadequate, or non-existent, evacuation procedures. After the disaster, it took too long for the central government to identify needs on the ground and to meet them with financial and technical help. Too much was left to the legendary diehard patience of the people of northeast Japan themselves. Japan's response may have been far better than that of the US in 2005 after Hurricane Katrina, but it left much to be desired.

Still, great moments of crisis have proved decisive turning points in Japanese history before. Some hoped the country, literally jolted from its complacency, would rediscover its lost energy. John Dower, whose book *Embracing Defeat* is perhaps the greatest study by a foreign scholar of post-war Japan, talked of the clarity that can come from such moments. 'Things are cracked open and things can be put in motion,' he told me not long after the tsunami. The tragedy, he said, had provided a fresh opportunity for ordinary Japanese – not just its politicians and bureaucrats – to rethink priorities and to remake their society. 'The question is can they do it again?' he asked. 'Will these ideas be squelched because of the entrenched, gridlocked system? Or can this help create a more participatory democracy, can people be mobilized as they have on occasions in the past, and challenge what is going on?'[2]

The title of this book, *Bending Adversity*, comes from a Japanese proverb about transforming bad fortune into good. Japan has a remarkable track record of confronting and transcending adversity. Virtually alone in Asia, it resisted the colonial predations of western powers. After 1945, it overcame its own crushing defeat by blazing an economic trail that has had a profound impact on all of Asia, including China. In both instances, it found some sort of path through adversity. Sometimes, though, rather than bending adversity to its own advantage, Japan has instead been bent by circumstance. Its island status has provided it security and a firm sense of itself, yet too often it has been a prisoner of its geography and an island mentality. Its nineteenth-century struggle to ward off colonial intent ended up in an imperial endeavour of its own that caused the death of millions and its own near-annihilation. If this was bending adversity, it had perhaps been better left unbent. Even its post-war economic miracle, so impressive in so many ways, could seem to some like a soulless exercise in wealth accumulation, a search for international prestige through manufacturing and commerce where war and conquest had failed. Though Japan had found the key to economic development, it had perhaps lost something of itself in the process.

Now it has lost its economic vigour too. Paradoxically, as Haruki Murakami, the best-selling author, once suggested to me, this may give it a better chance of finding itself again. Along with post-bubble drift has come an existential angst, a probing for a way forward. Japan was lost, he said, but to be lost is not always a bad thing. A friend, echoing those sentiments, recently wrote to me of her fellow Japanese, 'People are lost. They lost their model and they lost themselves.' But in the disappearance of something old lies the possibility of something new – at least a chance to bend adversity and turn it into something better.

I arrived in Japan in the winter of 2001. Before I started my job as a foreign correspondent in Tokyo, I spent a month beginning to learn the language while I was living with a family in the castle town of Kanazawa, a sort of mini-Kyoto on the rugged Sea of Japan coast. Kanazawa was a charming place with much of its medieval heritage preserved. It had samurai and geisha quarters, a famous garden called Kenroku-en – like most famous sights in Japan, diplomatically said to be one of the 'best three' in the country – and a thriving artistic community of potters, gold-leaf craftsmen and amateur Noh dramatists. On my first day, fresh off the plane from London, I was taken to the sixteenth-century moated castle, an imposing whitewashed structure set on huge stone walls, to attend a tea ceremony. Dozens of people had gathered on a gazebo-like platform in the castle grounds, where the ritual was to take place. I was ushered by my 'host mother', Mrs Nishida, to the very front so that I could sit as close as possible to the proceedings. A woman in kimono prepared the hot water in a sunken hearth, spooning out green powder with a wooden scoop and whisking it with a long brush. Every action she performed, from the way she knelt to her handling of the tea bowl, was precise and rehearsed – a mirror of the actions made in countless other tea ceremonies down the ages. I sat, as did everyone else, in *seiza* style, legs and feet folded beneath my buttocks, back straight. After a few minutes of initial pain, my limbs grew used to the position and I concentrated on what was going on around me. When the tea was served, we first ate an exquisite handmade sweet, separating it into bite-sized pieces with a small wooden utensil like a large toothpick. Then we earnestly examined the tea bowl's shape and glaze, and felt the heat of the tea penetrate the fired clay. We rotated the bowl two quarter-turns, before downing the pleasantly bitter, jade-green liquid in quick, noisy slurps.

Japan is a country of performances and role-playing: here we were all actors in a centuries-old pageant, our every action dictated by custom. When the ceremony was over, the other guests rose and took their leave. My lower limbs, however, had lost all feeling and standing was impossible. I was left, alone on the stage, waiting for what seemed like several minutes while a painful tingle slowly crept up my legs as sensation returned. I still regard the experience as my initiation into the pains and pleasures of Japan.

From my first days in Kanazawa, I resolved to embrace the new culture in which I found myself. I ate the food I was served, whether it was crab brains, sea urchin or raw octopus. Slowly I discovered that almost everything the Japanese prepared, however unfamiliar, was fresh and delicious – better, in fact, than any food I had tasted before. At the age of thirty-seven, I plunged into the study of the Japanese language, working my way through a series of exams that obliged me to learn more than 2,000 *kanji* characters and obscure grammatical constructions. (I eventually learned to read fairly fluently and to conduct stilted interviews, but my Japanese remained like Samuel Johnson's description of a dog walking on its hind legs: it was not done well, though at my age it was perhaps surprising to find it done at all.) In Kanazawa, I learned to love the routine of living on tatami, the traditional rush-mat flooring. One removed one's shoes at the house entrance known as the *genkan*, knelt on the floor to watch TV and unrolled one's futon at night. The tatami had a comforting, musky smell. Bathing was in a square upright tub, in which you sat only after a thorough scrub in a separate shower area. Sometimes we would walk to the local public bath with its old-fashioned municipal tiles. It had outdoor communal pools of cold, warm and hot sulfurous water and vibrating massage chairs of worn leather in the changing room.

I loved that Japanese people always put their hands together to thank their food before they ate it, and the way they apologized before they asked for money in a shop as though payment sullied the otherwise pleasant human interaction. I learned the correct place at which guests should sit at a table – furthest from the door, a position in former times that was safest from surprise attack. I gained an appreciation for small, considerate gestures. My teacher had told me, for example, that it was rude in a business conversation to say that you were busy, since this might imply that you were more in demand than the person to whom you were speaking. I liked it that even cheap restaurants handed out a hot hand towel before you ate and that, when it rained, there was a machine at the department store to seal your wet umbrella in a plastic cover. I marvelled at how social convention trumped laws. The streets were entirely litter-free. No one would dream of answering their mobile phone on the train or in a lift, not because it was illegal but because consideration was expected. Even in the street, people cupped their hands over mouth and phone to muffle the sound of their voice.

When I got to Tokyo to start my job, I was enthralled all over again. Its urban thrum, theatres and galleries and astonishing variety of restaurants, clubs and bars made it the New York of Asia, only far bigger, with a population, in the greater metropolis, of 36 million people. Yet Tokyo was anything but the faceless conurbation I had imagined. Most big cities have been described as a collection of villages. But Tokyo, more than any other, deserves that description. City neighbourhoods, including the one I moved to in Higashi Kitazawa, are still organized into village-sized units. At festival times, bankers to bricklayers gather to pound rice into soft *mochi* cakes. At night, they dress in short cotton indigo *happi* coats, with bare legs and sandals, and heave the local shrine like a palanquin through the narrow, paper-lantern-lit streets. Tokyo is a maze of hundreds of *shotengai*, crowded little shopping streets with tiny, almost shack-like shops offering homemade tofu, traditional sweets, flowers, sushi, fruit or sacks of rice. The back streets are so narrow they are difficult, if not impossible, to access by car. In most of Tokyo, the favoured mode of transport is the bicycle. The city doesn't have enough big parks, but the back alleys are a jumble of potted plants and greenery sprouting out of every crack and crevice. Tokyo feels surprisingly close to nature as though the buildings could, at any point, fall back into the soil. In the summer the deafening trill of cicadas drowns out the traffic. Some restaurants turn off the lights and let loose fireflies so customers can watch them flash in the night air. There are little shrines to foxes and fish and even one to eels. One of my most abiding memories is the sight of three blue-uniformed policemen standing outside Shinjuku Gyoen park in springtime, staring up in deadly earnest at the petals of a single cherry blossom. With a scandalous lack of crime to go around, they were examining the tiny pink flower with as much intensity as if they had chanced upon a corpse and a bloodstained knife.

I set about meeting as broad a cross-section of society as possible, from authors such as Haruki Murakami and Kenzaburo Oe to the prime minister of the day, Junichiro Koizumi. I met industrialists and bankers, politicians and bureaucrats, geisha, kabuki actors and sumo wrestlers. I interviewed people ordinary and extraordinary: car workers and health workers, activists and conservatives, liberal schoolteachers and traditionalist Shinto priests, teenagers and octogenarians. There were many irritants and things to dislike, but all in all I found Japan an enchanting place in which to live, particularly as a foreigner enjoying all the benefits of a smooth-running society with none of the responsibilities. If quality of life meant individually wrapped biscuits and an impeccably maintained aquarium at your local metro station, then Japan won hands down. Where else would it be possible to leave your laptop on a café table safe in the knowledge that it would still be there on your return? What other country had gone through years of severe financial crisis with few obvious signs of social strife?

There was a relentless pessimism, even sneering bitterness, in much writing about Japan that I found hard to reconcile with the largely comfortable society around me. Though I arrived at the end of Japan's first 'lost decade' and in what was supposed to be a deep recession at the start of its second, there was scant evidence of deprivation, certainly much less than I was used to seeing in my native Britain. Japan had huge problems: an ageing society, a scandalously high suicide rate, school bullying, a large and growing public debt, a stuttering economy and an imploding electronics industry. But there was little sense of crisis (though some people claimed that was precisely the problem). Overall it seemed an affluent, and in many ways a vibrant, society, one comfortable with being both very Japanese and very modern.

Many people told me that if I wanted to find hardship, I should leave the Tokyo bubble, and visit the poor provincial towns or isolated rural communities abandoned by all but the very old. In my subsequent travels around the country, which took me to nearly all of Japan's forty-seven prefectures, I certainly came upon pockets of misery, a general foreboding about the future and even outright poverty. There were shuttered high streets and depressed industries and villages full of octogenarians struggling on without much outside help. Some people, especially the young, seemed to be drifting and directionless. But in most places I found a society largely intact and comfortable in its assumptions, albeit one struggling to adapt to new circumstances.

Whether one sees in another country a glass half full or one half empty may be largely a matter of temperament. If this book occasionally puts a more positive gloss on modern Japan than some accounts, I hope that this will not be mistaken as naivety. The reader will find much that is negative too. Yet the relentless pessimism of much coverage of Japan is, in its way, as misguided as the hopeless boosterism of the 1980s. Then, Japan was said by many experts to be taking over the world with its unstoppable economic machine. Today, the default position is to see a glass not so much half empty, as one cracked on the bottom with the remaining contents fast draining away. Japan, we are told, is unable to rejuvenate and so must continue to sink. Its industry is dying, its women are suppressed, its people are suicidal, its society closed and its debt unpayable. There is an element of truth to much of this, but it does not tell the whole story. Some have sought to present a picture of Japan as almost psychologically sick, based on accounts of its infantile obsessions and hoards of 'shut-in' teenagers who never leave the house. But that would be like depicting the US solely as a country of mass shootings, drug addiction and urban segregation, or the UK as nothing more than a class-ridden society with an underbelly of hooliganism and nightly stabbings. These would be gross caricatures. Any country, including Japan, deserves to be seen in more rounded terms. For all its problems, Japan remains a resilient, adaptive society. Its history suggests it has the ability to confront and eventually overcome many of the difficulties it faces – some of which, incidentally, are not unique to Japan as often assumed.

The way change occurs in Japan has occasionally been compared to the rebuilding of the shrine at Ise, Shinto's most sacred site, which reputedly dates back to the third century. The shrine is not what one might expect. There are actually 125 separate places of worship, each dedicated to a different deity. All the surrounding woodland is sacred, making Ise less St Paul's Cathedral and more Hyde Park with gods. Every twenty years, the simple wooden shrines are razed to the ground≈and rebuilt to exactly the same specifications. The question of whether they are two decades – or two millennia – old is open to interpretation. Similarly, Japan has proven itself capable of extraordinary transformation, but always with reference to its past and own beliefs. It can remake itself, but it will use the same material. Henry Kissinger, former US secretary of state, once told Zhou Enlai, Mao Zedong's right-hand man, that he thought Japan's 'tribal outlook' made it capable of rapid change. Like other nations convinced of their own exceptionalism, including the US, Japan's historical ability to transform and rejuvenate in radical ways is rooted in a strong sense of itself. 'Japan believes that their society is so different that they can adjust to anything and preserve their national essence,' Kissinger said. 'Therefore the Japanese are capable of sudden explosive changes. They went from feudalism to emperor worship in two to three years. They went from emperor worship to democracy in three months.'[3]

Yoshio Sugimoto, a Japanese sociologist, says analysts are 'tempted to join either a "Japan-admiring camp", or a "Japan-bashing camp" and to portray its society in simplistic black-and-white terms'.[4] There are foreign observers, including those who have not been able to tear themselves away from the country for years, who regard it as an unredeemably xenophobic, misogynist society, hierarchical, shut off from new ideas, and unable to square up to its own history. Others see some of the things I glimpsed in Kanazawa – social cohesion, a sense of tradition and politeness, a dedication to excellence and relative equality. The two views are hardly irreconcilable. Sugimoto recommends a 'trade-off model', which focuses on the ways in which 'both desirable and undesirable elements are interlinked'.

Let's take one tiny example. We may admire the fact that an apprentice of *bunraku* puppetry – in which three puppeteers manipulate a single doll – takes thirty years to learn his trade. First, he must work the legs of the puppet for ten years before being allowed to take charge of the left arm. After another decade he can graduate to the head and right arm. Only after a further ten years is he considered a true master. In some performances, the face of the main puppeteer is visible to the audience, a sign of his accomplishment, while the heads of his two junior accomplices are covered in black hoods so as not to distract the audience from the action. Such fastidiousness is seen in almost all walks of life. Some sushi masters will not let their apprentices handle fish for years. A bonsai master told me he spent three years, without pay, before his teacher would allow him to prune a tree. Such obsessive respect for detail and decorum helps explain the exquisite standards encountered throughout Japan from restaurant kitchen to factory floor. Only in Japan will you regularly observe people cleaning the grout between tiles with a toothbrush. And yet, we may observe, how stifling of innovation and crushing of spirit it is to insist on such mind-numbing discipline, born of the outmoded idea of an apprentice absorbing received wisdom from an infallible master. The artist Yayoi Kusama, who coats her canvases in uncontrollable outbreaks of polka-dots, once told me that the master–pupil relationship made her 'want to vomit'. She escaped to the US to pursue her art. It is hard, if not impossible, to reconcile our admiration for the products of Japanese society with qualms about how they are produced.

To take another small example, we may mock morning calisthenics at Japanese companies as ridiculous, and evidence of 'groupthink'. In Tokyo, I often looked out amusedly as construction workers in their matching uniforms gathered at a building site for morning group exercises. At the same time, I couldn't repress a sneaking admiration for a practice that undoubtedly contributed to the health and well-being of the Japanese – many of whom remain enviably lean and agile into advanced age – and which 'democratized' exercise by removing it from the ghetto of the private fitness club.

Such trade-offs are present in any society. But they can be a useful way of thinking about Japan. In business, for example, Japanese companies are often criticized for being too reluctant to lay off workers and improve efficiency. This harms shareholders, whose returns are suppressed because a company's prime concern is not increasing profits. Such practices also cushion the forces of creative destruction through which dynamic economies, such as the US, are constantly shifting labour and resources to more productive areas, breaking down old industries to build up new ones. On the other hand, Japan has a far lower jobless rate than many other countries – about 4 per cent. That means the state pays less in unemployment benefits and society pays less in the social side effects of long-term unemployment, such as higher crime or illness. There may well be a trade-off in terms of lower corporate productivity. Perhaps more ruthlessly efficient economies do better in the long run. But striking an appropriate balance between stakeholder and shareholder capitalism is a legitimate matter for debate in any democratic society.

The same trade-off model might, at the extreme, even apply to what many identify as perhaps Japan's greatest flaw, its inward looking 'Galapagos mentality'. Understandably, this is usually described in a wholly negative light. It has hampered, and continues to hamper, Japan's proper integration into what Yukichi Fukuzawa, a liberal nineteenth-century thinker, called the 'give-and-take of the rest of the world'. Japan is too closed to foreign investment and immigration for its own good. On the other hand, Japan's sense of itself as a nation apart has helped preserve what many most admire about the country. Pico Iyer, who has lived in Kyoto for twenty-five years, told me that what he regarded as the strangeness and delight of Japanese culture would not exist if its society were more open. 'Having a very strong sense of who is inside the group and who is not is what allows Japan to function so seamlessly and harmoniously,' he said. 'The society reminds me of an orchestra in which everyone is playing from the same score and everyone knows her part perfectly, and everything goes beautifully so long as everyone does her bit.' Not all foreign visitors are so forgiving. David Mitchell, the author of *Cloud Atlas*, once told me a story about when he was living with his Japanese wife and two young children in the claustrophobic atmosphere of Hagi, an old samurai town in western Japan. The mothers at school routinely referred to his children as 'half', the standard – and to the Japanese inoffensive – term for someone who is half Japanese. The word upset Mitchell, who spent hours explaining that his children were not 'half', but 'both', a perfect whole. The Japanese, he concluded, were not good at living on cultural 'borders or thresholds'. After a year, Mitchell took his young family back to Ireland.

Sugimoto's 'trade-off model' doesn't work perfectly. It can set up false dichotomies. Japan could very plausibly be more open and international and just as civil and harmonious. Strong, confident societies can absorb foreign influences – and people – without disrupting their basic equilibrium. Japan would do well to throw open its universities to foreign students and encourage more of its own young people to fan out across the world, as its Meiji pioneers did, in search of new ideas. Perhaps Japan could even find a way of combining better business efficiency with low levels of unemployment, or learn how to foster a generation of rugged individualists nevertheless willing to participate in group calisthenics. Social systems, however, are not always easy to disentangle. Their strengths are often their weaknesses and vice versa. Cultures are not menus from which one can order à la carte.

Partly for that reason, this book is light on prescription. Those looking for a lecture on how the Japanese should revive their economy or overhaul their 'mindset' may be disappointed. For the record, I don't disagree with some of the standard prescriptions. In my opinion, Japan would indeed be a better place if it were less closed, less conservative, more aware of its recently violent history and more willing to unleash the talents of its women. It would benefit if it could foster a more participatory democracy and stabilize its dysfunctional political system. Doubtless, it should work harder too at generating more economic growth – perhaps through a combination of economic liberalization, more open trade and more aggressive monetary policy. It would be a more dynamic society if it had more entrepreneurs willing to take a risk and an education system that produced more original thinkers. In the medium turn, it may indeed need to raise taxes or cut spending, or both, if it is to clear up its fiscal mess. Yet to say so does not get us very far. It is not as if many academics and policymakers in Japan haven't said much the same thing. The shopping list of what Japan 'ought to do' may be obvious, but it can also be glib and unsatisfying.

This book, then, will concentrate on Japan as I find it, not Japan as I would like it to be. My assumption is that it is a society in the process of adapting and evolving, albeit in its own, sometimes frustrating, way. And if we should not think of Japan as fixed and unchanging, neither should we treat it as homogenous. Though the Japanese harbour an image of themselves as uniquely harmonious, theirs is a country, as any other, cut across by class, region, gender and age, challenged by subcultures and shaped by structural change. Any utterance that begins with the phrase 'the Japanese think' should be treated with utmost scepticism. In deference to that reality, these pages seek to allow, wherever feasible, the Japanese to speak for themselves, in all their diversity and noisy disagreement. Some of these opinions are critiqued along the way, but many are presented more or less unfiltered – as I found them.

Part I of the book, 'Tsunami', is an account of how ordinary people, especially in the coastal towns most affected by the catastrophe of 11 March 2011, confronted the disaster. I spent ten days reporting from Japan right after the earthquake and returned many times in subsequent months, as well as in the following year. From interviews and contemporaneous accounts, I try to reconstruct what went on in the terrifying moments right after the tsunami struck Rikuzentakata, a fishing town of some 23,000 residents in Iwate prefecture. I also report my own impressions from the nearby town of Ofunato in the days, weeks and months after the disaster. These chapters introduce the idea of Japanese resilience as witnessed in a single event. For a deeper understanding, however, of how Japan adapts and survives, we need to delve into the history and culture of a country that, constantly threatened by earthquakes, tsunamis, volcanoes and typhoons, has long been 'primed for adversity'.[5]

Part II, 'Double-bolted Land', contains a chapter about how Japan came to see itself as a nation apart. Geographically it lies in Asia, off the coast of China, whose national resurgence is the great story of our age. Part of its resilience stems from its own sense of separateness, though I will argue that this is as much a source of weakness as of strength. In the nineteenth century, confronted by the superior technologies of the west, Japan made a decisive break with the Sinocentric world and modelled itself on the 'Great Powers' of Europe. It ditched feudalism and modernized. Then it embarked on a brutal and disastrous imperial project, rooted in a racist imperial cult. The upshot was tragedy and near self-destruction. As a consequence, today, Japan stands isolated in its own region, its relations with neighbours, particularly China and South Korea, stalked by history. Neither European nor fully Asian, Japan can seem adrift, its only diplomatic anchor a 'client state' relationship with the United States. Even stockbrokers refer to 'Asia ex-Japan'.

Part III, 'Decades Found and Lost', begins by briefly tracing the country's remarkable recovery from the ruins of war to economic might in the 1970s and 80s. More recently, that has been followed by a long period of relative stagnation after the collapse of the bubble in 1990 and the twin crises of 1995, when an earthquake brought much of Kobe crashing down and a religious cult targeted commuters on the Tokyo subway. That year, as Murakami said, was a turning point for Japan: it brought home to ordinary people a realization that there was no going back to the pre-bubble era. During its fast-growth years, the drive to catch up with western living standards was, to a fault, the central feature of Japan's post-war national project. Though Japan has basically succeeded in that goal, the bursting of the bubble has deprived it of its sense of national purpose. It has lost what the Japanese call its *konjo* – its 'guts' or its 'fighting spirit'.

Part IV, 'Life after Growth', deals with how contemporary Japan has sought to adjust. The book will contend that the country has not stood still, as some would have it, though its transition has been imperfect and is far from complete. Two chapters dealing with the economy – 'Japan as Number Three' and 'Life after Growth' – argue that Japan has preserved living standards and social cohesion better than commonly acknowledged. Its economy, though hardly robust, has not performed as badly as many think. Japan has become a sort of lazy shorthand for everything that can go wrong with an economy. Yet, when considered from the point of view of Japanese living standards, rather than investor returns or the size of the Japanese economy in relation to others, the past twenty years have not been all that disastrous.

Japan has avoided deep damage to its living standards partly – perhaps largely – through the as-yet-unknown cost of accumulating a huge public debt. Some argue that this will inevitably end in crisis. At some point the state is likely to renege on these obligations, either by outright default (unlikely), cutting social welfare, or eroding it away through inflation. At that stage we may look back and conclude that Japanese leaders ought to have moved much more quickly to tackle deep-seated structural problems. Japan has prioritized stability over radical change. It might perhaps have done better to allow more bankruptcies and aggressive industrial restructuring in the interest of longer-term economic rejuvenation.

As Europe and the US are now finding out, however, recovery from a severe financial shock is not easy. When push came to shove, even the US, for which adherence to the free market is a creed, was not willing to allow its banks or its car industry to go bust. At the start of 2013, US unemployment was roughly 8 per cent and the economy still fragile, though showing signs of recovery. In Britain, unemployment was also nearly twice Japan's. The UK's economy had contracted 4 per cent since 2008. The situation in countries such as Spain and Greece was far worse still. Like Japan, then, other countries are having to grapple with higher deficits, lower growth and previously undreamed-of experiments in monetary policy needed just to keep their economies afloat. Japan is often viewed as a cautionary tale. The true lesson, though, may not be how badly it has coped with the collapse of an asset bubble, but, more worryingly, how relatively well. When it comes to asset bubbles, the most important lesson Japan may have to teach the world is: at all costs, avoid them in the first place.

The chapter 'Samurai with a Quiff' deals with the years from 2001 to 2006 when Junichiro Koizumi, the most charismatic prime minister in a generation, led the country. It was an extraordinary period when people rallied around a leader promising radical change. Koizumi sought to breathe new life into a political system that had festered in the new, lower-growth era. His threat to destroy his own party and end a fifty-year-old political hegemony eventually came to pass, though no robust two-party system has yet taken hold to replace the old status quo. Japan's political system remains unequal to its task. Two subsequent chapters – 'The Promised Road' and 'From Behind the Screen' – deal with the social change that followed the breakdown of Japan's post-war model. Life has become less certain and, for many, particularly women and young people, less secure. But with the erosion of old certainties comes opportunity. These chapters look at how Japanese people are grappling with these issues.

Part V, 'Adrift', discusses Japan's severe diplomatic challenge in an era when its power has faded and that of China is on the rise. China's awakening is uncomfortable for Japan given the unresolved issues of memory and territory that still reverberate around the region. A dispute with China over a tiny group of uninhabited islands between Okinawa and Taiwan has become a new focal point of rancour between the two countries. The perceived threat from China has opened old wounds in Japan about its place in the world and its sense of identity.

Part VI, 'After the Tsunami', attempts to look more closely at what has changed in Japanese society, and what has not. The events at Fukushima suggest that much of 'old Japan' remains intact. The failure to deal properly with the nuclear crisis or to act honestly with the public is evidence of a highly flawed political and bureaucratic system. Yet some good things emerged from the disaster too. Japan became more aware of its links with the rest of the world as donations poured in from far and wide. One foreign ministry official was nearly in tears when she told me that the city of Kandahar in Afghanistan had scraped together $50,000 to help reconstruction. The Japanese rediscovered the northeast of their country, revered by poets for its spectacular beauty, but long ignored by the rest of Japan as rural and backward. Now they came to appreciate the incredible endurance of its people: in Japanese it was called *gamanzuyoi* – steadfast patience. Volunteers flocked to the area to help clear up the rubble and dig out the mud. Civil society, bolstered by new laws passed in recent years, also came out stronger after the tsunami. Japan has not always been the harmonious society of repute. In the immediate aftermath of war, there were frequent ideological clashes between left and right over how the past should be remembered and how a future should be built. The fast growth of the 1960s dulled dissent, but in recent years, Japanese have begun to rediscover what it is to organize, to debate and to challenge the consensus. That came out more powerfully after Fukushima as an anti-nuclear movement gathered force and as people affected by the tsunami and nuclear contamination pressed for compensation.

Finally, in the fishing towns of northeast Japan, once the debris had been cleared and the bodies counted, ordinary Japanese citizens revealed tremendous humanity and fortitude as they tried to put their lives back together again. One Japanese playwright said their actions drew on 'an intriguing tradition of forging onward while holding on to a sense of our own impermanence'.[6] The only thing they could count on was that, one day, a tsunami would come again. In many cases, they showed a pioneering spirit more reminiscent of the rugged

American West than the uniformity and dependence on top–down authority sometimes mistakenly associated with Japan. After the great quake and tsunami of 2011, the people of the northeast didn't wait for a government in which they had little faith anyway. Instead, they took control of their own situation and started from the ground up. It is in their stories of perseverance and survival that we should seek both hope and inspiration.

# PART ONE

# Tsunami

# I

# Tsunami

It was in 1666 that the local potentate, a former engineer by the name of Heitazaemon Yamazaki, ordered the wealthy merchants of what became Rikuzentakata to plant pine trees. The sturdy black pines were to be located on a one-and-a-half mile strip of sandy beach that stood between the small town and the vast Pacific Ocean. The jagged stretch of coastline in this distant and isolated northeastern part of Japan, itself in those days a remote feudal island, was then, as it is now, among the world's richest in seafood. All along the coast, the waters were abundant in kelp and a startling variety of fish and crustaceans. But it could also be a deadly place. The salt winds and high tides were poison to the farmland. And once every generation or so – infrequently enough to push to the back of one's mind, but not so uncommon as to forget entirely – a monstrous wave would surge in from the horizon to wreak destruction upon the town.

And so, some 350 years ago, the residents of Rikuzentakata planted trees in the hope of providing their homes and farms with some protection from the wind, the salt and the sea. In the first seven years of their endeavour, 18,000 pines were planted. Subsequent generations added to the natural barrier. The project became more urgent when the goldmines in the nearby mountains were exhausted, obliging Rikuzentakata to step up its production of rice and other crops. By the mid-eighteenth century, there were no fewer than 70,000 pines lined up like a defensive army in close formation beside the ocean. Locals strolled through the grove's shaded pathways or took picnics by the shore. Young couples doubtless courted in its secret shadows. In more modern times, the 70,000 pines became a tourist attraction. In 1927, the year after Emperor Hirohito came to the throne, the beach was designated as one of the 100 most beautiful landscapes in all of Japan. The venerable trees stood along the white sandy beach, between the wooden houses of Rikuzentakata and the narrow cove that, together with the other steep inlets along this wild and beautiful coast, form a serrated pattern like the teeth of a hacksaw.

In yet more recent times, in 1989 to be exact, the year of Emperor Hirohito's death, a building went up just behind the beach. At seven storeys tall, built of little white bricks and boasting a spiral staircase to match the one on the *Titanic*'s first-class deck, the Capital Hotel was the tallest – and certainly the grandest – structure in town. In the lobby was hung a large painting depicting young children playing, carefree, by the beach. Glass doors led out to an oval-shaped swimming pool on the veranda. There was even a special retreat for the use of young brides as they changed for the wedding ceremonies that were held in the hotel's sumptuous surroundings. The room's location was such that, as the young women prepared for their nuptials, they were afforded a perfect view of Rikuzentakata's celebrated pines.

The Capital Hotel had been built with money made during the go-go years of the 1980s bubble era, a time of legendary excess. When the bubble burst, the hotel was taken over by the local municipality, as were so many bubble-era follies. The principal investors had been the president of a construction company and a local singer of tear-filled *enka* ballads, both of whom had wanted to put something back into the local economy. And the Capital Hotel was certainly something. In the rugged town of 23,000 people, its white-painted façade and beachside location made it the natural place for locals to hold their celebrations, their trade association dinners and their funerals. As Kazuyoshi Sasaki, the hotel's sales manager, said, 'For a small town in the countryside, this really was a beautiful hotel.'

Sasaki was stockily built for a Japanese man, with a pleasant round face and a self-deprecating sense of humour. Even when he was talking about the gravest of matters, there was always the faintest flicker of a smile on his lips. Now in his late fifties, he was born in Rikuzentakata, as were his parents and their parents and their parents before that. Indeed, it was in 1734, when Japan was almost completely shut off from the outside world, that Sasaki's ancestors had established a small business to extract tea-seed oil from camellias. Their shop was called Aburaya. Over the years, the business grew to become a general food manufacturer and wholesale distributor, passed down from generation to generation into the nineteenth, twentieth and, finally, into the twenty-first century. In 2006, after more than 270 years in business, Aburaya went bust, brought low as Rikuzentakata's population dwindled and amid stiff competition from bigger, slicker outlets. Sasaki's first impulse was to flee the town, unable to stand the shame, as he saw it, of having let down his employees and his ancestors. But the company needed to be wound up in orderly fashion. And so he and his wife stayed on in Rikuzentakata, and Sasaki found another job – at the Capital Hotel.

On the morning of 11 March 2011, a Friday, Sasaki had gone on behalf of the hotel to pay his last respects to Yukio Shimizu, a city council member who had just passed away. Many people had gathered for the vigil in which friends and relatives bid farewell to the deceased so that the soul can more readily make its journey to *yomi no kuni*, the other world. Mourners burn incense and stay up through the night, chanting prayers to keep the deceased company. Sasaki had gone to the house to discuss the final seating arrangements for the Buddhist funeral service that was to take place at the Capital Hotel on the following day. The house where Shimizu's vigil was held was on higher ground in the hills above the flat valley floor in which the town of Rikuzentakata was spread out. Sasaki would later note the irony. 'If they hadn't been at the wake,' he said, with a half smile, 'many of those people would likely have died.'

Sasaki himself did not stay long at the house. Instead, in the early afternoon, he returned to the Capital Hotel, where he entered his office at 2.46 p.m. He recalls the time exactly, to the minute in fact. For it was at precisely that moment that the ground started shaking.

The Japanese have long been accustomed to earthquakes. In years gone by, they blamed these periodic events on Onamazu, a giant catfish on whose back the Japanese islands were said to rest. Usually, the catfish was pinned beneath the mud by a mammoth slab of rock held in place by the powerful Shinto god of the earth, Kashima. But when Kashima let down his guard, Onamazu would twist free and thrash about, causing the earth to heave and shake.[1] Within days of the Great

Ansei Earthquake of 1854, which caused damage from Kyushu to Tokyo, woodblock prints of catfish went on sale in the capital. The Japanese also live with constant reminders of the tsunamis that frequently follow large earthquakes. The monumental bronze Buddha at Kamakura sits open to the elements, the hall in which it was once housed washed away by a giant wave in 1498. Japan's coastline is dotted with gnarled stone tablets, the size of mini-tombstones, warning future generations to build their houses further from the shore. Lafcadio Hearn, an Irish-Greek who spent fifteen years in Japan in the late nineteenth century, described it as 'a land of impermanence [where] rivers shift their courses, coasts their outline, plains their level'.[2] One Japanese seismologist calculated that, since the fifth century, the archipelago had been subjected to some 220 earthquakes of catastrophic force.[3] In modern times, the Japanese learned that the islands on which their ancestors had settled are, in fact, located on the most unstable section of the earth's crust, at a confluence of several tectonic plates along what is termed the Pacific Ring of Fire. Nine out of every ten earthquakes occur along this volatile section of Earth, making Japan the single most vulnerable nation to such disasters. On most days of the year, some part of Japan suffers a minor tremor. So used are people to these distractions that short earthquakes, even if they set wooden screen doors rattling or light shades swinging, barely elicit a pause in conversation.

But the earthquake at 2.46 p.m. on 11 March was no minor tremor. Everyone who felt the ground turn to liquid on that afternoon knew instantly that this was something entirely out of the ordinary. Measuring 9.0 on the Richter scale, it was the fourth most powerful earthquake in recorded history, unleashing the energy equivalent of some 600 million Hiroshima bombs. The epicentre was beneath the seabed, about forty-five miles off the northeast coast of Japan, somewhat to the south of Rikuzentakata. Geologists later said the so-called undersea megathrust earthquake – the sort that happens at the boundary of tectonic plates – had occurred where the Pacific plate had been pushing under the North American plate on which Japan rests.[4] That slab of the earth's crust had been pushed upwards as if, as one commentator put it, a playing card were being squeezed between thumb and forefinger.[5] When it bent too far, it suddenly released the pent-up tension, forcing the North American plate to snap back. In an instant, parts of the Japanese archipelago shifted as much as thirteen feet to the east.

This sudden rupture had occurred some twenty miles beneath the seabed, a relatively shallow depth that meant much of the energy was released to the surface. Throughout a large part of Japan, the earth-quake went on for a time-stopping six minutes. Many later recounted how the earth's movement seemed to build in intensity even as they prayed for it to stop. In Tokyo, the modern skyscrapers, many built on rubberized or fluid-filled foundations, lurched towards each other like bamboo in the wind. So violent was the swinging that, in the midst of their terror, some office workers felt as sick as if they had been on a boat in the heaving ocean. In Rikuzentakata, far nearer the epicentre, the shaking was more violent still. One witness described the accom-panying sound as being like thunder.[6] When the hellish shuddering finally stopped, there was only one thought in most people's minds: tsunami.

Sasaki, still clutching the papers relating to Shimizu's funeral, clam-bered up the staircase towards the roof of the Capital Hotel, three floors higher than the next tallest building in town. The lights of the hotel had gone out, as they had across all of Rikuzentakata, and the stairwell was dark as he and some thirty hotel employees fumbled upwards. From the roof, they looked out. Despite the intensity of the earthquake, there did not appear to be extensive damage to the buildings. Out at sea, the water looked flat and calm, though a tsunami-warning siren was already sounding. A few minutes later, the hotel manager announced that a bus was waiting below to evacuate staff. At around 3 p.m., after hotel employees had checked to see that no one was left in the building, the bus departed. The road directly in front of the hotel was blocked with cars trying to escape. The gate at the level-crossing a few blocks inland was down, causing traffic to back up behind it. So the bus took an alternative, longer route, skirting the coastline for a few minutes before heading inland towards the hills that ringed the cove. By 3.08 p.m., all the staff of the Capital Hotel, Sasaki included, had reached safety.

Far out to sea, where the earth's crust had jolted upwards, a great swell of water set off on what would be a journey of annihilation.

When, many hours later, it reached Sulzberger Ice Shelf some 8,000 miles to the south in Antarctica, the force would break off chunks of ice as large as Manhattan island.[7] Long before that, the surging tide had wreaked terrible destruction along more than 250 miles of Japan's northeastern coastline. Travelling initially at 500 miles an hour, the speed of a jet airliner, the wave slowed as it neared the shoreline, first to the speed of a bullet train and then to that of a car. Soon after 3.20 p.m., a little more than thirty minutes after the first tremors struck, it surged into the bay on which Rikuzentakata sits.

We have an image of a tsunami from the magnificent woodblock prints of Hokusai as a great, arched wave, curling its watery fingers over the land. Real tsunamis are more prosaic, but more dreadful. At sea, the height of the wave is nothing special, though a tsunami can be hundreds of miles long. They travel, often unnoticed by passing ships, as a forceful swell, gathering to great heights only as they approach land. Nor do tsunamis come as a single wave. Rather than through their initial impact, they often cause most damage as they suck back out to sea before thundering towards the shoreline in even greater volume. In Rikuzentakata, it was only a matter of minutes before the swell had breached the sea wall, built at what town planners had imagined was an impregnable height of twenty feet. Once the water had spilled over the concrete slabs, knocking parts of the wall over with its mighty force, the town lay before it. Water spilled into Rikuzentakata at different points, surging up the central riverbed and rushing up the valley floor until land and sea became indistinguishable. The only thing to do was flee.

From ground level, the first thing most people saw of the tsunami was a ghostly dust, rising from buildings that were collapsing in the water's path. The eerie white powder floated ahead of the wave like some terrible omen of death. It was accompanied by a crunching and wrenching of collapsing buildings, some of which were torn whole from their foundations and transformed into violent projectiles, smashing all in their path. Those who could fathom what was happening and had the wherewithal to escape drove or ran towards the hills as the water made its relentless surge up the valley floor. Many of those who died were too old to move, though many younger citizens of Rikuzentakata perished trying to help their older relatives and neighbours to escape. There were also some, within easy reach of safety, who didn't see the need to evacuate, so far were they from the shoreline. 'They stayed in their houses when they could so easily have made it to higher ground,' Sasaki said. The tsunami, according to witnesses, took just minutes to sweep across the entire valley, a distance of some three miles. 'The whole city just disappeared in four minutes,' Sasaki recalled, still shocked at the recollection. 'If you actually saw the tsunami, for you, basically, it was too late.'

Photographs taken by a high-school girl in Rikuzentakata document the first minutes of destruction. Early frames show water moving up the river that runs through the town. The river in the picture is swollen, but looks less than capable of causing widespread destruction. A few frames later, the water is wilder and about to wash away a small bridge. Before the first tidal surge could recede, another wave sloshed over the tsunami wall, increasing the volume of water. It was later reckoned the wave reached forty feet as it raced up the valley. By now, the photos show uprooted wooden houses, their tiled roofs still intact, carried up the valley as if in a stream of molten lava. An entire Mos Burger restaurant, Japan's equivalent of McDonald's, floats across the valley like some unmoored boat, its red roof and 'M' logo distinctly visible as it sweeps towards the hospital. By the time it gets there, it has been ripped in two. Now the water looks like raging mud. Another set of photographs, these taken by a volunteer fireman who had clambered to the top of an antenna, shows what looks like the high seas during stormy weather. The only clue that this is land is the incongruous sight of the town clock peeking out from the boiling waves.

As water churned back and forth, in and out of the cove, it dragged with it the deadly debris it had collected, hurling boats and houses and cars and factories and nails and glass at everything – and everyone – in its path. Neither wood nor concrete, nor bones nor teeth, were spared these waterlogged missiles. Whole tree stumps and mangled steel beams crashed through the third-floor windows of the Maiya shopping centre. At the public hospital, scenes of horror were unfolding. Water rushed into the fourth-floor ward, where many elderly patients lay immobile. They floated up on their mattresses on the rising water. Some were dragged to safety on the roof. Others drowned where they were in their beds. The survivors, sopping wet, were wrapped by staff in black bin-liners to protect them from the near-zero temperatures. Most spent the night on the rooftop. In the dark, the waters raged about them.[8]

Similar desperate struggles for survival were playing out all over town. At the city hall, government employees scrambled to the fourth-floor roof. From there, they scanned the ocean with binoculars and saw the first wave slop over the tsunami defence wall. Within a matter of minutes, the water was all around them, lapping over the top of the roof itself. Those who could, hauled themselves and others onto an elevated section of the roof, just out of the water's reach. From there, Futoshi Toba, the town mayor who would later achieve national fame, stared out at the elementary school where his two children were studying. 'I knew my children were at the school and that the teachers were looking after them,' he said.[9] He was more anxious about his wife. She had most likely been at home when the earthquake struck and, from his rooftop vantage point, Toba could see that his house had been inundated. All the phone lines were down. There was no way of checking on her safety until the following morning when the water had receded. Toba felt torn between his duties as a government official and those of a father and husband. 'I am also a human being,' he said later. 'And worry is worry.' In the event, his children survived. At Takata Elementary School, his son, twelve-year-old Taiga, had been told by a teacher to make a run for it. Later the boy told a reporter, 'It was like Godzilla. You could see the wave coming towards you, knocking down the houses. It was quite slow, but very powerful.'[10] Taiga's mother, the mayor's wife, was less fortunate. She was one of the more than 1,900 people washed away that terrible day.

Across town at Takata High School, the swimming team was missing. Before the earthquake struck, the ten or so members had set off on a half-mile walk to their practice at the city's brand-new indoor swimming pool. The B&G swimming centre bore a sign reading: 'If your heart is with the water, it is the medicine for peace and health and long life.' Neither the team, nor their young female coach, were seen again.[11]

More than seventy people had taken refuge in the gymnasium, one of several official evacuation centres. The experts who had produced tsunami hazard maps had judged the building beyond the reach of even the hugest wave. When people heard the first wave had breached the defence wall, they rushed up to the gymnasium's second-floor seating, where spectators from the town had, over the years, watched countless basketball matches and *taiko* drumming competitions. Water rushed into the building, where it became trapped, swirling around the domed interior as if in a washing machine. Sasaki later used the Japanese words 'guru, guru, guru' to describe the sound. Terrified people tried to clamber onto the metal girders arching along the gymnasium's roof. A few managed to hang on, but altogether sixty-seven perished there that night. The clock high above the second-floor seats stopped at 3.30 p.m., marking the moment when water neared the ceiling. At some point, the tidal force became such that it broke through the gymnasium's back wall and spilled out to continue its destructive journey. Locals call the ghastly, gaping hole it left in the gutted building the 'devil's mouth'.[12]

As these terrible scenes were playing out, Sasaki was watching the inundation from his hillside vantage point. He too was frantic about the fate of his wife, 57-year-old Miwako. With mobile networks down, he couldn't reach her by phone. He watched awestruck as water poured over the defence wall. The ghostly smoke rose as buildings crumpled under the tidal force, sending powdery debris into the air. It was then that he witnessed something he had thought he would never see. The pine forest of 70,000 trees gradually disappeared before his eyes as waves knocked down the towering trunks like so many matchsticks. It was a sight as unlikely as the marching forests of Dunsinane in Shakespeare's *Macbeth*. 'I was dazed and couldn't really understand what was happening,' Sasaki recalled.[13]

His wife must have been making her rounds delivering soba noodles when the earth started shaking. By the time the tsunami siren sounded, she would have been trying to drive back to the family home, about a mile-and-a-half from the shoreline. She didn't make it. A firefighter, one of the first emergency workers to enter the city, described the scene he encountered. 'People in the high places were crying, in shock, with their mouths hanging open. Along the river, we found no one alive, not a person.'[14]

By the time those few minutes were over, virtually the entire town of Rikuzentakata had been annihilated. There is no other word for it. Nearly one in ten of its population was dead or missing. Four-fifths of the buildings had been turned to matchsticks. Even the town's few sturdy concrete structures, including the Capital Hotel, were gutted, as debris-carrying water smashed through their interiors. As Sasaki had witnessed with his own disbelieving eyes, the 70,000 pines that had symbolized the town for hundreds of years had vanished in a few instants, swallowed by the raging flood. Even the beach on which they had stood was churned up and partially washed away. The very topography of the town had been altered, its coastline ripped and torn. Some of the land along the shoreline had sunk by nearly three feet.[15] Nothing was as it had been. Except, that is, for one thing. Almost miraculously, a single, straight pine stood, its 100-foot-high trunk – surrounded by shorn-off stumps – defiantly pointing skywards. The people of Rikuzentakata, those who survived that is, called it simply the Lone Pine.

# 2

# Bending Adversity

As the near-empty aeroplane slid through the piercing blue towards Tokyo's Haneda airport, I craned my neck to take in the scene below. In my mind's eye, Japan was no longer a solid island rooted to the earth's crust. Instead, it was a deeply unstable chunk of land erupting with orange flames and atomic explosions, a thin layer of earth floating on a boiling sea. But from this height at least, the runway looked perfectly normal and the land perfectly affixed. It was a beautifully clear afternoon. Around 150 miles to the north of Tokyo was the crippled nuclear plant at Fukushima, where the worst nuclear crisis since Chernobyl was unfolding. About 100 miles north of that lay Rikuzentakata. Tokyo had escaped the tsunami altogether. Yet the megalopolis of some 36 million people was still being thrown about by mammoth aftershocks, at magnitude 6.0 or above, big enough to cause huge damage in less well-constructed cities. The date was 15 March.

On the day of the earthquake itself, I had been working in Beijing. A couple of people I met that day swore they felt the earth tremble even there, 1,300 miles away. Yet when I received a call from a colleague telling me there had been some kind of earthquake off Japan's northeast coast, my first reaction was 'no big deal'. I no longer lived in Japan, but during my time there I had become inured to earthquakes, having felt many come and go with little consequence. Only when my phone vibrated again and I was told that a massive tsunami was heading for the Japanese coast did I rush back to my Beijing hotel to find out what was going on.

On the hotel TV I watched disbelievingly the footage that has now become so familiar. Few, if any, natural disasters of such magnitude can have been relayed live on television. When I first saw pictures of soupy water, thick with what appeared to be toy cars and match-sticks, I couldn't work out what I was seeing. Subsequent images revealed molten water choked with flaming houses sliding up the beach; whole ships crashing into buildings or caught in whirlpools out at sea; an airport runway disappearing under a blanket of water. One television channel showed before-and-after aerial shots of a town in Iwate prefecture, Minamisanriku. In the first shot the town was there. In the second it just wasn't. Most frightening of all were the images of an explosion at the Fukushima Daiichi nuclear plant, sending shreds of concrete wall high up into the air. A subsequent explosion was accompanied by a fireball and a plume of smoke.

But the two video images that stuck with me longest were on a smaller scale altogether. One showed supermarket staff at the moment the earthquake started. Instead of rushing for cover, employees ran to the shelves as they writhed and wobbled. Using their hands, arms and even bodies, the neatly uniformed staff tried to prevent bottles of soy sauce, cartons of orange juice and packets of noodles and miso soup from toppling to the floor. Mostly their efforts were in vain, but the dedication of Japanese to their work, it seemed, held good even in moments of extreme danger. In the second clip, a television crew had found a young woman walking in a daze around a field. She had been out riding, yet there was no horse to be seen. The landscape had become a wilderness without distinguishing features, save for a few mangled trees. Still wearing riding breeches and a tight-fitting riding top, the woman stared at the nothingness around her. 'The things that are supposed to be here are not here,' she said as if speaking to herself.

In the following few days, as the story clarified, the scale of what had happened became apparent. The quake had been so powerful that the earth was knocked slightly off its axis, altering its spin and shortening the length of the day, if only by 1.8 millionths of a second. The death toll was still officially in the hundreds, but tens of thousands were missing. Perhaps half a million more had been evacuated. The Fukushima nuclear plant appeared to be out of control. Tokyo Electric Power Company (Tepco), the operator, denied there had been a meltdown, but the company had decided to flood the reactors with seawater in what seemed like a desperate attempt to bring the situation under control. The government said radiation spewing from the plant was 1,000 times its normal level and ordered a two-mile evacuation zone around the site. That quickly widened to six miles, then twelve. People just outside the zone were warned to stay indoors.

Before I flew to Tokyo, I had tried calling Japanese friends. Some had fled to other parts of Japan, away from the jolting, unnerving aftershocks and the spreading fear of radiation. Those who remained were clearly shaken, their voices strained, even fearful, over the phone. One employee of a trading house told me the people from Tepco were doing their best. 'I have heard the French are telling everybody to evacuate. I don't think you should come,' he said. I'd contacted another friend, an adventurer and photographer called Toshiki Senoue, to ask if he would be prepared to travel north with me to the disaster zone. He replied by email that he might be willing to go. But please, he asked, could I bring a Geiger counter.

Tokyo was profoundly changed. It was also the same. At Haneda's stylish new international terminal, the escalators and moving walkways had been halted to save electricity, but an announcement still trilled in the high falsetto used on public address systems, exhorting passengers to hold on tightly to the moving handrail. My taxi driver was wearing the familiar white gloves and bowed as I approached the car. Across the back seat was spread the usual white cloth doily. Once I was seated, the door glided shut on its own. As we drove noiselessly away, the driver explained there had just been yet another big aftershock. The streets were virtually empty as we slid through a picture-perfect Tokyo. The sky, on this crisp spring day, was a lovely powder blue.

At my old office building, a black-glass skyscraper on Uchisaiwai-cho, not far from the moat and monumental stone walls of the Imperial Palace, the lobby was dark and deserted. The Starbucks was closed. The shelves of the in-lobby convenience store, usually crammed with rice balls, *bento* lunch boxes, dried octopus snacks, cream buns and rows of green tea cartons, had been picked bare. In the bathroom, the hand driers were switched off, covered with a paper sign reading *setsuden* – 'energy saving'. The toilet seats were still heated (some little luxuries you cannot do without). Yet in the next weeks, as the gravity of the post-nuclear-accident energy shortage became clear, even this most Japanese of basics was sacrificed. This was *setsuden* Tokyo, low-wattage Tokyo.

In the *Financial Times* bureau on the twenty-first floor, I found Mitsuko Matsutani, the loyal office manager, and Nobuko Juji, the long-serving secretary, still visibly shaken. They described how, on the day of the earthquake, the skyscrapers had careered towards one another, as they lurched from side to side. They had run downstairs, all twenty-one flights, and gathered in Hibiya Park, a European-style garden opposite. When a massive aftershock struck, they thought the tower block would surely topple. Now, a few days later, their work commutes were difficult. Trains that normally ran to the minute, if not the second, were subject to lengthy delays. Besides, it was frightening to venture underground with the earth still shaking. There were rumours of rolling blackouts to come and still worse disruptions to the transport system. Authorities had warned that another massive quake was likely within days. Perhaps this would be the 'Big One' for which Tokyo had long been braced. When I left the office for my first appointment with an old acquaintance, Kaoru Yosano, the 72-year-old minister of economic and fiscal policy, Matsutani handed me a hard hat. I didn't know whether she was joking or not.

At the old ministry building, a brick construction of utilitarian style, the mood was just as subdued. Two receptionists sat huddled under blankets to keep their knees warm. The heating, along with most of the lighting, had been turned off. Yosano, who usually wore a well-tailored suit, arrived in a blue boiler jacket and long rubber boots. That was now the official uniform of the cabinet, which had adopted the attire and demeanour of wartime. Naoto Kan, the prime minister, had warned that this was Japan's worst crisis since the Second World War: 'Whether we Japanese can overcome this crisis depends on each of us.'

Yosano slowly removed his boots and flexed his feet. His office was large but short on pomp. When I asked him if this disaster could galvanize the nation, he looked at me in silence before making a small, defiant fist. The minister answered questions about the extent of the damage and the likely economic impact. Since the ministry's offices were said to be particularly vulnerable to earthquakes, each time there was a tremor – and there was more than one during our hour-long encounter – his staff looked anxiously at the creaking ceiling and the swaying fixtures. Yosano, who had recently recovered from throat cancer, used the lull in the conversation to light up another cigarette.

I didn't know it then, but at virtually the same time, Emperor Akihito, the 77-year-old monarch, was making a televised address to the nation. It was the first such broadcast of his twenty-two-year reign. His father, Hirohito, had famously made a declaration, spoken in hard-to-fathom imperial language, on 15 August 1945. In a voice unfamiliar to his subjects, who considered him a living god and had never heard him speak, Emperor Hirohito had told his subjects of Japan's unconditional surrender, though he never used the word. The war 'had not necessarily developed to Japan's advantage', he said in his archaic, roundabout Japanese. The people should prepare to 'endure the unendurable and bear the unbearable'. That statement had been prompted by two nuclear bombs, which had made Japan's surrender, and subsequent occupation, inevitable. More than six decades later, his son was confronting both a natural disaster and a nuclear one in similarly sombre tones. Dressed in a dark suit with black tie and seated before a wood-and-paper screen, Akihito spoke for six minutes. Coincidentally or not, that was the length of time the earth had shaken. 'The number of people killed is increasing day by day and we do not know how many people have fallen victim,' he said. 'I pray for the safety of as many people as possible. People are being forced to evacuate in such severe conditions of bitter cold, with shortages of water and fuel.' As to the gathering nuclear catastrophe, he professed deep concern. 'I sincerely hope that we can keep the situation from getting worse,' he offered.[1]

The situation behind the scenes was even more desperate than the emperor had let on. That morning, while my plane was still in the air, there had been a hydrogen explosion at the Fukushima plant, the third blast in as many days. Kan, the prime minister, a former social activist, marched into Tokyo Electric's headquarters in central Tokyo. An investigation into the nuclear crisis later concluded that Kan had reacted with fury at suggestions by Tokyo Electric that it might abandon the plant altogether.[2] In an angry confrontation with the company's president, Masataka Shimizu, the prime minister demanded 'what the hell is going on?' So dangerous was the situation that Kan began to discuss a worst-case scenario with his cabinet. If Fukushima Daiichi were abandoned, the plant might spiral out of control, forcing the evacuation of nearby plants and risking further meltdowns. Yukio Edano, the down-to-earth-looking chief cabinet secretary whose regular television appearances made him the face of the crisis, privately warned his colleagues of a 'demonic chain reaction' that might force the evacuation of the capital. 'We would lose Fukushima Daini, then we would lose Tokai,' he said, referring to two other plants. 'If that happened, it was only logical to conclude that we would lose Tokyo itself.'[3]

There was certainly a sense of buttoned-down fear in Tokyo, though no one at that point knew anything about the panicked deliberations going on inside the cabinet. Later there were rumours that some people with close government connections had quietly been tipped off to slip out of the city. Tokyo at night was stranger still than in the day. It was, as a colleague of mine wrote, like a city 'operating on the lowest dimmer setting'.[4] Of all the cities in the world, Tokyo in normal times burns perhaps the brightest. The fashionable avenues of the Ginza and the teeming streets of Shibuya, Ikebukuro, Shinjuku and Akasaka are a blaze of neon. The roads are jammed with yellow, green and red cabs, the pavements clogged with swaying salarymen, office ladies and dolled-up bar hostesses in evening gowns. Now, they were shadowy and deserted. The sushi bars, *tonkatsu* pork cutlet outlets, the high-end and low-end restaurants, the holes in the wall, the noodle shops, the *izakaya* pubs, the clubs, the jazz bars, the karaoke lounges and the drinking establishments of this, the most bedazzling of night-time cities – all had closed up the shutters by eight or nine o'clock. This in a city that usually thrums until two or three in the morning. But in *setsuden* Tokyo, a few days after the quake, people hurried nervously home before the power failed or the trains stopped running. In one less than brightly lit subway carriage I spotted a man wearing a miner's hat, with torch attached, the better to read his newspaper. Even the lights of Tokyo Tower, an Eiffel Tower lookalike that is a symbol of the city, were turned off. The antenna at the top, it was said, had been bent by the earthquake.

That night, I telephoned an old friend, Shijuro Ogata. He is a charming man with impeccable English and a lively, liberal mind. Though he was once deputy governor for international relations at the Bank of Japan, a job of not inconsiderable prestige, he has none of the pomposity that sometimes attaches itself to important men in Japan. On the phone, Ogata was his usual cheerful self. He was fine, he said. He had hardly left the house since the earthquake, only venturing out to pick up a few essential supplies from the neighbourhood shops. He had been impressed with the stoicism of his fellow Japanese, many of whom had battled to get to work on time in spite of the chaotic train system and fears of a second earthquake. Where he lived there had been very little hoarding, he said. People had restricted themselves to one carton of milk, one packet of tofu.

Ogata was less thrilled with the officials at Tepco, who, he believed, had little handle on the nuclear crisis and appalling communication skills. 'They are very clumsy and don't seem to be so knowledgeable about what's going on,' he remarked in his understated way. But overall, he thought Japan would pull through its latest crisis. 'My wish is this,' he said. 'I am hoping this may awaken the Japanese spirit, which was demonstrated after the war to rebuild Japan.' Then he used a Japanese saying that I had never heard before: *wazawai wo tenjite fuku to nasu.* After I put the phone down, I looked it up. The dictionary rendered it, rather prosaically to my mind, as 'make the best of a bad bargain'. I thought about it and settled on a more literal translation – 'bend adversity and turn it into happiness'.

I had been here before. Except that no one had been *here* before. Four years earlier, almost to the day, I had come to this little fishing town of Ofunato on Japan's northeast coast about 250 miles north of Tokyo. Tohoku is Japanese for 'northeast' and that is what people call the region where the tsunami struck. Back then, I had come to research a story about how mackerel, amberjack, blue-fin tuna, spear squid and dozens of other types of seafood are brought from these teeming fishing grounds to sushi counters and supermarket freezers around the country. Early one morning – very early one morning as I recall – I went out on a boat with one of the crews. We had left in the dark and returned to port after several bitterly cold hours of fishing. We drank homemade liquor together in the boat's cramped mess and slurped down fish stew as we steamed through the darkness to the fishing grounds. I ate a piece of grilled meat that turned out to be dolphin. We watched the huge nets go down empty and come up alive with a silvery thrashing. It was a memorable experience and an insight into the salt-bitten lives of the men who catch fish for their urban countrymen. Now I had come again. Except the fishing boats had gone. And Ofunato was no longer there.

In the days after the quake, there was no easy way of getting to Ofunato – or rather the place where Ofunato had once been. Sections of the roads leading north from Tokyo were virtually impassable. The airport at Sendai, the biggest city in the north, was flattened and buried in mud by the tsunami. Flights to other airports in the three most affected prefectures – Fukushima, Miyagi and Iwate, where I was headed – were fully booked with volunteers and rescue workers bringing supplies. In the end I flew to Akita, a northern city on the opposite, Sea of Japan, coast about 100 miles from Ofunato. There, I met Toshiki, my photographer friend, for the drive down. Toshiki had studied in America and had a wild side to him. He was taller, more rugged and more unkempt than the average Japanese man, certainly those who put on suits and work for its big companies. He loved motorbikes and cars and sleeping in the wilderness. Still, he had needed some convincing to head into the disaster zone. We were to leave the following morning. The first thing I had to tell him was that I didn't have a Geiger counter.

That night, I watched television in my perfectly arranged, but coffin-sized hotel room. On one channel a woman was reading a never-ending list of names, of those missing and those found, in a slow, respectful monotone. After each name, read out with the family name first in the Japanese style, the announcer added the respect term *san*: 'Sato Yoshie-san, Takahashi Michiko-san, Suzuki Mitsuko-san'. The Chinese characters that the Japanese use can be read in different ways and it is not always obvious how to pronounce unfamiliar names. (Yuko, a common first name, can, for example, also be pronounced Hiroko.) So sometimes the announcer was obliged to offer alternative versions of the names of people feared dead or missing. 'Kawano or Kono-san,' she said. 'Kiyonari or Kiyoshige-san.' Not only were people missing. Their very names were losing substance.

20

I switched channel. Tokyo firemen in orange outfits were saluting before being sent in to douse the smouldering Fukushima nuclear reactor with their tiny hoses. As they marched unhesitatingly towards the plant, still gushing radiation, I thought of the *kamikaze* pilots sent on doomed missions in the final months of war. Another channel had turned a variety show into a fundraiser. Doraemon, a blue-and-white cat-like creature with capacious pockets from which he extracted useful and whimsical items, had been recruited to the cause. He was urging viewers to send in money. After an hour or so, I switched back to the original channel. The woman was still reading out the names of people in her respectful monotone. 'Ono Megumi-san, Uchiyama Tomoe-san, Uchiyama Mitsuo-san.'

The next morning we set out for Ofunato. We loaded the car with food and water since both were said to be scarce on the tsunami-afflicted coast. We needed a few extra provisions, Toshiki said, including protective boots for clambering over the rubble. The hardware store had posted a sign on its automatic doors specifying all the unavailable items, sold out due to panic buying. It was not a short list: fuel containers, batteries, radios, flashlights, portable heaters, gas canisters, mobile phone chargers, water, tea. Toshiki said that the disaster had revealed what was elemental: 'Water, fire, communication.'

The drive to Ofunato was uneventful. The roads were virtually empty. We had managed to wangle an emergency pass and only cars like ours were allowed to buy petrol. Tolls were waived. The landscape was mountainous, with trees stretching to the horizon. Snowy fields, small hamlets, fir trees, a tin-metal sky. We passed occasional convenience stores, most with their lights dimmed and signs proclaiming: 'We have boxed lunches.' They didn't appear to have much else. Just a few miles from the coast we passed the Maruhan Pachinko Parlour, the sort of place where the Japanese play noisy arcade games involving streams of metal balls. Toshiki shook his head at the sight of the car park full of vehicles. So near to tragedy, the people inside were in a sea of cigarette smoke and clanging machines. A few minutes later we rounded the corner and entered the valley that was once Ofunato.

For those who haven't seen it with their own eyes, it is practically impossible to imagine the devastation left behind by a tsunami.

A colleague of mine described it as like walking into a photograph of Hiroshima after the nuclear bomb. I wrote in my notebook that it was as if the man-made world had vomited up its innards. The things that were usually hidden – piping, electric cables, mattress stuffing, metal girders, underwear, electricity generators, wiring – were suddenly on full display, like secrets expelled from the intestines of modern living. Amid the shreds of wooden houses, twisted steel and old soy sauce bottles, one of the first things I noticed was a deer on its back, its glazed eyes staring up blankly at the sky. Next to it were a stoat, its snarl fixed in death, an eagle, an owl, a peacock and a second deer. It took me some time to realize what I was looking at. This must have been someone's taxidermy collection. The hooves of the deer and the other animals were attached to a green baize board.

These were the things that were not meant to be here. Those that were – houses, streets, shops, factories – had mostly vanished. Even solid concrete buildings were reduced to frames, doll houses with their walls ripped off by an explosive force, their shredded contents flapping like paper in the wind. Then there were the mangled cars, perched in trees, or on their side, or on their back or even, by some fluke, the right way up. A coil of green mesh sat on top of a collapsing balcony, like some metal python surveying hell. There was an oil truck, nose down in the ground as if flung from the sky. Scattered in the mud was a collection of salacious magazines showing half-naked women emerging from the shower. There were dead fish washed far inland. The smell of sea salt hung on the frigid wind.

Suddenly, amid the rubble, I spied two tiny figures, picking their way along a twisted train track, bound uncertainly for a train station that was no longer there. There was something faintly shocking about seeing life stirring on the dead valley floor. I thought of *The Road*, Cormac McCarthy's novel about a father and son moving their way through a charred, post-nuclear landscape. As the figures drew nearer, I saw that one woman was carrying a red cane. She wore a blue woollen hat and scarf, a sweater, jeans and a pink backpack. Her cheeks were red from the bitter cold. Her companion was younger and slimmer. She was wearing spectacles and her mouth was covered with a white facemask. She was also carrying a backpack. The two were staring intently at the ground as they inched along, occasionally raking the rubble with the cane or stooping to examine something more closely.

I approached and asked what they were doing. I felt as though I had encountered fellow travellers in the desert. They bowed slightly, their politeness out of place in these surreal surroundings. Hiromi Shimodate, the red-cheeked lady, explained they were searching for possessions, something from the café she and her friend ran together. 'We are looking for anything of ours. Just something, a chair, anything,' she said. Just a week before, they had both been in the café when the earthquake started. Shimodate waved her hand in the direction of the shore, indicating an area of rubble indistinguishable from the other rubble around it. On the morning of the earthquake, she had gone to the city hall to file taxes. She had returned to the café with some packages just as the last two customers were leaving after lunch. 'I was with Kimura and I thought: Maybe we should get something to eat,' she said, indicating her companion with the facemask. 'That's when the shaking started. It was very unusual. It lasted such a long time. I had never felt anything like that before.' Even before the motion had stopped, Shimodate ran outside to check on the elderly couple who were the landlords of the café. 'They were huddled behind the house, next to the train tracks, holding on to each other.'

When the tremor stopped she had gone back to find Kimura. 'We went to the parking lot. Only my car and Kimura's car were there. There's a small river. Usually, there's several feet of water. But it was only a few inches deep, and it was black and filled with fish thrashing about. We thought: This is definitely bad news.' Water was seeping out of the tarmac in the parking lot, which had liquefied. They made it to their respective vehicles and drove off. Kimura's car went to the left and Shimodate's to the right. Shimodate immediately ran into traffic, all of it heading for the hills. So she took a detour. If she hadn't, she thought, she would not be alive today. After she had reached her sister's hilltop house, she looked back down into the valley. A massive wave was already surging on to the shore.

Shimodate fell silent. Yasuko Kimura, her companion, brought out her mobile phone and showed me a photograph of the café. It had a pink interior and framed pictures on the wall. It had been taken a few days earlier, in a different era. Shimodate said the tsunami had altered the shoreline. 'I was born and brought up here. My family has always been here. A lot of people here have always been here,' she said. 'We all know it. The landscape that we saw everyday has changed. The water is definitely higher than it was before. Everyone says it. The sea has come closer.'

Suddenly, she let out a shriek. 'Look, there's something.' She darted forward and retrieved a silvery object from a pile of crumpled wood a few feet away. Once she had brushed it off, it became clear what it was – a flat metal sieve with a simple wire handle. It was the sort you might use for straining scum from boiling soup, or for lifting tofu from hot water. She held it up, half in delight, half in regret for the lost world it evoked. 'I knew it was mine straightaway. It's something I used every day,' she said, rubbing her fingers along its familiar handle and metal grid, not much bigger than the palm of her hand. She looked up to contemplate once more the destruction around her, the broken buildings, the mangled cars, the flattened houses. Then she looked anew at the sieve, a small, familiar object in the midst of desolation. 'It's a bit pathetic, isn't it?'

Kimura broke the silence. 'A lot of old people died here. They didn't escape,' she said. The older people of Ofunato, some of whom had witnessed three deadly tsunamis in their lifetime, remembered the biggest one that followed the Chile earthquake of 1960. That was the largest earthquake in recorded history and though it happened halfway round the world it sent a massive tsunami thundering towards the Japanese coast. 'At that time, the tsunami only went up to here,' Kimura said, indicating a place not far from us. 'The older people didn't think the water could come so far, so they didn't move.' It was a common tale, she said. Those who thought they understood the lessons of history were fooled into complacency. Even so, given the extent of the physical destruction, the toll of dead and missing had not been as bad as it might have been, she added. 'Over in the next valley, they've had it far worse,' Shimodate said, pointing at the hills to the south. I didn't know it at the time. The town she was talking about was Rikuzentakata.

The town of the 70,000 pines was just eight miles south along the coast from Ofunato, on the other side of a mountain. By the time we got there, night had fallen. We stopped the car and absorbed the stillness around us. You could sense the destruction, but you couldn't see it. As we drove slowly along the streets, many strewn with debris, we saw glimpses of rubble in the headlights, the odd carcass of a car or the marooned hull of an upside-down fishing trawler. In the dark, we couldn't make out any buildings. In fact, there were no buildings left to see, none, that is, apart from a handful of concrete structures that had survived the oceanic onslaught. Among them was the Capital Hotel.

I went up north again with Toshiki in August 2011. This time we drove the 250 miles from Tokyo. Nearly half a year after the earthquake, the capital was returning to some kind of normality. The number of aftershocks, several a day in the weeks after 11 March, had abated. The city was gradually, if uncertainly, rediscovering its rhythms. The rowdy *izakaya* pubs where students and salarymen wash down copious quantities of sashimi, grilled fish and chicken skewers with even more copious quantities of draught beer and sake, were full again. The trains and buses were back to their punctilious schedules. Still, the buildings were dark and clammy (air-conditioning was set to 'low' or not on at all). Many of the city's escalators were stopped dead in their tracks, cordoned off with yellow tape as though they were a crime scene. One employee of a large company told me he carried a torch to work so that in the shadowy corridors of his ultra-modern office block he could identify his colleagues. (No use bowing at ninety degrees to the boy from the post room.) A few months before, the traditional *hanami* cherry-blossom viewing parties, a boisterous rite of spring, had been less raucous than in less shaken times. Shintaro Ishihara, the rightwing Tokyo governor who had mused aloud that the tsunami must be divine retribution for Japanese 'egoism', had deemed it inappropriate to be guzzling sake in the city's parks while fellow Japanese suffered in the north.

In Tohoku, the frost and snow of March had given way to flies and mosquitoes. If Rikuzentakata was anything to go by, the clean-up operation had advanced significantly in just five months. The town was still a wreck, but it was a pretty ordered wreck. Much of the rubble had been cleared away or piled into neat mountains. Cars, bent, twisted and crushed almost beyond recognition, were carefully stacked as if ready for sale. Lumber was piled to one side, household bric-à-brac to another. Local authorities were struggling to figure out what to do next. There simply wasn't enough space in Japan to bury the millions of tonnes of rubble. In neighbouring Miyagi prefecture alone, rescue services piled up 16 million tonnes, the equivalent of nineteen years of general refuse. In Rikuzentakata, the city grid had been neatly exposed, cleared of debris. A casual observer might have thought this was a new town, with a neat scheme of intersecting roads already marked out. The Capital Hotel stood silhouetted against the flattened landscape, like some post-modern version of the Hiroshima A-Bomb Dome, the solitary and skeletal building left standing near the hypocentre.

I met Sasaki outside the shell of the hotel that used to employ him. I had been given his number by one of the tens of thousands of volunteers who had travelled up to Rikuzentakata, and other similarly devastated coastal towns, to help pile up the rubble and dig out the mud. Sasaki gave me a tour of the hotel's wrecked interior. His itinerary was as well thought out as if he were an estate agent showing me around a new building and trying to clinch a sale. From the outside, the hotel looked reasonably intact, though the wall of the ground floor had been ripped away in several places. There was a large jaunty logo in red and pink above the main entranceway, but the hotel itself was quite deserted. Inside, it smelt of the sea. There was shattered glass everywhere. Wire and strips of metal dangled from the ceiling. There were piles of splintered wood, and a few pine trunks that had come crashing through the picture windows facing the ocean. We walked up the stairwell, its thick carpet matted with mud and scattered with pine cones. Broken chairs lay everywhere. We headed up, following the same path that Sasaki had taken after the earthquake. There was less mud and rubble on the fourth floor. The fifth floor was basically fine. By the time we reached the roof, Sasaki was pouring with sweat. We looked at the bay and the ocean, calm and unthreatening. He pointed out where the beach and its 70,000 pines had once stood and the single remaining tree. 'It has become a symbol of our hope,' he said.

There's another, less heartwarming, story associated with the 70,000 pines of Rikuzentakata, one that speaks less well of the ability of Japanese to pull together in times of strain. Sasaki told me about it when we went to see his temporary house, a well-built wooden structure situated in the hills a little way from town. On a small table he had set out watermelon and Calpis, a milky coloured soft drink. A photograph of his wife was on a little altar in the corner, incense and apples placed before her likeness. 'Please have a seat in my palace,' he said with a grin, placing a cushion on the floor.

In March, after the tsunami waters had receded and many of the dead bodies had been recovered, the survivors wanted to mark the deaths of those who had perished. Not all had yet been identified. 'Some entire families were lost,' he said, studying the floor. 'So there's no one left living to look for the bodies. There's a lot of people like that.' Their ashes were placed in wooden boxes, wrapped in white muslin and stored in the Fumonji temple, like many Buddhist places of worship built on higher ground, and thus undamaged by the tsunami. Some bodies had been unidentifiable, at least by sight. In June, a corpse had washed up from the sea. 'He may have been trapped in the rubble and his body dislodged by an aftershock,' Sasaki said. It took a laboratory technician and a DNA test to determine that the corpse belonged to one of his school classmates.

What better way, thought the survivors of Rikuzentakata, to commemorate the dead than with the fallen pines. The townspeople carved some of the trunks into 340 woodblocks, on which they inscribed prayers and memorials for those who had died. The woodblocks were transported to Kyoto, Japan's ancient capital, 425 miles to the south, to be burnt in the August festival on Mount Daimonji. In that great spectacle, giant fires are lit on the hills around Kyoto shaped into the three-stroke Chinese character representing 'dai' or 'big'. The Gozan no Okuribi festival is a ceremony to send off the spirits of the dead, which, according to Buddhist tradition, come to visit their relatives in the hot, sticky weeks of mid-August.

There was a hitch. Residents of Kyoto protested that the woodblocks might be radioactive since Rikuzentakata was just 100 miles from the stricken nuclear plant at Fukushima; it might be dangerous to burn them. Officials refused to include them in the ceremony. Kyoto can be a closed, stand-offish city. It is to Japan what Japan is to the rest of the world. Its residents speak their own dialect, and many regard their culture as purer than that of other parts of the country. Tohoku, poor and marginalized for centuries, did not figure much on their radar. 'From Kyoto, us northerners must seem like *oni*,' Sasaki said, using the word for devil. 'The terrible thing is, there's this idea, this image that the radiation fell here,' he went on. 'Kyoto is supposed to be the spiritual centre of Japan. We put our effort into writing on those pines and in the end they just looked out for themselves.'

Japan's *hibakusha*, the survivors of the nuclear bombs, were often discriminated against by neighbours, who feared they might pass on contamination. After the tsunami, there were isolated instances of rescue workers refusing to evacuate people from close to the Fukushima nuclear plant and even evacuation centres turning people away until they had been screened for radiation. As for the 340 woodblocks, they were returned to Rikuzentakata, where they were incinerated in a square bonfire.

Even that was not the end of the saga. Feeling repentant and stung by the public outcry, Kyoto announced it had now changed its mind and was prepared to burn 500 woodblocks of Rikuzentakata pine. New blocks were duly prepared and dispatched. But when they were tested, tiny traces of radioactive caesium, which has a half-life of thirty years, were discovered. Once again, they were considered too dangerous to burn. Futoshi Toba, the mayor of Rikuzentakata who had lost his wife to the tsunami, even offered his apologies to the people of Kyoto for causing them anxiety. It was a dignified gesture. But it was the people of Rikuzentakata who deserved the apology.

Writing in the *Mainichi* newspaper, the columnist Hiroshi Fuse expressed sadness at the sorry affair. 'Some people have criticized the Kyoto municipal government and the organizer as being "narrow minded" over the latest case, while others have appreciated their decision as "calm judgement not being overwhelmed by emotion",' he wrote. Personally he wondered why people were afraid of such minute levels of radiation. 'I prayed to the Kyoto bonfire of 16 August that firewood from quake- and tsunami-hit areas can be burned in the Gozan no Okuribi festival next year.'[5]

While Sasaki was telling the story of the rejected pine, I noticed that Toshiki had quietly left the table. When I looked over, I saw he had lit some incense. He was on his knees, head bowed, quietly praying to the photograph of Sasaki's wife.

# PART TWO

# Double-bolted Land

# 3

# Shimaguni

Japan is an island nation. That is a fact of enormous, not to say exaggerated, importance to many Japanese. In the Japanese language, the word for island is *shima*. In written form, it is represented by the ideograph of a bird sitting on top of a mountain as though, exhausted in flight, it had found a place to perch in the vastness of the ocean. The word for country is *kuni*. When the two are run together, they fuse into the magical sounding *shimaguni*, or 'island nation'. The syllables have a sonorous heaviness about them, like the title of some lost epic. Even in everyday language, the term is occasionally invoked like an incantation, as though its very utterance settles everything. In the presence of foreigners, it can serve as the final word on the subject of Japan. *Shimaguni*. All there is to know – and all that can never be known – about an archipelago whose customs are felt to be beyond the understanding of outsiders.

Few would deny that Japan's island status has had tangible effects on its history and culture, even if the Japanese tend to make too much of it. To the outsider, Japan can seem a mysterious, even unknowable, place. Before it was opened up by American warships in the latter half of the nineteenth century, Japan spent long stretches of its history mostly shut off from western, if not Asian, influence. Both Japan and China, at one stage in their history, banned the construction of seafaring vessels capable of sailing far from land. In Japan's case, that was largely to prevent its people from being poisoned by foreign ideas, whether those were Christianity or rebellion against the shogun who topped the feudal order. Thus, for a quarter of a millennium, until the country was prised open like a shell, the Japanese government forbade most people from entering or leaving Japan on pain of death.

Under the system of *sakoku*, or closed country, which operated from the early seventeenth century, only minimal contact was permitted with traders from Korea, China and Holland. Dutch vessels were restricted to the tiny man-made island of Dejima. Built in the shape of a fan off the coast of Nagasaki in Japan's southwest, it was as much a prison as a port of entry.

Even before the period of *sakoku*, the waters that separated the Japanese archipelago from the Asian continent diluted the cultural influence exerted by China over Japan. At its closest point, roughly where the modern-day city of Fukuoka is located on the island of Kyushu, Japan lies some 120 miles from the Korean peninsula. That is nearly six times further than the mere twenty-one-mile gulch that divides Britain from continental Europe. China, the ancient civilization from which so much Japanese culture derived, is some 500 miles away, a formidable distance in centuries past.

Jared Diamond, an American thinker who has written extensively, and controversially, about the effects that geography can have on a nation's development, argues that Japan's location – 100 miles from the nearest continent – has had a distinct bearing on its culture.[1] Despite what many British like to think, the islands that form the United Kingdom have been closely integrated with the continental landmass for hundreds of years. There has not been a single century in the last ten in which British armies have been absent from the European continent. Britain itself has been invaded by Celts, Romans, Saxons, Vikings and Normans. By contrast, Japanese armies have ventured onto the Asian mainland only twice, in the 1590s, when the newly unified country invaded the Korean peninsula, and in the late nineteenth and twentieth centuries, when Japan annexed Korea and attacked China. Conversely, apart from what may have been a large influx of Koreans 2,300 years ago, Japan has escaped the military conquests that have shaped other nations.[2] The Mongols twice failed to invade, in 1274 and 1281. On the second occasion, the ships of Kublai Khan were wrecked by a typhoon, the 'divine wind', or *kamikaze*, from which the name of Japan's suicide pilots was later taken.

Even after its defeat in the Second World War, Japan was spared full colonization. The Americans, under the command of General Douglas

MacArthur, stayed only seven years and ran the country at arm's length through a local bureaucracy. That was not even long enough to leave a strong tradition of proficiency in the English language. Even today, Japan scores worse in English tests than almost all other Asian nations. When the Dalai Lama visits Japan, he is sometimes asked what would most benefit the country. Tibet's spiritual leader never fails to disappoint his audience. Instead of philosophy or religion, he has more practical advice on how Japan can better integrate with the world. 'Learn English,' he says.[3]

Japan's position on the extreme east of the Eurasian continent made it a backwater in which concepts developed on the mainland came late and took on their own form, like algae in a stagnant pond. From China, often via the Korean peninsula, came new ideas: written language, Confucianism, Buddhism, architecture, metallurgy and poetry. But once these concepts arrived, they fused with Japan's nativist traditions to undergo a subtle transformation. Undisturbed by a constant back and forth across land borders, ideas took their own course. In religion, Buddhism melded with animism, ancestor veneration and Shinto beliefs. Today, shrines dedicated to foxes sit alongside temples devoted to the Buddha. Acknowledging their religious syncretism, the Japanese like to say they are born Shinto, marry Christian and die Buddhist. In surveys most describe themselves as atheists. In language too, Japan absorbed Chinese characters developed on the mainland several thousand years ago. By the late Shang Dynasty (1600–1029 BC), the Chinese were scratching characters on the back of turtle shells as part of royal divination ceremonies. Many hundreds of years later, Japan, which had no native writing system, adapted the same characters to their own, entirely distinct, language. Partly because the fit was imperfect, the Japanese created two more phonetic alphabets known as *kana*. Today's written Japanese is a mixture of the three scripts, one Chinese and two homegrown.

This cultural appropriation and subtle subversion of outside influence is hardly unique to Japan. But the distance between Japan and the outside world, both physical and psychological, perhaps exaggerated the phenomenon. The Japanese adapt what comes from outside. They mix strips of seaweed or sea urchin in their pasta. They use the term *sebiro* to mean suit, mostly unaware that the word is a distortion of Savile Row, a London street famed for its men's tailors.[4] More recently, they have taken western technology and modified it. In the inventive hands of Japanese engineers, trains became bullet trains, and mobile phones morphed into powerful computers (and electronic wallets) well before the onset of Apple's iPhone. Even the humble western toilet, adapted to the Japanese mania for cleanliness, became a high-tech contraption of sprays, massage nozzles and hot-air dryers. Yet the modern rarely supplants the old entirely. In many public lavatories, these lavatorial wonders sit alongside old-fashioned squat toilets just one up from a hole in the ground.

The oceans around Japan are not merely shock absorbers that break the intensity of foreign influence. The sea itself has become part of Japanese culture. Its people have a relationship with their surrounding waters perhaps more intimate than inhabitants of any other large nation. No part of the Japanese archipelago lies more than eighty miles from the ocean, still the country's main source of protein despite the relatively recent encroachment of milk and meat. Old Jomon mounds, some dating back more than 10,000 years, have traces of fish bones from multiple species, indicating how long the Japanese have been active fishermen.

The influence of the ocean on culture is ubiquitous. Sporting fans eat octopus balls at baseball matches and shopkeepers sometimes offer young children not sweets, but raw shrimp, as a treat. In the same way that people discuss the weather or football in England, the Japanese talk excitedly about the coming into season of a particular fish. In Tohoku and other coastal regions, the years when great tsunamis struck the coast are remembered like the dates of battles. The very language is awash in watery imagery. A lackey or sidekick is a 'goldfish poo' trailing behind its master. What we would call a 'spike' in English, say in the price of gold, is *unagi nobori*, or 'surging eel'. (A canned drink by the same name was launched a few years ago.) Prime ministers have been known to compare themselves to fish: one likened himself to a loach, an unflashy bottom-dwelling creature well suited, he said, to muddy politics.[5] Even in moments of extreme distress, the ocean may be the first thing that comes to mind. A mother who witnessed the atomic mushroom cloud spreading malevolently over Hiroshima mouthed in horror: 'It moves like a sea slug.'[6]

\*

34

Japan is not a single island, but an archipelago. Its four main islands–
Hokkaido, Honshu, Shikoku and Kyushu–stretch 1,200 miles from
the northeast to the southwest, forming an apostrophe on the edge
of the Eurasian landmass. That makes Japan roughly the same length as
the east coast of America, though its total area is no bigger than the
state of Montana. Even then, over two-thirds of Japan's territory
comprises steep mountains that are virtually uninhabitable, while
only 17 per cent of its land is arable. Thus, the country's 127 million
inhabitants are squeezed into an area about the same size as Bulgaria.
In other ways, though, Japan is not small at all. If it were in western
Europe, it would be the continent's most populous nation by far, with
more people than Britain and Italy combined. Economically, notwithstanding two supposedly 'lost decades', it remains a giant with an
output half as big again as Germany.

Japan's island status has helped foster the idea that it is somehow
unique among civilizations. Of course, it is not the only country to
consider itself unique. During the US 2012 presidential campaign,
Mitt Romney, the Republican nominee, made it clear he put his
faith in 'that special nature of being an American'. Barack Obama, the
US president, has been taken to task for questioning the concept of
American exceptionalism. Still, the idea of Japan's separateness
from other cultures has gained currency among both foreigners and
Japanese themselves, though many, as we shall see, vigorously, and
properly, contest the notion. Samuel Huntington's 1996 book *The
Clash of Civilizations* divides the world into seven categories, of
which Japan–alone – has a category of its own.

At its most benign, discussion of Japan's uniqueness is an attempt
to define the country by explaining what makes it different, in the way
that all cultures are different from one another. Yet obsession with the
idea of Japan's supposedly uniquely homogeneous, group-oriented
society has become a fetish. At its worst, it has slipped into a dangerous assertion of racial superiority. It was, after all, a sense of Japan's
uniquely divine origins and its emperor-centred system – a mythology
largely manufactured in the late nineteenth century – that stoked its
poisonous sense of manifest destiny in the 1930s and 40s.

It is not only the Japanese who have laboured the country's supposed uniqueness. *The Chrysanthemum and the Sword*, written in

1946 by Ruth Benedict, an American anthropologist, painted a picture of the Japanese as 'the most alien enemy the United States has ever fought in an all-out struggle'. Explaining why it was incumbent to study Japan's culture so closely, she wrote: 'In no other war with a major foe had it been necessary to take into account such exceedingly different habits of acting and thinking.' The underlying assumption of the book – of a people with codes of behaviour entirely distinct from those of westerners – made it respectable to see Japan as a nation apart. After the war, the success of *The Chrysanthemum and the Sword* helped breathe life into an entire genre of writing called *Nihonjinron*, or 'treatise on what makes Japan separate'. The form had its origins as far back as the seventeenth century but reached an apogee in more modern times. In 1977, Joji Mori, a poet and English teacher, wrote a treatise on Japan's group-oriented society called *The Shell-less Egg*.[7] The book postulated that Europeans and Americans were like eggs with their own shell, self-contained individuals. The Japanese, by contrast, were shell-less – sticky rather than hard, amorphous rather than rigid. They did not, the book argued, conceive of themselves as individual human beings unless defined in relation to family, village, workplace, superiors and inferiors, insiders and outsiders. By the 1980s, when some Japanese became convinced their nation's unique characteristics would propel it past America to become the world's economic superpower, whole sections of bookshops were devoted to these self-absorbed tracts.

*Nihonjinron* builds on the phoney concept of a racially homogenous society. One only has to look at the faces on a Tokyo or Osaka subway to realize that the Japanese originated from many different parts of Asia. Nevertheless, the idea of a pure Japanese essence persists. This would have it that the Japanese are cooperative, sedentary rice farmers, not garrulous, mobile hunter-gatherers; that they have a unique sensitivity to nature; that they communicate without language through a sort of social telepathy; that they use instinct and 'heart' rather than cold logic, and that they have a rarefied artistic awareness. Much emphasis is placed on the advantages of a harmonious society. Taiichi Ono, considered the father of the 'just-in-time' manufacturing method that revolutionized Japanese productivity after the war, cheerily told a documentary filmmaker, 'With a racially homogenous workforce, it's much easier to discuss things. In fact, it is perfectly natural for us to have a unanimous agreement in whatever we undertake.'[8]

By the beginning of the twenty-first century, when I moved to Tokyo as a foreign correspondent, talk of Japan's uniquely admirable qualities had faded somewhat along with the vigour of its economy. 'When I hear people talking about *ishin-denshin*, I wonder what they have in their heads,' Noritoshi Furuichi, an academic, told me, referring to a belief in a unique Japanese ability to communicate non-verbally. 'The interesting thing about *Nihonjinron* is the extent to which the Japanese want to believe it.'

Indeed the idea of *Nihonjinron* had not died completely. In 2005, Masahiko Fujiwara, an essayist and mathematics professor at Tokyo's Ochanomizu University, published a slim volume called *Dignity of the Nation*. In it, Fujiwara did not argue, as had been common in the 1980s, that Japan's unique qualities destined it to beat America at its own economic game. Nearly two decades of sub-par growth since the spectacular collapse of Japan's twin asset bubbles had seen to that. Rather, he harked back to Japan's supposed essence, captured in notions of samurai honour and codes of practice that would have been familiar to readers of Ruth Benedict. He yearned for a time before Japan had been sullied by contact with western capitalism. His was a call, in sometimes strident nationalistic language, for a return to a prelapsarian, mythical land.

It was tempting to dismiss all this as the ravings of an eccentric. But in the months following its publication, Fujiwara's book came up time and again in conversations with businessmen, politicians and bureaucrats. Within a short time it had sold no fewer than 2 million copies. Only the translation of the latest Harry Potter had done better. I decided I ought to hear Fujiwara out for myself. At first, he was reluctant. Somewhat defensive on the phone, he appeared to have little interest in explaining himself to a foreigner. In any case, he was busy. He could not meet in Tokyo, since he spent summers in the coolness of the mountains. In the end, he relented. If I would take the two-hour train ride to Nagano in central Japan, he would talk over lunch.

We met in a Scandinavian-style restaurant in an airy and verdant valley a world away from the sweltering heat of Tokyo. I took a taxi from the tiny, immaculate station at Chino. Even out here, the driver wore white gloves. The GPS system blinked reassuringly. There was something of the Swiss Alps about the neatness of the surroundings. Fujiwara was waiting for me at the restaurant. In his early sixties and skinny, he appeared slightly gawky, dressed in a check shirt and casual white slacks. His greying hair sprouted hither and thither like untamed weeds. He spoke decent, if slightly strained, English, an interesting touch for someone who advocated the wholesale abandonment of English-language teaching in schools. English was so intrinsically different from Japanese, he said, that it was almost impossible for Japanese children to master. 'Only one in 10,000 can acquire both languages,' he said. 'I spent so much time on English, I now repent it.' Besides, he said dismissively, failure to communicate preserved the image among foreigners that the Japanese were thinking deep thoughts. Only when Japanese broke the language barrier did they reveal to the outside world that they had nothing to say.

The first course of our exquisitely presented set lunch was a single prawn, with a few meticulously arranged chickpeas. So precisely did his arrangement match mine that I found myself counting the chickpeas to check whether the kitchen staff had, as I suspected, given us exactly the same number. I never discovered the answer since Fujiwara was in full flow. I had asked why he thought *Dignity of the Nation* had so caught the *Zeitgeist*. Japan, he was saying, had been pursuing the chimera of wealth for sixty years. That rush to prosperity had blinded it to the foolhardiness of the capitalist model it was pursuing and, more importantly, to its own virtues. Nearly twenty years of stagnation had brought a sense of perspective. 'Japan used to despise money, just like English gentlemen,' he said. 'But after the war, under American influence, we concentrated on prosperity.' He harked back to the golden age of the Edo period (1603–1868) when *bushido*, the ethical and spiritual code of the samurai, spread from the elites to the general population via books and popular theatre like kabuki. 'People believed in *bushido* and for 260 years there were no wars,' he said, referring to the peace established between clansmen under the strict control of the Tokugawa shogun. 'When *bushido* started in the twelfth century, it was a kind of swordsmanship, but since there were no wars in the Edo era, swordsmanship became a [set of] values, like sensitivity to the poor and to the weak, benevolence, sincerity, diligence, patience, courage, justice.'

Much of that had been lost through exposure to what he called the dog-eat-dog values of the west. He cited recent controversies over western companies seeking to bring alien concepts of 'shareholder value' and hostile takeovers to Japan. 'Hostile takeovers might be logical and legal, but it's not a very honourable thing for us Japanese,' he said, smiling benevolently. 'I find the idea that a company belongs to its shareholders a terrifying piece of logic. A company belongs to the staff who work in it. That goes without saying.'

Another plate arrived, this one a perfectly arranged display of scallops. 'Chinese dishes, of course, are very delicious. But we pay greater attention to aesthetics. In writing we have *shodo* and for flowers we have *ikebana*,' he said, referring to the calligraphy and flower arrangement that lift everyday experiences above the routine. In England, he had been appalled, though perhaps secretly delighted, to see esteemed Cambridge professors slurping tea from cracked mugs. 'In Japan, we have tea ceremony. Everything we make into art.'

Fujiwara blamed Japan's descent into militarism on its abandonment of samurai values and its embrace of prevailing western thought. In its quest to become a Great Power, it aped the colonial ways of that other island nation, Britain, he said. 'I always say Japan should be extraordinary; it should not be an ordinary country. We became a normal country, just like other big nations. That's all right for them. But we have to be isolated, especially mentally. For the past 200 years, after the industrial revolution, westerners relied too much on logical thinking. Even now, they tend to think that, if you really depend on logic and reason, then everything will be all right. But I don't think so. You really need something more. You might say that Christianity is something that can come on top of those things. But for us Japanese, we don't have a religion like Christianity or Islam. So we need to have something else – deep emotion. That is something we have had for twenty centuries.'

Such deep emotion, the sticky albumen of the shell-less society, is said to explain numerous facets of Japanese behaviour, from the way people interact with the each other to, of all things, their supposedly distinct way of hearing insects. Not long into our conversation, Fujiwara, almost inevitably, cited the infamous studies of Dr Tadanobu Tsunoda of Tokyo Medical and Dental University. Dr Tsunoda's research – and one can almost see the electrodes attached to the heads of earnest volunteers – concluded that the Japanese brain was different from that of most other peoples.[9] The Japanese, he found, heard the sound of temple bells, insects and even snoring with the left half of the brain, the opposite of westerners. In Fujiwara's book there is an excruciating description of how a visiting American professor, on hearing the sound of crickets, asks: 'What's that noise?' Fujiwara feigns to be appalled. How can the professor not recognize this as music? How, he wonders, could we have lost the war to these imbeciles? 'All Japanese listen to insects as music. When we listen to crickets in deep autumn we hear it as music. We hear the sorrow of autumn because winter is coming. The summer is gone. Every Japanese feels that. We feel the sorrow of our very temporary, short life.'

I was looking sceptical, but he ploughed on. He explained another familiar, and related, concept, that of *mono no aware*. This is sometimes translated as 'the pathos of things', but can also mean sensitivity to the ephemeral. That is why, he said, in an explanation one hears trotted out every spring, the Japanese love cherry blossom – precisely because its bloom is so fleeting before it gently flutters to earth. 'If cherry blossoms were in full bloom for six months, no Japanese would love them,' he said. 'It's beautiful because it dies within a week.'

I said I had no doubt that these were important cultural reference points, handed down from parents to children and expounded upon by poets and philosophers. The idea of the fleeting cherry blossom was indeed a beautiful metaphor. But I saw no need for brain-mapping experiments or assertions of Japanese unique sensitivity to explain it. Wasn't the reaction to insects and cherry blossoms, and no doubt to countless other things, better explained as cultural association? I conjured up my own vision of a cricket match on an English village green. Where a Japanese might see red-faced men in white clothes panting aimlessly around a field, we British felt the beauty of summer, we tasted hops (and cheese and onion crisps) and, in our mind, heard the chatter of happy children. This didn't make us naturally sensitive to the sound of leather against willow. It was the association of a shared cultural experience.

Fujiwara partially conceded my point, but he was reluctant to let go of the idea that the Japanese had a unique love of nature. Why did they prune bonsai trees to within an inch of their life then, I goaded? 'They love nature so much, they want to keep it at hand,' came back his ingenious reply. Why, then, was a nation of nature lovers so inordinately scared of rain, I pressed? It takes but a scattered shower to bring out a forest of previously secreted umbrellas and the merest few drops – between taxi and kerbside – to send young women screaming at the thought of getting wet. I didn't mind getting drenched and never thought to carry an umbrella, I said defiantly. Didn't that make me more in tune with nature's bounties? I should have guessed the answer even as it was forming on Fujiwara's lips. 'British rain and Japanese rain are quite different,' he replied.

The idea of Japan as an impenetrable island culture is not easy to dislodge. I once wrote an essay in which I sought to refute the notion of Japanese exceptionalism.[10] Before I submitted it, I sent it to a friend, Sahoko Kaji, a professor of economics at Keio University who specializes, for her sins no doubt, in the macroeconomics of the European Union. Kaji speaks impeccable English. She is as comfortable in the company of westerners as in that of Japanese and she carries herself as would any modern woman in London or New York. Now in her early fifties, she helped write a slim, tongue-in-cheek volume called *Xenophobe's Guide to the Japanese*. In it, she and two co-authors poke gentle fun at Japanese customs – a fondness for 'love hotels', compulsive gift-giving, the art of bowing – as well as at foreigners' misconceptions about what such practices might mean. Given her worldliness and sense of irony, I was somewhat taken aback to receive the following email response to my essay:

It seems to me the only people on earth that are not worried about understanding Japan are the Japanese. Nobody can 'understand' Japan in the western sense of the word, because in Japan there is no absolute.

I sometimes feel sorry watching westerners trying to define Japan or the Japanese. There are even well intentioned Japanese who use western terminology to 'explain' Japan in their usual effort to be nice to guests and foreigners.

But it is futile. If you meet a Japanese who can define exactly what it is to be Japanese, he/she is not a true Japanese. In Japan, one thing blends into another seamlessly. And importantly, nobody (no Japanese anyway) worries about where the line is drawn. I would agree with the shell-less egg analogy.

I might add that my sister [a high-flier in the foreign ministry and also a friend] is the most Japanese of Japanese people. Maybe the most Japanese person I know. She has no borderline around her and it never even occurs to her to define anything at all. So you see, it has NOTHING to do with whether you can speak foreign languages or have lived abroad for years.

I cannot successfully engage in conversation with a westerner without defining things and showing borders. And yet I am certainly Japanese in the sense that I stand back and 'marvel' at westerners who keep trying to define this un-definable thing called Japan. Why bother? You cannot do it. I will not attempt it.

Japan will probably no longer be Japan if it is captured, defined, understood. I think I have confused you enough. I really should not have confused someone facing a deadline, but there it is.

Clearly it is hard to define things. How would you 'define' an individual, let alone something as complex and multifaceted as a national culture? But why should Japan be any harder to define than any other country? And, why should Japanese people not have borders – whatever that means – and exhibit less faith in absolutes than people in other parts of the world?

At the time, I had just finished reading a book, *Japan Through the Looking Glass* by Alan Macfarlane, a professor of anthropology at Cambridge University. Unlike me, Macfarlane was convinced that Japan was so different from other cultures that it could be understood only in reference to itself. 'The Japanese do not seem to me to be just trivially different from the west and other civilisations, but different at such a deep level that the very tools of understanding we normally use prove inadequate,' he wrote. One evening I telephoned him from Tokyo at his Cambridge home. He told me, quite as if he were discussing a hidden tribe in the Amazon, that, in contrast to other societies he had studied, Japan became less comprehensible the more he thought about it. 'When I go to India or China, I find lots of strange and amazing things. But I don't feel a growing sense of confusion. In Japan, I start off with a feeling of similarity and then, growingly, things become more strange.'

It would be disingenuous to pretend I have no idea what Macfarlane is talking about. Whenever I fly out of Japan, I sometimes sense my understanding of the country trickling away, like water through fingers. Even experienced Japanologists are not immune from finding Japan difficult to pin down. Lafcadio Hearn, who pitched up on the archipelago in 1890 only a few decades after it had opened to the west, wrote, 'The outward strangeness of things in Japan produces a queer thrill impossible to describe – a feeling of weirdness which comes to us only with the perception of the totally unfamiliar.' Hearn, who adored Japan, was no *ingénu*, much less a racist, though he might be accused of making Japan seem more exotic than it really is. A naturalized Japanese citizen, he was known as Yakumo Koizumi – or Koizumi Yakumo in Japan's 'topsy-turvy' word order. He married the daughter of a samurai family, spoke fluent Japanese and spent the last fifteen years of his peripatetic life in Japan. Yet of that country, he wrote, 'The wonder and delight have never passed away; they are often revived for me even now, by some chance happening, after 14 years of sojourn.' Foreshadowing a sentiment often expressed by today's long-time residents, puzzled at their inability to grasp what they imagine to be the essence of Japan, he added, 'Long ago the best and dearest Japanese friend I ever had said to me, a little before his death, "When you find, in four or five years more, that you cannot understand the Japanese at all, then you will begin to know something about them."' Hearn's book was tellingly entitled *Japan: An Attempt at Interpretation*. A year after his attempt, he was dead.

It is true that, in a hundred tiny gestures and assumptions, Japan can seem just slightly out of kilter with other countries, at least western ones, a modern society that nevertheless appears to move to secret rhythms. Well-travelled foreigners visiting Japan for the first time frequently describe an encounter with what strikes them as an altogether alien, if fascinating, culture. Pico Iyer, who has lived around Kyoto for a quarter of a century, describes Japan as being 'less like anywhere else than anywhere else I know'.[11]

Like Hearn and Iyer, I too am sometimes struck anew by patterns of behaviour as if observing them for the first time. I am rarely less than surprised when, in what is in many ways a conservative country, a female caretaker breezes into a public lavatory while men are urinating. I often forget that when Japanese people refer to themselves they point not to their heart, but to their nose. When they hand over a business card or a yen note, they always rotate it so that it is facing the recipient, since not to do so is considered quite rude. Linguistically, the Japanese revel in ambiguity. The first, second and third person often blend into one. The phrase 'I love you' contains neither the word 'I' nor 'you'. Businessmen introduce themselves as belonging to their company, as if their own identity and that of the business they work for is partially fused. 'I am Tanaka of Mizuho bank.' The word 'san', a polite appendage usually translated as Mr or Mrs, is also used for animals, as in 'Did you see Mr Elephant at the zoo?'

One should not, however, make too much of such differences. Perhaps one should make nothing of them at all. Any western-centric observer who assumes that what he does is 'normal' will find equally unfamiliar practices in Peru, India or Papua New Guinea. Macfarlane's argument, though, went further. He was saying the differences between Japan and other countries went beyond the superficial. According to him, whereas other modern societies had gone through a profound separation of the spiritual from the everyday, no such division ever took place in Japan. It never underwent, he says, what German philosopher Karl Jaspers called an 'Axial Age', a separation creating a dynamic tension between the world of matter and another world of spirit. Japan had no heaven or hell against which to benchmark its worldly actions. 'Japan rejected the philosophical idea of another separate world of the ideal and the good, a world of spirit separate from man and nature, against which we judge our actions and direct our attempts at salvation.'[12]

A retired geisha in Kyoto, whose life provided some of the material for Arthur Golden's *Memoirs of a Geisha*, once spoke to me in similar terms. 'I have read the Bible,' she said disapprovingly. 'In comparison, our gods won't test us to see whether we are bad or whether we are good.'[13] Out of interest, I asked several Japanese friends how, if at all, they conceived of god. One young woman, who worked as a telephone sales clerk, said she immediately thought of her dead grandmother, not an answer I would imagine hearing in the west. Another, Akira Chiba, a friend who works for the foreign ministry, said, 'I don't know much about Christianity, but seen from the outside it looks as though there's a difference between your role and god's role, your terrain and god's terrain. In Japan, gods are floating around and they're together with the people. Essentially, we live together with the gods.'

Macfarlane saw what he called this lack of separation everywhere. Thus sumo, with its purification rituals, was both sport and religion. A garden was both nature and art, as was the food I shared with Fujiwara. A temple was a place of worship in a country without faith. Economics, as Fujiwara said, was not a science to be placed outside the moral sphere. 'Gardens, ceremonies, people cannot be understood in themselves, but always in relation to something else,' Macfarlane wrote.[14] His idea of a world 'without partitions' echoed my friend Kaji's insistence that Japan was 'without borders', a place where 'one thing blends into another seamlessly'.

In art, too, Macfarlane detected this lack of separation. The Japanese, he said, did not distinguish between art and craft. Their best artist-craftsmen – potters, swordsmiths, papermakers, lacquer workers and calligraphers – were afforded enormous respect, designated 'National Living Treasures'. Like many observers of Japan, he found art everywhere, in the exquisite arrangement of flowers, food laid out on lacquerware or ceramic, even in the movements, passed down the generations, with which people sliced fish or swept a stone garden. 'For the Japanese, in Keats's words, truth is beauty, beauty truth.'

The haiku, a poem of just seventeen syllables that includes an obligatory allusion to the season, supports the idea that little in Japan makes sense without reference to something else. The best-known haiku by the poet Basho is:

furu ike ya
kawazu tobikomu
mizu no oto

Hearn rendered it:

old pond
frogs jumped in
sound of water

In English, it sounds like doggerel. The beauty in Japanese comes from its reference to things outside; the season (spring is mating time for frogs), the setting, the sound of water conveyed by the onomato-poeic word *oto*. A master of wine who is also an expert in sake once told me that the most elegant Japanese rice wines are defined by the absence of taste, the reverse of what one looks for in a claret or a Chardonnay. 'Sake is about what's not there. With wine it's about what's here. It's like in speech. The pauses and the silences, the things that aren't there give a hint of the meaning. The most elegant sakes are barely there at all.'

The idea of thinking about Japan as different from anywhere else is seductive. Yet there are many reasons to reject the notion. Those feelings that Japan moves to rhythms incomprehensible to most outsiders have reinforced an almost morbid sense of separateness. The Australian academic Gavan McCormack sees Ruth Benedict's *The Chrysanthemum and the Sword* as 'one of the great propaganda coups of the century'.[15] In stoking Japanese fantasies about their own separate identity, he says, the book helped sever Japan's psychological ties with its Asian neighbours in the years after the war, making it more dependent on the US.

If we look closer, much of Japan's supposed 'essence' turns out to be a relatively modern distillation. Nineteenth-century nationalist leaders found it useful to create emperor-centred myths around which a new, post-feudal nation could rally. They elevated Shinto, an animist set of folkloric beliefs, to the status of national religion. The various strands of Shintoism were united under the banner of the emperor. Amataresu, the sun goddess from which the imperial line supposedly sprang, was placed at its centre. From the 1880s, history textbooks in school began not with Stone Age man but with the birth of the Sun Goddess and the start of the imperial line. Much of Japanese uniqueness, in other words, is propaganda. Blending nativist animism with the cult of emperor worship was a political artifice. The emperor became so powerful an expression of the Japanese state that even the occupying Americans preserved the institution, exonerating him from any responsibility for the war fought in his name. 'All of this left him as the supreme icon of genetic separateness and blood nationalism, the embodiment of an imagined timeless essence that set the Japanese apart from – and superior to – other peoples and cultures.'[16]

It is all too easy to attach cultural explanations to what were, in fact, exercises in the consolidation of political power. It turns out, for example, that the practice of recording dates according to imperial reign is not – as some would have it – an expression of Japan's uniquely cyclical view of time. Rather, it dates back merely to the mid-nineteenth century when the imperial cult was being created. Of today's nationalists pining for a supposed Japanese essence, McCormack writes: 'What they believed to be ancient tradition was quintessentially modern ideology.'[17]

After the war, when the Japanese traded in emperor worship for the 'cult of gross domestic product', new notions of what it was to be Japanese arose. Noriko Hama, a professor at Doshisha University in Kyoto, a delightfully brusque iconoclast, disputes the common notion that there was anything fundamentally 'Japanese' about Japan's post-war economic model. At the turn of the twentieth century, she says, Japan practised an energetic, cut-throat form of capitalism that had little to do with the communitarian values later put forward as the secret of its economic miracle. According to Hama, some post-war arrangements, such as lifetime employment and seniority pay, which promotes people according to age not ability, were practical responses to demographics and the need to keep a manufacturing industry supplied with labour. They did not reflect any underlying Japanese proclivity for a gentler form of capitalism. As growth has slowed and society aged, many of the post-war arrangements once hailed as essentially Japanese are fast evaporating. By some measures – for example in the high percentage of casual labour – Japan now has a more flexible labour force than many western countries. For some, the lifetime employment system and seniority pay had been a modern version of Fujiwara's *bushido* sensibilities. If that really is the essence of Japan, then such essence is fast vanishing, like drops of ink in water.

Contrary to the views of essentialists, cultures are not immutable. Like language they evolve and adapt, though they may take generations to do so. To seek to explain the history of a country – let alone its future – on the basis of supposedly fixed national characteristics is to succumb to a determinist view of the world. We should challenge some of the assumptions that give rise to such opinions.

The starting point is the belief that island Japan is a racially homogenous society. But where do Japanese people actually come from? There were two distinct phases. The first people who came to the islands probably walked there over land bridges that connected the Japanese islands to the continent during the low sea levels of the Ice Age. The existence of stone tools suggests humans may have arrived, probably from both the northeast and southwest, some half a million years ago. By about 12,000 years ago, shortly after the glaciers had melted all over the world, these hunter-gatherers were thriving.[18] These so-called Jomon people were making the oldest examples of pottery yet discovered. They lived not unlike the Native Americans of the northwest and had a varied diet. They ate nuts, berries and seeds. They harpooned tuna, killed porpoises and seals on the beaches and fished with nets and hooks carved from deer antlers. There was little sign of hierarchy.

But the Jomon lifestyle, which remained largely unchanged for some 10,000 years, underwent a radical transformation around 400 BC. At that time, the inhabitants of Japan began to use iron tools and to produce rice in paddies with sophisticated irrigation systems. These people, since named Yayoi, adopted customs previously unknown to Japan. They wove, used bronze objects, glass beads and rice storage pits. They buried the remains of their dead in jars. Who were they? The evidence of geneticists and archaeologists points to an influx of Koreans, a theory resisted by some Japanese scholars. They could have come from the peninsula through mass migration, overwhelming the Jomon population. Alternatively, they may have arrived in far fewer numbers, but their superior agricultural techniques would have meant that, over time, their population grew much faster than the Jomon people. Either way, the new Yayoi lifestyle spread rapidly from the southern island of Kyushu, where it first took hold, to Shikoku and then up the spine of Honshu. It did not reach the much colder island of Hokkaido. The view of the Japanese as a mixture of Korean-like Yayoi people with an indigenous Jomon population is now largely accepted by academics. But it does not sit well with those who would like to portray Japan as an essentially island civilization, whose culture and genetic inheritance arose in isolation from the mainland.

Neither is modern Japan quite as monocultural as is often presumed, though it is certainly more so than societies with large immigrant populations. One scholar, exaggerating a little for effect, calls Japan a 'multi-ethnic, multicultural society in denial'.[19] Japan has about 2 million 'non-Japanese' in a population of 127 million. At about 1.5 per cent of the total that is small compared with more open countries such as the US, the UK and Spain. But it is not negligible. About 1 million of those so-called foreigners are, in fact, ethnic Koreans, most of them born and brought up in Japan, the descendants of those who came, sometimes involuntarily, between 1910 and 1945 when Korea was a Japanese colony. In less closed societies, they would already be classified as Japanese. Even so, that still leaves 1 million registered foreigners and at least 200,000 illegal residents – many of them students, temporary workers or 'tourists' who have overstayed their visas.

There are also between 1 million and 3 million so-called *burakumin*, the descendants of an 'untouchable' class known as *eta* in feudal times. As in India, they were a caste restricted to 'polluted' work in slaughterhouses or tanneries. Theoretically liberated with the abolition of the feudal caste system in 1870, the *burakumin* continued to suffer discrimination well into modern times.[20] In addition, there are the roughly 1.3 million people living in Okinawa, many of whom trace their heritage back to the independent Ryukyu kingdom before it was annexed by Japan in 1879. Finally, there are still scattered descendants of Ainu hunter-gatherers in the northernmost island of Hokkaido. The Ainu, who speak an entirely different language from Japanese and are lighter skinned and with more body hair, were pushed into the north some 2,300 years ago. Like Okinawa, Hokkaido is a fairly recent addition to Japan's landmass. For centuries the lands in northern Honshu, where the 2011 earthquake and tsunami took place, were known by the derogatory term of Ezo, which could also refer to its native Ainu people.

Divisions of class, gender and geography are often played down in a society that has grown to think of itself as uniformly middle-class. But they are just as real as in other societies with no history of claiming, as Japan did in the war, that 'a hundred million hearts beat as one'. Yoshio Sugimoto, a Japanese academic, rejects the idea that 'the national character of the Japanese [is] cast from a single mould'.[21]

The leaders of the Meiji Restoration of 1868 needed to concoct a new sense of what it meant to be Japanese. The old feudal order had been dismantled in the name of modernization. Samurai had to dispense with swords and topknots. Commoners, who had previously been forbidden from carrying weapons on pain of death, were suddenly required, if necessary, to die for the state. Manufacturing a sense of national identity became essential. As Japan's imperial ambitions grew, the idea of Japanese identity became more enmeshed with the psychological preparation for war. The Imperial Rescript on Education of 1890 was treated as a sacred text and committed to memory by students. In it, the sons and daughters of Japan swore loyalty and filial piety to the emperor and pledged, should they be required, to sacrifice their lives in his name. What Benedict saw as indelible cultural traits – she described how a Japanese schoolmaster would sacrifice his life to rescue a painting of the emperor from a burning building – might better be described as brainwashing.

Half a century later, on New Year's Day 1946, newspapers carried an imperial proclamation declaring as false the 'conception that the emperor is divine and that the Japanese are superior to other races and fated to rule the world'. The very terms of the announcement suggest that these were precisely the assumptions of pre-war Japan. Even today, myths surrounding the imperial family have not been expunged. More than 150 gigantic *kofun* tombs built for emperors between AD 300 and AD 686, are off limits to Japanese archaeologists. Presumably, the Imperial Household Agency suspects they may contain some unpleasant secret, for example the possibility that Japan's imperial line can be traced back to the Korean peninsula.

Some modern writers and intellectuals have stressed the importance of thinking and acting individually rather than following received practice. One is Haruki Murakami, whose protagonists tend to be loners and drifters. In 2009, Murakami won the Jerusalem Prize, Israel's highest award for foreign writers. Standing next to Shimon Peres, Israel's prime minister, he gave an acceptance speech that many interpreted as pro-Palestinian. 'If there is a hard, high wall and an egg that breaks against it, no matter how right the wall or how wrong the egg, I will stand on the side of the egg,' he said. The speech, with its echo of Joji Mori's shell-less egg, the idea that Japanese society is communal and sticky, could also be heard as a defence of the individual. It expresses the opposite of the idea that the Japanese are homogenous. 'Because each of us is an egg, a unique soul enclosed in a fragile egg,' he went on in words that implicitly challenged many of the tenets of *Nihonjinron*. 'Each of us is confronting a high wall. The high wall is the system.'[22]

Chiba, my diplomat friend, said education played a fundamental role in moulding Japanese people's self-image. 'There are things we are taught at school, for example that the Japanese bring in things from abroad and then adapt them to how things are done on these islands. That's our self-image. That's how we teach our children: that the Japanese are different.' Such reinforcement through education, he said, could become a mantra. 'We have to do the same as everyone else or else it's very shameful. Conformity and preservation of tradition: that sort of mentality is very strong.' He was sceptical about any notion that this made Japan unique. 'In the past, we were very different because we ate raw fish. But now everybody eats raw fish, so that's a point less,' he said in his tongue-in-cheek style. 'We have sumo wrestlers, very fat people trying to beat each other up. But now we have Mongolians and Belarusians doing the same thing. So that's another point less.' Chiba said the Japanese tended to compare themselves to Europeans and Americans, rarely to fellow Asians. By that measure, it was only natural that Japan should appear an outlier in a world still seen mostly from a European, Judeo-Christian perspective.

That affects not only Japan's view of itself, but also the world's view of Japan. It is worth conducting a thought experiment. Imagine for a second that, rather than Japan, Thailand had startled the world in the latter half of the twentieth century by attaining western levels of wealth and technology. In that case, there would have been shelves of books explaining Thailand's success based on its unique culture, the unique position of its king, its uniquely Thai way of conducting business, the unique properties of Thai cuisine and so on. If we stop comparing Japan with Europe or America and look at it in relation to China and Korea, it suddenly looks less of an outlier. 'Korea has its own forms of animism, which are not so hugely different and China is full of folk beliefs that often derive from Taoism, which is not a million miles removed from nature worship and Shinto,' says Ian Buruma, a thoughtful scholar of northeast Asia.[23] According to him, the problem is that foreigners take at face value what the Japanese say about themselves. 'But the reason the Japanese nativists describe their own culture as completely different from China was a form of defensiveness. They were, of course, deeply influenced by China. But precisely because of that, in order to carve out their own space, they have tended to exaggerate the differences.'

Yoichi Funabashi is one of Japan's most respected journalists and international commentators. He's also an old friend. I asked him whether he agreed with those who said that Japan's sense of unique self-identity had been manufactured in the interests of nation-building and maintaining political power. 'I think to some extent that may be the case,' he said. He mentioned a number of books – all written around 1900 – including Nitobe Inazo's *Bushido, the Soul of Japan* and Kakuzo Okakura's *The Book of Tea.* 'Although they did not use the word *Nihonjinron*, what they had in common is that they were searching for a new Japan. It's a revolutionary concept. They believed that tradition was very much relevant to Japan's future. So even though they learned so many things from abroad, from Germany, France, Britain and eventually the United States, what they sought was a combination of the national soul with foreign expertise. That is what we call *wakon yosai*,' he said, using the words for 'Japanese spirit and western knowledge'.

Japan, he said, lost the balance of those two concepts in the run-up

to its military expansionism of the 1930s and 40s. 'We were intoxi-
cated with Japanese-ism.' After defeat in the war, some equilibrium
was restored as Japan sought to learn again from advanced countries,
particularly the US. 'Now I think we are losing this delicate balance
again. This is the Galapagos phenomenon, an intoxication on the part
of the Japanese with their own things, their own Japanese-ness.'

The idea of Japan as a Galapagos island, whose culture is perfectly
adapted to its own environment but not to the rest of the world, has
become fashionable. It has been applied to the business environment,
particularly to the creation of products tailored too narrowly to local
tastes or local operating systems. 'This Galapagos-ization doesn't just
apply to mobile phones,' Funabashi said. 'It applies to nuclear safety
regulations, to English-teaching methods, to almost everything. In my
view, this Galapagos mentality is really toxic because it inflates our
narcissism, our belief in Japan's unique way. "We don't need to learn
from other countries. Other countries should emulate our way because
our products have been tested by the most picky consumers in the
world."' He paused for effect. 'This is a myth.'

I asked what the word *shimaguni*, 'island nation', meant to him.
He told the story of when he took six months off to write a travelogue
about Asian waters. 'The more I travelled the Japanese seashore, the
more affectionate I became for this small island,' he said. But then he
went to China. He started off in the northern port city of Dalian, moving down the lengthy eastern seaboard to Tianjin, on to Shanghai, the
ancient city of Hangzhou and ending up in the Pearl River Delta trading port of Guangzhou in the far south, near Hong Kong. 'I was struck,
overwhelmed even, with the vastness of the Chinese maritime world.
That was a rude awakening for me.' The journey upended Funabashi's
long-held view of Asian geography, that of Japan as a seafaring nation,
a lone island, and China as anchored to the great continental landmass.
'We have to understand the reality that China is a maritime nation too.'

His point made me think of something Hama, the Doshisha professor, had told me. An island nation, she said, could choose either to
look inwards or outwards. 'There was a time when Japan was – though
not quite on a British scale – a nation of pirates. We weren't afraid of
going out to sea, we were adventurous and risk-taking. To the extent
that we are a maritime nation, I think we ought to assume that there

is that underlying trait in the Japanese psyche. But the more we isolated ourselves from the rest of the world, the less of that boisterousness and buccaneering spirit we were able to retain. I like the buccaneering image of *shimaguni*. But when it is used as shorthand in conversation, it is definitely used to mean an isolated island mentality, inward-looking, not looking beyond your shores.'

Funabashi said it was true that Japan had once been outward-looking but had turned in on itself during the Edo period of the Tokugawa shogunate (1603–1868). However, even in the so-called period of *sakoku* isolation, the country maintained more links to the outside world than generally realized. '*Shimaguni* can mean an island that separates itself from the world or an island that connects with the world. In Japan's case, our island mentality makes people tend to believe that we can go back to being a secluded island of peace. But that's never going to happen, and never did happen actually, not even in the Edo period. It's a fantasy of Japanese seclusion.' He paused again. 'I think it's dangerous. We cannot go back to the Edo era, we cannot seclude ourselves. One way or another, we will have to live with the world.'

# 4

## Leaving Asia

Island Japan has for hundreds of years had a complex and difficult relationship with the outside world. It was true before Japan's first contacts with Europe in the sixteenth century, when China – though the admired fount of culture and learning – was resented as an overbearing influence. It was true in subsequent centuries when Europeans brought their 'wicked cult'[1] of Christianity, and later their unequal treaties and threat of colonization. And it is true today in an era when Japan is mistrusted by its former wartime enemies in Asia, and allied to a power halfway round the world, the US.

Even at the height of its economic prowess in the 1980s, when there was overblown chatter about Japan becoming the world's most powerful economy, it lacked geopolitical clout. Stripped of its right to have an army by its American-written pacifist constitution, it was an economic giant but a diplomatic dwarf. That fact was painfully underlined during America's first war in Iraq in 1990. Tokyo bankrolled the military campaign to the tune of $13 billion, but when Kuwait published a list of countries to be thanked for its liberation, the bankroller-in-chief was not mentioned.

Frequently referred to as a 'western power' – a reference to its advanced economy rather than its geographical location – Japan is isolated in Asia. Some regard it as a client state locked in a semi-colonial relationship with its US master.[2] A member of the Group of Seven, a post-war cartel of rich nations now fast losing relevance, Japan has never been admitted into the club that really counts as one of the permanent members of the United Nations Security Council. Nor has it ever taken the leadership role in Asia that its economic dominance once promised. Though its massive investments have helped power economies from Indonesia to Thailand, and though it blazed a development trail emulated by every successful Asian economy, including China, its hopes of a leadership position have been undermined by simmering wartime hatreds.

Japan's struggle to find a place in the international hierarchy goes back centuries. Its self-imposed isolation from 1630 only delayed the necessity of joining the international discourse. When it finally did so, through its embrace of western learning in the Meiji Restoration, it was initially triumphant: a 'European' Great Power in Asian garb. But Japan's timing was terrible. It became a colonial power just as the naked colonialism practised by the likes of Britain, Spain and Portugal was fading as a 'legitimate' practice. Its hopes of becoming the Great Britain of the Orient were dashed. That Japan's colonial campaign was out of step with history was only compounded by the disastrous miscalculations of its semi-fascist government, whose adherence to the fanatical cult of emperor worship blinded it to the inevitability of defeat. Japan's near-annihilation by war's end closed for good any hope of achieving international 'status' through military means. All that was left was to take the economic route.

One scholar says Japan's fraught relationship with the rest of the world has given it 'a shrill sense of inferiority and a sometimes obsessive preoccupation with national status'.[3] Kenneth Pyle, a US historian, describes brilliantly the semi-feudal society that emerged blinking into the glare of western enlightenment following the collapse of feudal Japan in 1868. 'Japan's worldview, the way in which it conceived of . . . the world of nation-states that it entered, was a projection of the ideas it held of its own internal society,' he writes. 'Its hypersensitivity to its rank in the world owed much to its distinctive honour culture nurtured over centuries of feudal life.'[4] It brought into the international system 'a confidence in hierarchy'. In conversation, he elaborated, 'If you go back to Meiji, the Japanese are constantly measuring their steps up the ladder: "We are ahead of Turkey now, but behind Spain." That kind of concern with international status has been more or less a constant theme.'[5]

Naoki Tanaka, an adviser to former prime minister Junichiro Koizumi, once described to me how Japan had turned its back on Asia in its pursuit of international status. 'After Meiji, our leaders thought that Chinese and Korean leaders were very corrupt,' he said. 'In order to survive the pressures coming from Europe, they thought that "leaving Asia" should be priority number one.'[6]

This sense of Japan's 'geographic tragedy' – a 'European' Great Power somehow trapped by location and history – is a powerful theme. In the nineteenth century, as Japan struggled to break free of the intellectual yoke of China, some of its boldest scholars began to conceive of Japan in strongly European terms. Japan wanted to escape the indignity of becoming a colony, a fate to which many of its Asian neighbours, such as the Philippines, had succumbed. Even the mighty China, once considered the infallible centre of the world, had been defeated in the first Opium War of 1839–42, subjected to the indignity of unequal port treaties and eventually 'carved up like a melon' by colonial powers. By 1878, European nations and their offshoots controlled 67 per cent of the world's landmass, a figure that would jump to an astonishing 84 per cent by 1914. The only way to resist this unstoppable force was surely to abandon Asia altogether and become 'European' too. That would require industrialization and the adoption of a modern constitution. It would also mean the acquisition of colonies. This was seen as the right, even the duty, of any self-respecting nation aspiring to Great Power status.

It is this process of rejecting Asia but failing – ruinously – to become a successful imperial power that lies at the heart of Japan's still fraught relations with the outside world. Having tried and failed to join the western club, Japan finds itself in diplomatic limbo, surrounded by the resentful neighbours it once tried to conquer. How this came about is the subject of this chapter.

Japan's modernization has proved what was once unthinkable to Europeans, whose colonialism was built on racist theories: non-whites could match or even surpass western nations. For many Asians, though, its achievements have been inexorably tarnished, not only by the brutal facts of its war against its neighbours, but, more subtly, by the belief that Japan had sought to wrench itself free of Asia altogether.

Most of what we know today as Japanese culture had its origins in China. The Middle Kingdom, as its name implied, was the centre of the known world and the origin of all culture, technology, religion and ethics. Rice cultivation was brought from the mainland, via the Korean peninsula, as were techniques in the use of both bronze and iron. From around the first century, some of the many tribal chieftains who ruled Japan sent delegations to Korea, itself under the influence of China.[7] From around AD 400, Japan was sending regular missions to imperial China, to Nanjing and then to distant Chang'an, capital of Tang Dynasty China. They returned inspired by all manner of Chinese practices and doctrine, most importantly the teachings of Buddhism (which had originated in India) and Confucianism. The Japanese 'constitution' of AD 604, an explanation of ethical codes attributed to Prince Shotoku, is full of Confucian and Buddhist assumptions.

George Sansom, a historian of pre-modern Japan, writes that Buddhism represented not merely a new form of worship, but a comprehensive set of beliefs. 'It was as if a great magic bird, flying on strong pinions across the ocean, had brought to Japan all the elements of a new life – a new morality, learning of all kinds, literature, the arts and crafts, and subtle metaphysics which had no counterpart in the native tradition.'[8] Prince Shotoku commissioned the magnificent Horyuji temple, a miracle of wood carving situated between the ancient capitals of Nara and Kyoto, in dedication to the Buddha. It stands, perfectly preserved, today. Chinese ideas on tax, land tenure and bureaucratic rank became deeply engrained elements of Japan's social and political order.

Even then, when there was no disputing China's cultural superiority, relations were not always smooth. In AD 607, the Japanese ambassador presented credentials to the court of Chang'an implying that the two nations were equal. That was a laughable suggestion to the Chinese court, where Japan was considered a peripheral non-entity.[9] The Japanese continued to pay intellectual, if not monetary, obeisance to China. 'From the beginnings of civilisation in Japan, the model had always been China, directly or indirectly,' writes Donald Keene, a scholar of Japanese literature. 'Inevitably Chinese ideas had been considerably modified in Japan, and some Japanese aesthetic and spiritual concepts were never vitally affected by Chinese example; but by and large China was admitted to be the fount of all wisdom.'[10]

The break with China – for it was nothing less than that – took several hundred years. It began, in piecemeal fashion, during the

Tokugawa period, named after the family of military rulers who brought Japan under their control from around 1600 until the Meiji Restoration of 1868. 'As knowledge of the world grew, the Japanese began to realize that China was not the centre of the world and to recognize the weakness of China,' the scholar and author Ian Buruma told me. 'So they thought: "We better start repositioning ourselves." Japan did not free itself decisively from China's intellectual yoke until the modernizing Meiji reformers had overthrown the Tokugawa regime itself. That was the year, if one can pinpoint such a thing, that Japan can be said to have ditched its Sinocentrism in the hope of becoming the first 'European' power in Asia. It was the beginning of Japan's spectacular modernization, but also of its eventual descent into militarist adventurism and wartime defeat.

The Tokugawa shogunate, which ruled over Japan for more than two and a half centuries, came into being after the battle of Sekigahara of 1600. There, Ieyasu, the first in the Tokugawa line, destroyed opposition forces to become the unassailable ruler of all Japan. The emperor, a figure of more symbolic than actual authority, conferred upon him the ancient hereditary title of shogun. Ieyasu established a centralized system from what had been, only a few decades earlier, a fractious polity fragmented into several hundred warring domains. From his new capital of Edo, later to become Tokyo, Ieyasu Tokugawa imposed, by brute force, an unprecedented peace. The period from 1600 to 1868 was marked by a total absence of warfare, so much so that the samurai warriors, whose *raison d'être* had been to fight for their *daimyo* lords, sank into a state of indulgent idleness. As they consolidated power, the Tokugawa shoguns neutralized all possible opposition –from Buddhist priests and peasants to the *daimyo* and the emperor's court at Kyoto.

The Tokugawa brooked no external opposition either. A clampdown on Christianity, begun in the 1590s, accelerated in the first years of Tokugawa rule. There was to be no competition, particularly from a foreign god. The first missionaries had arrived with Portuguese traders in the 1540s. By 1600, some 300,000 Japanese had been converted to the Catholic faith.[11] The Portuguese habit of taking slaves, as well as souls, had not endeared them to Japanese rulers even before the Tokugawa family had established absolute control. The subsequent clampdown on Christianity blended with a policy of severely restricting relations with all Europeans, Christian or otherwise. From 1633 to 1639, Iemitsu, the grandson of Ieyasu, issued a series of edicts designed to control, if not entirely sever, Japan's relations with the outside world. The teaching of Christianity was banned. Japanese ships were prohibited from sailing west of Korea or south of the Ryukyu islands, an independent kingdom later to be incorporated into Japan as Okinawa. Foreigners were forbidden from travelling inland or distributing books.[12] The British had already given up on Japan, since there were greater riches to be had in India. With the Portuguese expelled, among Europeans only the Dutch, confined to their artificial island, had any sort of contact with the Japanese at all.

These restrictions may strike us as hideously xenophobic today. But it is worth bearing in mind that contact with Europeans in those days rarely ended well. The Dutch, who were polite decorum itself in Japan, had, in 1740, carried out a massacre of some 10,000 ethnic Chinese in Batavia, present-day Jakarta. Japan's prickly relations with the outside world have by no means always served it well, but virtually alone among Asian nations, the country escaped the indignity of outright colonization.[13]

Nor was its 'seclusion' ever as absolute as suggested by Herman Melville's description of a 'double-bolted land'. Marius Jansen, a historian of Japan, describes Tokugawa foreign policy as 'more of a bamboo blind than a Berlin wall'.[14] Trade and diplomacy continued, at least to some extent, with both Korea and China. Japan's seclusion, Jansen argues, was aimed principally at the west. By keeping a close watch on outside events, he says, 'the world of the Japanese was far from closed mentally, culturally, or even technologically'.[15] Still, there were costs to Japan's policy. It had chosen to restrict relations with the west at what proved to be a momentous period of European history – the start of the Industrial Revolution and the acceleration of European colonial expansion, including to the New World.

Technologically, despite what Jansen says, Japan did suffer. An obvious example was firearms. In the sixteenth century, many Japanese warriors fought with weapons made by Japanese gunsmiths modelled on those brought by the Portuguese. The Japanese even improved on the originals by adding a device to prevent the matchlock's ignition from glowing at night.[16] But in the nearly 270 years of peace that accompanied Tokugawa rule, knowledge of gun-making faded. The samurai, no longer required to fight for real, in any case preferred the sword. When Commodore Matthew Perry first stepped ashore in 1853 determined to prise open Japan, many of the warriors who faced him were armed with seventeenth-century flintlocks.[17]

By the eighteenth century, few Japanese had ever seen a foreigner, let alone a modern weapon. Some who lived in Nagasaki may have peered at Chinese merchants and sailors from afar. Those who lived along the road to Edo may have caught the briefest glimpse of a Dutchman being carried by palanquin on the annual mission of homage to the shogun. According to Keene, most Japanese regarded foreigners, particularly hairy Europeans, as 'a special variety of goblin that bore only superficial resemblance to a normal human being'.[18] The Dutch knew no classical Chinese, a barbarous omission in itself, and were widely thought to lift one leg, like the dogs to which they were often compared, when they urinated.

These vulgarities notwithstanding, it was necessary to speak to the Dutch with whom trading was conducted. By 1670, there were a number of interpreters who could read and speak Dutch, if not always fluently. Twenty families in Nagasaki had been given hereditary jobs as interpreters. The Dutch had much to teach the Japanese in terms of medical science and astronomy. But the Japanese government remained suspicious of western learning and its association with Christianity. Chinese books on western religion and science were banned, though a few illegal manuscripts found their way to private libraries. Kageyasu Takahashi, a court astronomer, paid dearly for his curiosity for western knowledge. When in 1828 he swapped Japanese maps for four volumes of Adam Johann von Krusenstern's *Voyage*, an account of the circumnavigation of the globe, he was imprisoned for espionage and died awaiting trial. When a guilty verdict was finally delivered, his corpse, pickled in brine, was sent to the executioner so that it might be properly beheaded.[19]

The ban on western learning began to ease in 1720 when Yoshimune

Tokugawa encouraged the study of the western calendar. Yoshimune had heard that Europeans could measure the passage of time more accurately than the Chinese. That might, he thought, better serve the needs of Japan's hard-pressed, and occasionally rebellious, farmers.[20] There arose a small, but dedicated band of scholars, known as *rangaku-sha*, acolytes of Dutch learning. It was the slow recognition by these scholars that European learning was not merely the match of Chinese scholarship but, in important ways, superior, that helped foster the eventual break with the Sinocentric world.

One significant hint of western scientific superiority came in the field of anatomy. In 1771, Gempaku Sugita, a Japanese physician, came across *Tafel Anatomia*, a book written by a German physician forty years earlier. 'I couldn't read a word, of course, but the drawings of the viscera, bones and muscles were quite unlike anything I had previously seen, and I realized they must have been drawn from life,' he wrote.[21] At that time, dissections in Japan were uncommon and performed only by *eta*, an untouchable caste of butchers and tanners who were considered unclean.[22] Not long after Sugita had found the book, he attended a dissection on an execution ground at Kotsugahara, near Edo. The procedure was carried out on a fifty-year-old woman called 'Old Mother Green Tea', who had been put to death for some unknown crime. Sugita writes,

> The dissections that had taken place up to this time had been left to the *eta*, who would point to a certain part he had cut and inform the spectators that it was the lungs, or that another part was the kidneys ...
> Since, of course, the name of the organ was not written on it, the spectator would have to content himself with whatever the *eta* told him.[23]

When Sugita compared the actual arrangement of the organs with the illustrations in his European book, he found that it was exactly as depicted. That was not the case with the old Chinese books of medicine, previously considered irreproachable, whose drawings of internal organs had one flaw – they failed to correspond to reality.

Such discoveries marked the beginning of a slow recognition that, in matters of science at least, the European 'goblins' were more advanced than Chinese scholars. That the world did not revolve around China must have been a revelation on a par with the discovery that the sun did not revolve around the earth. To accept such a reality – that the

Dutch 'dogs' were, in some areas, more advanced than the Japanese or Chinese – demanded painful intellectual contortion. Until then, the guiding ideal of Tokugawa Japan had been Chinese knowledge paired with the Japanese 'spirit'. There was no room for a third set of accomplishments. To the extent that western learning was accepted, it would have to supplant Chinese influence.

The break with China did not come about only because of the attraction of European learning. China itself had also lost its sheen. In 1644, the Ming Dynasty had fallen to invading Manchurians. As one writer put it, 'The fall of China to an alien, "barbarian" dynasty certainly contributed to the demotion of China in the estimation of Japanese and tarnished the once burnished image of a cultural ideal.'[24] Japan had a movement called *kokugaku*, literally 'country learning', which sought to break with China and fall back on nativist traditions. The idea was to discover in home-grown literature and religious belief a complete culture such that Japan could break loose from its intellectual bondage. Much emphasis was placed on the purity of Japanese poetry. 'The evocation of nature and praise of emotion that they found there seemed to them to be far removed from the formal didacticism of Confucian teaching,' writes Jansen.[25] These ideas resonate even today. Shintaro Ishihara, the nationalist politician known for his anti-Chinese sentiments, once told me about something the French novelist André Malraux had mentioned to him. 'He said the Japanese were the only people who can grasp eternity in a single moment.' Ishihara smiled, his eyes blinking in their owl-like way. 'For example, the haiku is the shortest poetic style in the world. This was not created by the Chinese but by the Japanese.'

The life of Yukichi Fukuzawa (1835–1901), a great liberal thinker of his age, encapsulates the break with China. Fukuzawa was different from most of the young samurai caught up in the Meiji Restoration of 1868. For them, the object was not so much to embrace the west, but to learn the barbarians' techniques the better to expel them. Fukuzawa, by contrast, thought that, by opening up to western ideas, Japan could join the modern world and be accepted as an equal. Instead of looking inward, he believed that only through embracing the west would Japan stand as a strong, independent nation.

Fukuzawa's life straddles the extraordinary gulch in history that separates pre- and post-Meiji Restoration. As Carmen Blacker writes in the foreword to a translation of Fukuzawa's captivating autobiography:

> At the time of his birth Japan was almost entirely isolated from the outside world, with a hierarchical feudal system based on a Confucian code of morals. Her notions of warfare were medieval, her economy largely agricultural, her knowledge of modern science confined to the trickle of Dutch books which found their way into the country through the trading station at Nagasaki. At the time of his death Japan was to all effects a modern state. Her army and navy were so well disciplined that [in 1895] they had defeated China and [in 1905] they were to defeat Russia.[26]

Blacker says that, for Fukuzawa, 'it was not enough for Japan merely to have the "things" of civilization – the trains, the guns, the warships, the hats, the umbrellas – in order to take her place with dignity and confidence among the nations of the modern world. It was also necessary for her to comprehend the learning which in the west had led to the discovery and production of these things.'

Fukuzawa, a low-ranking samurai, was attracted to western thinking from an early age and set out to learn Dutch so that he might unlock its secrets. His writing brims with the thrill of learning. His fellow students, he writes, 'were interested in dissecting animals, stray dogs and cats, and sometimes even the corpses of decapitated criminals. They were a hardened reckless crowd, these aspirants for western learning.'[27] Having studied Dutch to a high level, he was dismayed to find during a visit to the port city of Yokohama in 1859 that all the foreign signs were in English. By that time, the Black Ships of Commodore Perry, 'veritable castles that moved freely on the water',[28] had appeared menacingly off the coast. The US had made significant progress in opening up Japan. In the very year that Fukuzawa visited Yokohama, the city had been designated a treaty port along with several others. As in China, where the humiliation of the unequal treaties and 'extraterritoriality' had long been known, foreign traders were not subject to Japanese law, but answerable only to consular courts.

Fukuzawa seemed more upset by his lack of English than by the dangers to Japanese sovereignty posed by the treaty port system. He quickly set out to learn English – like Dutch, a language 'written sideways' – and somehow got himself appointed as an interpreter on Japan's first mission to America in 1860. Of his voyage across the almost unimaginable distance to San Francisco, he writes: 'I trusted in western science through and through, and as long as I was on a ship navigated by western methods, I had no fear.'[29]

Though they took place 150 years ago, these early encounters with western culture are still part of Japanese folklore. A few years ago, I met Ichizo Ohara, a wonderfully animated Diet member then nearing retirement, who conjured up for me the comedy of one of the early expeditions to America. 'They were dressed in traditional clothing with Japanese knives. They needed to dress as westerners, but they didn't have shoes,' he said, laughing at the thought of it. 'When they went to buy them from the trading house, they were so big you could fit two people's feet in. So when they went to the US they went "karang, karang, karang" down the street. Their shoes were like musical instruments. They arrived in San Francisco in these big baggy clothes and these outsized shoes and people made fun of them. Japan's plenipotentiary didn't even know how to use a knife and fork.'

To read Fukuzawa's autobiography today is to be struck by his modernity. He championed the individual. He hated the feudal traditions that saw his father despised as a low-ranking samurai and that blocked personal advancement based on merit. 'The feudal system is my father's mortal enemy which I am honour-bound to destroy.' In the school he was later to set up, which became Keio University, one of Japan's best, he banned the practice of students bowing to teachers on the grounds that it was a waste of time – a rule that holds today. Of 'iron-bound feudal' custom, he writes, 'I did not care to hold my head above others any more than to bow down before my superiors.' One of the surprising things about reading Fukuzawa, whose words appear as fresh as the day they were penned, is how vehemently antagonistic he was to what he called 'the degenerate influences' of Chinese scholarship. For him the feudal system, with its backward codes and practices, was the embodiment of a Chinese value system that had to be jettisoned whole. During his student days, he recalls, 'We came to dislike anything that had any connection with Chinese culture. Our general opinion was that we should rid our country of the influences of the Chinese altogether.'[30]

When Commodore Perry sailed into Uraga harbour at dawn on 8 July 1853, there were few people who thought like Fukuzawa. Most Japanese were terrified by the awesome display of firepower from the smoke-belching seaborne monsters, the largest of which, the 2,450-ton *Susquehanna*, Perry's flagship, was more than twenty times the size of Japan's biggest vessel.[31] Knowledge of how a few thousand British sailors had brought the mighty Chinese empire to its knees a decade before in the first Opium War must have added to the sense of doom. The barbarians were coming. Japan may have been the land of the gods. But these westerners had technology that even the most divine country could not withstand.

In a sense it proved exactly thus. It took just fifteen years from Perry's arrival to spark the Meiji Restoration, a social and political upheaval of extraordinary profundity that was a revolution, a resistance and a capitulation all at once. Staying on the periphery, in its splendid isolation, was no longer an option. Japan had to work out how to deal with the outside world. In this, the young leaders of Meiji proved ruthlessly pragmatic. 'For them, when push came to shove, the importance of power and the preservation of the nation took precedence over the preservation of Japan's own cultural practices,' writes Pyle.[32] In the name of the emperor, the feudal system was dismantled, the samurai disarmed and a process of rapid industrialization set in motion. Yet for most leaders of Meiji, the driving force was not change for change's sake. Change was rather a means of national preservation. As so often in its history, Japan was altering so that it might remain the same – like the shrines at Ise. 'Unlike most other modern revolutions, the Meiji Restoration was a profoundly conservative event.'[33]

Many of the leaders of the Meiji Restoration came from the lower samurai orders. They were military men who valued samurai codes. The revolutionary qualities they possessed lay in their willingness to set aside the feudal form of Japanese culture so that they could preserve what they regarded as its essence. As such, their determination to learn from the west was often wholly practical. Japan must learn how to make the trains, guns and floating battleships mastered by westerners, not because these were inherently honourable things to do, but because they were the tools with which they could stand up to western aggression. Their working thesis: know thine enemy.

Japan's decision to end its isolation was reluctant from the start, a fact that has influenced its international relations ever since. Those behind the Meiji Restoration were military men who 'readily adopted the vocabulary of Social Darwinism and spoke of *jakuniku-kyoshoku* (the strong devour the weak) to describe the mores of international politics'.[34] From this beginning, Japan's evolution from would-be victim of colonization to Asian predator has a certain predictability. We are so used to judging the Japanese – for the unspeakable violence and suffering their colonial campaign caused – that it is easy to forget how almost natural it was to slip into empire-building and war. 'From the opening up of the country in the Meiji period, the Japanese idea of what westernization meant was to be a good imperialist,' John Dower told me.[35] 'Japan's pre-war success, its emulation of the west, is not simply industry, it's not simply culture. Westernization also means imperialism.'

Even Fukuzawa, by the standards of his age a most liberal thinker, never doubted his country's duty to bring 'enlightenment' to other parts of Asia. Of Japan's victory over China in the war of 1895, he wrote, 'How happy I am. I have no words to express it . . . I am often brought to tears of pity for those who died too soon [to see it].'[36] Some years previously, an anonymous newspaper article had appeared that was later attributed to Fukuzawa. In 'On Leaving Asia', he wrote that China and Korea, which had failed to emulate the modernizing Meiji reforms, were too backward to join Japan on the road to 'civilization'. Japan should therefore 'leave the ranks of Asian nations and cast our lot with the civilized nations of the west'. It was not a big leap from there to suggest that it should emulate the great 'civilizing' endeavour of the European powers by acquiring colonies of its own. 'Fukuzawa saw the future of East Asia as pivoting on a Chinese–Japanese conflict,' Masamichi Komuro told me when I went to see him in his office in Keio University, the institution Fukuzawa founded. 'This would resolve the issue: was East Asia to become a Confucian bloc or a modern bloc?'

By the end of the nineteenth century, just thirty years after the Meiji Restoration, Japan's relations with the outside world had been transformed. From being a marginal backwater on the edge of Asia, it had won a dominant regional position and was fast to be counted, at least formally, among the world's Great Powers. Its expansionism had begun in the 1880s, when it had imposed unequal treaties on Korea, much as America had forced such treaties on Japan. In 1894, a few weeks before the start of the Sino–Japanese War, Japan achieved its long-desired diplomatic goal of overturning the unequal treaties it had been forced to sign a quarter of a century earlier. That ended its status as a quasi-colony. In 1895, it gained control over Taiwan after its victory over China in war. China paid Japan reparations and Japanese ships were allowed to ply the river Yangtze. In 1902, the Anglo-Japanese alliance was signed, suggesting – at least on paper – that Japan had finally achieved Fukuzawa's improbable dream of becoming 'a great nation in this far Orient [to] stand counter to Great Britain of the west'. In 1905, Japan stunned the world by defeating the Russians and gained an early, ill-fated, foothold in Manchuria. By 1910, it had formally annexed Korea. The victim was turning victimizer. What was expected of a 'civilized' power was neatly summed up by Kakuzo Okakura, author of *The Book of Tea*. 'The average westerner was wont to regard Japan as barbarous while she indulged in the gentle arts of peace,' he wrote. 'He calls her civilized since she began to commit wholesale slaughter on the Manchurian battlefields.'[37]

In addition to its external conduct, there was a systematic attempt, much of it rather po-faced, to adopt foreign practices at home. Japanese high society took to attending balls, to wearing tailored suits and top hats, to shunning the pleasure quarters and to eating beef, which Fukuzawa said would improve their physique. Kabuki, a ribald form of entertainment that had its origins in riverside performances by Kyoto prostitutes, became staid and classical. Danjuro Ichikawa IX, whose descendants are still acting on the stage today, decried the traditions of a kabuki theatre that he said had 'drunk up filth'. Instead of wearing a dashing kimono or dressing as a demon on stage, he donned white tie and tails.[38] The establishment took to pressing western morals on its populace, for example forbidding public nakedness and mixed bathing. One such ordinance proclaimed that although 'this is the general custom and is not so despised among ourselves, in foreign countries this is looked on with great contempt. You should therefore consider it a great shame.'[39]

Yet for all its efforts, both on the battlefield and in its ballrooms and bathhouses, Japan never won the acceptance it craved. At the Paris Peace Conference of 1919, Tokyo pressed for the principle of racial equality to be made part of the founding covenant of the League of Nations. The western powers refused, causing immense bitterness among the Japanese, who took it to mean – perhaps rightly – that a nation of 'yellow-skinned' people would never be accepted as equal by racist westerners.

The sense that Japan would always be excluded from the white man's club is an important psychological backdrop for its eventual descent into aggressive militarism. The Japanese saw Woodrow Wilson's newfound championing of the sovereignty of nations as hypocritical. Now that western powers had seized their colonies and established their control over the world's natural resources, their aim was to shut out latecomers such as Japan. As early as the 1880s a popular song spelled out Japan's view of what lay beneath the deceitful civility of the new world order. 'There is a Law of Nations, it is true, / but when the moment comes, remember, / the strong eat up the weak.'[40]

Japan's victories over China and Russia and its full annexation of Korea set it on a tragic course. These early triumphs instilled an over-confidence and sense of manifest destiny that ended with its brutal campaign throughout the region. Before the fighting was over in 1945, several million Chinese had been killed (the United Nations estimated 9 million in the war alone, not counting those who died of hunger and disease) and several million more Asians had perished as a direct or indirect consequence of war. Tens of thousands of forced labourers, from Indonesia, Korea, Malaysia, China and elsewhere were worked to death in the mines or in the 'death march' construction of railroads. After the war, the French sought reparations on the basis that 5.5 per cent of the European population and 2.5 per cent of the native population had died during Japanese rule in Indochina. In the Pacific theatre, the American armed forces lost 101,000 men with a further 291,500 injured. The Japanese themselves were not spared. Some

1.75 million military personnel died, as did nearly 400,000 civilians, including those in the bombing raids on Tokyo and the atomic bombing of Hiroshima and Nagasaki. The total of more than 2.1 million dead represented some 3 per cent of the Japanese population.[41]

Yet as Japan had been gearing up for war after its unprecedented victory over Russia in 1905, some Asians had celebrated its military ambitions as a blow for Asian liberation, proof that non-whites could be a match for Europeans. Sun Yat-sen, China's nationalist leader, said, 'We regarded that Russian defeat by Japan as the defeat of the West by the East.'[42] Jawaharlal Nehru, the first prime minister of an independent India, wrote in his autobiography, 'Japanese victories stirred up my enthusiasm ... Nationalistic ideas filled my mind. I mused of Indian freedom and Asiatic freedom from the thraldom of Europe.'[43] John Frederick Charles Fuller, a British army officer and military historian, had no doubt about the significance of Japan's victory. 'Above all it was a challenge to western supremacy in Asia,' he wrote. 'The fall of Port Arthur in 1905, like the fall of Constantinople in 1453, rightly may be numbered among the few really great events of history.'[44]

That initial reaction lent a veneer of credence to Japanese propaganda that its invasion of neighbours was a war of liberation not of subjugation. It proved to be a lie. The claim was quickly undermined by the blatantly racist attitudes that the Japanese exhibited towards fellow Asians. Imperial ideology, with its faith in Japan as the 'land of the gods', had taught its subjects to believe that other Asians were inferior, even subhuman. Japanese working in the hellish Unit 731 in the puppet state of Manchukuo – where vivisections and biological and chemical experiments were performed on mainly Chinese and Korean prisoners – referred to their victims as 'logs', not human beings. Throughout Asia, those 'liberated' by Japan's Imperial Army soon found their new masters to be worse than the old ones. General Aung San, father of Nobel Peace Prize winner Aung San Suu Kyi, helped the Japanese to invade Burma, but quickly saw how repressive the Japanese 'liberators' turned out to be. 'I went to Japan to save my people, who were treated like bullocks by the British,' he said in 1942. 'But now we are treated like dogs.'[45]

\*

Domestically, it was a failure to deepen the institutions established by the Meiji Restoration that allowed Japan to fall under the spell of a quasi-fascist imperial cult. Fukuzawa feared his country would not be able to embrace the philosophy of individual inquiry that he thought necessary to the success of a modern state. 'His fundamental belief was that this spirit of inquiry was essential and that the only way to achieve it was to oppose hierarchical structures,' said Komuro of Keio University. 'Only with the autonomy of the individual could the nation also become autonomous.' Contrary to Fukuzawa's hopes, the early decades of the twentieth century saw the gradual snuffing out of individualism and the reassertion of hierarchy. Japan's feudal order had been overturned not, as in some European states, by a revolution from below, but rather by one imposed from above by a modernizing clique of samurai. It had a parliament, elected by a narrow franchise of male voters, political parties and a prime minister, but it lacked the sense of a sovereign people characteristic of modern democracies. That made it easier for a conservative elite to rally people around a national project, namely rapid industrialization and colonial conquest, wrapped in the shroud of an imperial cult.

The Meiji era came officially to a close in 1912 with the death of the Meiji emperor. For a reign associated with startling modernization, the emperor in whose name it was conducted was afforded a fanatical devotion reminiscent of the feudal order Japan had supposedly discarded. On the day of the emperor's funeral, 13 September 1912, General Maresuke Nogi, the hero of the Russo-Japanese War, stripped to his undergarments while his wife donned a black kimono. After bowing to a picture of the emperor, General Nogi plunged a knife into his wife's neck and then committed ritual suicide by thrusting a short sword into his belly.[46] It was the classic act of a loyal samurai, not that of a modernizing general bent on the assimilation of western learning.

The emperor who followed Meiji gave his name to the Taisho era (1912–26), one associated with a febrile political debate that could plausibly have developed into a more participatory democracy. The emperor himself was prone to bouts of mental illness and his reign was cut short, ending with it the putative development of a functioning civil society. The political system during his reign had evolved more quickly than the leaders of the Restoration had intended. Political parties grew stronger. The new labour movement engendered by rapid industrialization began to seek rights and influence. The number of street protests, often violent, mushroomed, culminating in 1918 with a push for universal male suffrage. In that same year, rice riots spread across the countryside. Troops were called in to quell disorder. Tenant militancy spread partly as a result of growing literacy among all classes. Masato Miyachi, a historian at Tokyo University, called it 'the era of the popular riot'.[47] Some elements of the labour movement even flirted with the Marxism that was energizing Europe. The constitution was ambivalent on quite where power resided. The emperor was sovereign yet the constitution rejected the idea of direct imperial rule.[48] For a while, Japan's democratic future hung in the balance.

'Taisho democracy' was a chimera. The 1923 earthquake, which flattened large parts of Tokyo and killed around 140,000 people, proved to be a turning point. In the wake of that disaster, police exploited the chaos to round up leftists and anarchists. Although universal male suffrage was enacted in 1925, other freedoms were rolled back. Political groups with radical agendas were banned while the Peace Preservation Law made criticism of the emperor, or of the system of private property, an offence punishable by up to ten years in prison.[49] As the economy slid into recession towards the end of the decade, the scene was set for a further lurch to the right. In 1928, after general elections in which workers' parties had participated, there was another mass roundup of leftists.[50] In the end, party politics, with its inevitable divisions and competing ideologies, was jettisoned as an idea: it was regarded as incompatible with Japan's principal national interest, namely the cranking up of a war economy. 'Two-party politics can be a meaningful way to generate good policy for a wealthy, advanced nation,' wrote Kazushige Ugaki, a moderate military leader, in 1931, in an argument beloved of authoritarian leaders even today. 'But a weak, poorly endowed late-developer needs to seek the welfare of the people not only at home but in development abroad. That requires national unity, and the two-party system is not welcome.'[51]

Things shifted decisively into the hands of the military after the assassination on 15 May 1932 of Tsuyoshi Inukai, a liberal-leaning prime minister who had tried to restrain the armed forces. He was killed by fanatics seeking to 'restore' the emperor to his place at the centre of the system. From the time of his murder, prime ministers were no longer drawn from political parties but from the military or its sympathizers. With his death, descent into militarism and all-out war was sealed. At political rallies, anyone who criticized the military was silenced. Yet even then, radical parties struggled on. The Social Masses Party won nearly 10 per cent of the vote in the 1937 election, a sign that not everyone was swept up in the imperial cult. Still, the Japanese system came more and more to resemble the fascist states of Germany and Italy. There was a fanatical emphasis on the supposed purity of the Yamato race, a near religious devotion to the emperor and a strong desire, shared by some on the left, to spread Japanese 'values' to other countries. At the time of Meiji, Japan's leaders had been determined to 'leave Asia' in order to join the Great Powers of Europe at the head table. Having not been invited to dinner, Japan felt humiliated. Many of its intellectuals were spoiling for a fight. 'We are the so-called "yellow race". We are fighting to determine the superiority of a race that has been discriminated against,' wrote Sei Ito (1905–69) in his diary. 'Our destiny is such that we cannot realize our qualifications as a first-class people of the world unless we have fought with the top-ranking white men.'[52]

That looked more and more inevitable as Japan's campaign to be treated equally went nowhere. The number of naval vessels Japan could own in relation to Britain and America was frozen by international agreement. In 1933, after the League of Nations had condemned the seizure of Manchuria, Japan walked out in disgust. It had effectively given up on its long-held ambition to be accepted as a member of the western colonial club. Shorn of its moorings, Japan's military flew out of control. By 1937, it had moved from Manchuria deeper into China proper, and in 1940 into northern Indochina. When Japan pushed further into Indochina, Washington responded with a full-blown international oil embargo. Boxed in, Japan's leaders mounted what they portrayed as a 'defensive' attack on Pearl Harbor in December 1941. The following February the Japanese seized Malaya and Singapore and, within weeks, the Dutch East Indies, modern Indonesia, fell into its hands. Not long after, it grabbed a large part of the Philippines and much of Burma.

The attack on Pearl Harbor was greeted with euphoria at home, where many saw it as revenge for Commodore Perry's assault on Japan all those years before. It was celebrated by one poet, Kotaro Takamura (1883–1956), who saw in the bold act against the Anglo-Saxons revenge for years of humiliation and an affirmation of Japanese superiority.

> Nippon, the land of the gods
> Ruled over by a living god[53]

Yet now America had been provoked into entering the war, it was only a matter of time before the military tide turned. Just six months after Pearl Harbor, the Japanese navy lost the decisive battle of Midway, which severely depleted its fleet and left its new empire in the Pacific exposed. The Americans pursued an island-hopping strategy, moving ever closer towards Japan. When, in July 1944, they captured Saipan, within bombing range of Japan, the great air raids on the Japanese cities began. Unfortunately, Japan's military leaders were unable to face the inevitable. The navy was perhaps prepared to accept a negotiated surrender, but not the unconditional capitulation the Allies were demanding. Terrible battles ensued, not least the one for Okinawa, so catastrophically violent it was known as the 'Typhoon of Steel'. The battle, in which kamikaze pilots mounted some 1,500 attacks on American ships and Okinawan civilians committed mass suicide, often instigated by Japanese troops, was one of the most ferocious of the Second World War. Then came the two nuclear bombs on 6 August and 9 August of 1945, followed by the unconditional surrender that Japan's deluded leaders had so long resisted.

Japan lay in ruins. For the next seven years it would be a supplicant of America and the occupying force of General Douglas MacArthur, Supreme Commander for the Allied Powers. Japan had left Asia. But the price of doing so was to become subordinate to another power – the United States.

# PART THREE

# Decades Found and Lost

# 5

# The Magic Teapot

Two months before Japan surrendered to the Allies, Shijuro Ogata, the seventeen-year-old son of a famous newspaper editor, secured a ticket for the Japanese Philharmonic Orchestra. The concert was Beethoven's 9th Symphony. It was to be held in the Hibiya Public Hall, a brick construction erected as part of the capital's modernization effort after the Great Kanto Earthquake of 1923. On the evening of the concert, Ogata remembers taking a tram from Shibuya to Shimbashi, a distance of some three miles. The journey covered what are now some of the city's most expensive neighbourhoods, a choc-a-bloc jumble of neon, skyscrapers, office buildings, parks, homes, department stores, boutiques, bowling alleys, arcades, cinemas, theatres, clubs, museums and thousands of cafés, restaurants and bars. Back then the scene was desolate. From early 1945, the US had sent dozens of low-flying B-29s to drop incendiary bombs on the Japanese capital, much of which was constructed of wood. On the night of 9–10 March, some 300 bombers had roared over the city, dropping bombs that destroyed sixteen square miles of buildings and unleashed raging fires. That night alone, an estimated 100,000 civilians died and a million homes went up in flames. It is considered the most destructive bombing raid in all human history, more deadly, even, than the atomic bombs. The Ogatas' house in the then up-and-coming Shinjuku district survived the March raid only to succumb to another in late May. 'Tokyo was completely devastated,' Ogata recalls of his journey through the charred wasteland to the concert in Hibiya Hall. 'Everything was flat, just flat.'[1]

Now in his eighties and retired from the Bank of Japan, where he spent most of his professional life, Ogata has a kindly face and a ready wit. It was he who had introduced me to the proverb about 'bending adversity' and who had professed his faith that Japan could recover again, both from the devastation of the tsunami and from its current economic and political malaise. In ordinary people's dignified response to adversity, he had seen something of the post-1945 spirit that had enabled the Japanese to confront adversity and build something positive from the wreckage of war. Ogata loves a political discussion and to venture opinions that many would consider a little risqué, especially those on the right of Japan's political spectrum. Much of his time is spent in the Japan Press Club and the Foreign Correspondents' Club of Japan where he attends lectures and press conferences and talks about issues of the day. He has his stock of little sayings, rarely delivered without a twinkle in his eye. 'Japan is a country of good soldiers but poor commanders' is one of his favourites. It is a lesson perhaps learned from Japan's wartime experience, but one that he finds applicable to modern Japan too, particularly in its current phase of drift. For him, the aphorism captures the diligence and decency of common people – exhibited again in the aftermath of the tsunami – but the disappointment he feels in the nation's leaders. Although he was a senior figure at the Bank of Japan, he likes to introduce himself with a self-deprecatory, 'I am Sadako's husband,' acknowledging the greater renown of his wife, former United Nations High Commissioner for Refugees and one of Japan's most famous citizens.[2]

Ogata's grandfather and great-grandfather on his father's side, both born well before the Meiji Restoration, had been students of Dutch learning. His father, Taketora, was editor-in-chief of the liberal *Asahi* newspaper and a proponent of greater democracy in the late 1920s. Despite this liberal upbringing, Ogata remembers celebrating the fall of Nanking as a primary school student. As the rape and slaughter of civilians unfolded, archive photographs show innocent-faced ranks of Japanese schoolchildren like Ogata waving Rising Sun flags outside the Imperial Palace. Four years later, the surprise attack on Pearl Harbor had shocked the teenage Ogata, but he confessed that news of the distant hostilities brought a certain thrill. 'The initial victories excited most of us, including those who had been opposed to the war,' he writes in his memoirs.[3]

Because of his father's connections to the newspaper business Ogata was better informed about what was going on than most Japanese, for whom censored news media spewing imperial propaganda was the only source of information. He guessed before most that Japan would lose the war. By 9 August, less than two months after he had attended the Beethoven concert, he learned from navy officers that Hiroshima had been destroyed by a fearful new weapon and that the Soviet Union had torn up its non-aggression pact with Japan. Though Ogata did not yet know that a second nuclear bomb had been dropped on Nagasaki, he realized the end of the war was close. The entry in his diary, six days before Japan's unconditional surrender on 15 August, reads, 'The arrival of a very tragic day of history seems imminent.' It is hard to imagine now the psychological devastation. Japan's dreams – if that's what its fantasies of Asian domination can be called – were over. The emperor, previously distant, divine and unerring, came on the radio to announce the surrender. Villagers and city dwellers alike gathered around crackly radios, their heads bowed in disbelief. No one had heard the emperor's voice before, let alone speaking such unimaginable words. Shintaro Ishihara, who grew up to become Tokyo governor, was twelve years old. 'I thought his voice was high and sounded very feminine,' he told me. 'Like the shriek of a cat.'[4]

Japan lay in ruins, its ideology as well as its buildings reduced to rubble. Aerial photographs of Tokyo, Osaka, Nagoya, Hiroshima and Nagasaki in the days following surrender look strangely like those of the towns along the northeast coast after the 2011 tsunami. The street grid is visible, but most of the buildings have vanished. Only the odd industrial chimney or brick building sticks up from the rubble. Japan's defeat was absolute. Four-fifths of its ships, a third of its industrial machinery, and nearly a quarter of its rolling stock, cars and trucks had been destroyed.[5] Documentary footage from just after the surrender shows ragged children in wooden clogs picking through the debris.

My own father-in-law, Gene Aaroe, a member of the US coastguard in 1945, remembers landing at the northern port of Aomori shortly after the surrender. He had half expected to fight. After all, he had witnessed the planes of kamikaze pilots explode in flames as they attempted to sink the ships around him in the Battle of Okinawa. Like other Americans, he had heard stories of a fanatical race of emperor-worshippers who would never surrender and were prepared to fight to the last man, woman and child.[6] Instead, he found a submissive and devastated nation. People in Aomori lined the streets with their pots, pans, kimonos and other possessions at their feet, items for sale to the conquering Americans. He bought a *harakiri* ritual suicide knife, which he still keeps in a cupboard in Seattle. Doubtless the few dollars he paid for it were exchanged for desperately needed food.

Two weeks after the emperor's message, General Douglas MacArthur, Supreme Commander for the Allied Powers in Japan, landed at Atsugi aerodrome near Tokyo. Dressed in khaki army fatigues, he struck an imposing figure. His apparent nonchalance at becoming Japan's potentate was emphasized by the enormous corncob pipe stuck jauntily between his teeth. A subsequent picture taken with the emperor shows a relaxed American towering over a slight and nervous Japanese man. Not long after, the emperor himself endured the unendurable: he told his people that stories of his divinity were misplaced.

For the first time in its history Japan was to be occupied by a foreign power. The Americans stayed less than seven years. It was to be one of the most extraordinary encounters of the twentieth century, a 'sensual embrace' of victor and vanquished in John Dower's memorable phrase. Though MacArthur was a conservative, many of the officials around him were Roosevelt New Dealers, idealists who wanted to fashion a peaceful and democratic society from the broken shards of Japan's failed modernization. Acting through the existing bureaucracy, they began to implement a series of far-reaching policies, including land and labour reform, the breakup of oligopolies, equal rights for women, an amnesty for leftwing political prisoners and the drafting of a new pacifist constitution. They also set about purging the government and armed forces of those associated with militarism, though MacArthur took the controversial decision to shield the emperor from prosecution and preserve him as a figure of national unity.

Among many thousands who came under initial suspicion was Ogata's father, Taketora. Despite his liberal background, he had overseen the *Asahi*'s shift towards a more pro-government line and in

1944 was drafted into the cabinet to head the information bureau. After the war, he was briefly designated a war criminal and placed under house arrest. In March 1946 he was summoned by the prosecutors to give evidence to the Tokyo War Tribunal about the pre-war political situation. At the trial, seven men, including former prime minister Hideki Tojo, were sentenced to death. Sixteen more were given life sentences. Outside this show trial, Asia's equivalent of Nuremberg, hundreds of lower-ranking officers were executed for atrocities. Ogata's father was purged from public activities but subsequently cleared of war crimes. Still, Ogata remembers a shrine festival when a drunken man repeatedly pounded on the wooden wall of their house, calling out, 'Taketora Ogata, you are a war criminal.' It was, Ogata recalls, a miserable evening.

At the time, millions of Japanese were engaged in an urgent attempt to understand how their society could have gone so badly wrong. In the years immediately following the war, support for the socialist and communist parties surged, so much so that the American occupiers were frightened into clamping down on the forces they had let loose. In the so-called 'reverse course', which took hold in around 1948 as the contours of the Cold War began to freeze into shape, there was a crackdown on organized labour and on leftwing political leaders. As early as 1947, MacArthur had personally intervened to head off a threatened national strike. Eleanor Hadley, who had been given the job of breaking up the powerful *zaibatsu* business conglomerates, noted the hypocrisy. 'They had been told to organize, that there was a right to strike,' she said. 'Then at the moment of their power they were cut off.'[7] By 1949, the idea of a Red Purge against 'troublemakers' in the labour unions, media and private sector had become so prevalent that the phrase had migrated into Japanese where it was rendered *reddo pa-ji*.

Such was the intellectual turmoil, everything came under discussion. Ogata remembers a conference at his high-school campus to discuss the pros and cons of dropping Chinese characters and, instead, Romanizing written Japanese. One theory claimed that Japan had been held back because it took so long for children to master thousands of complex characters, leaving insufficient time to study modern science. Even in its defeat and humiliation, the impulse to escape its Asian inheritance and join the ranks of 'civilized' western nations had not been extinguished.

The means of achieving this had clearly changed. Japan was occupied and, from November 1946, had a constitution that renounced its right to wage war or to maintain a standing army, navy or air force. The colonial route to international status was blocked. That left the economic path. Ogata says that, even then, amid the ruins of war, he did not despair. 'We were quite optimistic really,' he recalls cheerfully, speaking more than sixty-five years after his tram ride through a flattened Tokyo. 'Because, you see, there was no way to go down. The only way to survive meant going up.'

The world now takes Japan's economic rise for granted. Its startling achievements from 1950 to 1973, when the economy was torpedoing along at an average growth rate of 10 per cent a year, loom much less large today than its more recent economic failures. The past two 'lost decades' – though they have not been quite as lost as some believe – have convinced many detractors that the nation's supposed economic strengths were a chimera and that the true, hidebound Japan now stands before us. The country that some in the 1980s predicted would surpass the US as the world's most powerful economy has instead fallen flat on its face. As a result, the once supposedly essential components of Japan's economic rise – its particular corporate culture and its managed industrial policy – are sometimes derided as the very reasons for its twenty years in the wilderness. 'The state of Japan is a scandal, an outrage, a reproach,' wrote Paul Krugman, a Nobel prize winner in economics, in a series of papers about Japan's post-bubble disease. Subsequently, when economic crisis and paralysis hit the US and Europe, Krugman changed his tune, citing Japan instead as a model of how to weather an economic storm.[8] Even after twenty years of malaise, Japan still stands as the world's most successful example of a catch-up economy. No other non-western nation, save city-states such as Singapore and Qatar, has achieved the standard of living the Japanese now take for granted.[9]

It is all too easy to forget just how unpromising Japan's economic prospects looked in 1945. We forget too that Japan, understandably vilified in Asia for its wartime aggression, nevertheless became an inspiration for much of the region in the latter half of the twentieth century. Japan may not have been loved, but it had proved what should always have been obvious: non-whites were every bit as capable of achieving economic and technological success as Caucasians. That simple truth was not self-evident even in 1958 when Kenneth Galbraith began his book *The Affluent Society* by defining wealthy nations as those 'in the comparatively small corner of the world populated by Europeans'.[10] Japan's implicit message proved an inspiration for technocrats and political leaders alike in Singapore, Taiwan, South Korea, Malaysia and Hong Kong, all of whom emulated its export-led development model. The image of flying geese, first dreamed up in the Japan of the 1930s, took hold, this time with an economic, rather than military, meaning. Japan was the lead goose and the nations of Southeast Asia its followers. Japan had proved to arrogant westerners and to self-doubting Asians alike that colour was no bar to development.

None of this was foreseeable in 1945, at least not to outsiders. Japan's economy, built up since Meiji, was a smoking wreck. Its industrial misery was compounded by the failure of the harvest in the year of its defeat. Bad weather combined with lack of fertilizer and labour to produce a food shortfall of some 40 per cent. *Grave of the Fireflies*, an animated feature film produced four decades later, started gruesomely with the child protagonist dying of starvation in Ueno station, a fate that befell countless people in those early desperate months.[11] Hungry Tokyoites clambered aboard trains leaving Ueno for the countryside, loaded with kimonos and other family heirlooms to swap for food. So crowded were the trains that people hung onto the outside of the carriages and railway staff put wooden slats across the windows to stop them cracking. Kazue Matsumaru, a farmer's wife in a village near Tokyo, described the ravenous crowds that descended from the trains. 'They'd buy anything. Even the leaves off the potato plants.'[12] There was a good deal of stealing too. Much food made its way onto the swelling black market. In the cities, some young women earned money or received scarce items such as nylon stockings or canned food by sleeping with American GIs. 'In the dark corners of certain downtown areas, prostitutes, called "*panpan* girls" in those days, emerged every evening to wait for American soldiers,' Ogata recalls.

Such hardship notwithstanding, America's first concern was not to boost Japan's economy but to dismantle its wartime industrial complex.[13] Japan had been one of the fastest-growing economies in the world since the 1880s when the Meiji leaders set out to modernize their country. From the 1930s, its industries had been marshalled for a war economy. The Americans were determined this would never happen again. Shipyards that had turned out warships were banned from building anything other than wooden fishing boats. The US originally planned to dismantle most of the factories left standing and pack the machinery off to Japan's former enemies as war reparations. Those plans were gradually scaled back. The softening was initially out of sympathy for Japan's desperate economic plight and concerns about social unrest. But, as the Cold War set in, Washington's ideas shifted. It decided that its strategic needs were not best served by a Japan on its knees. Rather, it wanted a bulwark against communism. Yet, even when America started to think about how to build up Japan economically, the 'image always remained of a fundamentally second-rate economy at best'. Only days before the outbreak of the Korean War, John Foster Dulles, special envoy of President Harry Truman, said Japan should concentrate on exporting items such as cocktail napkins.[14]

If the US saw Japan as a maker of trinkets, the nation's bureaucrats had other ideas. Even before the war had ended, government officials had secretly planned for life after defeat. Saburo Okita, a post-war economic planner, sent out a notice at the start of August 1945 to arrange a meeting. 'The idea was to discuss the future of the Japanese economy after the war,' Okita said of his surreptitious plans. 'But if we'd advertised a meeting with a title like that we would have been arrested by the military police.' The gathering of experts took place in a burnt-out building on 16 August, the day after Japan surrendered. Okita remembered how desperate the situation seemed. 'If you looked out of the windows, it looked like a scorched plain. Everybody was starving. But the committee discussing the future worked really hard. They thought, It's bad now. But with a big effort, Japan will get back on her feet again, not by military means, but with new technology and economic power.'[15]

These early planners discussed various models for rebuilding Japan, with some arguing that it should concentrate on agriculture. The consensus that eventually emerged, however, was to employ the same methods that had been marshalled for all-out war to create powerful peacetime industries. From the early 1930s, Japan had shifted from light to heavy industrialization, emphasizing warships, bombs and chemicals over textiles and handicrafts. *Fukoku kyohei* – 'rich country, strong army' – had been the centrepiece of the Meiji project, an objective that slipped into militarism. Now that Japan was forbidden from fighting, it could concentrate solely on building a strong economy.

Washington was soon to regret writing the pacifist clause into Japan's constitution. But in what became known as the Yoshida Doctrine – after Shigeru Yoshida, prime minister for much of the decade after the war – Japan used its lack of international obligations to its own advantage. Released from the burden of defence and protected by the US military, it was able to throw all its energies into economic development. Wealth creation was seen as an alternative way of generating national prestige. The link between pre- and post-war ambitions, and the means of achieving them, was sometimes explicit. Kiyoshi Tomizuka, a professor of engineering at Tokyo Imperial University, wrote in his diary in April 1945, 'An army in uniform is not the only sort of army. Scientific technology and fighting spirit under a business suit will be our underground army.'[16]

For all these aspirations, by 1948, the economy had reached crisis point. Prices had risen a cumulative 1,200 per cent in the three years since the war. Labour conflict was rife. The Americans called for Joseph Dodge, a Detroit banker, who as 'economic tsar' oversaw a drastic plan to rein in government spending and fire public workers. Inflation was gradually contained, and the exchange rate massaged lower to stimulate exports. The Red Purge started and policies intended to break up conglomerates were quietly abandoned. Unemployment rose, consumption dropped and many companies went bankrupt. Depression beckoned. Then, in 1950, the Korean War came to the rescue. What remained of Japan's industrial base cranked into action to supply the Americans with military equipment. Yoshida called it 'a gift from the gods'. Long-idle factories hummed as the US, setting aside its scruples about Japan's military complex, put in orders for barbed wire and munitions. Some factories went the other way, from pre-war military production to the manufacture of civilian goods. An aircraft factory in Osaka started making nails for houses. Makers of radio parts turned their thoughts to light bulbs. In due course, companies such as Nikon, which had ground lenses for gunsights, started producing cameras and binoculars.

The Americans lifted the ban on shipbuilding. The naval yards at Kure, which had built the *Yamato*, the largest battleship ever made, converted production to tankers and other merchant vessels. At that time, Britain was producing half the world's ships. But even during the shipbuilding ban, Japanese engineers harboured what looked like fantastical dreams of surpassing it. Universities continued to churn out shipbuilding engineers even though there were no jobs for them. As soon as the ban was lifted, they were put to work. In Kure, managers adopted the so-called block construction method of shipbuilding in which prefabricated sections of a ship are welded together. They were soon turning out ships in seven months, less than half the time in other countries. A secret mission was sent to study shipbuilding on the Clyde in Scotland. Its members discovered that Japanese methods were already more advanced. Less than a decade after work at the shipyards resumed, Japan had overtaken Britain as the biggest shipbuilder in the world.

It was shortly after Dodge arrived that the Ministry of Trade and Industry, the legendary MITI, was formed. The ministry that was subsequently credited by many with overseeing Japan's economic renaissance was a direct descendant of the Ministry of Munitions. In that incarnation it had beseeched Japanese companies to work together for the purpose of increasing weapons production. Now the bureaucrats of MITI rallied Japan's industrial potential in the interests of peacetime revival. One of its priorities was steel, what one official called 'the food of industry'. If steel was sustenance, it was thin on the ground. In the aftermath of the war, Japan was turning out just 5 million tonnes against the 90 million tonnes being produced in America. Every tonne produced took seven times more man hours. In a strategy reminiscent of the post-Meiji Iwakura mission, in which

Japanese had scoured the world for tips on modernization, steel study groups were sent to the US. MITI concluded that new mills would be needed in strategic port locations. Using the tools of what was then a semi-command economy, it ordered the reclamation of large tracts of land on which ultramodern steel plants could be built. As was to happen with other favoured industries, the government gave mills preferential access to cheap finance and foreign currency. Meanwhile, Japanese engineers were quick to see the potential of a new steel production technique using blown oxygen. They proved rapid learners. By 1960, Japan had quadrupled steel production to 20 million tonnes and had vastly improved efficiency. Five years later, it had more than doubled it again.

Something similar was repeated in the auto industry. In the 1920s, there were only a few thousand cars in Japan, all of them foreign made. General Motors and Ford dominated. As Japan militarized, this was considered a threat. American companies were expelled and Toyota and Nissan were asked to build military trucks. Toyota, which had hitherto made textile looms, began building vehicles only from the mid-1930s. Quality was poor. Yet days after Japan's defeat, Kiichiro Toyoda, Toyota's president, told his engineers they must catch up with American technology within three years. Even for Toyota that proved a fanciful goal. When the company started exporting cars to the US in 1957 under the Crown brand, they flopped. The car could not accelerate fast enough to get onto American freeways. Still, at home Toyota was doing better, helped by high protective tariffs on foreign imports and by cheap finance. The men at MITI had fought with the more economically 'rational' officials in other parts of the government, who had argued Japan should leave car production to the far more advanced Americans. As in other industries, car manufacturers received a huge boost from the Korean War, Toyota's 'salvation', according to Toyoda. 'I felt a mingling of joy for my company and a sense of guilt that I was rejoicing at another country's war.'[17] Although Toyota went it alone, other car companies signed tie-ups with foreign manufactures. MITI made sure that the country was not swamped by superior foreign technology. Instead, Japanese companies were given strict timetables to indigenize the manufacture of components and finally to build entire cars in Japan.

Certainly, MITI officials were not averse to practising a mercantilism that came to be known as 'industrial policy'. Of their protection of start-up industries behind high tariff walls until they could fend off foreign competition, Yoshihiko Morozumi, a senior MITI official, said, 'Until we were strong enough, we kept the doors tight shut. If we opened them too early, the winds might blow everything flat.'[18] It would be wrong, however, to suggest that MITI and other ministries orchestrated Japan's industrial and economic revival singlehandedly. Some recent studies have even suggested that those industries left alone by government were the ones that did best.[19] That view is exaggerated. But there was a great deal of bottom-up entrepreneurial activity as well as state planning. One example is Honda, which became a car manufacturer in direct contravention of MITI's orders. Soichiro Honda, a self-taught engineer who began his career tuning racing cars, turned his attention to motorbikes after the war. He built his first by attaching a small engine to a standard pushbike. After he launched the Honda Cub, he was determined to graduate to cars and trucks. He recalled a meeting with the officials at MITI, who tried to block his entry into an already crowded arena. 'The bureaucrats still had their heads full of the old notions of central control,' he remembered more than three decades later. 'They were absolutely no help. You wouldn't believe what a hard time I had with MITI. When I wanted to make cars, they said, "Keep out. Toyota and Nissan are doing it already." I said, "I'm free to do what I want. The war's over you know."'[20]

Honda was by no means the only entrepreneur to invent a business from scratch. More than any company, Sony exemplifies Japan's rise from the rubble and its transformation from a producer of shoddy trinkets to a manufacturer of world-beating technology. It began its life, quite literally, in a bombed-out building, the shell of the Shirokiya department store in Nihombashi, where Masaru Ibuka opened a radio repair shop in late 1945. The following year, he and Akio Morita, who had been expected to take over his family's 300-year-old sake business in Nagoya, founded a company with the unpromising name of Tsushin Kogyo, or Tokyo Telecommunications Engineering Corporation. The initial investment was $500.

Morita and Ibuka had met the year before the war ended when they were both put on a project to develop a heat-seeking missile. Ibuka, an electrical engineer with thick spectacles, 'shovel hands'[21] and a working-man's accent, was an inveterate tinkerer. After the war, whenever he travelled to America, he would return with toys, but never presented them to his children without first pulling them apart and putting them back together again. Sometimes he bought two sets so that he and Morita could dismantle them together. Early on Ibuka experimented with electric rice cookers (a flop) and reel-to-reel magnetic tape recorders, the first to be sold in Japan. The big breakthrough came in the 1950s when he paid $25,000 to Bell Laboratories to license its transistor technology. His aim was to adapt transistors for use in radios. Bell told him it was impossible. Ibuka persisted and in 1955 Sony became the first company to make transistor radios a commercial success. The transistor was actually a little large for most pockets. So Morita, a marketing genius, had salesmen wear shirts with slightly bigger pockets to foster the illusion of portability.[22]

Morita, thirteen years younger than Ibuka, was the company's commercial brain. His entrepreneurial attitude was exemplified by one incident in 1955 when he was in New York. The Bulova watch company had offered to buy 100,000 units of Sony's transistor radio, an order that was worth more than the entire capitalization of the fledgling company. The only stipulation was that they be sold under the Bulova name. Against the advice of Sony's board, Morita turned the offer down, arguing that Sony needed to build its own brand. He later called the decision the best of his career. 'Morita was an entrepreneur in precisely the American sense of that word, a bold venturer in the mould of John D. Rockefeller and Bill Gates,' said John Nathan, who wrote a superb history of Sony.[23] 'He relied on his gut feeling about products and disdained market research.'[24]

Sony, like Honda, at first struggled in its home market, where it lacked the retail connections of more established, and officially favoured, companies. Both made their initial breakthroughs in the US. Morita criticized some aspects of Japanese business practice, for example the obsession about which school and university an employee had attended. Sony was one of the first companies to introduce merit pay. Though everyone, from the president down, wore the same uniform – still common in many Japanese manufacturers today – the outfits were designed by Issey Miyake.[25] Morita, for all his success, was considered an arrogant maverick by the men at MITI.

I met James Abegglen a couple of times towards the end of his life. In 2006, we had lunch in the modern surroundings of his private club, where he was treated with the deference you might expect to be accorded one of the first people who had 'got' Japan. Abegglen was somewhat frail by then but it was clear he had once been an imposing figure. He possessed what seemed to be an unshakable faith in his own convictions. The other time I met him was when I semi-crashed his eightieth birthday party held in a swanky Tokyo hotel. The celebrations were presided over by his Japanese wife and family and attended by some of the great and the good of the business world. He gave a speech in which he recapped the main episodes of his lifelong entanglement with Japan. The son of a Wisconsin cheese maker, Abegglen first got to know Japan when he was trying to invade it. As a US Marine he was wounded in Iwo Jima. Later, as part of the US Strategic Bombing Survey, he spent time assessing wartime damage to Tokyo and Hiroshima. He returned in 1955 when, as a Ford Foundation fellow, he began a study of what was then the virtually unknown world of the Japanese company, or the *kaisha* in the Japanese word that he helped to internationalize. He was given unprecedented access to several companies, unglamorous cogs in Japan's industrial machine, including Nippon Electric Company, Sumitomo Chemical and Fuji Seitetsu, which would later become Nippon Steel.

Abegglen was the first to identify what became some of the best-known features of the Japanese model, lauded by many in subsequent decades as the 'secret' of the country's industrial success. In his 1958 book *The Japanese Factory*, he emphasized the importance of company-based unions, whose leaders had a stake in raising productivity as well as their members' wages and conditions; lifetime employment; and an emphasis on continuous improvement in production, known as *kaizen*. Abegglen viewed Japanese companies as 'social organizations'. The expectation, at big companies at least, was that people would stay for their entire working lives. From the workers' point of view that meant absolute job security and the prospect of continuous promotion and wage increases until retirement. It was a career escalator determined not by merit but by length of service, a system that encouraged loyalty and cooperation, not a battle among employees to prove who was most worthy of advancement. These companies hired graduates en masse, partly because they wanted to train (or indoctrinate) their workers in-house and partly because it made sense to grab them early in an era of rapid growth and potential labour shortage. 'Especially for Japanese men, companies play the role of a religious community,' one Japanese academic told me.[26] There were company songs, company dormitories, company holidays and, of course, lots of company overtime and company drinking sessions. Matsushita's official song, performed by workers wearing identical grey jumpsuits, went:

> *We will send our products to the people of the world*
> *Our hard work and toil like the sound of water*
> *Gushing from the spring; industrial progress, industrial progress*
> *Number one for harmony, Matsushita Electric*[27]

'Japanese companies are not simple economic machines with the purpose of rewarding shareholders and executives,' Abegglen wrote.[28] 'The Anglo-American notion that all is owed the shareholder has no currency in Japan. The primary stakeholders in the *kaisha* are its members, the employees.' Westerners looked at the peculiar characteristics of large Japanese companies with bemusement. 'The conclusion in the west was that you couldn't possibly run a company that way,' Abegglen said.[29] The fact that companies were not beholden to their shareholders, in his view, enabled them to play a longer game. According to a senior partner at the Boston Consulting Group, where Abegglen later spent much of his career, he would say, 'Profits are for now or for later. Westerners want their profits now. Japanese want growth now and profits later.'[30] That view enabled Japanese companies, liberated from quarterly earnings targets, to prioritize market share and to plot multi-year takeovers of entire industries. From steel and shipbuilding to cars and semi-conductors, that is exactly what they did.

Success certainly wasn't all down to Japanese business practice. Many techniques, both organizational and technical, were borrowed from abroad. William Deming, an American consultant, became revered in Japan, more so than in his native America, for his lectures in the 1950s on quality control and testing. Japanese executives were almost fanatical about learning 'best practice' and they took ideas from wherever they came. In the early 1950s, Eiji Toyoda, who went on to become president of Toyota, spent three months at Ford's River Rouge Plant in Michigan learning about quality control and efficiencies of scale. There were, though, some peculiar features of the Japanese model that later came to be seen as important.

The Americans had attempted to break up the old *zaibatsu* conglomerates, which they had seen as part of Japan's war machine, but these lived on in other forms. Companies retained close links with each other through cross-shareholdings and close relationships with suppliers. These horizontal and vertical ties, which in later decades were almost impossible for foreign entrants to penetrate, were known as *keiretsu*. These loose groupings, often served by a 'main bank' acting more like a sponsor than a profit-driven lender, became instruments of mutual support. In the so-called 'convoy system', companies moved together, ensuring that no one in their group fell behind. That did not mean, as was sometimes assumed, that there was no competition. In many ways, it was quite the reverse. Some studies concluded that Japanese industry was more fiercely competitive than in other countries since competitors did not simply go bust and leave the field to a few dominant players. There were at least ten car companies, five steel makers and later ten semi-conductor manufacturers. Overcapacity meant slim margins. That made the pursuit of volume, including the conquering of foreign markets, vital to success. Vertical *keiretsu*, between large companies and their myriad suppliers, were different from horizontal ones. Small companies, many not much more than family workshops in big industrial cities such as Osaka, were the equivalent of the German Mittelstand. They acted as shock absorbers for big business. Larger companies squeezed them mercilessly, placing orders at short notice and demanding absolute flexibility of working practice. In this way, the price of components was kept low and Japan's famous just-in-time system, whereby manufacturers kept inventory at a minimum, was sustained. Small companies, where conditions were less generous and jobs less secure, took the strain. This allowed bigger organizations to fulfil the generous social contract of lifelong employment and ever-rising wages for which Japan became famous.

The system had obvious flaws. Industrial production was prioritized over consumer goods, market share over profits, saving over spending and large companies over small ones. The entire economy revolved around exports – a legacy that Japan still lives with. At home, thrifty households were given meagre interest by banks and the post office, allowing the government to lend cheaply to industry. Big businesses were allowed to pollute the environment in the interests of profit and to charge Japanese consumers more than foreign ones in the interests of the nation's balance of trade. Some of the fruits of Japan's rapid growth were, in other words, sacrificed to the greater, abstract, goal of nation-building. These were the seeds of what some have called Japan's 'empty affluence'.[31]

As far as nation-building projects go, though, Japan's was supremely successful. In 1960, after a period of political turmoil surrounding the renewal of the US–Japan Security Treaty, Prime Minister Hayato Ikeda announced his national income-doubling plan.[32] Japan was progressing faster than anyone imagined. That year, Charles de Gaulle, the French president, had referred snidely to the Japanese prime minister as 'that transistor salesman'.[33] Two years later, the transistor salesman was running a country with a larger economy than France. In 1967, Japan also overtook Britain, and in the following year it surpassed West Germany to become the world's largest capitalist economy after the US. If Japan had been hopelessly lost in the 1930s and 40s, surely now it was found.

Something of the excitement of those catch-up years is captured in a trilogy of films, *Always: Sunset on Third Street*, the first of which was released in 2005. As Japan's economy has slowed, it has been common to look back nostalgically at the high-growth years for clues as to the spirit that drove rapid development.[34] In the first of the trilogy, set in the back streets of Tokyo, the country is getting back on its feet in the 1950s. A young woman comes from Aomori, in the poorer, rural north, to work at Suzuki Auto, a tiny repair shop catering to the few cars then on the road. She represents the mass exodus to the cities that took place in the decades after the war. By the end of the film, the main protagonists, though poor, have traded in their ice-coolers for refrigerators and one or two have bought black-and-white televisions. In the late 1950s, in a play on the imperial regalia of sword, mirror and jewel, the Japanese talked of the three 'sacred treasures' of refrigerator, washing machine and black-and-white television. The film and its two sequels take place in the shadow of Tokyo Tower, a fire-engine red version of the Eiffel Tower completed in 1958 that became a symbol of Japan's economic resurgence. Built in part from the carcasses of US tanks used in the Korean War, Tokyo Tower was thirteen metres higher than the French original and the tallest self-supporting steel tower in the world. In the third of the films, set in 1964, the neighbourhood prepares for the Tokyo Olympics by buying colour televisions, one of the three new must-have items – the other two being air-conditioner and car – that had replaced the earlier sacred treasures. At the end of the film, the country girl from Aomori befittingly embarks on her honeymoon by boarding the *Shinkansen* bullet train to Osaka, unveiled in time for the Olympics. Just nineteen years after its surrender and seeming total devastation, Japan had built the fastest train in the world.

Certainly there were further adversities to bend during Japan's seemingly inexorable rise. Most serious was the oil shock of 1973 when oil prices quadrupled after Arab members of the Organization of the Petroleum Exporting Countries proclaimed an embargo in response to US help for Israel during the Yom Kippur War. Japan had only four days of reserves. Inflation rose to 30 per cent and consumption slumped. But Japan turned on a dime, both diplomatically and economically. Tokyo sent envoys to the Middle East, distancing itself from US policy and swearing loyalty to the Arab world. At home, workers, tamer than their western counterparts, were persuaded to moderate wage demands. Robots, another American technology, were rapidly adopted and companies strained to reduce their energy consumption as oil prices skyrocketed. MITI promoted 'brain-power industries', such as electronics and computers, over the energy-intensive heavy industries it had formerly favoured. A decade later, Japan had nearly halved its energy imports from 3 per cent of GDP to 1.6 per cent.[35] The country emerged from the twin oil shocks of the 1970s – there was a second after the Iranian Revolution of 1979 – with greater energy efficiency and faster growth than any other advanced nation.

Yet, as well as enthusiasm for what was being created, there was concern for what was being lost. As early as 1953, cinematographer Yasujiro Ozu's masterpiece *Tokyo Story* depicted a rapidly changing urban society in which the communitarian values of rural Japan were vanishing. Two elderly parents from a seaside town visit their children in Tokyo only to find that their offspring have become too self-absorbed to pay them much attention. Against a backdrop of cranes, cars and construction, the parents traipse between households much as King Lear is shuffled between his daughters' castles. Some social commentators were highly critical of Japan's 'progress', particularly as concern grew about the environmental destruction that accompanied breakneck urbanization. Speaking of the decade in the run-up to the Olympics, Minoru Morita, a leftwing commentator, said, 'I felt we had created a monstrous society for ourselves. In the city our atmosphere was contaminated, our rivers were dirty, our seas were polluted and our natural environment was destroyed. As far as our people were concerned, they'd come to desire economic profit above all else. They had abandoned all the greater humanistic ideals. I thought it was an era of despair.'[36] That was not a typical view. More common was the opinion of Masaya Ito, the press secretary of Ikeda, the prime minister who had initiated the income-doubling target. 'How far could the economy go on growing?' he asked. 'It was like a magic teapot that just kept on pouring.'[37]

Japan's growth had inevitably slowed a little in the 1970s, but by the 1980s its living standards had caught up with those of many western countries. The features of industrial Japan first described by Abegglen were widely recognized as important elements of its success. There were even suggestions that western companies would do well to emulate some aspects if they were to survive the Japanese onslaught. In 1979, Ezra Vogel, a US academic, produced a book, *Japan as Number One*, in which he laid out the country's social and industrial strengths and suggested America needed to watch its back. The book presented a Japan that was organizationally, educationally and technologically equipped to take on the world. Although primarily intended to wake US policymakers from what Vogel considered their complacency, *Japan as Number One* was a bigger success in Japan than it was in America. It became, in fact, the all-time best-selling work of non-fiction by a western author. The reasons for that were not hard to fathom. Its very title appeared to be an affirmation of what Japan had so ardently sought for more than a hundred years since the Meiji Restoration, a Japan that could take on westerners at their own game – and win.

The Japanese became swept up in their own hyperbole. As early as 1967, the year Japan's economy overtook that of Britain, one professor of Kyoto University had relegated Europe to the status of a nice place for sightseeing. The following decade, books on 'the British disease' became popular. One writer defined it as a social disease that causes 'a diminished will to work, overemphasis on rights and declining productivity'. Books on 'the American disease' inevitably followed. The US was said to be wasteful and inefficient, its companies devoted to short-termism. It was also deemed to lack a work ethic. Japanese engineers who visited foreign factories often expressed their amazement at overseas workers' penchant for tea breaks and knocking-off early. American society was considered to have been corroded by violent crime, drugs and divorce.

In a 1983 government survey, one question revealed the long-held obsession of the Japanese state, the 'shrill sense' of inferiority and superiority that had driven its catch-up project for more than a century. 'Compared to westerners,' the pollsters asked, 'do you think, in a word, that the Japanese are superior? Or do you think they are inferior?' By the 1980s, in a word, 53 per cent of Japanese answered that they thought themselves superior against just 20 per cent who had so responded in 1953 when the same unpleasant question had been asked. In neither survey was there a box asking whether the question itself was objectionable.[38]

By the late 1980s, many in America were beginning to talk about Japan in terms of threat. Japan's trade surpluses were swelling to unheard of proportions, its cars were displacing petrol-guzzling US models and its companies were snapping up trophy assets – an iconic building here, a Hollywood film studio there. A group of commentators, who collectively became known as 'the revisionists', had an explanation for Japan's success. They built on the pioneering work of Abegglen to suggest that Japan represented an entirely new way of doing business. Unless the US dropped its laissez-faire approach and adopted some of the same 'industrial' and 'strategic trade' policies as Japan, they argued, it would continue to lose ground.

The revisionists included Chalmers Johnson, who had written about the state planning undertaken by MITI in 1982; James Fallows, who wrote *Looking at the Sun*; and Clyde Prestowitz, a former trade negotiator under Ronald Reagan whose frustrations at trying to open Japan's semi-conductor, telecoms and medical markets confirmed his belief that Japan was playing a smarter game. His 1993 book was called *Trading Places: How We Are Giving Our Future to Japan and How to Reclaim It*. Prestowitz says he and others were far from the 'Japan bashers' sometimes alleged. 'We were, in fact, admirers of the Japanese system and promoted the idea that in order to compete with it, the US would have to imitate it in important ways. Our frustration was not so much with the Japanese as with the US government.' Orthodox US policymakers, he says, could not understand how Japan was beating America at its own game. 'I tried to explain to the top officials of the Reagan administration that Japan was playing football while we were playing baseball.'[39]

A third book, less about trade and more about Japan's political and social organization, also depicted a society unlike anything the west had encountered before. Karel van Wolferen's *The Enigma of Japanese Power* presented a portrait of a country without central authority in which decisions were taken almost organically. From the perspective of orthodox free traders trying to negotiate with Japan, this meant by definition that the people on the other side of the negotiating table were powerless to affect change. Van Wolferen's was a subtle take on the story. The more common version, a crude popularization of the revisionists, was of a sinister Japan Inc in which clever planners outsmarted competitors. Abegglen, who tried to portray Japan as having 'a complex combination of cooperation and competition', was always opposed to the notion of a government-directed machine. He told one journalist about a widely held notion that somewhere in the recesses of Japan's bureaucracy was 'a guy with a long beard and a big computer, and if we could find and shoot him, we'd solve the problem'.[40] If van Wolferen's thesis was correct, there was nobody to shoot.

Whatever the reasons for Japan's success, the idea was taking hold, in the popular press at least, that it was on the verge of challenging America to become the world's largest economy. Given that its population was half the size, that was a bold prediction, requiring that every Japanese on average become twice as wealthy as every American. In 1988, the well-known financier George Soros responded to a huge stock market slide in New York and London by predicting nothing less than 'the transfer of economic and financial power from the United States to Japan'.[41] Just at the time such notions were gaining credence, however, Japan was in the midst of its own grotesque financial bubble. When it burst, the idea of Japanese economic supremacy would be for ever discarded.

# 6

## After the Fall

It was never clear whether Nui Onoue herself or her large ceramic toad was the true oracle. Either way, when Onoue held her weekly séances over which the one-metre-tall, brownish toad presided, there were lines of limousines parked outside Egawa, her exclusive restaurant in the Sennichimae entertainment district of Osaka. This was the height of the 1980s bubble and her clients came for tips about which Japanese companies would perform best and thus on which shares to place their lavish wagers. A former hostess, by then in her early sixties, Onoue had established the exclusive *ryotei* restaurant in the ardently commercial western city of Osaka. As time went on, her clients came not so much to dine as to invest.

For some reason, in Osaka toads had come to be associated with wealth. Japan's second-biggest metropolis had been the commercial hub for hundreds of years, a centre of rice trading and home to the world's first futures market, established in 1730. It was a city where people sometimes greeted each other not with *konnichiwa*, but with *mokkari-makka*, 'are you making money?' Because of the amphibians' reputed money-making properties, some Osakans refer to their wallets as 'toad mouth', or *gama-guchi* in Japanese.

Onoue's toad was extra special. It received trading tips from the gods and at one stage, through the auspices of Onoue herself, controlled a portfolio of some $20 billion, an astronomical sum even for the heady days of the Japanese bubble. Word of the toad's remarkable track record – for it was rarely wrong – spread far and wide. The sort of people who came for advice were executives of some of the country's most prestigious financial institutions. They included officials from Industrial Bank of Japan, the *crème de la crème* of the banking world and, at the time, one of the largest financial institutions in the world. Executives from Yamaichi Securities also regularly attended. A prominent securities trading firm, Yamaichi was to become one of the biggest casualties of the stock market crash, ceasing all operations in November 1997. A financial subsidiary of Matsushita, the company that made the Panasonic brand, was another firm that put its faith in Onoue, entrusting her with Y50 billion. When the bet went sour, Matsushita's humiliated president did the honourable thing. He resigned.

Japan's Nikkei stock average, the one most often quoted on the pages of the business press, came within a whisker of 39,000 on the last trading day of 1989. That proved to be its last hurrah. When the price of shares began to sink the following year, Onoue was presented with a problem that not even her toad knew how to fix. It was then she hit upon the idea of keeping the whole thing going by getting managers of one bank to issue fake deposit receipts, which she used to free up cash and securities lodged with other institutions. It was a convoluted scheme that got her deeper into trouble as shares continued to slide. In August 1991, she was arrested for fraud. An investigation discovered that a senior executive from Yamaichi Securities – not the gods after all – was the true source of the toad's inspiration. As her financial empire crumbled, it was almost inevitable that Onoue became known as 'The Bubble Lady'. She was sentenced to twelve years.[1]

Onoue's story encapsulates the madness of the bubble, which lasted from the mid-1980s to the end of the decade. Stories from that era are legendary, and quite possibly apocryphal. They tell of how businessmen would think nothing of giving thousands of dollars in tips to a favourite hostess, asking little in return save that she laugh coquettishly at their jokes. They tell of people sprinkling gold leaf on their food like salt and pepper, a practice that – if truth be told – persists in some of Japan's more upmarket restaurants to this day. They tell, too, of the golf memberships that traded on the secondary market, bought and sold by speculators with no intention of ever actually donning golfing apparel and teeing off.

The bubble was encouraged by the belief, derived from post-war experience, that when it came to property prices, the forces of Sir Isaac Newton no longer applied in Japan. It was further puffed up by a heady mix of easy money, financial deregulation, a strong yen and low interest rates. The main human ingredients, as so often, were fear and greed. The bubble is sometimes presented as proof that Japan's economic system, so lauded by credulous admirers only a few years before, was deeply flawed. It is true that Japan's economy chased market share over profits. It is true too that the system worked best during the catch-up years, but less well once Japan had reached a western standard of living. But the country's bubble was partly just an inevitable consequence of decades of rapid growth, an exuberant overshooting. As Americans and Europeans have themselves become all too aware in recent years, irrational exuberance can grip the western imagination too.

In Japan, property prices were driven ever higher as companies, many with entirely unrelated businesses, borrowed money to put into escalating real estate. Those that didn't participate found their performance falling behind competitors that were bingeing on property. At one stage, the choicest buildings in Ginza, the most upmarket commercial district in Tokyo, were fetching $20,000 a square foot. By comparison, in 2011, property in London's Knightsbridge, one of the city's most exclusive areas, cost a tad over $3,000.[2]

The other favoured investment was shares. These also seemed a safe bet, partly because their prices kept ascending and partly because their value was propped up by friendly shareholders who held them as cross-shareholdings in the *keiretsu* system. Share prices rose beyond what was considered normal, but, as usually happens in such circumstances, market gurus came up with explanations for why the Tokyo market was different. Shares in Nippon Telegraph and Telephone, for example, were trading at what stockbrokers call a price-earnings ratio of 300, implying that it would take 300 years of profits to cover the share price.[3]

Many date the start of Japan's extraordinary excesses – and hence its drastic decline – to a meeting of the finance ministers and central bank governors of the US, Germany, Britain, France and Japan held in New York's Plaza Hotel in September 1985. It was a very upmarket mugging. The upshot was that Japan, together with the other countries present, agreed to intervene on the currency markets in an effort to strengthen the yen and weaken the dollar. The idea was to help the

US clamber out of recession and to close what had become a yawning trade gap between Japan and America, a cause of increasing friction. The effort proved all too effective. Over the next two years, the yen doubled in value from Y240 to Y120 against the dollar, making Japan's products twice as expensive for the rest of the world to buy. The Bank of Japan, the central bank, convinced that the higher yen would tip Japan into recession, lowered interest rates to keep the economy afloat. It was also acting in response to western requests – of the sort these days being made of China – to boost domestic consumption and serve as an engine of world growth.

There were domestic reasons for the crisis too. The government had deregulated the capital markets, making it easier for companies to issue debt rather than borrow from banks. That left banks looking for alternative places to invest their deposits. All too often they lent to those who wanted to speculate on property. Japan had also failed to make the transition from exporting powerhouse to what Yasuhiro Nakasone, prime minister in the mid-1980s, called an 'importing superpower'.[4] The post-war political economy had been built around production and exports. Shifting to a consumer-led model was easier said than done. For that, one needed to overcome vested interests and an entire political structure built around big business rather than the ordinary citizen. As a result of the central bank's effort to stimulate the economy, money became easier and cheaper to get hold of, fuelling a speculative frenzy. The price of shares and property began to escalate in what looked to many like a one-way bet. Even Onoue's ceramic toad appeared incapable of making a wrong move. Of course in finance, as in life, bets can go both ways. When the central bank, realizing how far things had got out of hand, tried to tame the euphoria by raising interest rates, the bubble was pricked. Japan, which had been floating on air for so long, landed with a thud. There would be no return to the economic vigour of the past. The dream of Japan as Number One was over.

It took many years for the Japanese to understand that collapsing asset prices marked more than a temporary setback. Hype about the unique strengths of the Japanese economy – based naturally on the unique virtues of the Japanese people – led many to believe that it was only a matter of time before shares and property prices bounced back to 'normal'. In the first years of the 1990s, the economy grew reasonably well. Only as the decade wore on, did growth slow and some financial institutions begin to come under pressure. Gradually, it became clear there was to be no return to the good old days. This was the new normal.

To breathe life into the flagging economy, over the course of the 1990s successive governments implemented several big stimulus packages of the sort that Europe and America tried after the 2008 Lehman crisis. They spent on public works – later derided as 'bridges to nowhere' – on tax cuts and on social security. At one point, they even sent shopping coupons, worth around $200 each, to more than 30 million households. If the aim was to return to pre-bubble growth rates, these stimulus packages didn't work, though no one knows what would have happened without them.[5] Whatever the effect, growth in the 1990s averaged just 1.2 per cent – about one-quarter of its rate in the 1980s – and Japan suffered no fewer than three recessions. While living standards held up reasonably well, it was a far cry from what 'catch-up Japan' had been used to. Worse was to follow. From 1997, a few big banks, laden with bad debts, started failing. Among the casualties was Yamaichi Securities, none other than the source of trading information for Onoue's ill-fated toad. Japan faced the very real prospect of serious financial crisis.

In the political sphere, there had been intimations of crisis in 1993 when, for the first time in four decades, the Liberal Democratic Party lost power. The coalition that replaced it was fragile and divided, and the Liberal Democrats were back in office within a year. Still, nothing would be quite the same again. From that time on – at least until the party was rejuvenated under the extraordinary premiership of Junichiro Koizumi in 2001–6 – the Liberal Democrats could cling on only with the support of coalition partners. Successive governments' failure to mount anything other than a sporadic response to deepening economic gloom meant that the political system, so stable in the post-war period, limped from crisis to crisis. Over the course of the decade, no fewer than seven prime ministers came and went. It marked the start of a period of political dysfunction that persists to this day.

*

It was the novelist Haruki Murakami who first put the year 1995 into my head. It is not the most obvious year to pick as the decisive turning point in Japan's post-war history. One might just as easily nominate 1973, the year of the first oil shock, when toilet paper disappeared overnight from supermarket shelves, as the year when post-war innocence vanished. Growth more than halved, from an average of 9.5 per cent since the 1950s to 4.2 per cent in the 70s and 80s. It was the end of what Shijuro Ogata, my friend from the central bank, had called Japan's 'golden era'. Then there was 1989, the year in which, on 7 January, the Showa era ended with the death of Emperor Hirohito at the age of eighty-seven. Hirohito's reign had begun on Christmas Day 1926. Few reigns could have seen such highs and lows. By contrast, the Heisei era, as the period that followed is known, has proved altogether less riveting, marked as it has been by comfortable affluence, gentle decline, and political and economic drift.

By many measures, 1990 is the most compelling candidate of all for Japan's post-war turning point. Not only was that the year the bubble burst, but there were also momentous geopolitical changes. The Berlin Wall had fallen and the Soviet empire was entering its death throes. Those political earthquakes ended at a stroke what for Japan had been the comfortable certainties of the Cold War, in which its place in the world order as an American ally in the Pacific had been clearly delineated.

Murakami, however, thought 1995 was the year I should be looking at. Neither the death of the emperor, nor the collapse of the bubble, nor even the fall of the Berlin Wall had perfectly crystallized for the public the fact that Japan had entered a new era. Rather, he said, it was the twin psychological shocks of 1995 – an earthquake in Kobe and a terrorist attack on the Tokyo subway – that brought home the country's changed circumstances with absolute clarity. 'That was the year the post-war myth of the miracle years ended,' he told me. When the modern city of Kobe collapsed, he said, faith in Japan's engineering prowess, its very modernity, crumbled with it. More frightening still was the attack by members of a murderous doomsday cult. That shattered the illusion, he said, of a harmonious nation whose people would always pull together in the same direction. Japan's very social consensus was rotting from within.

I once spent an afternoon with Murakami in a quiet restaurant called Tamasaka in the Aoyama district of Tokyo. The street, like so many in this city of secret neighbourhoods, had no pavement save for a white painted line, and was flanked in parts by a large, uneven stone wall, which gave the surroundings an almost medieval flavour. A casual observer might have missed the restaurant altogether, so discreet was the sign and so narrow the gravel path leading to its unmarked door. Having removed our shoes, we were directed upstairs to a bare, squarish private dining room with tatami-mat flooring and wooden panels. We sat on cushions on the floor facing each other across a low table set with chopsticks. When the waiter stepped outside and slid the paper-slatted screen door closed with a gentle clunk, we were left together in a room as silent and contemplative as one of the wells in which Murakami's characters have sometimes found themselves.

Murakami was wearing a deep blue suit and a collarless shirt. His short haircut emphasized the wideness of his face. There were a few lines around his mouth, but he still looked good for a man in his mid-fifties. He wouldn't have a lunchtime beer, he said, as he intended to go for a swim afterwards. Murakami had an intense, slightly pensive gaze. He spoke in English. His style was to pause for long periods, weighing up the words, and then to squeeze out everything at once, like toothpaste. Every sentence had a heaviness about it, as though it was his definitive word on the subject. We began our conversation not in 1995, but in the 1960s, in the fast-growth years when Murakami was growing up. 'My parents expected me to join the system, to go to some big company and to marry a good girl. That's the course I was expected to follow. But I just didn't want to live that way,' Murakami was saying. 'Japanese society has a kind of power system. If you are part of it, you are OK. But if you are out of it you are not OK. I was out of it by choice. When I graduated from university, I just dropped out.'

Murakami was born in 1949. His parents were both teachers of Japanese literature. His grandfather on his father's side had been a Buddhist priest. His maternal grandfather had been an Osaka merchant. A teenager during the income-doubling decade of the 1960s, Murakami had felt from an early age that not all was well with Japan's economic miracle. Something troubled him about the ceaseless quest for growth and status. His own life had been a rebellion of sorts against the easy certainties into which he had been born. At Waseda University, where he studied drama, he met and married his wife, Yoko, much to the annoyance of his parents. When Yoko went to meet them for the first time, tension was so high she suffered a temporary attack of paralysis.[6]

Alongside his studies, Murakami worked in a record shop and, before graduation, started a jazz bar in Tokyo called Peter Cat. Clearly he loved it, though he described it as hard labour. 'I had to work until two or three o'clock in the morning. It was full of cigarette smoke and drunks. I had to kick those drunks out sometimes. I had to do everything.' While he was working at the bar, he began to write fiction for an hour every night, eventually producing *Hear the Wind Sing*, which was published in the literary magazine *Gunzo* in 1979. He sold Peter Cat and devoted himself full time to writing, winning wider recognition in 1985 with *Hard-Boiled Wonderland and the End of the World*, a story set in a surreal version of Tokyo inhabited by flesh-eating creatures living underground called INKlings. After that came *Norwegian Wood* (1987), a novel about love and suicide that unfolds against the background of student agitation in 1960s Tokyo. It went on to sell 4 million copies in Japan. Murakami became so uncomfortable with his growing fame that he fled the country, first to Europe and then to the US, where he taught at Princeton. Partly he sought to escape the furore his novels had created. But partly it was to extract himself from the late-1980s excesses of the bubble economy and what he called the mindless 'Number-One-ism' overwhelming society. 'I just wanted to escape from Japan. I was so sick of living here. We were too confident, too arrogant, too rich.'

Murakami returned from self-imposed exile in 1995. It was quite a year in which to make his reappearance. The first of the twin shocks took place in the port city of Kobe where he had been brought up. At 5.46 a.m. on 17 January, a powerful earthquake measuring 6.8 on the Richter scale ripped through one of Japan's most prosperous cities, killing 6,500 people and injuring thousands more. In *After the Quake*, a book written several years later, Murakami describes the destruction and chaos of an imaginary temblor.

Derailments, falling vehicles, crashes, the collapse of elevated expressways and rail lines, the crushing of subways, the explosion of tanker trucks. Buildings . . . transformed into piles of rubble, their inhabitants crushed to death. Fires everywhere, the road system in a state of collapse, ambulances and fire trucks useless, people just lying there dying.[7]

Although the disaster was a natural phenomenon, its impact was worsened by man-made decisions. Buildings and highways that Japanese engineers had confidently proclaimed to be earthquake-proof collapsed like cards. Reclaimed land around the city of 1.4 million people turned to mud. The Hanshin expressway, a showcase of modern engineering, crumpled and buckled. Only months before, Japanese experts had gone to Los Angeles to investigate the recent earthquake there. Their arrogant conclusion was that such destruction could never occur in Japan because of the superiority of its building techniques. The damage in Kobe turned out to be far worse.

Japan's institutions proved just as fragile as its supposedly unshakeable buildings. In Tokyo, it took politicians several hours to work out what was going on. A cabinet meeting in the morning had been told erroneously that a quake had hit Kyoto, fifty miles from the actual site of the disaster. Communications had collapsed, meaning little information was getting in or out. Authorities dithered about whether they should send in the Self Defence Forces, Japan's army-equivalent, which was still mistrusted by the public half a century after the war. The rescue response was so haphazard that *yakuza* gang members, famed for their tattoos and supposed honour code, were reported to be first on the scene with food and blankets. Into the institutional vacuum poured hundreds of thousands of volunteers whose actions began to seed the idea that people, not governments or bureaucrats, were the ones who could get things done. It was an unsettling turn of events for a population that had, by and large, trusted the authorities for four decades to do the right thing.

'The structure of society is very unstable,' Murakami told me, adding that the Kobe earthquake and the authorities' ill-judged response to it brought that home. In one of the stories in *After the Quake*, a collection of short stories that takes place in the weeks between Kobe and the subsequent poison-gas attack on Tokyo, a child has nightmares about 'Earthquake Man'. In another, a giant frog and an unassuming loan collection officer at a trust bank, Mr Katagiri, team up to save

Tokyo from Worm, a malevolent serpent bent on unleashing a second, even more devastating, quake. The blurb on the book jacket speaks of the 'inconsolable howl of a nation indelibly scarred'.

As if Kobe were not enough, just two months later, on 20 March, members of a religious cult called Aum Shinrikyo caused terror by scattering deadly sarin poison on the Tokyo subway, injuring thousands of people. Aum was a quasi-religious organization led by Shoko Asahara, the son of a tatami-mat maker who had been born in 1955 as Chizuo Matsumoto. Asahara had begun his destructive career as a peddler of make-believe when he made $200,000 by selling Almighty Medicine – tangerine peel in alcohol – at $7,000 a dose to desperately ill elderly people. In 1984 he had set up the Aum Association of Mountain Wizards, a yoga and health club that became even more sinister when it was renamed Aum Supreme Truth. Asahara stitched together a set of beliefs from Shiva the Destroyer, Nostradamus and biblical notions of Armageddon. He began to predict a nuclear war that would soon lay waste to civilization. Before long he had set about trying to hasten that end. Only paid-up followers of Aum would survive.

Asahara attracted a better class of cultist. Many were drawn from Tokyo University and other top-flight academic institutions where the bureaucrats – the midwives of the national miracle – had been trained. Members signed over all their possessions to Aum and cut ties with their families. They took part in bizarre rituals, including one in which they paid to drink Asahara's dirty bathwater, otherwise known as Miracle Pond. Improbably, Aum acquired thousands of members. Asahara sent his lieutenants, known as monks, to search for chemical and even nuclear weapons. Fortunately they never got their hands on the latter. But they did discover sarin, a nerve gas developed by Nazi German scientists in the 1930s.

On the morning of 20 March, Aum members boarded several different subway lines, each of them rattling towards Kasumigaseki, Japan's bureaucratic nerve centre. They punctured plastic bags containing sarin, at least one with the tip of a specially sharpened umbrella. As the gas spread through the crowded metro tunnels, thousands fell ill. By the end of that horrible day, 5,500 people had been struck down. Some were left in a vegetative state. One woman, whose contact lenses fused to her pupils, had to have both her eyes surgically removed. Thirteen people, including station staff, died.

The rise of the Aum doomsday cult was the sort of freak occurrence that could have happened anywhere. Yet Japanese intellectuals, Murakami among them, sought to link its emergence with a broader crisis in Japanese society. In *Underground*, a book of interviews with victims and perpetrators of the poisoning, he wrote, 'I can't simply file away the gas attack, saying: "After all, this was merely an extreme and exceptional crime committed by an isolated lunatic fringe."' Rather than seeing the event as 'Evil Them' versus 'Innocent Us', he raked over mainstream society for clues about what could have led to Aum. 'Wasn't the real key,' he wrote, 'more likely to be found hidden under "Our" territory?' To me he said, 'The cult people got out of that system and they entered the right system, or at least a system they thought was right . . . They decided to live for something good. But they committed a crime.'

Other writers, including Kenzaburo Oe, Japan's only living recipient of the Nobel Prize for Literature, also spoke sympathetically about Aum. Of Asahara's mad brigade, Oe once told me, 'They wanted to show the Japanese people how we have reached a dead end in our mental situation, a dead end in our soul.'[8] I thought it was strange that two of Japan's leading authors should have spoken about Aum in such terms. It was true, though, that people had long been looking for inspiration beyond the cult of gross domestic product, which had become a national obsession before the bubble burst. They were not short of alternatives. L. Ron Hubbard's Church of Scientology, the Unification Church of Reverend Sun Myung Moon and Bhagwan Shree Rajneesh all vied for acolytes. In the Japan of the 1980s, dozens of new religions had taken hold, prompting one academic to term the restless era 'the rush hour of the gods'.[9]

'Nineteen ninety-five was the most important year after the war,' Murakami told me.[10] 'It was a critical year, a kind of milestone for our country.' He fell silent while a waiter placed bowls, dishes and small pots on the table. We listened to the gentle scraping sound of clay against wood. The waiter's every movement seemed precisely choreographed as though he were performing a martial art. It struck me that his task was a little like the stage hands in kabuki drama, the *kuroko* or 'black people'. Dressed from head to toe in black, they glided about the stage in full view of the audience, moving props and changing actors' costumes. Yet, by convention, they were treated as invisible to the spectator's eye.

The Japanese are good at role-playing and suspension of disbelief. But 1995, Murakami said, awoke them from their reverie. 'We believed in our system. We had been getting richer and richer and we thought our system would be stable for ever. We believed that, if you were part of the Mitsubishi Corporation, you would be all right for ever. But after 1995, we are no longer so confident. We have come to think that there is something wrong with our system. It is a time of great change in our way of thinking.'

For Murakami, the events of that year were connected with the collapse of the old economic model. They marked the violent death throes of a system that he had always felt was somehow rotten. 'I think the burst of the bubble economy was good for Japan. When we were rich, I hated this country. It was stupid, foolish and arrogant. We were so confident about our system. This system was right. Japan was Number One, stupid things like that,' he said. 'The bubble burst and we have problems these days. But I think it's good. I think our society is healthier than it was ten years ago. Back then, we thought we were right. But now we are kind of cool and we are thinking, What am I? What are we? I think that's good. It happens in history. I think it is only a matter of time before we recover, economically and mentally.'

# PART FOUR

# Life after Growth

# 7

# Japan as Number Three

The envelope was stiff with ice. It sat in the icebox of the Tokyo house I moved into in the winter of 2001. On it, in neat, handwritten characters, were the words 'Cat Money'. Inside, as crisp as the day they were printed, were three Y10,000 notes, at the time worth around $250. The envelope in question had been left by the previous residents of the house in Higashi Kitazawa, a lovely, upper-middle-class neighbourhood of little lanes, topiary pine and walled-off homes in central Tokyo. Sometimes, when they were gone for the weekend, they would ask neighbours to look after the cat. The money was for anything the indulged feline might require while they were away.

Two things occurred to me about the cat money. The first was how expensive it appeared to be to feed a pet in Tokyo. Many people in the capital, even in those supposedly straitened times, maintained an extravagant attitude towards money. Certainly, well-to-do Higashi Kitazawa, known for its artists and authors, was not typical of Tokyo living standards, let alone those of Japan's more economically depressed regions. Still, I had been struck by how willing even ordinary people – secretaries, students, telephonists and office workers – were to spend quite large sums on little luxuries. Some seemed happy to splash out $200 per head on an exquisitely prepared meal or $400 a night per person for a room at a hot-spring resort. Luxury goods makers such as Louis Vuitton had made a killing in a country where young women would line up for hours just for the privilege of purchasing an overpriced handbag. Naturally, such outlays were only occasional. Naturally, too, many Japanese – including the increasing number without work, those retired on meagre pensions or people in the new category of 'working poor' – could never afford such items. Japan felt much more economically divided than before. Even so, though I arrived in what was said to be the midst of a deep recession, many Japanese appeared to have a lot of money. A visiting MP from northern England, on seeing the bright lights of Tokyo and throngs of people waiting outside overflowing restaurants and bars, remarked, 'If this is a recession, I want one.'

The second thing that occurred to me was less obvious, but more important. Although the cat money lay forgotten in the refrigerator, it was actually appreciating in value. Because of the deflation that had been gnawing at prices since the mid-1990s, the crisp notes could acquire more goods the longer they remained in their frozen vault. If, for example, someone had stashed Y100,000 in the fridge in 1995, by 2012 its purchasing power would have risen to Y112,000. By contrast, if that money had been invested in the Japanese stock market, it would have halved in value to just Y50,000.[1] At the time I moved to Higashi Kitazawa, the interest rate on a typical Japanese savings account ran to a derisory 0.01 per cent. That made the refrigerator a better bet than the high-street bank, since the refrigerator had neither withdrawal charges nor account fees.

I came to think of the cat money as a metaphor for the strange, almost Alice in Wonderland state into which the economy had slipped since the burst of the bubble. Because of prolonged deflation, normal economic assumptions no longer applied. Companies didn't want to borrow money even if they could do so for free. A worker's wages might fall, but he or she could still feel better off. In a normal economy, it made no sense to hoard cash. Besides the risk of theft – admittedly negligible in Japan – the value would be constantly eroded by inflation. In Japan it was the reverse. The longer you held cash the more it was worth. For years, the central bank had kept interest at zero in a losing effort to get prices moving. They kept edging downwards anyway. 'We've been suffering deflation for twenty years and no doctor has diagnosed it,' one frustrated Bank of Japan official told me. The Japanese had a similar concept to my cat money, though they spoke not of the icebox but of *tansu* savings, named for the traditional wooden chests in which they kept their kimonos and family heirlooms. One economist calculated that by 2003 as much as $300 billion – roughly the annual output of Denmark – had simply vanished into people's cupboards and under their futon mattresses.[2]

No economy can function properly when all the incentives are to hoard cash. 'The most significant fact about Japan is that prices are falling,' Martin Wolf, a celebrated economics commentator, once wrote. For him, deflation was the root of all Japan's post-bubble evil. Deflation was 'a sorcerer's apprentice of debt – a machine for making a bad situation worse'.[3] If prices are falling, past debts – including the national debt – get progressively larger relative to current income. That is the opposite of what happens in a normal economy when mild inflation steadily erodes the value of past borrowings, making it easier to pay off a mortgage, a business loan or government borrowing. With deflation, debts incurred in the mad bubble years became increasingly hard to repay, clogging up the banking system with the detritus of long-forgotten exuberance. Companies stopped borrowing to invest, concentrating instead on paying back loans. Besides, if future revenues were to be continually worn away by the drip-drip of deflation, debts taken on today would inevitably become harder to repay in the future. Deflation was sapping what economists call 'animal spirits', the expectation of future growth that encourages investment and risk-taking. 'If Japan cannot ever get out of deflation,' says Takatoshi Ito, an economist at Tokyo University and former government adviser, 'that means stagnation and slow death, right?'[4]

Deflation may be the underlying cause, but the litany of economic woes now associated with Japan does not stop there. While thirty years ago the country inspired awe as an economic trailblazer, today it is more likely to elicit a sorrowful shaking of the head. Among bankers and businessmen especially, 'What has happened to Japan?' has become a common refrain. So low has its economic reputation sunk that Japan has even become a verb. Like Americanization, we now have 'Japanization', at least on the pages of the business press. But unlike Americanization, which carries both positive and negative connotations, Japanization is all bad. It means to stagnate, to shrink, to stop competing, to lose one's entrepreneurial and industrial edge and to be crushed by a mountain of debt. It means to suffer permanently falling prices. It means a stock market that hasn't budged for years and property prices that make the US housing market look buoyant. It means a shrinking population, fading international visibility and domestic policy drift. It means lack of innovation, insularity and a broken political system. Ultimately, it carries with it, as Ito says, an intimation of death. An economy that cannot grow surely must eventually die. One so indebted must eventually default. Japanization is a disease that no other nation in its right mind would wish to catch.

Such an interpretation – the strong consensus – is overblown. Japan's policymakers have undoubtedly made many mistakes and its economy has fallen into a rut. High public debt and rapid ageing do, as pessimists suggest, make the future uncertain and, quite possibly, not all that rosy. But Japan's economic performance has not been as grave as the economic obituaries make out. As we shall see, measured in per capita terms and accounting for deflation, Japan's growth compares reasonably well with that of other rich nations. It has also managed to maintain a level of social cohesion, reflected in fairly low unemployment and extremely low crime, that contrasts with the social friction in supposedly more successful economies. Certainly, the go-go years of the 1980s, when the Japanese were living a credit-fuelled fantasy, are gone. Its economy overshot, crashed and has paid the price in subdued growth ever since. That much is true. Before long, though, we could be saying much the same thing about the once credit-enhanced economies of the US and Europe, still struggling several years after the 2008 financial crisis.

In one sense, Japan's slowdown tells an obvious story. It is much easier to catch up with rich countries than to overtake them. Predictions in the 1980s that Japan's economy would outstrip that of the US were always implausible. Now that Japan has fallen, there is a hint of *Schadenfreude* in seeing an upstart challenger brought low. The Japanese compounded the problem by believing the hype themselves. The drunken salaryman giving the western visitor a bar-stool lecture on Japanese superiority is a cliché for a reason. Edwin Reischauer, a scholar and former ambassador to Japan, once said jokingly that *Japan as Number One*, the 1979 book proclaiming Japan's formidable strengths, should be required reading in the US – and banned in Japan.

If we take a longer-term view, Japan's post-war economic performance remains impressive. Its income per head[5] jumped from a fifth of US levels in the 1950s to nearly 90 per cent in 1990, a spectacular, indeed unprecedented, catch-up. Japan is the only Asian economy, outside the city-states of Singapore and Hong Kong and the smaller countries of Taiwan and South Korea, to break out of what economists call the 'middle-income trap'. By comparison, China is still at about one-fifth of US income per head, roughly where Japan was in the 1950s. It is commonly heard today that China's leaders are desperate to avoid Japan's post-bubble catastrophe. The truth is that China will be lucky if it can engineer the same standard of living, quality of life and social wellbeing that exist in Japan today.

It is true, though, that, when the bubble imploded, Japan's convergence on American living standards went into reverse. By 2010, its per capita income had fallen to about three-quarters of US levels. It is not hard to make the case, then, that Japan entered the economic wilderness in 1990 and has stumbled about in the dark ever since. It has suffered, by this account, not one but two 'lost decades' in which its economy has barely grown and its industry has lost its competitive edge. A few data points appear to settle the case. In nominal[6] terms, Japan's gross domestic product – the total value of its output of goods and services – has been treading water since 1991. To be exact, Japan's economy grew from ¥476 trillion in 1991 to ¥477 trillion in 2012, an increase of a staggeringly low 0.2 per cent in two whole decades. By comparison, the US economy – again measured in nominal terms – grew from roughly $6 trillion in 1991 to $15.6 trillion in 2012, an increase of 160 per cent. Britain's economy, which went from £600 billion to £1.5 trillion, did nearly as well, expanding 152 per cent.[7]

Those nominal figures don't tell the whole story. But they do explain why Japan is diminished internationally. In the mid-1990s, its share of global GDP was 17.9 per cent, a proportion that had halved to 8.8 per cent by 2010.[8] Over roughly the same period, its share of world trade has fallen just as steeply to around 4 per cent. The fact that Japan's economy has stood still while others have raced ahead (in nominal terms) has a real impact. It affects Japan's global visibility and influence. It is the reason that, in 2010, China surpassed Japan as the world's second-largest economy.[9] Japan was Number Three. In terms of international prestige nominal GDP clearly counts.

Another measure of Japan's decline can be found on the stock market pages of any business newspaper. As we have seen, the Nikkei

225 average, which tracks the share performance of Japan's largest listed companies, peaked in December 1989 at 38,916. By July 2012 it was around 9,000. The fall of share prices, coupled with an equally precipitous collapse of land values – now roughly 60 per cent below their 1991 peak[10] – has destroyed wealth, or at least the illusion of wealth, and sapped confidence. If we measure an economy's performance in terms of returns to investors, again Japan's performance has been catastrophic. The fall in asset prices also crippled companies and banks, both of which bought shares and property in the 1980s when prices were in perpetual upward motion. Banks extended loans to companies in return for collateral backed by overvalued land. When prices collapsed, the fantasy was exposed. As well as being saddled with bad loans, many banks owned huge portfolios of near-worthless shares. Since those shares were counted as capital, it left banks effectively bankrupt. Rather than owning up, most maintained the fiction their loans were good. Some even lent money to indebted companies so they could repay interest. The banks and their borrowers were like two drunks leaning up against each other for support. As a result, banks virtually stopped lending to new businesses. That made sense for individual institutions. For the economy as a whole it was disastrous. In the ten years from 1995, total bank loans shrank by a third.[11] By 1997, the crisis bubbled into the open and some large institutions started collapsing.

Even if banks had wanted to lend, companies were in no mood to borrow. When they realized the good times were over – and many assumed for years that the stock market crash was a blip – they battened down the hatches. Companies cut overtime, bonuses and even wages. That took money out of the pockets of consumers, exacerbating a chronic lack of demand. Today, businesses hire far fewer permanent staff, taking on lower-paid part-time workers instead. As a result, nearly one in three Japanese employees is now temporary, compared with one in five in 1990. The creation of a labour underclass is hardly unique to Japan. But it has wounded Japan's sense of having an egalitarian society and put a cap on consumer spending.

Tadashi Yanai, president of the clothing company that makes the Uniqlo brand and a specialist in provocative statements, told me, 'Japan is shrinking. It will become like Greece or Portugal.' In their comfortable affluence, the Japanese were living a fantasy, he said. 'People who believed that they were middle class will realize they are poor. Japan has been in a slump for twenty years. So that day will come soon.'[12] Many outsiders agree with his assessment. Not untypical was the prognosis of Nicholas Eberstadt, a political economist at the American Enterprise Institute in Washington, who went so far as to suggest that Japan's young and old alike should consider abandoning their blighted archi-pelago altogether. 'Given the cost of ageing, Japan might establish "health care colonies" in places like India or the Philippines, spots where large populations of elderly Japanese could enjoy a good quality of life at a fraction of the cost at home,' he wrote cheerily. 'Younger Japanese, for their part, might find it attractive to embrace new oppor-tunities abroad, rather than stay in a shrinking, dying Japan.'[13]

Viewed through a different lens, Japan's post-bubble experience has been less ghastly. First, let's look at growth on a real basis, adjusted for inflation and for population. That is a sensible thing to do if we want to know how individual Japanese have fared. Adjusting for inflation – or in its case deflation – makes Japan's numbers look better. That's because deflation means people can afford to buy more with the same amount of money. Japanese incomes may have been falling, but the price of everything from newspapers and haircuts to housing and sushi have been stuck at 1981 levels.[14] Likewise, Japan's population has not grown much in the past twenty years. Since 2007, it has even started shrinking, albeit still very slowly. Some countries look 'richer' in aggregate merely because their population has grown. But unless growth outstrips population increase, individuals don't feel better off. So, if we're interested in standard of living rather than investor returns, we should look at growth on a per capita basis.

In nominal terms, you'll remember, Japan's economy has barely budged in two decades, while the UK and US economies have grown 152 per cent and 160 per cent respectively. Much of that increase, it turns out, is down to the simple fact of rising prices and a growing population. Adjusted for both, Japan still underperforms, but not by nearly as much. If the size of the three economies in 1989 is rebased at 100, Japan's economy reached 127 by 2013, compared with 137 for the US and 144 for Britain.[15]

Japan had a genuinely lousy 1990s. But it turns out that, relative to other rich countries, the last decade has not been quite so bad. As we shall see in the next chapter, during the years Junichiro Koizumi was prime minister (2001–6), the country actually went through a mini-growth and productivity boom. Even after the Lehman shock, which devastated Japan's export markets, and the tsunami, which destroyed production and hit the energy supply, remarkably Japan has done marginally better than either Britain or the US on a real per capita basis in the past decade. Expressed as an average growth rate, Japan's real per capita income has risen 0.9 per cent a year since 2002. That compares with 0.8 per cent for the US and 0.7 per cent for Britain and 0.5 per cent for Norway. If we are to describe Japan's past decade as 'lost', perhaps fairness dictates that we do the same for both the UK and the US.[16]

Other numbers also suggest Japan has not done quite as badly as widely assumed. Unemployment, 4.1 per cent at the end of 2012, never rose above 5.5 per cent even in the dog days of recession. That is much higher than the full employment Japan is used to, but it compares favourably with other advanced countries. According to statistics from the Organisation for Economic Co-operation and Development, in March 2012 the US had a jobless rate of 8.1 per cent, France 10 per cent and Spain a massive 24.1 per cent.[17]

Sceptics, pointing to overstaffed Japanese construction sites and department stores, argue that headline numbers hide underemployment. That is true. In more market-oriented societies, excess workers might indeed have been sacked. Instead of the company paying them, they would then have needed support either from the state or from their family. Japan's low unemployment is, then, arguably achieved at the cost of suppressing productivity or, to put it another way, subsidizing work. One can disagree with such a policy. Shareholders would undoubtedly prefer companies to increase profits by laying off workers. But Japan's 'stakeholder' capitalism, which has similarities with continental Europe, is a legitimate policy option. The Anglo-Saxon model, which favours capital above labour, has sometimes helped investors at the cost of higher unemployment.

Economists might counter that the reluctance to sack workers hampers creative destruction. Only by allowing uncompetitive businesses to fail can labour be directed to more productive parts of the economy. There is some truth to that. Japan's 'zombie banks' have indeed propped up 'zombie companies'. But different economies reorganize in different ways. In Japan, there has been more corporate restructuring than is widely recognized, often behind closed doors and with less resort to bankruptcy or hostile takeovers. This may be slower and less efficient than in more market-oriented economies. Yet persistently high, and long-term, unemployment may be the inevitable price of the creative destruction process in many western countries – certainly if sacked workers are not properly retrained to move into new industries. In Japan, the industrial re-engineering process, though slow, and perhaps inadequate, is more likely to take place within a large company, at least for those fortunate enough to have a full-time job. Thus Canon shifted its emphasis from cameras to photocopiers without being taken over by a rival company or private equity firm and broken up as might have happened in a more aggressively capitalistic country. Japan's low unemployment figures, sceptics will point out, also mask 'discouraged' workers, who do not bother looking for non-existent work. Nor do they tell the story of high youth unemployment, now at 8 per cent. Such phenomena, though, are hardly unique to Japan. The headline unemployment numbers may disguise the true picture, but they are broadly comparable across nations. However you make the comparison, Japan has lower unemployment than most advanced economies.

Japan has never been quite as egalitarian as it likes to think, but its income gap has widened less sharply than in some other advanced nations. In the US, the top 1 per cent of earners has captured nearly all the economic gains of the past thirty years.[18] Everyone else has stood still or fallen behind. The same is broadly true of Britain, where the share of the top 1 per cent of income earners rose from 7.1 per cent in 1970 to 14.3 per cent in 2005. That means that most of the growth in the UK and the US has brought little benefit to the bulk of the population. In Japan, what growth there has been has been more evenly distributed. In the mid-1990s, the average income of the top 10 per cent of Japanese was eight times higher than the bottom 10 per cent, a ratio that widened to ten times by 2008.[19] Japan's inequality has widened, but not to the extent of many other nations. Nor has its equality deteriorated as much as the Japanese themselves imagine. Yoshio Sugimoto, emeritus professor at La Trobe University in Melbourne, says the fast-growth years produced an 'optical illusion' of equality since everyone was moving up the escalator. Now the escalator has stopped, he says, 'it becomes difficult for the illusion to be sustained'.[20]

Quality of life is hard to quantify. It is also largely subjective. But in some measures, Japan does extremely well. One is the safety of its citizens. By international standards, Japanese crime rates are ridiculously low. In Japan – where it is an offence to own a gun, another to own a bullet, and a third to pull the trigger – you are ten times less likely to be murdered than in the US.[21] You are thirty-six times less likely to be robbed.[22] Dropped wallets are almost invariably returned, cash untouched. Violent crime is very rare. Japan feels safe not because all the criminals are locked up. In fact, Japan imprisons very few people. It has some 80,000 prisoners compared with 2.3 million in the US.[23] Even as the country's economy has slowed, its society has held together remarkably well. In 2009, newly laid-off workers built a 'tent village' amid the fountains and shrubbery of Hibiya Park to draw attention to their plight. But there have been no sprees of burning and looting as there were on the streets of London in 2011, nor the mass demonstrations prompted by a collapse of living standards seen in Greece and Spain.

One mustn't get carried away. To say Japan has done better than generally acknowledged is a useful antidote to some of the more hysterical analysis. That is not to say everything has been fine. Far from it. Japan has gone from being the fastest of catch-up economies to an also-ran among mature ones. That has caused national soul-searching at home and lessened Japan's prestige abroad. 'A nation is happiest when you are chasing someone and there's no one behind you,' says Richard Koo, a well-known economist resident in Japan. Since the bubble burst, Japan has stopped chasing, he says. 'It's been pretty horrible.'[24]

We must also take into account the huge public borrowing, which has softened the blow for the current generation but left a huge bill, and a potentially massive problem, for future ones to deal with. In the words of one economist, 'Living standards have been propped up by

an unsustainable accumulation of debt.'[25] Japan's 'solution' to its
slowing economy has tended to favour the older over the young.
Deflation has preserved the savings of baby-boomers at the expense
of creating a vibrant economy for younger generations. In a later
chapter we will see how youth, deprived of the certainties and the job
opportunities enjoyed by their parents and grandparents, has borne
the brunt of Japan's strung-out economic adjustment.

In 2005, the finance ministry helpfully drew my attention to the fact
that, if Japan's debt were stacked up in Y10,000 notes, it would reach
1,400 times higher than Mount Fuji. Why anyone would want to do
such an odd thing was never adequately explained. But the point was
clear: Japan's debt mountain was unsustainably high. That was back
then, when gross public debt amounted to Y538 trillion, about
$4.5 trillion at the time, and equal to 150 per cent of Japan's GDP.
The government was constantly adding to the pile. For every Y100 it
was spending, it was obliged to borrow Y40 by issuing yet more debt,
since taxes – depressed by years of deflation and non-existent nominal
growth – were insufficient to meet its spending needs. Now it is borrowing even more. By 2012, more than half of what the government
spent was being borrowed. Gross public debt had ballooned to more
than 230 per cent of GDP.[26] I didn't dare go back to the finance ministry to discover how high the debt mountain reached now.

'Things that can't go on for ever, don't,' an old economists' adage
has it. As long ago as 1999, Japan's then prime minister Keizo Obuchi
pronounced himself the 'king of the world's debtors'.[27] Debt as a proportion of GDP has more than doubled since then and some economists
believe it is only a matter of time before the whole house comes crashing down. For several years, the ratings agencies have put the country
on notice. A decade ago, Moody's infuriated Japan by downgrading its
sovereign debt – an assessment of the likelihood of defaulting – to the
same level as Botswana.[28] More recently, ratings agencies downgraded
Japanese debt again. Standard & Poor's, which in 2011 caused a furore by removing the US AAA rating for the first time in seventy years,
gave Japan an AA-minus rating. That still meant Japan had between
a 'very strong' and a 'strong' capacity to meet its financial commit-
ments. But the downward trend suggested its position was becoming

less tenable. Moody's went so far as to say that the shock to the economy of the March 2011 tsunami and the vast rebuilding costs could push Japan's bond markets towards a 'tipping point'. Kaoru Yosano, the minister of economic affairs whom I met in his office in the immediate aftermath of the earthquake, warned that Japan 'faced a dreadful dream'.[29] Ito of Tokyo University said issuing more and more bonds merely staved off the inevitable. The fundamental problem was that the government spent more than it raised in taxes. 'Who is going to pay?' he asked. 'You can't just keep shifting it to the next generation.'[30] Ito had long been a thorn in the side of the Bank of Japan, urging it to set an inflation target. Modest inflation, he argued, would help Japan to float off the rocks of perpetual deficit. In a normal economy, public debt would fall as the economic pie grew. One of the main reasons Japan's debt had risen so quickly as a percentage of GDP was that nominal GDP itself had been stuck in a rut – at 1990 levels.[31]

However it got out of its current bind, Ito said, Japan would not be able to rely for ever on the huge savings amassed by previous generations. As things stood, those savings provided the state with an easy source of cheap finance. Companies and individuals deposited savings in banks – when they were not under the mattress, that was. The banks, in turn, bought government debt. Ito said that merry-go-round couldn't go on indefinitely. Pensioners would start to spend down their savings, reducing the pool of assets to be recycled. Younger people were saving less. 'Once you hit a ceiling, it is all quite easy to unwind. And once people start selling [government bonds], the prices will go down, there'll be more selling and the price will go down further.' Then there would be capital flight as Japanese rushed to safety overseas. 'It's a giant Ponzi scheme. I think the end is near.'

That is plausible. Yet people have been saying much the same thing for years. The markets – imperfect though rational people must now accept them to be – have resolutely refused to endorse this pessimistic view. Bond prices have not crashed as so long predicted. Instead, they have done quite the reverse. The markets regard Japanese government bonds not as a time bomb but as a safe haven. As bond prices have risen, yields have fallen. The Japanese government can borrow money for ten years at below 1 per cent, more cheaply, says Peter Tasker, a Tokyo-based strategist, than any government since Babylonian times.

That means Japan's debt repayments are actually pretty low. 'For the past decade the Japanese bond market has been making monkeys out of not just the credit rating agencies, but also academics, trigger-happy short sellers [who seek to profit by selling Japanese bonds] and politicians and bureaucrats who see fiscal austerity as a virtue in its own right,' Tasker says. 'All have been proclaiming that out-of-control public debt has set Japan on the road to fiscal perdition.'[32]

One reason things haven't blown up yet is that, contrary to common perception, Japan is far from being the world's biggest debtor. In fact, it is the world's biggest creditor. It has vast claims on foreign assets. According to Jesper Koll, an economist at JP Morgan who calls himself 'the last Japan optimist', every week $4 billion more flows into Japan than flows out. The country's private sector runs a financial surplus large enough to cover the government's deficit and still have plenty of capital to export abroad. Japan's much talked-about public debt, then, is not money that Japan owes the rest of world, but money that the government has borrowed from its own people. For most of the past two decades nearly 95 per cent of Japanese debt was domestically owned, although this had fallen (perhaps worryingly) to a record low of 91 per cent by 2013. Still, in the case of Greece and nations that have defaulted in recent years, such as Argentina and Russia, most of their debt was owed to foreigners who wanted their money back. It is possible that Japanese banks and individuals will also develop a sudden craving for their cash. Yet, even at that point outright default is unlikely. One way the Japanese state could default over time would be to cut pension payments or health benefits, something that – in common with governments everywhere – it has begun to do. If push came to shove, the government could also resort to the aggressive use of the printing presses, hoping to float the debt away through inflation. The danger would be that inflation might get out of hand, turning into hyperinflation.

Still, nothing of the sort has happened yet – not, anyway, until Shinzo Abe came along with his deflation-busting plan in 2013 (see Afterword). And with prices still falling, it seems premature to worry about excessive inflation. Some economists have even gone so far as to argue that Japan's debt pile is not so bad, but actually evidence that the government has been doing more or less the right thing. Richard

Koo, an economist at Nomura, talks about a 'balance sheet recession'.[33] As he sees it, ever since the bubble burst in 1990, massively overstretched companies have dedicated themselves to paying down debt. Even those that have managed to restore healthy balance sheets are so traumatized they have no more desire to borrow or invest. Their unwillingness to borrow makes conventional monetary policy useless. Richard Jerram, now chief economist at Bank of Singapore, compared Japan's failure to reboot the economy through monetary expansion to a pub where endless free beers are lined up at the bar, but whose customers are so past the point of inebriation, they are in no mood to imbibe further.

We should not forget the magnitude of the shock caused by the bursting of Japan's bubble. According to Koo, so deep was the fall in land and equity prices that it cut the value of all Japanese assets by a sum equal to 2.7 times the country's entire 1989 GDP. That is bigger than the loss sustained by the US after the 1929 Wall Street crash.[34] For all its problems, in Japan there has been no Great Depression. The big mistake was allowing the bubble to inflate and pop in the first place. But having done so, according to this reading, Japan's authorities were correct to compensate for a massive fall in private sector spending by ramping up government spending and loosening monetary policy. It is a classic Keynesian argument for counter-cyclical spending.

For many years, arguments about Japan's strange economic circumstances were a matter mainly for Japanese specialists and academic economists. That is no longer the case. After the collapse of Lehman Brothers and the subsequent global financial crisis, nearly every western government faces similar problems to Japan. They too are suffering balance sheet recessions. Their companies and households have also stopped spending. Their central banks have lowered interest rates to practically zero and started printing money to buy bonds, a policy known as 'quantitative easing' that was pioneered by Japan from around 2003. In seeking to learn the lessons of Japan, economists have drawn diametrically opposite conclusions. The debate has been particularly shrill in the US, which now has gross public debt above 100 per cent of GDP and, like Japan, borrows more than 50 cents for every dollar it spends.[35]

At the Republican National Convention in Tampa in 2012, a giant clock showed the national debt ticking ever upwards towards $16 trillion. Mitt Romney, the Republicans' presidential candidate, even said the US should consider a return to the gold standard, a policy that would severely restrict the Federal Reserve's ability to print money. Many Republicans have also opposed spending to compensate for the fact that the private sector is in sharp retrenchment. In a *Wall Street Journal* opinion piece called 'Arigato for Nothing, Keynes-san' ('Thanks for Nothing, Mr Keynes'), the US business newspaper said the lesson of Japan was that Keynesian fiscal stimulus didn't work, precisely the opposite of Koo's conclusion. Japan was a 'rebuke to those who argue Keynesian sprees help unleash private-sector-led growth down the road'.[36]

Japan's debt, however, has not risen primarily because of spending on 'bridges to nowhere' as its critics often say. Undoubtedly, there has been some of that, though most such spending happened before the bubble burst, not after. Big stimulus packages ended in the late 1990s. Under Koizumi, as we shall see in the next chapter, public works spending was sharply scaled back.[37] In fact, there are two main reasons for Japan's ballooning debt: falling tax revenues and the stagnation in nominal GDP. Government tax revenues have halved since 1990, an extraordinary fact that reflects the prolonged slump in nominal growth – a sign of how damaging deflation can be. The pay of many workers has fallen below the income tax threshold, corporate tax revenues have dropped and the slump in land prices has hit inheritance tax. That suggests that Japan's main problem has not been too much spending (and printing), but too little growth. With the mildest of inflation over the past fifteen years, Japan's debt problem would not look nearly so bad.

Paul Krugman, the *New York Times* columnist, is famously on the Keynesian side of the debate. In one column he characterized the 'debt worriers' in his country as misunderstanding the nature of national debt. They thought of it as if a family had taken out a mortgage it would have trouble repaying, he wrote. That was a bad analogy. While families had to pay back their debt, governments didn't. All they had to do was ensure that their debts grew more slowly than their tax income – precisely what Japan has failed to do. US debt from the Second World War was never repaid, Krugman said. It just became increasingly irrelevant as the economy outgrew it.[38]

Some economists regard Krugman's analysis as fantasy. For Japan, like the US, they argue, the only way back from perdition is to cut government spending and raise taxes. Cranking the printing presses will merely lead to hell down the road. In Japan's case, one reason for saying that is the assumption that it has a bloated state, with an overly generous social security system and an unsustainable penchant for laying concrete. Money is wasted, no doubt. But the size of the Japanese state is not especially big compared with other advanced countries. According to the OECD, general government spending, which includes central and local outlays, was 43 per cent in 2013. That compared with 40 per cent in the US, 47 per cent in Britain and an average of 49 per cent in Europe. Still, no state can go on for ever spending more than it can raise in revenue. Japan's finance ministry has been advocating higher taxes for years. Political realities and economic emergencies mean it has mostly not had its way, although the government of Yoshihiko Noda, prime minister from 2011 to 2012, passed legislation preparing for a doubling of sales tax to 10 per cent by 2015. 'Our thinking is that economic growth and fiscal consolidation are compatible rather than contradictory,' Koji Omi, a former finance minister, once told me.[39] The logic is that, if the public knows the national finances are on a sound footing, it will be less inclined to make precautionary saving and more relaxed about spending.

Japan has never been able to test out that hypothesis since it has never got its fiscal situation under control. But in Britain, David Cameron's government put the theory into practice by implementing what has been called 'pre-emptive austerity'. Rather than increasing government spending to counteract the effects of falling private investment, it has sought to cut expenditure.[40] So far the results are not encouraging. By the summer of 2012, Britain's GDP was marooned at 4.5 per cent below its 2008 peak and the country had entered a double-dip recession. (It's true that by this time Japan was into recession number three.) Anatole Kaletsky, an economics commentator, declared the UK's experiment in fiscal tightening a failure. From 2010, when Cameron's government started cutting, Britain's performance diverged sharply from the US, which had continued to relax its fiscal policy.

Since the UK adopted austerity, the American economy had done almost three times better, Kaletsky wrote. As a result, Britain's debt had risen more as a proportion of a diminished GDP. His conclusion was that 'any country determined to control public borrowing should forget about fiscal austerity and instead do everything to grow as fast as it can'.[41]

So what, if anything, should the Japanese government have done differently to revive its flagging economy? It has been lambasted for ponderous policy decision-making, but there is no clear consensus, even among professional economists, as to quite what it should have done. It's a little like the Woody Allen joke about the restaurant with lousy food and overly small portions. Japan should have moved faster, though there is no real agreement as to which direction it should have taken. The sharp divide in opinion about how the US and Europe should tackle their own economic crises suggests that, even today, we don't really know – even with the benefit of twenty years' hindsight. Should Japan have cut spending and refrained from printing money? Or should it have printed and spent with greater abandon?

Of course, there were other steps it could have taken to breathe life into the economy, whole swathes of which were protected for the benefit of vested interests. As we shall see, even Koizumi, the only prime minister to take on the issue seriously, was better at talking about economic revolution than delivering it. 'What we need are opening and deregulation. Electricity, nursing, childcare, agriculture, fishery, forestry,' says Sahoko Kaji, the economist at Keio University. 'We are doing none of it.'[42] She thought that Japan's economy could be spurred to much greater efficiency and innovation through competition if Tokyo allowed the private sector a more unhindered role and signed meaningful free trade agreements with international partners. But because of strong opposition, particularly from the conservative and influential farming lobby, Japan had failed on both counts. Meanwhile, South Korea, a direct competitor, had concluded trade deals with both Europe and the US, giving its manufacturers preferential access to those huge markets.

One clear lesson from Japan's twenty years of economic difficulties is: don't get into a mess in the first place. Once the bubble burst in 1990, the government failed to recapitalize the banking system, leaving the Koizumi administration to clear up the mess finally more than a decade later. Many, though, reserve their severest criticism for the Bank of Japan, which they blame for allowing the economy to fall into a deflationary funk. Here the lesson also seems clear: the central bank should have acted earlier and more aggressively, pulling out all the stops until the economy was back on track. It did lower interest rates to near-zero, but since companies didn't want to borrow, that did little good. The bank, however, refrained from unorthodox policies – such as printing money to buy bonds – until much later. It even briefly raised interest rates in 2001, suggesting it didn't take the deflationary threat seriously enough.

In 1999, Ben Bernanke, who would later take over the US Federal Reserve, lashed out at Japan's central bank for what he said was the country's self-induced paralysis. He urged the bank to experiment more boldly in an effort to stimulate demand and slay deflation. It could, he said, print money to buy government bonds, foreign currency or any number of assets – anything to get things moving. Japan's central bank did eventually undertake unorthodox measures, even at one stage printing money to buy shares. Some sceptics said the limited effect of those measures proved that quantitative easing didn't work. Others said it was a case of too little too late. Whatever the faults of Japan's central bank, Bernanke found dealing with an economic crisis harder in practice than when he was lecturing Tokyo on monetary policy theory. The US recovery has been painfully slow. Four years after the Lehman shock, real median annual household income had fallen 5 per cent.[43] Bernanke is said to have privately admitted that he had been too hard on Japan.[44]

# 8

# Samurai with a Quiff

They called him *henjin*. Literally it meant 'strange person', though perhaps it was better rendered as 'oddball' or 'eccentric'. The Japanese are not as conformist as they are sometimes made out to be, but to be 'odd' or 'strange' is not usually considered desirable. In the case of Junichiro Koizumi, however, the most charismatic Japanese prime minister in a generation, it was different. Koizumi was different. And in his case, to be different was good.

Koizumi sidled on to the main political stage like some larger-than-life dandy in 2001. He took office just six months before I had arrived in the country. Japan was embarking on what looked like a second lost decade and was in yet another recession following the brief flurry of the dotcom bubble. There was little sense of crisis, but there was a quiet despondency, a feeling that Japan's best days were behind it and that the political system had run out of ideas. Countless stimulus packages had failed to breathe life into the economy. There were fewer good jobs for graduates. Koizumi's promise of 'reform without sacred cows' offered what seemed like a radical alternative to accepting decline as a *fait accompli*.

Koizumi was sixty-one years of age. By the grizzled standards of some political ancients that was not old. If anything, he came across as brash and youthful. Physically in good shape, he had lean, lively features. A flicker of amusement often lurked beneath his fixed expression and sleepy, half-closed eyes. There was something dapper about the way he dressed, even if it was just that he was wearing an open-necked shirt or a suit a few shades paler than it really ought to have been. Above all, it was Koizumi's hair that caught people's attention. His silvery grey, wavy mane lent him a passing resemblance to Richard Gere and gave rise to his nickname of 'Lionheart'.[1]

Many women, even young ones, found Koizumi devilishly hand-some. His speeches were sometimes interrupted by squeals from the audience and, on at least one occasion, a female devotee fainted with the excitement of it all. (With perfect aplomb, Koizumi stopped in mid-sentence to check if she was all right.) The attraction was, if any-thing, magnified by Koizumi's cheerful admission to spending nights in Ginza hostess bars. He was, after all, a bachelor, long-since divorced from his wife, the mother of his three sons. He somehow managed to combine an urbane stand-offishness with a Ronald Reagan-like feel for what moved ordinary people. It was a combination reflected in his love of both opera and heavy metal. When, after a few months as prime minister, he released a CD featuring his twenty-five favourite Elvis songs, this act of cocky self-promotion confirmed his reputation as the man for whom Japan had long been waiting.

Koizumi came from nowhere to grab the presidency of the Liberal Democratic Party, and hence the premiership of Japan, in April 2001. After the carousel of recession-dogged politicians in the 1990s, Koizumi was like a breath of sweet air. People wore Koizumi T-shirts, bought Koizumi posters and shouted out during his speeches as though he were a rock star. Unlike other politicians, who employed the noncommittal flowery ambiguities in which the Japanese language excels, Koizumi spoke in simple, easy-to-understand soundbites. He told a country bemused by a decade of economic logjam and political merry-go-round that there would be 'no growth without pain'. He would 'change the Liberal Democratic Party, change Japan', he said in a catchphrase that preceded that of Barack Obama by many years. If he couldn't persuade his party to alter its tired old ways, he would smash it to pieces. His blunt slogans offered the exciting, if unnerving, prospect of overhaul and renewal. Much of the Japanese public hun-gered for a radical shift of direction after years of confidence-sapping drift, though many wanted the sort of change that would merely reboot the old model. Rather than someone who would destroy the system, as Koizumi professed to want to, many of his followers sought someone who could revive it and, in so doing, preserve the comfort-able society so painstakingly built after the war. In short, they wanted the sort of change that would allow Japan to stay the same.

If Koizumi captured the mood of the nation at the start of a new century, his rise to the top was a fluke. Even when his name began to infiltrate the headlines in early 2001, few expected him to become prime minister. His popularity with the public had seemed almost irrelevant. Under Japan's parliamentary system, it was the governing party, not the electorate, which chose the prime minister. That meant the Liberal Democratic Party, which had governed Japan for forty-nine of the previous fifty years in one of the world's great feats of political longevity. Even China's Communist Party wanted to know how the mighty Liberal Democrats had managed to preserve power for so long, all the while holding regular elections and maintaining the trappings of a parliamentary democracy. The party was Japan's government and opposition rolled into one. It picked the prime minister on the basis of horse-trading between the heads of powerful factions that coexisted within the party's loose framework. In normal times, its leader was decided long before the vote reached the floor of the Diet, Japan's parliament. In a typical case of factional rigging, Koizumi's predecessor, the pitifully unpopular Yoshiro Mori, was said to have been chosen by just five men.[2]

The faction bosses, as much mafia dons as politicians, had done for Koizumi twice before. He had campaigned to become head of the Liberal Democratic Party in 1995 and again in 1998. His views on vested interests and his avowed determination to break the bonds between money and politics made him an unlikely leader for a party that thrived on patronage. Both times he had been soundly beaten, spat out by a party machine that did not want an unpredictable eccentric running the show. In 2001, it looked as though the same would happen again. Koizumi was up against Ryutaro Hashimoto, a black belt in kendo and faction boss who had been prime minister from 1996 to 1998. Party elders were looking for an experienced pair of hands after the disastrous premiership of Mori, whose popularity rating had sunk to an embarrassing 7 per cent. That was low even by the standards of recent prime ministers, many of them ineffective men of wan personality. The party was preparing to rally around Hashimoto in its hour of need.

But Koizumi had an unexpected advantage. The party had recently altered its voting system to give it at least a semblance of democratic accountability. This time, as well as parliamentarians, 3.2 million rank-and-file members were to be consulted. Grassroots supporters would account for a little less than one-third of the total votes, enough to have their say but not enough to determine the outcome. Still, that gave Koizumi, with his simple message and showman qualities, the opportunity to appeal over the heads of the grandees to those in the base. Party hacks had not intended to take the votes of rank-and-file members too seriously, but they made a crucial mistake by allowing the local chapters to vote first. When the tally came in from the prefectural offices, Koizumi had won an astonishing 87 per cent of the vote. The message from the grassroots was overwhelming. Many parliamentarians felt they could not simply override the verdict of the rank-and-file. One young MP expressed the changing attitudes, saying, 'I am going to vote for who I want to support, not just on the orders of my faction. People are rejecting the party's way of handling politics. This is the last chance for the Liberal Democratic Party to restore trust.'[3] Koizumi won the parliamentary vote too, albeit by a slimmer margin. Against the odds, and by popular demand, he would become prime minister.

Sochiro Tahara, a Koizumi confidant and host of an influential political chat show, said the daring new prime minister had subverted the norms of what he called 'the village'. 'Koizumi has not followed the village rules at all,' Tahara told me in the champagne bar of ANA Intercontinental Hotel where he habitually held court. 'He is not top of a faction. He has never made contributions to factions or to his superiors, so he has never been named to one of the party's three big posts. Yet without doing any of these things, he has risen to become prime minister. This is exceptional.'[4] Heizo Takenaka, the professor whom Koizumi would pluck from academia to sort out the banking system, called him simply 'the miracle prime minister'.[5]

The very manner in which Koizumi chose his first cabinet seemed to confirm his radical agenda. Instead of conferring with faction bosses, he handpicked his own team, barely consulting even close advisers. When the newly anointed chosen stood in stiff formation for the traditional group photograph, with the men dressed in frock coats and grey pin-stripe trousers, there were five women among their ranks, an unusually high number. Most prominent among them was

Makiko Tanaka, the new foreign minister, a woman every bit as out-spoken and popular as Koizumi himself.[6] Koizumi also broke with tradition by picking three people from the private sector, an affront to long-serving party elders, who saw cabinet positions as their due. Most prominent of the private sector appointments was Takenaka, a professor of economics at Keio University, who went on to serve as a loyal lieutenant for Koizumi's entire five-and-a-half-year tenure. Takenaka would later describe the excitement of the dawning of a new age. When his boss took to the floor of the Diet, answering questions off-the-cuff without recourse to the usual dry documents prepared by bureaucrats, Takenaka admitted to feeling 'quite giddy' with the thrill of it all.[7]

Koizumi had a different kind of presence in parliament and an entirely different rapport with the press and public. He took to appearing twice daily before television cameras when he would pep-per the audience with pithy soundbites. He gave the impression of speaking directly to the public, not to the party bosses or vested inter-ests who were seen to have run Japan from behind the *shoji* screen for so long. In his inaugural speech to the Diet on 7 May 2001, a set-piece occasion of great import, he laid out his reform agenda. He promised to deal swiftly with the non-performing loans that were clogging the banking system a decade after the bursting of the bubble. He hinted that he would allow companies, even whole industries, to die if neces-sary. 'After the Second World War, Japan achieved dynamic economic development, resulting in a tremendous increase in the standard of living,' he told the solemn ranks of assembled Diet members. 'Since the outset of the decade of the 1990s, however, the Japanese economy has been unable to break free of long-term stagnation as trust in our political leadership has been eroded and our society has become enveloped in a spirit of disillusionment. It is now apparent that the structures that hitherto served us so well may not be appropriate for our society in the twenty-first century.'[8]

The new prime minister promised doubtless nervous parliamentar-ians that his so-called 'Ceaseless Reform Cabinet' would bring about economic rebirth through structural reform. He would repair Japan's international standing, which had declined along with the size of its chequebook. (For a discussion of foreign policy under Koizumi, see the later chapter 'Asia Ex-Japan'.) He would carry out his goals of fiscal repair and economic revitalization without 'fear, hesitation or constraint'. In concluding, he told the story of the Nagaoka Clan at the start of the Meiji era. Defeated militarily and suffering dire poverty, the clan one day received a donation of 100 sacks of rice from a neighbouring province, enough to feed its hungry people for some time. But instead of distributing the rice, the 'wise clan leader' sold it, investing the proceeds in a school, 'thereby ensuring a future harvest of thousands and even tens of thousands of sacks of rice for his people', Koizumi said. The message was clear. He was prepared to put Japan through pain in pursuit of a better future. There was one hitch. In his speech, he never specified whether all the clansmen of Nagaoka had made it alive through the hungry years.

Ichizo Ohara, a fellow Diet member, knew Koizumi more than three decades before he became prime minister. Some fifteen years Koizumi's senior, he remembered him as a skinny thirty-year-old in his first term as an MP. In 1969, the young Koizumi had been studying economics at the University of London when word reached him that his father had died. He was summoned back to Japan to run for his father's parliamentary seat in Yokosuka, a port city about thirty miles from Tokyo and home to America's most important naval base in the western Pacific. That time Koizumi lost. But he won three years later on his second attempt. 'I remember this sassy, smart-looking guy showed up. Nobody else in the Diet had this Regent-style quiff. I thought, what a strange fellow,' Ohara chuckled, still amused, years later, by his first glimpse of Koizumi's distinctive hairstyle. 'I thought he was a kind of fool.'[9]

Koizumi, he said, displayed not the faintest sign of either political or material ambition. Most of Ohara's memories of the freshman MP revolved around carousing. 'We'd go out drinking or to yakitori bars in Akasaka, just rough-and-ready places.' Koizumi liked *fugu*, the poisonous fish that can kill if wrongly prepared and is, for that reason, a delicacy forbidden to the emperor. At around the time Ohara and Koizumi were visiting Akasaka bars, a well-known kabuki actor, Mitsugoro Bando VIII, died of convulsions after boasting he could eat four servings of *fugu* liver. 'We used to visit a lot of geisha too.

Koizumi was very charming and a good talker. He had this nice way of laughing. He was really cute,' Ohara recalled. 'He used to really enjoy the banter with the geisha. We never had to call for them. He was so popular, they just came.'

Nor did Koizumi seem to be motivated by money. That was almost unheard of for a politician. When he was first elected to the Diet in the early 1970s, Kakuei Tanaka was prime minister. Tanaka, a construction contractor and son of a horse dealer, perfected the pork-barrel politics that kept the Liberal Democratic Party in perpetual power. In the fast-growth period, money was sucked in through taxing the big corporations operating in the cities and spread liberally around the countryside where the party had its deepest roots. Tanaka, born in the relatively unpopulated prefecture of Niigata, the 'snow country' on the Sea of Japan, famously brought the bullet train to his home town in a classic display of patronage politics. The 'construction state', as it came to be known, was awash with money. There was plenty left over for the politicians who made it happen. Tanaka, whose premiership ended amid scandal in 1974, continued to dominate the party as the 'shadow shogun' from behind the scenes. This despite the fact that he had been charged with, and subsequently convicted of, taking bribes from Lockheed in return for advocating the purchase of aircraft. Ohara remembered how Tanaka had once tried to tempt him into politics by presenting him with ¥1 million in cash. Ohara, eyes bulging, mimed his struggle to fit the thick stack of notes into his pocket as he escaped down the corridor. As he recalled it, Tanaka called after him, 'Remember, politicians as well as thieves need big pockets.'

Koizumi hated everything about money politics. He was influenced by Takeo Fukuda, an upright politician he had served as political secretary after his return from London. Fukuda was Tanaka's political arch-enemy and he taught Koizumi to dislike everything about the way the party sloshed money around. 'Koizumi knew back then that Japanese finances were going nowhere, that the government was spending too much on bridges and rice fields,' Ohara said. Perhaps because he came from a comfortable background – in contrast to Tanaka, who grew up with six sisters and a drunken father – Koizumi had little taste for the perks of political life. 'As far as I know he has only one house. He doesn't have golf membership. He doesn't own

land. He doesn't own stocks,' said Yasuhiro Tase, a journalist who
followed Koizumi's career for decades.[10] Years later, on the twenty-fifth
anniversary of his election to parliament, Koizumi became entitled to
a stipend, a chauffeur-driven car and a portrait of himself by a master.
He turned down all three state-funded privileges. 'Before he was prime
minister, he lived in the politicians' dormitory. He still lives a humble
life,' said Tase. 'That's the samurai in him, I think.' Takenaka too
recalled Koizumi returning gifts, including a bouquet of flowers and
a necktie. Koizumi's ethics also put Ohara in mind of the austere
*bushido* code. 'He is a samurai,' he said. 'A samurai with a quiff.'[11]

Koizumi was hard to fathom. Even his closest colleagues admit to
not knowing what he was thinking. Sadako Ogata, whom Koizumi
appointed as Japan's special representative on Afghan assistance, was
one of many thrown off by his behaviour. Once, she had just returned
from Kabul and was summoned to the prime minister's office to relate
her findings. Koizumi simply sat there with his eyes closed. When she
had finished, he thanked her and she left without a clue as to what
he thought.[12] Takenaka remembered similar encounters, including a time
before Koizumi became prime minister when he briefed him on the
Japanese economy. 'He listened to my speech this way,' Takenaka told
me, cocking his head to one side and closing his eyes tightly shut. 'He
didn't take any memo. I thought he must be sleeping, that he wasn't
listening to what I was saying.' Later he recognized that this was simply Koizumi's way of doing things. 'He is cutting out the minor issues
and thinking about the main points,' was how Takenaka explained it.
'This is his main style as a leader.' Isao Iijima, Koizumi's loyal political
secretary over many years, attributed his boss's style to a calculated
ambiguity designed to unsettle those around him. 'No matter how
many times you meet the prime minister, you will never find out what
he is really thinking,' he boasted.[13]

If the man known as Japan's great communicator was silent for
much of the time, that was not the only paradox. His status as a
maverick outsider was belied by the fact that both his father and
grandfather had been cabinet ministers. Koizumi's grandfather,
Matajiro, was a stevedore who became a powerful labour organizer
rounding up people to work on the docks unloading ships. His back
was tattooed with a large red dragon of the sort usually favoured by

yakuza gangsters. He became known as the *irezumi* minister after the word for tattoo. Matajiro parlayed his various influences into a parliamentary seat. In government, he was put in charge of the post office, an entity that his grandson would later seek to privatize in dramatic fashion. Matajiro's adopted son, Koizumi's father, was elected to the same Yokosuka seat. In time he rose to become director-general of the defence agency. It was quite a pedigree for a self-styled political outcast.

Nor was Koizumi's popularity with women entirely logical. After his divorce, Koizumi was awarded custody of his two sons, but famously did not allow them to have contact with their mother. His wife, who was pregnant at the time of the separation, had a third son whom Koizumi never tried to meet and who was, it was reported, turned away from his grandmother's funeral. It was an acrimonious, if not altogether untypical, end to a marriage that had been celebrated with a wedding cake carved into the shape of Japan's ornate parliament. As one journalist commented about the politician who had stolen Japan's heart, 'Touchy-feely? Not in his private life he isn't.'[14]

Iijima, who spent much of his career by Koizumi's side, knows him better than most. As his political fixer, he was also the man who helped make him. When Koizumi was in power, I went to see Iijima a couple of times at the Kantei, the prime minister's official workplace. It is a beautifully designed minimalist building, decorated with bamboo and with something about it of an upmarket Ikea showroom. Once Iijima called me in because he was furious about an article I had written in which I had painted a rather unflattering portrait of Koizumi's 'guard-dog-in-chief'. I had suggested that Iijima – a stocky chain smoker with a taste for chunky jewellery – had carefully crafted Koizumi's media image by working his relationships with the staff of Japan's weekly magazines, salacious publications that combine soft-porn and scandal with investigative reporting. Although these magazines make Britain's tabloids look like choirboy song-sheets, they apparently found no dirt on Koizumi. Instead, they turned him into a household name. Iijima had helped create Japan's first truly media-savvy politician, one who owed his position not to the favours he had done colleagues, the palms he had greased or the years of political drudgery he had put in, but rather to the popularity he enjoyed with ordinary people. One of Koizumi's press secretaries once told me, half in admiration and half in disgust, 'Iijima is a top-class salesman and Koizumi is his number one brand.'

As I went to sit down on a chair in the small meeting room, Iijima shooed me out of the seat usually reserved for guests. That was the only time in my seven years in Japan that such a standard courtesy was so deliberately flouted. Iijima was shaking with pent-up anger and he embarked on a twenty-minute tirade about my offending article. The one indubitable mistake was that he could not, as I had described, have been wreathed in plumes of smoke as he sat at his desk. As he pointed out, his office had been designated a non-smoking area, obliging him to step outside whenever he needed to light up.

Once Iijima had calmed down, he began to talk freely about Koizumi, the 'thin and stylish' man he had met all those years ago. Initially, he confessed, he thought Koizumi lacked the guts to take on those he called the 'big frog' politicians squatting on power. But Koizumi surprised him. He proved more than a match for the political amphibians, shunning factional politics and sticking to his convictions. That style influenced the way Koizumi's cabinet functioned, Iijima said. Previous administrations had worked bottom up, with legislation filtering upwards through the party's Byzantine structures, agreed at every stage through a complex process of consensus-building known as *nemawashi*, or digging around the roots. In Koizumi's case, the process was the exact reverse. Koizumi would decide what he wanted to do and give orders that it be implemented. One of the mechanisms he used to enforce his agenda on bureaucrats, who were used to having things their own way, was the Council on Economic and Fiscal Policy. Although the body, designed to bring decision-making more firmly into the cabinet, had been established a few years earlier, neither his predecessors nor his successors knew how to use it to full effect. Koizumi attended almost every meeting of the council, which Takenaka managed and which included a few heavyweight members of business and academia. During Koizumi's tenure, the council became a focus of policymaking. The bureaucrats often had to do what they were told.

'The reason he is top down is because he doesn't have any followers,' Iijima said. 'He is not at the top of any faction. He is his own man.' As a result, he could pursue a radical agenda of the sort implemented by 'Satcha san', he said, referring to Margaret Thatcher, the revered former British prime minister credited by Koizumi's followers with shaking her country from its 'British disease'. Japan had had a Meiji Restoration and a Showa Restoration, Iijima said, the latter referring to its rise from the cinders of war under the Showa emperor, Hirohito. The name of the current emperor's reign was Heisei. Koizumi would, Iijima said with a triumphant flourish, lead Japan's Heisei Restoration.

Invocation of the Meiji Restoration, one of the most dramatic transformations in modern history, was bound to end in disappointment. Sure enough, nothing nearly so momentous took place. Those who had taken Koizumi at face value as a man who could revolutionize Japan and put it back on a vigorous growth path were to be disappointed. Even if Japan could kick-start its economy, its demographics and relative wealth meant there would be no return to the fast-growth years. Yet such language was symptomatic of the hype surrounding Koizumi throughout much of his premiership.

If one man was supposed to implement this radical agenda, certainly in the field of economics where Japan needed it most, it was Takenaka, the academic who ended up with not one but two cabinet posts. The newspapers called the round-faced professor Koizumi's 'economic tsar'. Crucially, in the second year of his premiership, with the stock market falling precipitously and frightened talk of financial meltdown, Koizumi gave Takenaka the job of salvaging the teetering banking system. Takenaka had long ago raised the issue of Japan's banks, weighed down with bad loans left over from their exuberant lending in the 1980s. Before Koizumi became prime minister, he had invited Takenaka to his study group, which took place at the Royal Park Hotel, an anonymous brick structure in Hakozaki, a little way outside central Tokyo. Takenaka, a man of strong conviction, gave his diagnosis of what he called Japan's 'economic pathology'. Since the bubble had burst in 1990, Japan had gone through three recessions and had grown at an average rate of only 1 per cent a year. Nothing could be done to revive the economy, he said, until the banks were purged of bad loans. If banks did not function properly, by lending money to promising businesses, the entire economy would remain sick. Banks had not dealt with their problems aggressively enough, he said. The strong continued to prop up the weak. There were such tight links between banks and corporations, which held a web of cross-shareholdings in each other's shares, that banks could not afford to deal too harshly with debtors. If too many companies went bust or if the value of their equities dropped beneath a critical level, they could drag the banks down with them.[15] So intimate were the connections between corporate and financial Japan that some banks even lent to struggling companies so they could maintain the fiction of paying interest on the debts they owed.

No one knew the precise value of bad loans. By the time Koizumi set about seriously tackling the problem in 2003, non-performing loans were officially recognized at Y43 trillion, some $355 billion at prevailing exchange rates.[16] Some economists put the number far higher, with one controversial estimate placing it at a horrendous Y237 trillion, some $2 trillion, or nearly half of Japan's entire economic output.[17] Takenaka suspected that the Financial Services Agency, which was supposed to be regulating the banks, was in collusion with the financial institutions. There were even stories of bank inspectors tipping off bank managers before each visit so they could hide incriminating evidence in secret vaults. In 1998, a finance ministry official had hanged himself after prosecutors found evidence pointing to collusion. Inspectors had been lavishly entertained, sometimes at outrageously expensive *no-pan shabu shabu* restaurants, where waitresses (minus their *pan*, short for 'panties') served preparations of extortionately priced beef to goggle-eyed customers.[18] At one point, before regulatory changes split bank supervision from the finance ministry, banks and brokers had whole departments dedicated to building cosy relationships with bureaucrats. Known as MoF-tan – or those in charge of looking after the Ministry of Finance – they specialized in entertaining bureaucrats at restaurants and hostess clubs. Takenaka was scathing about such links. Later he would write contemptuously of bank presidents as 'a bunch of incompetents' and buddy-buddy friends propping up the 'old convoy system'.[19]

After he was put in charge of financial regulation in 2002, Takenaka swiftly set about taking on the banks. Koizumi's role was to provide political cover as flak rained down on his economic tsar, particularly when Takenaka let slip to one interviewer that he considered no company 'too big to fail'.[20] The phrase became notorious, used to summon up a vision of the ruthless free-market monster that Koizumi was seeking to let loose. Takenaka compared the constant criticism to 'lying on a mat of needles'.[21] He ordered banks to halve the amount of bad loans on their books in two-and-a-half years. Then he forced them to comply by strengthening the way they accounted for capital. The aim was to push them into a corner. Either they would get rid of bad loans faster and bolster their capital – no easy task – or they would expose themselves as needing government help. If the government injected capital, it would be able to sack the management and take charge of a speedier bad-loan resolution itself. That is precisely what happened with Resona, the country's fifth-biggest bank, when auditors discovered in May 2003 that it was short of capital.[22] The government swiftly injected $17 billion of public money and installed new managers to run the bank. This was a foretaste of what was to happen in the US and Europe where, in 2008, authorities bailed out some of the world's biggest financial institutions to forestall a systemic meltdown.

In Japan, the bailout of Resona proved a turning point. Previous governments had been reluctant to inject sufficient state funds for fear of a public backlash against using taxpayers' money to bail out incompetent bankers. They had preferred to maintain the fiction that the banks were healthy. Under Koizumi, the issue was brought to a head. Investors took comfort from the revelation that, when push came to shove, the government would guarantee the solvency of the financial system. The stock market immediately began to recover. That ignited a virtuous circle in which the shares owned by banks gained in value, improving the banks' capital position. Three years later, the stock market had more than doubled, albeit from a post-bubble nadir, and bank shares had risen more than threefold.[23]

Meanwhile, as business conditions improved, the ratio of bad loans to total lending began to edge down in line with Takenaka's demands. Many of the companies responsible for the bad debts started to recover as a result of strong global demand, particularly from Japan's booming neighbour, China. Japanese companies had not stood still.

From the mid-1990s, they had been quietly restructuring, taking on fewer new recruits, ditching unprofitable lines of business and merging with rivals. The steel sector, for example, written off in the late 1990s as a has-been industry, had consolidated around four big companies and had staged a spectacular recovery by concentrating on specialist, high-grade steel. By 2003, the sector was producing the same amount of steel as in 1998, roughly 110 million tonnes, with a labour force one-third lower at 92,000 people. That revival was mirrored in other industries. As profits increased, companies could more easily repay their debts, normalizing what had previously been categorized as bad loans. By the end of 2004, the Bank of Japan, until then openly alarmed about the state of the banking system, had declared the worst to be over.

By 2006, non-performing loans had dwindled from an alarming 8 per cent of total bank lending to just 2 per cent.[24] Corporate balance sheets returned to healthy levels and profits reached a record high. By mid-2006 the Bank of Japan started raising interest rates – prematurely since deflation had still not been fully conquered – nudging them up to 0.25 per cent. (They had been stuck at zero almost constantly since the late 1990s.) Koji Omi, the finance minister at the time, told me, 'Fundamentally speaking, the state of the economy is very good.' Compared with the pessimism and self-flagellation of the previous decade, his quiet affirmation was tantamount to a whoop of victory.

Japan did, indeed, glide to a fairly strong economic recovery under Koizumi. This probably owed more to the efforts of the private sector and the favourable external environment, particularly insatiable demand from China, than to specific government policies. Measures put in place by the Hashimoto government of the late 1990s had also helped, particularly changes to accounting rules that made it harder for companies to hide losses. Whatever the cause, technically Koizumi oversaw the longest continual period of growth since the war, more than five years of non-stop recovery. The previous longest expansion period, the Izanagi boom – named for a Shinto god no less – was deemed to have ended in 1971, when growth slumped to the then disastrous level of 4.4 per cent from an average 11.5 per cent in the previous five years. Under Koizumi, of course, Japan's mature economy couldn't match anything like that. Still, it did grow at a respectable average rate of 2.4 per cent a year in real terms, with productivity gains by some calculations outpacing those of Britain, France, Germany and the US during most of that period.[25]

For many of the companies that had been paying down their debt and quietly getting in better shape, the Koizumi years were good. Although the consumer electronics industry had become a pale shadow of itself, other businesses were doing well. Car companies continued to go from strength to strength, and were now considered the best in the world. Toyota became a symbol of quality and was fast on the way to selling more cars than General Motors, which would need a government bailout before the decade was out. Exporters were helped by a change of heart at the usually hair-shirt finance ministry, which ordered massive intervention on the currency markets to keep the yen cheap. That helped exporters by making their products more competitive. Companies that had been on their knees only a few years before found themselves shipping steel, chemicals, components, machine tools and construction equipment to China. Koizumi had said 'No growth without reform'. A more accurate slogan might have been 'No growth without China'.

Besides cleaning up the banks, Koizumi's economic agenda had two other broad elements: cutting public expenditure and deregulating a heavily controlled economy. In his inaugural speech, he had set an overly ambitious goal of limiting Japanese borrowing to Y30 trillion ($260 billion) a year. His cost-cutting had a few key elements. First, he sought to rein in public spending on what he considered white elephant projects – the so-called 'bridges to nowhere' that had become a symbol of the failing construction state. Public works accounted for a large slice of expenditure and the construction industry employed no fewer than one in ten Japanese workers.[26] His opening assault came when he tried to privatize the debt-laden road corporations, which were financed largely through postal savings. That precipitated a pitched battle with the so-called 'road tribe' within the Liberal Democratic Party, many of whom owed their seats to popularity earned through supporting lucrative construction projects. Backing up the 'road tribe' was the powerful ministry in charge of construction. The man Koizumi entrusted to fighting this battle quipped, 'In the past Japan had the Imperial Army. Now we have the Ministry of Land, Infrastructure and Transport.'[27]

Koizumi's drive to cut wasteful spending was mirrored by a few local governors. Best known was Yasuo Tanaka, the leader of Nagano prefecture, a picturesque region in the Japanese alps, who was thrown out of office by the local legislature after declaring a suspension of all dam construction. Tanaka showcased his campaign for transparency by working in an all-glass office known as his 'crystal room' and, perhaps less relevantly, by publishing diaries about his hectic sex life under the title *Bump and Grind*. 'My no-more-dam policy is not only about the environment but also about how to spend our taxes properly,' he said. 'These things cost a huge amount of money and most of it goes to general contractors.'[28] Tanaka was subsequently re-elected in a blaze of publicity, though not all of Nagano's residents appreciated his cost-cutting drive. 'I can't stand the sight of him,' one vegetable farmer remonstrated. 'There are a lot of people – farmers and construction workers – crying at night because there's no work.' Though Koizumi remained wildly popular, there were not a few dissenters saying similar things about the crusading prime minister himself.

Koizumi pushed on regardless. In addition to his assault on public works spending, which slowly bore fruit, he cut state pensions and – controversially in an ageing society – raised the amount patients had to contribute towards the cost of medical care. He also sought to reduce the amount of tax revenue the central government transferred to local authorities. None of this proved enough to limit public borrowing as much as Koizumi had hoped, at least not initially. The government missed Koizumi's pledge to cap borrowing at Y30 trillion. In fiscal 2003, it issued debt worth more than Y36 trillion. Many economic commentators thought that was no bad thing. In a foreshadowing of recent debates in Europe and America about the merits of austerity versus Keynesian counter-cyclical spending, some experts argued that Koizumi's government needed to spend more in order to offset the parsimony of a private sector still too scared to invest. In his early days, Koizumi actually oversaw an expansion of government borrowing, not the contraction he had promised with his slogan of 'No growth without pain'. Only in subsequent years, when businesses revived and tax revenues improved in line with profits, did it become safe to shrink spending. By the end of his term in office, he had succeeded in whittling back the fiscal deficit from 8.2 per cent of GDP in 2002 to about 6 per cent.[29]

The final part of Koizumi's economic agenda was deregulation. This was what supply-side economists such as Takenaka regarded as a necessary loosening of controls over economic activity in order to release pent-up entrepreneurship – and hence growth. That meant shrinking the state and being less queasy about allowing so-called 'zombie companies' to go bust. It also entailed loosening labour codes and curbing the power of bureaucrats who liked nothing more than a bit of power-enhancing regulation. Despite Koizumi's ambitious rhetoric, actual progress was slow. He undertook a number of small, if symbolic, battles, but big vested interests, such as farmers and energy producers, escaped largely unscathed. One fight he did take on was over whether to allow regular shops, not just pharmacies, to sell over-the-counter cold medicines, a minor assault on the powerful medical profession which wanted to control prescriptions, for pecuniary as much as safety reasons. Yasuo Fukuda, Koizumi's chief cabinet secretary and later briefly prime minister himself, once mentioned the cold-medicines victory to me as one of Koizumi's crowning achievements of deregulation.[30] Convenient as this piece of regulation-busting doubtless was for millions of sniffling office workers, it was hardly enough to propel stratospheric growth.

Getting rid of regulations was clearly not going to be easy so Koizumi championed the establishment of special economic zones in which some national rules could be waived. The plan carried with it the echo, if none of the sweeping effect, of the special economic zones that had jump-started growth in Communist China. Fukuoka, a large and forward-thinking city in southern Japan, announced it would take advantage of the scheme by allowing, of all things, robots to walk down the street. Along with neighbouring Kita Kyushu, Fukuoka was a centre of robotic research and city officials wanted to give the industry a push. 'At the moment, you can't have robots on the sidewalk or in the street because of traffic and radio-signal regulations,' the governor of Fukuoka told me earnestly. 'We are asking the government to deregulate to allow these kind of experiments.'[31]

Robotic emancipation, like more readily available cold medicine, was probably not going to cure the economy of all its ills. Still, there was a flurry of applications for special-economic-zone status, with no fewer than 650 proposals: hospitals asking for greater leeway on treatment, schools to conduct their lessons in English and farmers in Nagano to be able to brew sake. Who knew they couldn't? Few of these proposals, on their own, seemed likely to spark a national revival.

Koizumi did push more substantive, if more divisive, attempts at deregulation. Most far-reaching was the further liberalization of labour laws to allow companies to hire more temporary workers, even in manufacturing where big businesses had generally offered full-time – often lifetime – employment. Such policies were credited by some with helping to make Japanese business more competitive, but blamed by others for widening income disparities. 'If the gap between rich and poor increases, we will see the emergence of an American-style society,' Ryusuke Kaneko, a 25-year-old musician working as an estate agent, told me with obvious alarm. 'If things go that way, it will not be a happy time for Japan.'[32] Takenaka, for one, was bemused by criticism that Koizumi had destroyed Japanese society with his radical economic agenda. 'There were many things left undone,' Koizumi's former economic tsar told me years later. 'If we are criticized because we only did a few things, I accept that. But many people criticize the Koizumi administration for too much reform. I find that really strange.'

If economic reform was patchy, Koizumi was more successful in the field of what might be called the 'political economy'. The most potentially far-reaching and controversial policy he pursued during his tenure was his attempt to privatize the post office, an institution where politics and economics overlapped. Really a huge state piggy bank, the post office had been raided by the Liberal Democratic Party for years as a source of easy income for public works and other popular endeavours. For Koizumi, it was a sprawling symbol of the money politics he so despised.

In the autumn of 2005, by then more than four years into his premiership, Koizumi electrified Japan by calling a snap general election over the improbable issue of postal privatization. That year, he had introduced a bill into parliament that would split the post office, which had 24,000 branches up and down the length of Japan, into four parts, each of which would subsequently be privatized. The bill squeaked through the lower house, but it was defeated in the upper house after a mass defection by Liberal Democratic Party legislators opposed to privatizing a beloved national institution. That was when Koizumi sent in the 'assassins'. Most of them were women, and glamorous ones to boot. Carrying out his threat to destroy his own party if it did not bend to his will, Koizumi dispatched his 'female ninjas' – as the press revelled in calling them – to run against the rebels from his own party who had defied him by opposing postal privatization. The 'assassins' were mostly celebrities, drawn from all walks of life to 'kill off' the professional politicians Koizumi had targeted. Among their number were a former beauty queen, a female newscaster and a television chef, Japan's equivalent of Martha Stewart – minus the criminal record.

His decision to dissolve parliament had been against all the advice of party grandees who had considered it electoral suicide. But Koizumi was furious at the disloyalty of those who had brought down a privatization bill that had been his lifelong obsession. He took his revenge by sacking the entire government – and rolling the dice. The opposition Democratic Party of Japan could not believe its luck. It began to prepare for office. Initial polls suggested Koizumi's Liberal Democrats might, indeed, be heading for a crushing defeat. Postal rebels and loyalists alike were terrified of losing their seat or even seeing their party shatter into pieces. If the Liberal Democrats lost power, it would bring to an end half a century of almost uninterrupted rule. Koizumi was visibly animated during the campaign. He toured the country, standing on the rooftop of party buses to defend his policies in an ever-hoarser voice. 'This election is about postal privatization. Are you for it or are you going to oppose it,' he challenged a crowd outside Tokyo's Kamata station.[33] On another occasion he hammed, 'If I am able to achieve postal system privatization, I don't care if I am killed.'[34]

Koizumi wanted to bolster the power of politicians by engaging the public more actively. For years, bureaucrats had been so powerful and skilful that politicians had been considered something of a sideshow. As in the British comedy *Yes Minister*, in which Sir Humphrey, an articulate and deliciously crafty bureaucrat, runs rings around his supposed political masters, so Japanese politicians were considered little more than front men. New foreign correspondents were sometimes advised by old Japan hands not to bother reporting on politics at all, since real decisions were made deep in the bowels of the bureaucracy. That view was a little overstated. Japanese policy had always been the product of a complex tug-of-war between bureaucrats, politicians and business. Koizumi's achievement – half rhetorical illusion and half substantive – was to render that policymaking process more open. The matter up for discussion in the 2005 election, among the most dramatic in Japan's post-war history, was the apparently dry subject of postal privatization. Were you for it, or against it?

For Koizumi it was not a dry subject at all, but an obsession. For him, the post office was a symbol of all that was wrong with modern Japan. The institution had its roots in the Meiji Restoration. When the leaders of the new government were casting around for ways of uniting the country, one of the things they hit upon was a universal postal service like that of Britain. Rich merchants were asked to donate land on which post offices could be built. Former samurai, their top-knots cut and swords confiscated as part of Meiji's sweeping modernization, were offered jobs as postmasters. In return, they were given generous stipends, tax exemption and the right to hand down their position like a feudal title. Those privileges remain largely intact today. Even in central Tokyo, let alone the countryside where post offices hold most sway, postmasters are often third or fourth generation.

Delivering letters was only part of it. The post office gradually evolved into Japan's biggest savings bank and provider of life insurance. In 2005, its savings and insurance assets amounted to an astonishing Y360 trillion ($3.3 trillion), about a quarter of the vast savings pool amassed since the war by thrifty households. That made it, by some measures, the biggest financial institution in the world, more than twice the size of Citibank. The pool of savings had proved incredibly tempting for economic planners, who recycled the money to chosen industries. The Liberal Democratic Party directed the savings, via a web of semi-state bodies, towards public works programmes. It had also been tapped to fund the 'second budget', a murky pool of money administered by the Fiscal Investment and Loan Programme that Koizumi was trying to kill off. Post office cash was, in short, the grease that oiled the Liberal Democrats' re-election machine. The post office's 280,000 full-time employees – more than those serving in Japan's army, navy and air force combined – could mostly be counted on to vote for the party and to get out the vote of friends and family.

All this made the post office the embodiment of the money politics Koizumi had promised to destroy, the most sacred of the 'sacred cows'. His advisers told him that privatization would unleash pent-up market forces by allowing the vast postal savings to be allocated, not according to the whim of pen-pushers and politicians, but according to market rationale. Getting rid of the state-controlled piggy-bank could also force the government to live within its means. Koizumi saw postal privatization not only as an end in itself, but also as a symbol of his determination to tear down the old Japan. When I interviewed him on the subject in his sleek office, Koizumi compared postal privatization to the sacking of an impregnable medieval fortress. 'Osaka Castle is surrounded by moats,' he said, smiling enigmatically. 'If you want to attack the headquarters, you have to attack the outer moat first, fill it in, and then attack the inner moat. The postal services are the outer moat.'[35]

For Koizumi's opponents, including the rebels within his own party, the post office was much more than a moat. Its 24,000 branches played a crucial social role, they said, particularly in remote areas that had been abandoned by young people and left to the elderly. I travelled by train to one such district in the mountainous Yamagata prefecture in northern Japan where the snow can be metres deep in winter. In that rugged, sparsely populated environment, it took Yoshihiko Suzuki, an earnest 42-year-old postal worker, one hour to deliver letters on his red-and-white moped to just four remote houses. His entire route consisted of only fifteen homes. At each residence, almost all of which were inhabited by elderly people, some living alone, he would pop his head around the door to ask how they were getting on and offer to bring them shopping. The town mayor, who saw Koizumi's privatization as an assault on Japan's social fabric, said, 'In these parts, the postman is more like a welfare officer. Elderly people who can't walk into town wait for the postman to visit and he calls out, "Is everything all right today grandma?"[36]

For the post office's detractors, Suzuki's work was a dreadful waste of money the state could no longer afford. For its supporters, it was an indispensable public service, the essence of a caring society. Even in the cities, the post office was a well-loved institution famed for its reliability. In the year Koizumi announced its privatization, for every one million letters delivered, only eleven were misdirected. The equivalent figure in Britain was 7,000.[37] An expert on the post office described the debate thus, 'One vision, represented by the postal lobby, places great store on state paternalism, informal social welfare, risk avoidance and predictability. The second [represented by Koizumi] champions the virtues of globalization, small government and self-responsibility.'[38] Shizuka Kamei, a grandee of the Liberal Democratic Party and a leading 'postal rebel', saw things even more starkly. In trying to destroy everything that was good about Japan, he said, Koizumi was worse than Adolf Hitler.[39]

Whatever people thought about postal privatization, there was huge public excitement about the election. Koizumi had depicted it as a fight to the death over the future direction of Japan. Noriko Hama, a professor of economics who was no great fan of Koizumi, nevertheless admired the choice being offered. 'This is a marvellous moment, something for which Japanese democracy has been waiting for half a century,' she told me. 'In this election, people have to say what they mean and mean what they say. They can't get away with being wishy-washy. This is something unprecedented in Japanese politics.'

The election, of course, went Koizumi's way. After he set out the choice, opinion polls began to shift dramatically. From being an issue to which Japan's public gave scant thought, postal privatization was suddenly elevated to its number one concern. The rationale seemed to be: if it meant so much to Koizumi it must be important. Throughout the campaign, fought under the slogan 'Don't Stop Reform', Koizumi never once allowed the opposition to distract attention from his chosen central issue. He brushed aside any attempts to talk about the mountainous public debt, the parlous state of pensions or the diplomatic imbroglios into which he had led the country. As far as Koizumi, the master of ceremonies, was concerned, the election was about one thing and one thing only: the post office. The result was an overwhelming victory. Voters turned out in the highest numbers for years and Koizumi's party won a landslide of 296 seats, giving it a two-thirds majority in the powerful lower house of parliament. That made it the biggest victory in the party's more than fifty-year history.

The following month, parliament duly passed a bill to split the post office into four units: savings, insurance, mail and counter services. By 2017, some way off even by Japan's careful standards, the state would run down its holding in the banking and insurance businesses to nothing, completing the privatization. It would retain ownership of the mail and counter services. Many of the 'postal rebels' had lost their seats to Koizumi's 'assassins', who now became known as 'Koizumi's children'. Some of the rebels who had managed to get re-elected as independents crawled back to the Liberal Democrats. They swallowed their pride and voted for Koizumi's hated bill. Kamei, the man who had likened Koizumi to Hitler, won back his seat standing for a new party. He was not so easily cowed. 'If things keep going like this, this will be the end of Japan,' he proclaimed darkly.[40] Koizumi said with his customary directness, 'We've destroyed the old Liberal Democratic Party.'[41] The party of factions, money politics and rural patronage was gone, political analysts said. In its place had emerged a new organization that was more responsive to the floating urban voter, with a mandate to change Japan. The legislature appeared to be at Koizumi's feet.

It was at precisely this point that Koizumi seemed to lose interest in the fight. The euphoria of the postal election turned out to be the high point of his premiership. Many expected him to use his newly won authority to push through the radical programme of deregulation and spending cuts he had so long advocated. The prime minister himself stoked expectations that he was about to embark on a Thatcherite crusade. At a press conference following his electoral landslide, he said, 'We've heard the people's voice in favour of structural reform. We will not stop, but will press on.'[42] He seemed to have *carte blanche* to do anything he liked. Instead he spent another rather inconsequential year in office and then declined to seek re-election as party leader. His popularity meant that he could, perhaps, have stayed on for several more years. Instead, he quietly departed.

Minoru Morita, a left-leaning political commentator, said Koizumi's actions betrayed an intellectual shallowness. The usual view, he
once told me, was that Koizumi had a grand vision but, opposed by
reactionary elements within his own party, lacked the political clout
to enact it. The anti-climax after Koizumi's triumphant victory suggested exactly the reverse. 'Koizumi has skilfully raised his popularity
by waging battle against the forces of resistance,' he said. 'But now
that he has secured power, he doesn't know what to do with it.'[43] Gerald Curtis, professor of political science at Columbia University and
one of the shrewdest observers of Japanese politics, said the same.
'Koizumi has not said what he will do after postal privatization
because he doesn't really have a clear agenda of reform,' he said
shortly after Koizumi's electoral triumph. 'He's going to be scrabbling
around figuring out what to do for an encore.'[44]

In the event, there was no encore. Koizumi simply left the stage like
a rock star with the sense to quit with his popularity at its zenith. In
some ways, it was a heroic gesture worthy of a 'kabuki premiership'
in which spectacle had been such a vital element. Koizumi retired, to
enjoy Italian opera and – if the gossip magazines were to be believed –
a series of younger girlfriends. Much of this was pure speculation,
though one businessman who entertained him at a high-class restaurant told me with a strange precision, '60 per cent of the time he talked
about sexy things'. Yet the truth was that, for a figure who had loomed
so large in the public imagination, little was known about his private
life. Koizumi kept to himself, rarely giving interviews or making public pronouncements. After a premiership of drama and impassioned
rhetoric, he simply shrank from view. The rest really was silence.

Once Koizumi was gone his party reverted more or less to norm. Politics returned to its old, unstable ways. None of his shortlived successors
had anything like his charisma, undermining the idea that the Japanese electorate would never again tolerate a colourless time-server
nominated by party grandees. The public also turned against Koizumi's neo-liberal agenda. His emphasis on light regulation and the
wisdom of markets became less fashionable in the years after the
2008 Lehman crash. There was nostalgia for Koizumi the man and
for Koizumi's style of leadership, but not many people appeared to

miss his policies. In particular, he was blamed for exacerbating the gap between rich and poor and creating the so-called *kakusa shakai*, the unequal society. His policies were said to have produced a harsher, dog-eat-dog Japan of winners and losers. Masahiko Fujiwara, the author who pined for the communitarian values of feudal Japan, criticized Koizumi for ripping the fabric of society. 'Koizumi is reform, reform, reform,' he told me. 'But of course reform does not necessarily mean improvement. Sometimes it means deterioration.'[45]

It is true, as we have seen, that, on some measures, the gap between rich and poor had widened, although at a probably slower pace than in many advanced countries. Still, people's perception was of greater income inequality thanks to the introduction of merit-based pay and, especially, the decline in the number of full-time jobs. Studies showed that the Gini coefficient, a measure of inequality, was not that far behind the US, a society many Japanese regarded as ferociously unequal and the antithesis of Japan's more egalitarian values.[46] In the last year of Koizumi's term, a survey in the *Nikkei* newspaper showed that only 54 per cent of Japanese considered themselves middle class, with a once unthinkable 37 per cent classifying themselves as lower class. For much of the post-war period, three-quarters of Japanese had consistently described themselves as being in the middle class.[47] During Koizumi's time in office books on the phenomenon of inequality, such as Atsushi Miura's *Lower Class Society* (*Karyu Shakai*), became bestsellers. There was also a rush of books advising people how to live on a meagre Y2 million a year, less than $20,000 at the time. 'Many Japanese have preferred a society of equals to one where people freely compete against each other,' said Yoshio Higuchi, a professor at Keio University. 'Analyses that show social and economic disparities widening have shocked the people.'[48]

Koizumi's policies may have contributed marginally to the widening wealth gap. Cuts to health provision undoubtedly made life more difficult for some. A further liberalization of the labour market allowed manufacturers to hire casual staff with lower wages and benefits. There were record numbers on welfare. Koizumi also broke his party's *modus operandi* of siphoning money from the cities and spreading it around the countryside. In stemming public works and clamping down on tax transfers to local governments, he may have exacerbated the already widening gap between isolated rural communities and Japan's giant metropolises where wealth tended to concentrate. In truth, though, his policies probably didn't make a huge difference. Mainly, he was channelling trends already in progress since the economy had slowed in the 1990s and the transition from manufacturing to knowledge-based industries had intensified. It was true that some of Koizumi's advisers did advocate an end to what they saw as the paternalistic, 'socialist' policies of the past and the creation of a society where individual responsibility and hard work were better rewarded. Yet the truth was that inequality had been rising for many years before Koizumi took office. Much was the consequence of international trends, particularly the incorporation of hundreds of millions of Chinese workers into the global workforce after Beijing's accession to the World Trade Organization in 2001. The middle class has been squeezed all over the world. Yuriko Koike, a prominent politician who had become close to Koizumi, dismissed the idea of yawning inequality. 'Among the capitalist societies, Japan is almost like a socialist country. The disparities in Japan are 0.01 of an inch,' she said, holding her well-manicured thumb and forefinger in the air by way of illustration. 'The disparities in the rest of the world, in places like Russia or China, are more like the distance between the moon and the earth.'[49]

Yasuhiro Nakasone, prime minister from 1982 to 1987 and the only Japanese leader in three decades to rival Koizumi's influence, agreed with Takenaka that Koizumi had done too little, not too much. I spoke to him shortly after Koizumi had refused to allow him to stand for re-election on the very un-Japanese grounds that he was too old. Koizumi had set an age limit of seventy-three for parliamentarians as a way of flushing out what he considered the reactionary old guard of his party. At the time, Nakasone, who had been a parliamentarian for six decades, was eighty-five. He was still fuming at the affront to his dignity and quoted me a haiku, of his own composition, on his feelings about being pushed out. ('Everything is human theatre/ The autumnal sun is now setting.') Koizumi, he said, was a showman who lacked gravitas. 'Reform has ended up as a mere slogan.' Nakasone pointed to his own record of privatizing the railways, a far more meaningful endeavour, he thought, than tampering with the post office. 'I believe that politics should focus on constitutional reform, education, social security, financial reform and diplomacy, particularly relations with other Asian countries,' he said at the time. 'His tendency to get sidetracked by less important projects rather than more substantial concerns facing the country has earned him criticism, which, in my view, is well-founded.'[50] Nakasone was not the only critic of Koizumi, whose reputation for grandiloquent rhetoric had earned him the nickname 'Nato' – short for 'No Action, Talk Only'.

Like a kabuki actor, whose garish make-up and larger-than-life gestures are meant to enrapture spectators, Koizumi loved nothing more than playing to the gallery. When he wanted to privatize the road corporations, he set up a televised commission that brought to light the lavish expenditure of those opaque bodies. Critics charged that the privatization itself was a fudge. For Koizumi, though, the grand gesture of opening up wasteful spending to public scrutiny (and outrage) *was* the policy. It sharpened the appetite for change by engaging and energizing the public. To call Koizumi a showman was not necessarily to criticize him. It was to identify his strength as a politician.

Takatoshi Ito, the Tokyo economics professor and a one-time government adviser, praised his leadership skills. 'I think Koizumi was wonderful. He demonstrated what strong political leadership could achieve and how to make people rally behind him . . . I still think it was a good moment in history.' Although Ito, like Nakasone, believed Koizumi ought to have pursued more radical change, he argued that the charismatic prime minister galvanized national morale. 'There has been very little optimism in the past twenty years, when people finally started to believe in the recovery and saw the light at the end of a long tunnel,' he said. 'That kind of optimism was limited to Koizumi's years in office.'[51]

Koike, who served as Koizumi's environment minister, also felt he had brought a sense of direction. 'Leaders must make decisions and then convince people to do it,' she said. 'We are no longer in an age when we should base everything on consensus.'[52] Iijima, Koizumi's crafty political secretary, said much the same thing. 'For the first time in decades, a prime minister has tried to assert top-down authority,' he told me. He had also been the first to take Japan's budget deficits seriously, he said. 'People say a lot of things about Koizumi. That he's not good at economy. That he doesn't know a thing about finance or monetary policy.' But Koizumi knew one thing, Iijima told me. 'Japan is the most indebted country in the world. We have to stop pouring money away like this. We have to turn the tap off.' Many, including Koike, said that what the prime minister had tried to start had been blocked, even reversed, after he left office. Ippei Takeda, a friend who ran a business in Kyoto, compared Koizumi's agenda to a seed that had been planted but not properly nurtured.[53]

In the past thirty years, Koizumi stands out as Japan's most exceptional prime minister, perhaps the only one with a truly international reputation. He was, in many ways, Japan's Barack Obama, promising change his nation could believe in. But the public, it turned out, didn't always know what kind of change it really wanted and Koizumi was not always able to deliver. Koizumi was as much a manifestation of structural shifts already in progress as the actual agent of change. Societal convulsions had long been in train, brought about by the collapse of the bubble, the end of the Cold War and the intensification of international competition. Koizumi's skill as a politician was to recognize those new realities and to try to articulate a response. 'Japan has changed so much since the 1990s,' Gerald Curtis of Columbia University told me in October 2011. 'The changes are societal and Koizumi has been riding them.'

Ezra Vogel, who had boosted public morale three decades previously with his book *Japan as Number One*, told me that, for all Koizumi's radical break with the past, Japan remained in political transition. A new sustainable system had yet to be built. 'The country needs a political system with the capacity to respond effectively to problems in a long-term way,' he said.[54] 'This coherence ended in the 1990s when there was a collapse of the parties. Japan hasn't built the right political system to put things back together again.'

A symbol of Koizumi's ultimate failure to enact change was the fate of his beloved postal privatization. After he left office, the legislation he had fought so passionately to enact became associated with the ills of rising inequality and a less caring society. 'There has been a very significant move away from the past, more inclusive, way of doing things,' said Hama, the economics professor who had been so invigorated by the 2005 election. After Koizumi, she said, Japan looked for ways of going back to a more inclusive society, what she called 'protection against the jungle' of the free market. If a private post office had become symbolic of an overgrown free market, in 2012 legislators brought out their machetes by passing an amendment to Koizumi's bill, scrapping the deadline for postal privatization. In theory, that would allow the state to own the post office indefinitely. For Koizumi loyalists, the amendment ripped the guts out of his bill and proved that politicians lacked the nerve to press on with his painful, but necessary, programme. For opponents, Japan had put the former prime minister's un-Japanese free-market ideas to rest. Of the handful of parliamentarians who voted against the amendment, one was none other than Shinjiro Koizumi, the 31-year-old son of the former prime minister and the fourth generation in the family to occupy the parliamentary seat at Yokosuka. Shinjiro, handsome and dashing like his father, was the great-grandson of Matajiro, the 'tattooed minister' who had run the post office eighty years before. Storming Osaka Castle turned out to be more difficult than anyone had imagined.

# 9

# Life After Growth

It was actually a Japanese health minister who raised the spectre of the Japanese people one day disappearing altogether. 'If we go on this way, the Japanese race will become extinct,' Chikara Sakaguchi said melodramatically in 2002.[1] Sakaguchi was basing his alarmist prediction on extrapolation. If you continue any downward-moving graph far enough into the future it will eventually reach zero. Japan's fertility rate fell below 2.1, the level needed to maintain a population, in the 1980s.[2] Between 2005 and 2010, it averaged just 1.27.[3] Although it has edged back up again, not nearly enough babies are being born to replenish the population. Japan's case is particularly stark since it is more resistant to immigration than most countries in its less-than-fecund position. Britain's population would be at risk of falling too were it not for a steady influx of outsiders.[4]

Part of the 'problem' is that people are living too long. Japan's life expectancy has risen dramatically. It is now the highest in the world, with men living to an average age of eighty and women to a remarkable eighty-six. In 1947, the average was fifty and fifty-four respectively. As a result, Japan's population is ageing rapidly. In 1950, only 5 per cent of the population was over sixty-five. Today that figure is 25 per cent. By 2035, one in three could be that age. As people retire and fewer youngsters enter the job market, the workforce is shrinking, by roughly 0.6 per cent a year. In 1960, there were eleven people of working age to support every person over sixty-five. By 2010, that number had dwindled to 2.8. On current trends, by 2055, there will be only 1.3 people of working age for every person theoretically retired.[5]

The seemingly inexorable maths leads many to depict Japan as a ticking time bomb. It implies there will be fewer workers paying taxes to fund the pension payments and medical bills of an increasing number of retirees. That is true so far as it goes, though as people grow older, they also tend to work longer, thus lowering the notional 'dependency ratio'. Still, in modern times, we have become accustomed to ever-rising populations. George Magnus, an economist who has written extensively about demographics, describes Japan, and other similarly placed countries, as being on what he calls a 'demographics death row'. By that he means that, barring a dramatic reversal, Japan's population will continue to shrink. On current trends, by 2050, there will be 25 million fewer Japanese, cutting the population to 102 million.[6] Under the most pessimistic assumptions, the population will drop to 45 million by 2100, the same as in 1910 Meiji Japan.[7] The proportion of Japanese in a still rising global population will also fall. In 2005, Japanese made up 2 per cent of the world's inhabitants. By 2050, they are likely to account for just 1.1 per cent. If population equals power, then Japan's national vigour is waning.

Before we proceed too far down the path of 'demographics equals destiny', it's worth peering a little below the surface gloom. For a start, and to state the obvious, longevity should be counted as a success not a failure. By 2050, according to some projections, there could be as many as 1 million Japanese over 100 years of age.[8] Doubtless this will present numerous challenges. Old people tend to fall sick and need caring for. Some are very poor. But the underlying reason for the existence of so many elderly people is that Japan is rich and medically advanced. Whether for reasons of diet, the quality and availability of healthcare, a sense of social wellbeing or some other factor, Japan does a better job of keeping its citizens alive and healthy than any other large nation. Life expectancy in the United States (fortieth in the list of nations to Japan's first) is a full five years below Japan, at seventy-five for men and eighty-one for women.[9]

Similarly, low birth rates, though not always desirable, are often a direct consequence of higher standards of development as women take greater control of their fertility. In Japan's case, one can certainly argue that women would be more inclined to have children if they felt more economically secure and if society did a better job of helping them juggle work and family. 'If you ask a married couple what is the ideal number of children, they would tend to say two,' says Takatoshi Ito of Tokyo University. 'They are somehow being discouraged from having families of an ideal size.'[10] Women are also postponing marriage. The average age for a woman to get married has risen steadily from twenty-three six decades ago to twenty-eight.[11] Another reason for the low birth rate may be the widespread availability of higher education. One British study found that 40 per cent of female graduates remained childless at the age of thirty-five.[12] Unless our remedy for Japan is to stop educating its women – and no doubt there are a few Japanese traditionalists who would advocate just that – we shouldn't spring too readily to the conclusion that a low birth rate is a sign of society gone wrong.

To present ageing in wholly negative terms can border on the absurd. One well-known Japanese sociologist told me a possible 'solution' to demographic problems might be 'to lower life expectancy'. He didn't specify how this happy outcome might be achieved.[13] That he mentioned it at all suggests we might be looking at the problem backwards.[14] Nor is Japan the absolute outlier it is sometimes made out to be. In fact, the world's lowest fertility rates are to be found not in Japan but in more than ten other countries, including South Korea, Poland, Belarus, Hong Kong and Singapore. Most of East Asia has sub-replacement fertility rates, as do many countries in South and Central America. In the Muslim world, Algeria, Tunisia, Lebanon and Turkey all have birth rates insufficient to maintain their populations over the long run. The fastest ageing societies turn out to be not in Japan or Italy, another country often placed in the category of 'demographic doom', but rather South Korea, Singapore and, because of its one-child policy, China.[15]

Japan then is not alone. Though some countries will have 'better' demographics than Japan for many decades and others will import people from abroad, the long-run global tendency is in the same direction. By 2050, there will be roughly 2 billion people aged over 60, three times the 673 million in 2010.[16] 'Some countries will age more slowly than others but, one by one, we are all moving into the third stage of ageing,' says Magnus.[17]

It would be foolish to suggest that rapid ageing doesn't present big challenges. Most pension and healthcare systems have not been designed with such large elderly populations in mind. 'A declining population is a negative for economic growth and a negative for any institution which is built on the assumption of increasing population or increasing GDP,' says Ito. 'You can live with a declining population [only] if all the institutions are built to cope with it.'[18] In the end, Japanese taxpayers will have to decide what kind of safety net they are willing to provide. That is bound to cause pain and will mean some people are not as well taken care of as they expect.[19] We should, however, put such problems in perspective. In 1920, the normal retirement age in advanced societies was seventy to seventy-four, hardly a burden on pension systems given that the average life expectancy was then fifty-five to sixty. Even in 1960, the average retirement age was sixty-five.[20] The pension problem, then, is relatively recent, born of over-optimistic assumptions when post-war welfare systems were being designed. Fixing it will require a combination of raising the retirement age and getting individuals to save more for their old age. It will mean adapting the healthcare system. It should not be beyond the wit of man.

Japan has taken tentative, though insufficient, steps. It has pushed through reform to link rising national life expectancy with an automatic reduction in pension benefits. It also mandated a steady increase in contributions to state pensions from 13.6 per cent of wages to 18.4 per cent. On the negative side – from a sustainability point of view, that is – it has not insisted that supposedly indexed pensions fall in line with deflation. The retirement age is, however, gradually being raised from sixty to sixty-five, with further rises expected.[21]

Those measures are enough to keep the existing pension system going, at least for now. Perhaps a bigger concern is that a large slice of the workforce has no pension coverage at all. Many part-time workers, a rising share of the labour force, are opting out of paying pension contributions entirely. That is partly, surveys show, because they do not believe the system will last long enough to pay them back. Savings rates are falling. Those in their thirties save only about 5–7 per cent of their income compared with the 25–28 per cent put away by today's retirees.[22] The huge nest egg on which Japan is now pleasantly slumbering is not likely to be around indefinitely.[23]

In general, there are three things societies can do to mitigate the effects of ageing, says Atsushi Seike, a labour expert at Keio University. They can raise fertility, productivity or labour participation. Japan has done poorly at increasing fertility compared with countries like France, which has successfully used incentives to reverse the long-term decline. (That, of course, is expensive. France's state sector is much bigger than Japan's.) Japan has been slow to establish affordable childcare for children up to five, essential if working women are to consider having babies. That is partly due to bureaucrats' anachronistic views about women and work and to pointless turf wars between ministries with overlapping responsibilities.[24] More could be done on productivity too, though in spite of Japan's image as an economic laggard, since the mid-1990s improvements in productivity per hour have not been significantly far behind those in the US.[25] Productivity in the service sector is still poor by some measures, suggesting there is some low-hanging fruit if Japan needs to harvest it.

As for participation rates, one way is to encourage people to work longer. 'The motivation and willingness of older Japanese to continue working is pretty high,' says Seike. Three-quarters of Japanese men aged sixty to sixty-five are still working, the highest level of any advanced country. Still, most large companies have traditionally forced their employees to retire at sixty. The seniority pay system, in which wages rise with length of service, means older workers are expensive. As a result, companies have opposed government efforts to raise the mandatory retirement age to sixty-five. Many have got around the problem by rehiring workers over sixty on contracts at lower wages.

More women are working as they delay marriage and childbirth. Still, a lower proportion of women work in Japan than in many advanced countries. The rate, at 48 per cent according to the World Bank, is higher than Italy, at 38 per cent, but much lower than Britain, at 55 per cent, the US, at 58 per cent, and Norway, at 63 per cent.[26] Even the increase in Japan is not all good news. Many women take low-paid, part-time work, either to supplement falling household wages or to provide for children as head of a growing number of one-parent families. Higher female participation is thus as much a sign of rising hardship as of women's emancipation.[27] Still, by one calculation, if women's participation in the workforce could be raised to the same level as men's,

Japan could increase its workforce by 8.2 million and expand the size of the economy by 15 per cent.[28]

Another potential source of labour is immigration. The Keidanren, the main business lobby, has periodically come up with eye-catching estimates suggesting Japan needs to import millions of workers if it is to make up a labour shortfall of 6 million people by 2025. Given that Japan is home to only around 2 million 'non-Japanese', many of them long-term Korean residents, it is impossible to imagine it opening the floodgates to that extent. Some years ago, I asked a senior Japanese official, urbane in the extreme, about the latest Keidanren report urging mass immigration. He visibly shuddered. 'For the rewards you get in terms of economic rejuvenation the costs are simply too high,' he said without explanation, though he was clearly alluding to the perceived social problems in multicultural western societies. 'We've seen what has happened in the US and Europe.'[29] After the Lehman shock, when the economy contracted, the Japanese government actually went the other way. It began a scheme to pay Japanese workers of Brazilian descent, many of whom were encouraged to come to Japan in the 1990s, to go back home. The stipulation of accepting a one-way ticket plus cash was that they never returned.[30]

There is a compelling case for opening up Japan to more immigration in order to spark fresh ideas, innovation and more fluid links with the outside world. Without big doses of youthful infusion, Japan's economic vigour could slowly seep away. In the absence of sufficient young people of its own, an influx of young immigrants might bring the economic vitality it lacks. 'The importation of labour would not be for the labour per se, but to bring in people with different mindsets, to shake things up a bit,' says Hugh Patrick, who has been studying the Japanese economy at Columbia University for half a century.[31]

The case for immigration, on purely numerical grounds, isn't always as compelling as it is sometimes made out to be. As we have seen, a little over 4 per cent of Japanese are unemployed, a figure that, as in other countries, underestimates the true number of those out of work. Youth unemployment is around double that.[32] That doesn't immediately suggest a serious labour shortage, although there are certain dirty, dangerous and low-paid jobs in construction and other industries many Japanese are not prepared to do. If manufacturing companies are looking for cheaper foreign labour they can get it in one of two ways. They can bring people to Japan or they can set up factories abroad. Japanese manufacturers have done both. At home, many have operated in grey areas of the law to employ foreign workers who sometimes lack the appropriate visas. More still have established factories abroad, in Southeast Asia, China, the US and Europe. By 2014, more than three-quarters of Japanese cars will be built outside Japan.[33]

In the services sector, Japanese companies employ less foreign labour, but still some. A few companies operate call centres based in China and some back office work is done in places such as India and the Philippines. In Japan itself, many of the ubiquitous convenience stores, such as Lawson and Family Mart, are staffed by Chinese workers with near-impeccable Japanese and an appreciation of the ultra-demanding service culture. Japan's service sector remains more 'inefficient' than that of other advanced countries, meaning there are more people to help the customer – wrapping items, pressing lift buttons and bowing graciously. This is the sort of thing that gets visiting time-and-motion consultants in a rage. If they are right that this is a hopeless waste of human capital – rather than part of one of the world's most pleasant service experiences – then Japan's much vaunted coming labour scarcity is surely exaggerated. Perhaps Japan won't need 6 million foreign workers after all. It can simply redeploy to other industries the hordes of lift girls and night-stick-wielding building site workers (who warn passing cars of construction ahead). 'Right now, I don't think we have a very serious labour shortage,' says Seike, who believes the real problem is a mismatch between jobs and skills and the precipitous growth of poorly paid work.

An obvious exception is the health sector, particularly when it comes to care for the elderly, where low wages make it hard to attract Japanese workers and there may be a shortage of up to 700,000 staff.[34] One option, if the money could be found, would be to raise salaries. For society as a whole that would be a way of transferring the excess savings of the elderly to younger generations who are being squeezed – through low wages, higher pension payments and so on – as part of Japan's adjustment to lower growth. Another way to solve the problem would be to allow in more nurses and care workers from countries such as the Philippines and Indonesia. Pilot schemes have been introduced, but numbers are pathetically small, restricted to a few hundred each year. Even then, care workers who want to stay have been subject to overly stringent language requirements, justified on the grounds of patient safety. I once watched a television documentary about an Indonesian healthcare worker who appeared to be devoted to her job in a nursing home where she was adored by her elderly patients with whom she communicated perfectly well. However, she was unable to pass the strict exam in written Japanese, since there weren't enough hours in the day to study the formidable lists of required characters, vocabulary and grammatical formulations. She was sent home.

Hiroshi Mikitani is a great believer in encouraging Japan to look outward. A successful financier at the Industrial Bank of Japan, he was exposed to new ways of thinking when the bank sent him to study at Harvard Business School. There he learned a new word, so unfamiliar he was forced to spell it out in the phonetic Japanese alphabet used for imported concepts: 'entrepreneurship'. He founded an internet company that evolved into Rakuten, today Japan's Amazon and eBay rolled into one. In 2012, Forbes put his wealth at $6.5 billion. Rakuten has expanded aggressively in countries such as Brazil, Indonesia, France and Russia. But Mikitani also wants to bring foreign influence to Japan. His boldest initiative, one that has attracted ridicule as well as praise at home, is to insist that his staff become proficient in English. His campaign bears the rather unfortunate name of 'Englishization'. Even the menu at the staff canteen is printed in English. Mikitani, who wears open-neck shirts and polo sweaters, told me that learning English and being more open to the outside world was vital for Japan's economic rejuvenation. 'If all the employees of Panasonic or Sony could communicate in English, they could be far better than Samsung,' he told me of the South Korean company that has left its Japanese rivals in the dust. 'A language will open your eyes to the "global", and you will break free from this conventional wisdom of a pure Japan. English is a tool to globalize you, to make you change.'[35]

Being open may be just as important as being fertile. Equating ageing with a dying economy implies that only countries with growing populations can be healthy. The late James Abegglen pointed out that, when Japan's population nearly tripled in the twentieth century, critics complained about its overcrowded islands where people had to live in 'rabbit hutches'. Now the prospect of a declining populace filled everyone with alarm. One need only consider Pakistan, a country whose population has nearly quadrupled to 190 million since 1960, to realize that we cannot draw any neat correlations between population growth and prosperity.

Yet unless we expect the population of the world to keep growing indefinitely, all economies will one day face the problems now confronting Japan. The idea that richer countries should simply import labour from poorer ones implies an endless supply of people from somewhere else. That proposition must also eventually run out of road. If we are not to argue for an ever-larger global population – or, perhaps, the importation of guest-labour from some far-off galaxy – societies will one day have to find a way of prospering without the impetus of ever-greater numbers. Japan is a stark example since its population is not merely stagnant, but on the verge of rapid decline. Much of the slowdown in headline growth over the past twenty years is the result of less favourable demographics. As the population shrinks, there will undoubtedly be severe strains as the country seeks to balance competing generational needs. Japan will need to come up with a serious policy and societal response. However, I'm willing to place a little wager with Sakaguchi, the doomsday former health minister. The Japanese will be around for a little while longer yet.

I was to imagine a grain of rice. Ippei Takeda, the avuncular chief executive of Nichicon, sat in his office in Kyoto, where the high-tech components maker has its sleek and rather daring offices. The spacious lobby looked more like an avant-garde art gallery than a corporate headquarters. I'd been escorted to the lift and along the corridor by one of his assistants to a large office on an upper floor. An immaculately dressed female attendant had just brought us both tea. She bowed as she entered the room, bowed as she silently set the little bowls of green liquid before us and bowed again at the doorway as she left. Takeda, engrossed in his story, appeared not to notice. He was blinking behind his silver-rimmed glasses and chuckling. The rice, he was saying, should be Japanese short-grained, about half the size of longer-grained foreign varieties. Now, he said, to make one of the aluminium capacitors that his company produced, I must imagine drilling 300,000 holes into that single grain, flipping it over and doing the same on the other side. It was vital that the holes didn't meet in the middle. An oxide layer, about eight to ten angstroms thick, must then be applied. He checked a little book with columns of figures before writing down the numerator, 1, followed by a denominator of 10,000,000. The thickness of the layer should be measured in ten-millionths of a millimetre. I must have looked nonplussed. 'It's very thin,' he clarified.

The point of Takeda's story was that there were still some things Japan did well. Making very small things was one of them. Nichicon's energy-storing capacitors went into almost every conceivable electronic device from air conditioners to mobile phones. Though his company had many foreign factories, including in China, where it made some capacitors at three-quarters of the Japanese price, the really complicated stuff was still produced at home. The quality and consistency were superior in Japan, he said, better even than in South Korea. Some capacitors cost only a few cents each but, if they went wrong, they could disable devices worth hundreds, even thousands of dollars. Manufacturers paid a premium for quality. 'If you're asking me can Japan survive as a manufacturing nation, my answer is, yes, without a doubt.'

That view is not shared by everyone. Japan is even more paranoid than other advanced countries about what it calls the 'hollowing out' of its industrial base. The proportion of Japanese workers employed in manufacturing has been steadily declining for years, from 27 per cent in 1970 to 17 per cent today. That makes manufacturing more important than in Britain or the US, where about 10 per cent of workers are engaged in industry, but slightly less important than in Germany and Italy with about 20 per cent.[36] Japan has been pressured by the emergence of lower-cost manufacturers in places such as China and by a strong rising yen. Since the tsunami, the drift of manufacturing abroad has accelerated, as companies worry about the safety of their supply chain and the reliability and cost of non-nuclear energy after the Fukushima disaster. 'If you look at it logically, it doesn't make sense to manufacture in Japan,' says Akio Toyoda, president of

Toyota Motor Corporation, still a symbol of Japanese manufacturing excellence.[37]

For a nation that prides itself on *monozukuri*, an almost mystical belief in the art of making things, this is a shocking conclusion for the boss of Toyota to arrive at. In feudal times, artisans came above merchants in the pecking order. Even today, the Japanese hold a residual suspicion of finance – 'money made from money' in the words of one economy minister, who told me that Edo Japan outlawed usurious interest rates.[38] The Japanese still consider making things to be more honourable. Some Japanese business leaders, perhaps remembering the disastrous forays abroad of banks, worry that the service industry is not cut out to compete internationally. Japanese standards of service are rightly legendary but not easily transferred abroad. When they have made bold gambits overseas, for example in banking in the 1980s, Japanese companies have tended to overpay for acquisitions and to struggle to convey a global vision to an international workforce. 'Japan's whole identity is tied to manufacturing,' says Yoshikazu Tanaka, founder of Gree, an online gaming company and one of the most prominent recent success stories outside traditional industry.[39]

Few companies epitomize the decline of manufacturing like Sony, a byword for Japanese quality and innovation after the war. The company that invented the Walkman, the world's first portable music player, and the Trinitron TV, with its revolutionary bright picture, has become shorthand for the dismal slide of manufacturing prowess. By 2012, Sony had not turned a profit in five years and, in that year, announced the sidelining of Sir Howard Stringer, the razor-sharp Welshman it had hoped could turn its fortunes around. For years, Sony has been outflanked by rivals such as Apple and Samsung. Though it has shed jobs by the tens of thousands, shipped out production to China and come up with device after unmemorable device, it has only fallen further behind. By mid-2012, its market value had dwindled to one-thirtieth of Apple's. Samsung, a company from the former Japanese colony of South Korea, now regularly makes more profits than the top fifteen Japanese electronics companies combined.[40]

Sony's biggest failing was its inability to navigate the industry's transformation from analogue to digital, or from 'knobs' to 'menus' in Sir Howard's clever phrase.[41] That was more a question of lack of imagination than of technical knowhow. Akio Morita, Sony's legendary co-founder, had thought hard about digitalization early on and Sony had a library of music that had come with its acquisition of CBS records. But Sony's engineers, the mainstay of its early success, resisted what they saw as flighty ideas about networks and convergence. As late as 2004, the company's devices did not support the standard MP3 format. Sony's PlayStation video console was more successful. But even that lost its lead, failing to stave off the challenge from cheaper rivals and online games.

Yasuchika Hasegawa, boss of a pharmaceutical company and chairman of the Keizai Doyukai business lobby, says Sony illuminates a broader Japanese failing. 'We continue to excel at developing and manufacturing the parts that go into machines and devices, but we miss the larger opportunities that developing new product concepts would bring,'[42] he says. Japanese companies knew how to make more than two-thirds of the parts that went into both the iPod and the iPhone. But they were so focused on 'partial optimization' that they missed out on what really mattered: creating and marketing a digital ecosystem. Where, in the commonly heard cry, is Japan's Google, its Twitter or its Apple?[43] Where is the Japanese Steve Jobs? For Hasegawa it comes as only mild consolation that many devices still contain Japanese components of the sort made by Nichicon. In his view, Japan has downgraded from 'Made in Japan' to 'Japan Inside'.

Manufacturers do still excel at making niche components as well as specialist equipment such as robots – in which Japan continues to be a world leader – and steppers, the machines used to produce silicon wafers for the electronics industry. Japanese companies manufacture all kinds of specialist chemicals, machine tools, automated systems, lenses, micro-controllers, tiny motors and dozens of other components and inputs indispensable for modern existence. Japanese car-makers, including Toyota, Nissan and Honda, continue to innovate and to excel. Japan, unlike Britain, whose manufacturing industry has shrivelled, is still good at making things you can drop on your foot. The decline of its electronics industry has been highly visible, since the brands that have faded – Sony, Sharp, Hitachi, Panasonic and many others – were once standard features in many middle-class homes around the world. That dramatic slide, though, has obscured the more enduring performance of companies that are less well known to consumers, whether they make industrial machinery, materials or tiny components. Take the case of South Korea's Samsung, whose success has caused so much damage to its Japanese rivals. Yet Samsung remains a huge importer of Japanese manufactured inputs, the quality of which it still cannot match itself or buy from other South Korean companies. For all its industrial success, South Korea still runs a big trade deficit with Japan, strong evidence of Japan's enduring competitiveness in certain fields. Japan, after all, continues to head the global league table of granted patents, beating even the US, though it trails in Nobel prizes and academic citations, suggesting perhaps that more of its innovations are incremental improvements rather than revolutionary breakthroughs.[44]

If, as Hasegawa suggests, the Japanese are somehow better at perfecting existing manufacturing techniques than inventing entirely new concepts, Japan's best days could indeed be behind it. That would fit the theory of those who argue that the country's rigid social structure and strong work ethic were better suited to the catch-up phase of industrial development than to the post-industrial era. I once visited a Canon factory on the outskirts of Tokyo where workers in identical jumpsuits perfected techniques to keep their movements to a minimum, the more efficiently to assemble complex devices such as colour photocopiers. There was something of the discipline of karate about the way they moved. So skilled had they become at eradicating both temporal and spatial 'waste' – *muda*, they called it – that the workers were now huddled together in smaller and smaller working zones. Whole areas of the factory floor had been 'liberated' by their perfection of techniques to build photocopiers in ever tighter spaces. One rather wondered to what avail. These were the sort of obsessions suited to the production age, when Japan was chasing the world's leading manufacturers by making incremental improvements to existing techniques. These skills may be less useful in a post-industrial era where the goal is to invent whole new ways of doing things. 'You need a different mentality to fend off the guy coming from behind. You need different talents, a different organization of society,' says the economist Richard Koo. Japan, he argues, lacks people who can think independently and 'not just regurgitate what the professor says'.[45]

Part of Japan's problem, say some, is what Yoichi Funabashi had referred to as the 'Galapagos syndrome'. Named after Charles Darwin's observations about how animals adapt to specific environments, in Japan it had come to mean the development of technology too narrowly catered to the obsessively finicky home market. Mobile phones are Exhibit A. Japan had phones capable of surfing the internet nearly a decade before the iPhone. Sharp was the first company to attach a camera to a mobile phone. But producers failed to market their innovations abroad or radically rethink their designs. As a result, Japan was eventually invaded by smartphones made by Apple and Samsung. Similarly, Sony invented an e-reader several years before Amazon's Kindle, but failed to commercialize its invention, which never caught on in the US or Europe.[46] 'Nuts and bolts are Japan's past, not its future,' says Masayoshi Son, the founder of Softbank, an internet company, and the man most often mentioned as an entrepreneur suited to the post-industrial age.[47] Son argues that Japan should give up on labour-intensive manufacturing altogether and focus instead on capital-intensive, high-tech industries such as information technology, alternative energy and pharmaceuticals. It should emulate Apple by concentrating on designing software as well as hardware, and by developing new business and marketing models, he says. Manufacturing can be done elsewhere.

Son's analysis suggests that a certain degree of 'hollowing out' may be inevitable, even a sign that industry is adapting as it should to a new era. Increasingly, companies locate routine manufacturing abroad but keep their 'black box' technology in Japan. They are also buying companies in what they hope are high-growth markets such as India, Brazil and Indonesia. That may not be good for employment, although, since Japan's labour force is shrinking anyway, this may not matter as much as it once did. It may not be good for tax collection either. Yet the fact that Japanese companies are buying more and more companies abroad – in record numbers in recent years – may be a sign that they are putting their capital to use where it has a better chance of counting. In 2012, Japanese companies spent $113 billion on foreign acquisitions, buying healthcare, telecoms and food companies among others. That was second only to the US, whose companies splashed out $174 billion in the same year. Japanese companies spent nearly twice the amount laid out by Chinese ones, perhaps surprising given the headlines about moribund corporate Japan and aggressive Chinese companies intent on snapping up assets around the world. Japan also outspent British companies by two to one.[48] To those who believe Japan's great strength is *monozukuri*, these trends are worrying. But in a world where more countries are getting better at making things and the domestic economy is flat, going abroad in search of profits and innovation may be just about the smartest thing Japanese companies can do.

A few years ago, an opinion piece in the *New York Times* caught my attention. Written by Norihiro Kato, professor of Japanese literature at Waseda University, it was titled 'Japan and the Ancient Art of Shrugging'.[49] It was a celebration of slow growth. Kato had written his essay just as China had overtaken Japan as the world's second-largest economy.[50] For the first time in more than four decades, Japan was back at Number Three. Rather than fretting about it, as the country's old economic warriors did, Kato said the national levelling off was something to celebrate. 'Japan doesn't need to be No. 2 in the world, or No. 5 or 15. It's time to look to more important things,' he wrote. Kato called it the end of the 'right-shoulder-up' era, a Japanese term for a graph that keeps ascending. Well before the burst of the bubble in 1990, there had been signs of a tapering off, he said. The population had risen by more than 1 per cent each year from 1910 to 1977, at which point it began to slow – until 2005 when it actually shrank.[51] Right shoulder down. Similarly, a graph of rice production between 1878 and 1980 showed a slowdown from the 1960s after nearly a century of steady expansion. 'Decades before China overtook Japan, the country had started downsizing, preparing for a smooth landing.'

Of course, the old guard would never let go of their dreams of endless expansion, Kato said. But Japan's youth seemed quite content with the new state of affairs. They had become, he said, 'non-consumers'. Japanese in their late teens and early twenties, 'did not have cars. They didn't drink alcohol. They didn't spend Christmas Eve with their boy-friends or girlfriends at fancy hotels downtown the way earlier generations did.' They worked hard at part-time jobs, and spent hours at McDonald's sipping cheap coffee. They ate fast-food lunches at Yoshinoya, a restaurant chain of good quality but very low prices, serving grilled beef over rice for as little as $3 a bowl. The Japanese, he suggested, were pioneering a new sort of high-quality, low-energy, low-growth existence.

I thought Kato's was a brave article. It was certainly open to ridicule. It challenged one of the unspoken tenets of the modern age – that an economy, like a shark, has to keep moving forward if it is to stay alive. But it broached a subject that was too often ignored. Was growth the be all and end all? Did decline have to mean death? After all, Britain was overtaken by the US as the world's biggest manufacturer in 1900, just as Japan had been pushed behind China in 2010. Yet most British citizens live far more comfortably today than their ancestors at the turn of the last century. Japan too was in relative decline, but accord-ing to Kato, it was learning how to live better.

Kato's was also an expression of something I had heard many times in Japan. Typical was a friend of mine, the photographer Toshiki Senoue, who travelled with me to the battered northeast coast in the days after the tsunami. 'They talk about Japan's decline,' he said once when we were driving up to the same coast another time. 'But there's no potholes on the street, there's good quality cars, no violence, clean air. It's OK.' Japanese food was the best and healthiest in the world, he said. Life was pretty comfortable. He paused. Decline wasn't too bad. 'And if you decline, maybe one day you can go up again.' Machiko Satonaka, a well-known illustrator of *manga* comics, had said some-thing similar. 'People talk of Japan as losing its economic power. But that's OK. We don't care. We don't want to be a superpower,' she said. 'Our values are evolving. Now our dreams should be how to create a safe society and a clean environment.' Such views can sound almost like heresy, but they are a powerful undercurrent of Japanese think-ing. Growth was not all it was cracked up to be, these people were saying. There was more to life than the endless pursuit of GDP.

I arranged to have coffee with Kato. We met, suitably enough, in the lobby of a hotel built during the bubble years. It was a little too garish for its own good, and looked dated in a Japan where the understated is once more a sign of good taste. Kato's hair, slightly tinged with grey, was sticking up as if responding to an unseen magnet hovering above his head. He was wearing blue jeans and a purple shirt. His face was animated, an ironic smile never far from his lips. His brain seemed to work faster than his mouth, and he occasionally struggled to order his thoughts properly.

Kato likened modern economies to the Hollywood action movie *Speed*, starring Sandra Bullock, in which a bomb is put on a bus full of passengers. The hijacker warns that, if the speed of the bus drops below fifty miles an hour, the bomb will go off. It was an interesting twist, Kato said. In a normal action movie, everything went faster and faster until the climax. In *Speed* it was the opposite. If the bus slowed down there would be an almighty explosion. 'It's the same with economies. We can't slow down without provoking a disaster,' he said. *Speed* was influenced by a script written by Akira Kurosawa (1910–98), one of Japan's most celebrated directors. His film, shelved for lack of finance, was to have been called *Shinkansen Explosion*. In the plot, a bullet train was set to explode if its speed dropped below 80 kilometres or rose above 120. 'But why do we have to stay between 80 kilometres and 120 kilometres an hour?' Kato asked. 'We understand what it is to maintain a certain sustainable growth speed, not above, nor below. Our growth was based on production. The post-growth period is about how to make better use of what we have. Rather than being larger our economy needs to be fitter.'

Kato reached for another metaphor. 'In the plant world, you can't constantly pursue growth. A plant can't bear fruit until it has finished growing and reaches maturity.' Growth in Japan's heyday was skewed. 'It was only growth if you excluded many things,' he said, referring to what economists call 'externalities', the unmeasured spillover effects of actions, for example on the environment or on people's health. 'Capitalism speaks in terms of limitless growth, but there are finite resources. What seemed possible in the 1960s and 70s is clearly no longer possible.' Kato reminded me of Walter Berglund, the heroic crank of Jonathan Franzen's *Freedom*, who argues that growth in a mature economy – as in a mature organism – is not healthy. It is cancerous. Kato is a professor of literature, not of economics. But even some economists are questioning how we should measure economic performance. At its crudest, people confuse growth with wealth. Bankers and investors tend to be more enthusiastic about a poor country, say China or India, which is growing rapidly than they are about a wealthy one that is maintaining a high standard of living. That viewpoint, in turn, gets reflected in the business pages of newspapers.

Kenneth Rogoff, professor of public policy at Harvard, has written about the best ways of measuring growth. In an essay called 'Rethinking the Growth Imperative', he says standard economic statistics do not measure life expectancy, literacy and so on. The United Nations Human Development Report ranks nations according to these broader measures of quality of life. In its 2011 report, Japan comes in at number 12. Norway is number 1, with the US at 4, Germany at 9, France at 20, Singapore at 26 and Britain at 28. As with rankings of the most 'livable cities', these exercises can be subjective, but the aim is to correct what Rogoff calls the 'statistical narrowness' of GDP.[52]

In his essay Rogoff argues that 'people are fundamentally social creatures [who] evaluate their welfare based on what they see around them'. Imagine, for example, the fabulous wealth of Nelson Rockefeller, the American businessman and philanthropist who died in 1979. For all his riches, Rockefeller could never have bought a laptop or an iPhone, items that have become standard fare for pimply teenagers in Tokyo and elsewhere. Rockefeller didn't feel cheated because none of his associates had an iPhone either. Yet such advances in technology are not captured in standard growth statistics. One only needs to think what kind of television set, computer or mobile phone an average Japanese of today owns compared with her supposedly more prosperous counterpart in the roaring 1980s. If you can buy higher-quality items with the same amount of money then you have become better off. In any case, Rogoff asks, how much we should care whether it takes 100 years or 200 years for an economy to grow eight-fold. An economy growing at 1 per cent would double in size in seventy years and grow eight-fold after 200, he says. One growing at 2 per cent would double in thirty-five years and increase eight-fold in just 100. But, Rogoff wonders, does that matter? 'There is a certain absurdity to the obsession with maximizing long-term average income growth in perpetuity.'

One can take such arguments too far. One objection is that, even if growth isn't desirable in itself, it may be necessary. Without growth, institutions such as pension systems are in danger of collapse. Without growth, it is hard to see how Japan can get out of its current debt trap. For Japan, the alternative to growth could be some sort of financial crisis that would deal living standards a further blow. Perhaps national economies, like sharks, really do have to keep moving forward. The search for measures of economic success beyond GDP is also open to abuse. Governments may be tempted to employ such definitions to justify their own lousy performance. Gross National Happiness was a term coined in the Bhutan of the 1970s. It was supposedly a measure of broader spiritual, as well as material, happiness. When it comes to things we can actually measure, however, Bhutan doesn't do so well. Today, it remains a poor country with a per capita income of $6,000, a life expectancy of sixty-six – a hardly creditable 134th in the world – and a literacy rate below that of Togo or Bangladesh.[53] Gross domestic product may be imperfect. But at least it means something.

In the case of Japan, one could argue that talk of 'life after growth' is defeatist nonsense, the result of failed public policies and national drift. Only a fool would embrace decline as a desired outcome. That is certainly the opinion of many. Takeda, the man who had taught me about the manufacturing prowess behind the capacitor, regarded such talk as revealing a national character flaw. 'To become Number One you have to have the will,' he said. 'But Japan never had that. Right now people say, "Why do you need to be Number One?" Unfortunately a lot of people have that attitude.' I understood Takeda's impatience. But I also thought that some Japanese were casting around for something important. The post-war period had been characterized by a national effort to increase GDP as much in the name of national pride as of the wellbeing of its people. Kato and others wanted Japan to find a more humanistic goal.

In recent years, it has become clearer that Japan's economic crisis, though prolonged, has not been unique. Nor has Japan, for all the mistakes, been uniquely incompetent in dealing with the litany of problems that followed the bursting of its bubble. 'Its historic experience – high economic growth, bubble economy, and subsequent economic stagnation, deflation and falling birth rates – will inevitably be replicated by countries around the world,' says the author Natsumi Iwasaki.[54] Japan may not look pretty. But it could be a taste of things to come.

James Abegglen, who was among the first to recognize Japan's industrial strengths in the 1950s, also warned against writing the country off too quickly. The 1990s, the so-called 'lost decade', he told me, had in fact been 'a decade of redesign', when many companies began to grapple with changed circumstances by paring their costs, paying down their debts and increasing their productivity. They had merged and moved some manufacturing abroad. They had ditched some lines of business and switched to others. That restructuring had carried on into the twenty-first century, he said. To call those years lost was 'simple nonsense'. Even so, Japan's most exhilarating days were behind it. 'In my era, Japan was a very exciting place. In the next era, it's going to be a very dull place. Very wealthy and very dull. It's going to be like a very large Switzerland – and that's not such a bad thing.'[55]

# 10

# The Promised Road

Kumiko Shimotsubo dated the start of what she called 'the ice age' to the winter of 1995. Like Haruki Murakami, she regarded that tumultuous year as the time when everything changed. For her, it was less about earthquakes and sarin gas attacks. Rather, it was when, she felt, many young people were 'frozen out' of the system their parents had taken for granted. In her final year of college, which she spent at the University of Tsukuba, a once futuristic science city built outside Tokyo in the 1960s, she sent off more than 100 applications to companies, each neatly handwritten on a postcard. She got perhaps fifty replies, a lower ratio than her male counterparts, she recalled with some bitterness, but enough to give her hope she could get a slice of the Japanese Dream. Now a slightly disenchanted 37-year-old, whose business card identified her as a Bilingual Writer/HR Consultant/ Intercultural Facilitator, Shimotsubo had found what she called 'the promised road' barred to entry.

We met in the elegant tea room in the Imperial Hotel, a mosaic by Frank Lloyd Wright covering one wall, the only remnant of the building he designed in 1915. Even such a prestigious hotel, still patronized by the imperial household, became swept up in the 1960s construction frenzy as Japan tore down the old in pursuit of the modern. In 1968, the hotel was redeveloped above the strenuous objections of Frank Lloyd Wright's widow, then in her seventies, who pleaded for it to be preserved even as the bulldozers moved in.

Shimotsubo was slim and fashionably dressed with a double string of pearls draped over her sweater. She started by telling me about her career expectations when, like all the other graduate hopefuls, she set out on the rite of passage known as the *shushoku katsudo*. Literally the 'find work activity', it was the mass screening of graduates by corporate Japan. Wearing a black suit, white blouse and sensible black shoes, her hair neatly trimmed (and on no account to be dyed), the then twenty-year-old followed the advice dispensed by make-up companies about how a young female graduate setting out in life ought to look. 'Fresh but not too sexy,' she recalled. The *shushoku katsudo*, or *shukatsu* in the inevitable contraction, was an urban phenomenon that might be compared to the migration of wildebeest. The passage traversed, however, was not to the pastures of East Africa, but to life in a big corporation, and hence a place in the Japanese Dream.

She applied to a who's who of elite companies, including the big trading houses such as Mitsubishi, Mitsui and Marubeni. But by the mid-1990s, fewer graduates were making the migration successfully. Companies had finally realized that the economic shock of the early 1990s, when asset prices started collapsing, was not an aberration. They would need to make adjustments. Because of their compact with existing employees – one that Shimotsubo likened to that of a *daimyo* lord with his loyal samurai retainers – there was almost no question of sacking existing workers who had implicitly been offered a job-for-life. The only option was to hire fewer fresh graduates or, *in extremis*, to suspend graduate recruitment altogether. Shimotsubo and millions of graduates like her bore the brunt of that decision. Shut out in the cold, they became the 'lost generation'.

Like many during that era, Shimotsubo had been caught unawares by Japan's changed economic circumstances. She had set her sights on being recruited as a so-called *sogoshoku*, the top intake of graduates whose careers were expected to progress smoothly into the higher ranks of a corporation. The second-tier intake, known as the *ippan-shoku*, the clerical workers on the 'non-career' track, was almost exclusively female and generally not expected to advance. Most likely such women would marry and leave to start a family. Shimotsubo aspired to a fast-track position. Attitudes were slowly changing, though some employers still thought these top-tier jobs should be reserved for men, the economic breadwinners. That and the deteriorating economic situation meant the sort of positions she was pursuing were few and far between.

Her dream of walking the promised road proved fleeting. She

received not a single offer. Only at the last minute did she get a solitary positive reply from a private publishing company, not the sort of elite firm to which she had aspired. 'I lost my motivation totally,' she recalled fifteen years after that bitter disappointment. Now married with a young daughter, she said of the years before she graduated, 'There used to be a promised career path. People were expected to join a company and then spend all their life in that company with the same colleagues. My father was a typical Japanese salaryman. He spent more than thirty years with one traditional Japanese company, the famous NEC. He followed the promised road.'

Shimotsubo did not. In Japan, where all serious hiring was – and still largely is – done *en masse* after graduation, there was no second chance. Most companies were inflexible about taking on people in mid-career. They wanted to get their hands on fresh graduates so they could train them from scratch and exercise what Shimotsubo called 'mind control' – to turn them into obedient employees. 'Once you dropped off the promised road, you'd be evaluated as "not a good person", just because you didn't belong to anything,' she said. 'To have a permanent job means to have a good social status. Not to have one means to lack social status. I am now thirty-seven and many people of my age are still desperately working in temporary jobs. They get a very low wage, the same as a new graduate, even though their careers have been going nearly twenty years. It's a kind of social discrimination.'

Shimotsubo had been luckier than most in her position. Because she spoke English, learned at her internationally minded high school in Yokohama, she had been able to build an alternative career working for foreign companies operating in Japan. They cared little, if at all, that she hadn't joined straight from university. At one, she even became head of the human resources department, something that would have been impossible at her age in a Japanese company. The irony of that job was that, after overseeing an aggressive western-style restructuring, she too was dispensed with. Now she worked as an 'intercultural consultant', operating in the penumbra between national employment practices. She remained bitter that the opportunities afforded her parents' generation had been snatched away. 'When I was a senior college student, I was so jealous of the bubble generation. They could eat and drink from the company's pocket,' she said of the famously lavish expense accounts. 'They got big bonuses even if their productivity was low. It was so easy to earn money in those days.' Looking back, she added, 'I was just a senior high school student when Japan was really booming. That generation had their very happy hour. But the people of the ice age, people like me, don't know what the bubble was. Today's younger generation don't know what growth is. Their experience is just downsizing and recession. That's all they know of the Japanese economy. That's why dreams are shrinking in Japan.'

Her work in human resources had led her to believe that the Japanese employment system needed to change. It was, she said, an all-or-nothing lottery that favoured those who gained an early foothold after graduation, but excluded the rest. 'I personally wish there were alternative paths to follow. But the current system is the only established one,' she said. The waitress came to pour more tea. Around us, an almost exclusively older clientele was chatting amid the reassuring clink of bone china. Looking around the tea room nervously, as though she were plotting a coup, Shimotsubo turned to me conspiratorially. 'For the younger generation to have any hope,' she whispered, 'I really hope the old system collapses totally.'

For Haruki Murakami, the fact that the promised road had forked off into a hundred unexplored directions was as it should be. Sure, because of a flagging economy, young people were having to make it on their own, he said. That was not always easy. But Shimotsubo's promised road had led to a false dream. When he was researching *Underground*, his book about the sarin gas attack, Murakami had become better acquainted with the foot-soldiers of the Japanese miracle. He had interviewed the stoic, uncomplaining office workers and bureaucrats who were gassed on their way to the offices from which they would seek to keep the Japanese Dream alive. 'It was love and hate of course,' he said, weighing up his words carefully. 'I admired them and, at the same time, they depressed me. I think their lives are absurd. They are consuming, consuming themselves, you know. They commute two hours between their house and the office and they work so hard. It's inhuman. And when they come back to their house, their children are sleeping. It's a waste of humanity.'[1]

Murakami felt more affinity with the post-bubble generation. He talked warmly of the *freeters*, the Japanese word for the casual, part-time employees who worked, mostly for minimum wage, in dead-end jobs. For most social observers, the idea of a *freeter* – moving from one precarious job to another – was the epitome of all that had gone wrong in the long years of slow-burn crisis. But where many Japanese saw low wages, lack of security and the extinguishing of opportunity, Murakami saw young people trying to build something new. It was, perhaps, easier to be optimistic from his position as a rich and successful novelist. He forked off the promised road of his own volition – and ended up with fame and money. Not everyone could be so lucky. Back then, the outlines of the promised road were still clearly discernible. Now, trying to make it as a young person in Japan was like charting an uncertain path through the desert. But Murakami admired a generation that had, albeit mostly by necessity, set out to find its own way. 'Our society has been changing,' he said. 'There are so many *freeters*. They chose to be free. They have their own opinions and their own lifestyles. I think the more alternatives we have the more open society will be.' The rigidities of the old system may have helped Japan in its catch-up phase, he was saying, but they were out-dated and harmful to individual development and personal choice. 'Most Japanese don't have any sense of direction,' he continued. 'We are lost and we don't know which way we should go. But this is a very natural thing, a very healthy thing. It is time for us to think. We can take our time.'

Noritoshi Furuichi, a 27-year-old Ph.D. student and author, was – at least on the face of it – more in Murakami's camp than in Shimot-subo's. Ten years younger than Shimotsubo, and three decades younger than Murakami, he was more optimistic about contempo-rary society, based both on his own, privileged, experience and on the research he had done as a budding social scientist. Furuichi, who dou-bled as the executive of a start-up IT firm established with college friends, dressed fairly typically for a twenty-something Japanese man. That is to say he looked nothing like the drab-suited salaryman of western imagination. If anything, he was more like the androgynous creation of a *manga* comic, a dashing, slightly effete young wizard from *Howl's Moving Castle*. His well-groomed hair had a delicate henna tinge and he wore casual clothes with no trace of a crease. He carried an iPhone 4S, then the latest model, and, over his shoulder, a capacious purple shoulder bag. When he waved goodbye, it was the cute salutation beloved of Japanese girls, elbow pressed against his hip, hand oscillating to and fro.

In his book called *Happy Youth in a Desperate Country*, Furuichi's main conclusion – quite counter to the prevailing narrative – was that Japan's youth has never been so content. 'The media have been unrelenting in their depiction of youth as poor, hapless, desperate and in dire straits,' he told me when we met on the top floor of a glinting new office tower near Shinagawa station, one of numerous showcase buildings that had shot up in Tokyo during the years of supposed stagnation. 'In fact, the government's own data shows that 73 per cent of youth are perfectly satisfied with their life,' he said, referring to an annual 'satisfaction survey' that had been going for decades. In the 1960s, when Japan was entering its high-growth sweet-spot, about half of respondents aged twenty to twenty-nine said they were happy. The 'happiness quotient', he said, had risen steadily ever since.

Those numbers looked wrong given what was generally said about the optimistic years of economic take-off and the directionless post-bubble decades. Furuichi's book had drawn criticism for downplaying real economic and social hardships. It was not unusual, though, he told me, for satisfaction levels to rise as an economy matured and slowed, partly because young people no longer had to delay their gratification like their parents and grandparents. Japan's miracle years, he said, were an era of happiness deferred. 'Half of Japan was still rural until the mid-1960s. So many people working in the cities were living for others. They were in the city on behalf of their home town and they needed to send part of their pay cheque back to the countryside. They functioned on behalf of another person. They were serving the future, serving the nation, serving the provinces. They were serving something other than themselves.' In sociological terms, Japan had transitioned from being what he called an 'instrumental' society, where actions served a larger purpose, to becoming a 'consummatory' society in which people lived for the moment. 'Now they're working for themselves, making their own decisions, taking their own responsibilities and reaping their own rewards.'

Despite all the economic insecurity of contemporary Japan, Furuichi said, few people of his age hankered after the old days. 'We knew our fathers were being called economic animals, that they were made fun of for being hapless cogs in the machine. Our mothers did what they could to be "happy housewives", but they were essentially maids and servants.' The job-for-life system was almost exclusively male and, even then, not all-encompassing, he went on. Many men worked for small companies without the benefits of absolute job security, ascending pay and generous pensions. 'Even in the best of times, the so-called lifetime employment system covered only 30–40 per cent of the population.' That number may have shrunk still further, but there were compensations. 'Fewer young people are buying cars. Instead, they're spending money on food, clothes, phones and spending time with their friends. "What should Japanese youth do?"' he asked rhetorically. 'I'm doing it. I'm not running for office, so I don't have a prescription for what everybody else should do. But for myself, and the people around me, I am being proactive. I'm establishing ways to use my knowledge and use the knowledge of people around me. I think people should look at the society that's near them and find ways to utilize each other's resources. They shouldn't worry about a united Japan, or the "Japanese people". Just find a group of people you can do something productive with and be productive. Everywhere you look you see the problems of the state ... I'm not saying we need to abandon the public sphere. But I am saying that small groups of smart people, ten or twenty people, getting together and seeing what they can do, that is definitely what interests me.'

Furuichi's breezy attitude about the present masked his deeper concerns about the future. I asked whether the current situation was sustainable. 'Among developed nations, our national debt is astronomical,' he said. 'Then we have an ageing population. So this is a transitory moment. Thirty years from now all these people living with their parents will need to care for them. I don't know whether they are prepared for that, either financially or emotionally.' Even Japanese housing was shoddy, he said, meaning little of what was built during the boom years would last very long. You couldn't rely on the wealth that had been built up in the past for ever. 'But in the meantime, young people are living quite happily with their parents, coexisting quite comfortably,' he added, downplaying the notion of inter-generational strife. Since stable jobs were harder to come by, younger people were absolved of the responsibility of trying to secure them. They could live with their parents, or share a house with friends, a growing trend. 'So long as their parents are healthy, there is no need for them to join the whole process,' he said. 'It's an open question whether this is a form of "twisted happiness" or not. But all I'm saying is that, if today's youth is in dire straits, they're not aware of it.'

Most Japanese still believed they had it relatively good, he said. When they looked at Europe and the United States, they tended to think things could be a lot worse. The world outside Japan could seem violent and frightening, filled with riots, drug addiction, home-lessness and a yawning divide between rich and poor. Those impressions might be exaggerated, filtered as they were through Japan's blinkered view of itself as a uniquely comfortable and harmo-nious society. Still, the self-image had made people wary of change. The old set-up might be creaking and groaning. But it still functioned. 'The previous system that developed in the high-growth era worked so well that everything has become fixed around it,' he said. 'Because the old system has not obviously come off the rails, conservatism rules. If it had fallen apart, we could have had a more radical renova-tion. But there has been no fundamental rethinking of whether that was the right way to organize a society. So instead we get entropy. That's precisely our crisis.'

'I don't feel as though I live in a desperate country, and I don't like it when people say Japan is in a desperate situation,' Yoshi Ishikawa, a 28-year-old who worked in the growing non-profit sector, said. I had asked him about Furuichi's idea that younger people were living in the moment, blind to the nation's larger problems. That made them sound rather like passengers on the Ship of Fools than confident navigators of their own destiny. Ishikawa thought they were more aware than that implied. Many young people, he said, had consciously rejected the values of their parents and were searching for fresh ways of living. 'There are so many young people trying to make something new.'

I first contacted Ishikawa through the organization he worked for, ETIC, or Entrepreneurial Training for Innovative Communities. ETIC had been active in the Tohoku region of Japan whose coastline had been so devastated by the tsunami. A government-supported body, it had been helping fishermen whose boats – even whole families – had been swept away. In Kesennuma, where large ships were washed up and the high street and much of the town destroyed, ETIC sent entrepreneurs to teach fishermen how to maximize profits by 'branding' their catch and selling direct to consumers. 'It was pretty impossible to do something like that before the earthquake,' Ishikawa said, referring to the difficulty of cutting out the middlemen with whom some fishermen had done business for generations. 'But now they feel more empowered and less afraid of the pressures from older generations.' Of his own motivation, he said, 'For us, the new frontier is to do something good for society or for our community. Even if we earn less money, so long as we can work with satisfaction, that is OK. I think that's how young people think these days.'

I had come to see Ishikawa at his office in Shibuya, a district of Tokyo where Japanese teenagers like to parade their fashions. On the way to his office, I'd seen two girls in matching yellow tartan with leggings pulled down around their knees to expose their thighs, and ruffles around their necks like clowns. Others clopped by in red cowboy boots, platform shoes or black patent leather boots with improbably narrow heels. Some of the boys wore beltless baggy pants riding low on their hips, knitted caps or pork-pie hats. There were skinny young men all in black, with drainpipe trousers and ghostly white faces. The fashions, so carefully individualized, still somehow contrived to look like a uniform. Ishikawa was casually, if much more conservatively, dressed, in a French-onion-seller-style stripy shirt and a dapper waistcoat. His hair was short with a studiously jagged fringe. The office was open plan. People, mostly in their twenties, sat at long benches made of rough-hewn wood, manufactured by one of the small businesses ETIC supported. There was a gentle clicking of laptops and the smell of freshly brewed coffee.

Ishikawa was brought up in Kira, a town of rice paddies and auto-parts factories about an hour from the industrial city of Nagoya where Toyota is based. His father worked at a small trading company, his mother was a housewife. His family was of fairly modest means. Neither of his younger brothers made it to university, though they both studied at technical school and landed good jobs in the motor industry. Ishikawa, an engineering graduate, could have worked in manufacturing too. But he chose a different path. His turning point, if it can be called that, came as a seventeen-year-old when he won a scholarship to spend a year as an exchange student in Alaska. He was in America when al-Qaeda terrorists flew planes into New York's Twin Towers. People from his home town had always thought of the US as a dangerous place. Several years before, a boy from Nagoya had been sent to Baton Rouge on the same scholarship as Ishikawa. One night he had been on his way to a Halloween party and had knocked on the door of the wrong house by mistake. The man, who thought he was a trespasser, shot him dead. 'We all knew this and felt scared of American culture,' Ishikawa said. But his time in Alaska turned out to be something of a revelation. He marvelled at how easily Americans socialized with each other and liked how openly affectionate his host parents were with their children. He even got a kick out of their tolerance for what, to his eyes, was the shoddy service and poor-quality merchandise Americans were used to. Perhaps the Japanese, who expected their petrol attendants to bow and their food to be always beautifully presented, were just too uptight, he thought.

Back in Japan, after postgraduate studies at Nagoya University, he landed a job as a management consultant. He worked in Texas, Barcelona and Tokyo, but felt unfulfilled. What was the point, he thought, of advising one Japanese beer company how to grab market share from another? That was the sort of thing that might have motivated his parents' generation, but surely there was more to life than that? The more he came into contact with corporate Japan, the more he became convinced it revolved around drudgery and pointless late-night drinking sessions. As a consultant, he had worked with one company whose employees spent millions of yen of the firm's money a month at a certain hostess club – a typical way for stressed-out salarymen to unwind with clients. His advice to the company, he said with a pained expression, was that it would make more sense to buy the club and run the hostess business itself.

Younger people thought differently, he said. The pre-bubble

generation had contributed to society by making the appliances – the fridges, air conditioners and cars – that people wanted. They felt strong loyalty to their companies, more than to the families they rarely saw. 'Our fathers didn't look so happy to us. They worked such long hours. They earned money, but families in those days led separate lives. Maybe we are asking ourselves, "What are we working for?" That's something we are trying to figure out.' He was into his theme by now. 'We call people in their late forties "the bubble generation". They think only about themselves and their family, but they don't think about social issues. They call us the "*yutori* generation, the anything-goes generation",' he said, using a word to suggest a less-conformist modern era in which youth had more leeway to express themselves.[2] 'They think we're into iPhones and video games and that's all. There is an inter-generational – I am not going to say conflict – but there's definitely a difference; an inter-generational gap.'

Of his new career, he said, 'I'm pretty sure we need entrepreneurs who can innovate. We should support small companies and entrepreneurs.' From his experience, many young people wanted to strike out on their own, or persuade corporate Japan to adopt new values. 'University students these days are asking the corporations they are hoping to join about their social values and CSR activities,' he said, casually throwing off the English abbreviation for corporate social responsibility. 'Even for me, it's incredible how they think about these issues. Social values is the big thing, even more than the environment. That means things like education, the family, equal rights for women, caring for the elderly.'

Ishikawa was not claiming that all young people had suddenly become idealistic, entrepreneurial and bent on refashioning Japan. 'Young people are divided into two. One group is more conscious and more passionate about going outside and doing something new. The other is getting poorer, and doing video games and internet all day.' He had two friends who he felt could be classified as *hikikomori*, people who shut themselves away. One, the daughter of a college professor, lived with him in a shared house. She had also spent a year abroad, but now she hardly ever ventured outside the house. She browsed the internet all day and took part in online forums such as 2channel, which attracted several million, sometimes incendiary or

**1.** One of Commodore Perry's Black Ships, as seen by a Japanese artist. The menacing boats became a symbol of the west's powerful technology and its imperialist intent.

**2.** Yukichi Fukuzawa (1835–1901), one of the greatest thinkers of the Meiji era. When he was born, Japan was isolated, hierarchical and feudal. By the time of his death, it was a modern state.

3. Citizens of Edo take their revenge on Onamazu, a giant catfish blamed for the city's devastating earthquakes.

4. The tsunami sweeps into the northeast coast of Japan. Scenes like this were repeated along a 250-mile stretch of coastline.

5. Ofunato after the tsunami. It was not unusual to see boats washed up many hundreds of feet from the shoreline.

6. Members of the Self Defence Forces were dispatched swiftly to the scene after the 2011 tsunami. After the 1995 Kobe earthquake, the government had been reluctant to deploy troops still associated with the war.

7. Hiromi Shimodate and Yasuko Kimura scour the ruined landscape of Ofunato a few days after the tsunami.

8. Happier times: Hiromi Shimodate and Yasuko Kimura re-establish Hy's café in Ofunato's temporary high street.

9. Seizaburo Sato, 82, works amid the wreckage of his home after the 2011 tsunami. He lost one eye in a previous work-related accident.

10. The author taking notes inside the wreckage of the
Capital Hotel, Rikuzentakata.

11. *Ippon matsu*: Rikuzentakata's solitary surviving pine has become
a symbol of hope, even though it is technically dead.

12. Tokyo after the massive fire bombing of 1945, the most destructive air raid in history. The scenes after the 2011 tsunami were eerily reminiscent.

13. Still from *Tokyo Story*, a 1953 film by the great director Yasujiro Ozu. As economic growth gathered momentum, the old ways were rapidly left behind.

14. Chewing gum and chocolates, Yokuska, 1959. America's military and cultural influence persisted long after the occupation ended in 1952.

**15.** Author Haruki Murakami: 'If there is a hard, high wall and
an egg . . . no matter how right the wall or how wrong the egg, I will
stand on the side of the egg.'

16. Cherry blossom against a castle wall in Kumamoto. For the Japanese, the fleetingness of the blossom is the essence of its beauty.

17. Tofu hotpot in Kyoto. Even the simplest dish is treated as art.

18. Foot *onsen* at a railway station in Kyushu. The Japanese never miss out on an opportunity to bathe.

19. Ginza. A visiting politician told the author,
'If this is a recession, I want one.'

20. Junichiro Koizumi campaigning in the dramatic 'post-office election' of 2005. He threatened to smash his own Liberal Democratic Party but ended up winning it its biggest post-war election victory.

21. Junichiro Koizumi visits Graceland with George W. Bush in 2006. Here, Priscilla Presley looks on.

**22.** A 21-year-old hostess shows her business card.

**23.** Natsuo Kirino: 'Men and women are not
on good terms in Japanese society.'

24. Yayoi Kusama with her phallus-filled installation 'Aggregation: 1000 Boats Show'. Japan left her so disenchanted with men and the male organ that much of her art was dedicated to 'obliterating' the offending appendage.

25. Noriaki Imai, several years after he returned from Iraq. To him, the public reaction in Japan was like being told 'you should have died in Iraq and come back a corpse.'

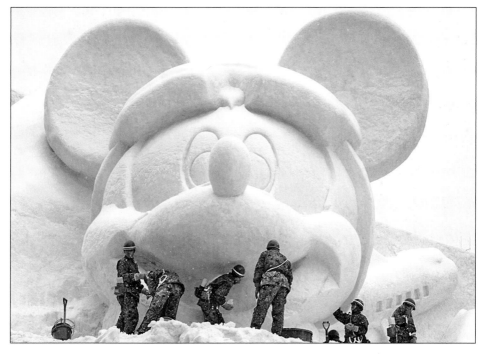

**26.** Members of Japan's Self Defence Forces work on an ice sculpture of Mickey Mouse at the Sapporo Ice Festival. Some seven decades after the war, Japan still has no official army.

**27.** Anti-Japan protestors take pictures of a burnt Japanese flag in Wuhan, Hubei province. Many in China were angered when Tokyo 'nationalized' the Senkaku islands, known as Diaoyu in China.

28. Testing for radiation after the Fukushima explosion.

29. Shinzo Abe waves from a tank belonging to the Ground Self Defence Forces in 2013. As prime minister he has not shied away from defending Japan's 'national interest'.

ultra-nationalistic, postings a day. Back in his home town of Kira too, one of his friends had never landed a proper job. Though he was in his late twenties, his room was decorated like a teenager's, with posters of pouting 'idols', heart-throb female singers or models. A nomad of cyberspace, he too rarely left the house. 'It's not a psychological problem,' Ishikawa said, after a long pause. 'He's just a bit scared.' He thought some more. 'He doesn't feel the need to work because he can live with his parents.' The *hikikomori* phenomenon was as much a product of affluence as poverty, he said. '*Hikikomori* people do come from both rich and poor families. But if you're really poor, you cannot lie around in bed all day.'

Affluence wasn't the same as economic momentum. Ishikawa recognized that the era of fast growth, with its sense of national rejuvenation, was over. 'I was born in 1983. I didn't get any benefit from the rapid growth of Japan. By the time I entered elementary school, the economy was going down. We don't believe the economy will grow so much in the next decades. It's not going to give us so many good things. I think that's something we all are feeling.'

Masahiro Yamada, a slightly dishevelled sociologist in his mid-fifties, had a different take still on the post-bubble generation. His was almost comically dark. I'd met the professor, a delightful man with a nervous giggle, several times over the course of a decade during which he had succeeded in becoming progressively gloomier. Known for coining the phrase 'parasite single' to describe twenty- and thirty-year-olds mooching off their parents, he recently wrote an essay with the fairly self-explanatory title 'The Young and the Hopeless'.[3]

I visited Yamada a few years ago in his cubbyhole of an office at Tokyo Gakugei University where he then lectured. Most Japanese academics are crammed into tiny spaces, smaller than some walk-in cupboards. Yamada's looked more cramped than most. Every available bit of shelf space and much of the floor were piled high with books and heaps of papers. On the way in I nearly tripped over a foot-massage machine buried somewhere in the debris. Yamada was a somewhat flustered host. Every now and again he would leap up to retrieve a document from the surrounding flotsam.

He sat opposite me on a moth-eaten couch and handed me a sheet of paper on which he had typed several phrases in Japanese. It was titled 'Winners and Losers in the New Economy'. Mostly he seemed interested in the losers. Top of the list was 'Sudden Increase of Suicides', a reference to a 35 per cent jump to nearly 33,000 in 1998, a year of big lay-offs. Suicides had remained above 30,000 ever since, about ninety a day, one of the highest rates in the world, although the rate did begin to fall again from 2010 and dropped below 30,000 in 2012. (One 'anti-suicide' measure the government had taken was to install large mirrors on some railway platforms. Apparently, the sight of oneself about to jump had a sobering effect.) Suicide was by no means the end of Yamada's list. It continued, 'Rapid Increase of Child Abuse ... Temporary Jobs ... Jobless Young People ... Wasted Labourers who Dream of Unrealistic Futures ... Twilight of Post-war Family'. In vain, I scanned the page for something more uplifting.

Yamada's view of contemporary Japan chimed quite closely with the version Shimotsubo had explained. The labour market had broken down, excluding more and more people from decent jobs by forcing them to take temporary work paying as little as $10 an hour. Yamada called those people 'liquid' labourers, sluiced from one part of the job pool to the next. Their existence in such large numbers was proof, he said, that the old system had stopped functioning. In its place had been created a sort of economic apartheid in which the winners were protected by the rules of the old system and the losers pushed out into an ultra-precarious new world. In his view, Murakami's part-timers and drifters were victims, not pioneers. The villain of the piece was the mass hiring of graduates, the *shushoku katsudo*, a fixture of the labour market for decades. It ought to be scrapped immediately, he said, though there were too many vested interests for that to happen. 'The time has come to do away with a system that apportions total stability to a shrinking elite of full-time employees while granting none to anyone else.'[4]

The old system worked in a fast-growth era when labour was scarce and companies put a premium on loyal employees, he said. But no one believed those days would ever return. He sprang up to fetch a survey. Taken among 25- to 35-year-olds, it showed that only 4 per cent expected the economy to improve over their lifetime. An overwhelming 61 per cent thought it would only get worse. Furuichi regarded low expectations as a sort of release from the treadmill of endless self-improvement, but Yamada had come to the opposite conclusion. Far from becoming independent risk-takers seeking their own path, he said, young people were 'conservatives' and 'fantasists'. The conservatives craved yesterday's certainties precisely because they were ever-harder to attain. Fantasists sought solace in make-believe, endlessly postponing decisions – on marriage, childbirth, career – in the Micawberesque belief that something splendid would turn up. It wasn't clear whether the conservatives or the fantasists upset Yamada more. He salvaged another survey from the surrounding piles, this one of newly hired workers. The question was whether they wanted to 'keep working for this company until retirement'.[5] In 2010, the percentage agreeing with that statement had risen to 57 per cent from just 20 per cent in 2000. 'Because opportunities for stability have been reduced, that's what they long for,' he said glumly.

The same attitude was reflected in surveys of young women. Far from seeking independence and career fulfilment, more than ever they wanted to become housewives, he said. (I once saw a flier for a hostess club called 'Badd Girls' in which one of the young women listed her favourite hobby as 'doing the washing up'.) More women in their twenties and thirties agreed with the statement 'the man works, the woman takes care of the house' than in any other age group, Yamada added. That was because most full-time jobs in Japan were not designed for women in the first place, especially if they wanted children, he said. Japanese employers demanded long hours of drudgery and too much overtime. Shimotsubo had said of her husband's job, 'I can't work like him. I am a mother, so I can't follow the company rules. That's the experience of women in Japan.' Unable to find security by following a male-oriented career path, Yamada said, women sought the next best thing – they married stability. But because the pool of eligible men with secure jobs was shrinking, more and more women were postponing marriage.

That was where conservatism blended into fantasy, he argued. The majority of unmarried Japanese between the ages of eighteen and thirty-five lived with their parents. Many had unrealistic dreams of becoming rock stars or fashion photographers or, if they were women, of marrying a wealthy man. The 'parasite singles' saved on rent and spent all their wages on maintaining a luxurious, but ultimately unsustainable, lifestyle. Much of their life was make-believe. Young men shied away from the attention of real women. Instead, they watched movies produced by Japan's vast pornography industry or went to 'maid cafés' where they were treated with old-fashioned deference by the sort of demure, pretty woman they could never hope to meet in real life. Women waited around for Mr Right, putting off marriage and childbirth. 'Not only are they living in a dreamland but they're not waking up.' Yamada despaired. 'They've given up. There's no idea about changing society, or changing their own life.' Perhaps, I ventured, they didn't want to change society because actually their lives weren't all that bad. Maybe they were contented as Furuichi said. 'Those who live outside the established system have no way of getting in,' Yamada said a little contemptuously. 'That's why they remain' – here he curled his lip mockingly – 'so-called happy and free.'

The words sliding along the bottom of the television screen left little room for ambiguity. Unless something was done, the 'children of Japan' would be burned alive. There were three of them. Nahoko Takato, a 34-year-old female aid worker, who had gone to Baghdad to distribute bread and jam and other staples to Iraqi street children. Then there was Soichiro Koriyama, thirty-two, a freelance photojournalist who had ventured to Iraq to cover a war in which Japan's Self Defence Forces, its version of an army, had been cast as a bit-player. But the person whose grainy image stood out for me was Noriaki Imai, a wan, handsome youth of eighteen years, cowering on the ground. All three were blindfolded. Behind them stood jumpy Iraqi militiamen, brandishing knives and Kalashnikovs.

It was 2004, the year Tokyo had sent its Self Defence Forces on a reconstruction mission to Iraq in Japan's biggest deployment of ground troops since the Second World War. The dispatch was considered unconstitutional by many. Public opinion was divided and volatile. The three 'children of Japan' had wound up in Iraq for humanitarian reasons, there to document, or to help alleviate, the suffering in a war that troubled them. Imai, a recent high-school graduate, had sneaked across the border from Jordan in a rented taxi. His objective was to study the effects of depleted uranium on civilians. It wasn't a well-thought-out plan. Within hours of his arrival, when his car stopped for petrol just outside the city of Fallujah, he was bundled into another vehicle by a group of militants shouting 'Kill the Japanese'. One held a hand-grenade to his head.

The events of 9/11 and the subsequent US invasion of Afghanistan and Iraq had transformed Imai from an out-of-touch video gamer living on Japan's northern island of Hokkaido into a young man vexed by some of the world's most pressing issues. 'When the bombing of Afghanistan started I felt very empty and useless,' he said of the US-led invasion of that country in 2001.[6] Imai had wandered the internet in search of answers to half-formed questions. He browsed topics such as the Rwandan genocide, and the possible connection between conflict in the Democratic Republic of the Congo and the scramble for coltan metal, a blackish ore used in Japan's then world-beating mobile phones. He felt that his generation was not interested in these moral and political questions, much less so when they involved people in far-away places. Somehow, it seemed like his duty to learn more. He knew it sounded pretentious, but he wanted to catalyse and energize his generation. That is how his cyber-odyssey led him to a real-world petrol station outside Fallujah.

For several days, Japan had been transfixed by the fate of the hostages. Parents of the three had been on television, both in Japan and in the Arab-speaking world, to plead for their children's lives. The young people had gone to Iraq to help the country, they said. None had supported the deployment of Japanese troops. To the fury of the Japanese government, the parents even reiterated the militants' call for Tokyo to withdraw its ground forces. For several excruciating days, the fate of the hostages hung in the balance. Only a few weeks later, Kim Sun-il, a 33-year-old South Korean missionary, was beheaded by his Iraqi capturers. The Japanese were more fortunate. After eight days, Imai and his two fellow hostages were passed into the hands of a cleric amid rumours that Tokyo had paid a ransom to secure their release. After debriefing and a medical check-up, they were flown back to Japan. It was then that the trouble really started.

Public opinion, or at least that reflected by the media, had turned quickly. After at first rallying in sympathy, Japan's powerful newspapers and television channels – which tended to ply the same party line – rounded on the three hostages, blaming them for ignoring foreign office warnings to avoid Iraq and for dragging Japan into a humiliating episode. The phrase *jiko sekinin*, meaning 'self-responsibility', became the stuff of the vacuous breakfast television shows, slapstick 'current affairs programmes' where men dressed in pork-pie hats and young starlets called *tarentos* ('talents') pondered the issues of the day with scant concession to substance or knowledge. From the media ether, the term bubbled into common parlance, muttered over sushi counters and through the smoke and background jazz of bars. The media started demanding that the three repay the government the cost of their flight home and post-kidnap medical check-up. Did the taxpayer really have to foot the bill for these hapless do-gooders? By the time Imai and his two fellow countrymen stepped onto Japanese soil, the mood was downright hostile. The former hostages emerged from the plane, heads bowed in shame. They shuffled past placards printed with angry slogans, one of which read simply, 'You got what you deserved.'

The reaction was difficult to fathom. Colin Powell, the US secretary of state, gave what seemed like the more rational response. 'I'm pleased that these Japanese citizens were willing to put themselves at risk for a greater good, for a better purpose,' he said. 'And the Japanese people should be very proud that they have citizens willing to do that.'[7] That was not how many Japanese saw it. When I caught up with him a few weeks later, Imai was still in shock at the reaction. 'It was a huge surprise. People were saying I needed to take responsibility for my own actions. But it sounded to me as if they were saying they wished I'd died. To my mind the meaning was, "You should have died in Iraq and come back a corpse."' He was inundated with hate mail. 'When I was just walking in the street in Sapporo, sometimes people would say, "Why did you waste so much taxpayers' money?" Twice someone punched me. That's why I became psychologically sick. I didn't talk so much. I wasn't friendly. It became a serious problem, like a phobia.'

Yoichi Funabashi, my friend at the left-leaning *Asahi* newspaper, said the government had manipulated the discussion through a pliant media. The three young Japanese, by offering humanitarian assistance outside the framework of Japan's official, military-led effort, had intruded onto the government's moral high ground, he said. In their small and shambling way, they had offered an alternative to the officially sanctioned policy of helping Iraq through the work of the Self Defence Forces. The Japanese mission was presented as a reconstruction effort, bringing water and electricity to ordinary Iraqi people. If there was good to be done, the government could handle it. A close adviser to Junichiro Koizumi, the prime minister who had promised George W. Bush he would get Japanese boots on Iraqi ground, confirmed Funabashi's suspicions. 'The families of the hostages self-destructed by appealing for the withdrawal of the Self Defence Forces,' he told me, adding that he suspected they were Communists. He applauded the public reaction. 'Such stern criticism reflects the growing maturity of Japanese public opinion.'

In their naivety, the three had stumbled into the hottest foreign policy issue of the day. But there was a broader symbolism to these youngsters' search for meaning in life and the sharp reproach they received at the hands of their elders. Years of less-than-stirring growth over the past two decades had put paid to the certainties of pre-bubble Japan. According to the academic Yoshio Sugimoto, as many as two in five young workers were now in non-regular employment, with many part of what had come to be known as the 'working poor'.[8] Non-regular workers were less likely to receive training, making it all the harder for them to break back into steady employment.

The upending of the old model forced a whole generation – or at least those shut outside what remained of the old employment system – to seek an alternative. Many, like Ishikawa, looked for something more fulfilling than the 'empty affluence' of their parents' middle-class dream. Fetching up in Iraq, as Imai had done, was a pretty drastic alternative, to be sure. Most youngsters stopped well short of that. But, in their own way, many were testing the boundaries of how to live. Some simply worked part-time, bouncing from job to job, or worked for employment agencies that dispatched them – like so many returnable packages – to the big companies that had refused to take them on as full-timers. That gave them a certain independence and time to pursue a better work–life balance. It freed them from the onerous demands of the typical large Japanese corporation. But in the bargain, they lost both long-term career prospects and a decent salary. Some even lost their identity since that had become so tightly bound up with being a member of a corporate family. Yet, outside the system, there was a life for some. Some set up businesses, though that was perhaps less common than in the west. Some worked for non-profit organizations, the numbers of which had mushroomed since the Kobe earthquake of 1995 where so many volunteers made their mark. Still others embraced 'slow living'. They established cooperatives or organic farms or just took it easy, dropping out like modern-day hippies. In 2003 one cigarette company caught onto this new lifestyle with the slogan 'Slow Down, Relax Up'.[9] Some local authorities tapped into the trend, declaring themselves oases of *gambaranai*, adherents of the almost un-Japanese philosophy of 'don't try too hard', or 'don't stress yourself'. Many youngsters certainly weren't trying quite as hard as their parents. They saved on rent by living at home, spending all their money on fashion, dining, foreign travel or the pursuit of hobbies. They were enjoying Japan's affluence – while it still lasted.

Then there were people like Noriaki Imai. I hadn't seen him for eight years. I wondered what had happened to him since his ordeal in Iraq and his painful homecoming. Quite coincidentally, I discovered that, now twenty-six, he had become one of the social entrepreneurs backed by ETIC, Ishikawa's organization. He was running a non-profit group to help disadvantaged children in Japan's second city of Osaka. I arranged to meet him in the spring of 2012, a few days after the first anniversary of the tsunami. I took an early-morning bullet train from Tokyo. Salarymen were drinking beer with their breakfast, going over papers or just sleeping as we sped past the industrial corridor that links Japan's two biggest conurbations.

Osaka had a completely different feel from Tokyo. It was grittier, more industrial, more casual. Young people dressed a little punkier than in the capital. People even stood on the opposite side of the escalator. Maybe it was the Manchester of Japan. Osaka had become the focus of some attention of late because it had elected a young mayor, Toru Hashimoto, who was making waves nationally. A brash politician and son of a yakuza gangster, Hashimoto – in the style of Junichiro Koizumi – had ridden the anti-political wave to become one of the country's most talked-about politicians. Recently, he had opposed the restarting of a nuclear plant in a nearby town, claiming that the government was ignoring safety. He had won notoriety for many other things: enforcing the early closing of nightclubs, insisting the national anthem was sung in schools and cutting budgets by firing bureaucrats. In one speech, later to haunt him, he had said Japan needed leadership 'strong enough to be called a dictatorship' to get out of its current funk.[10] His popularity even survived revelations in a weekly magazine that he had had an affair with a woman whom he got to dress up as a flight attendant during sex.[11] Some people thought he was dangerous, others were energized by what they saw as his vigour. Hashimoto was a one-man Tea Party. His arrival on the scene was another sign of youthful impatience with the status quo.

I met Imai at an *izakaya*, a Japanese pub where often high-quality food is served with sake, *shochu* spirit, beer and wine. The lighting was moody with artful use of spotlights. Jazz was playing over the speakers and, through the wooden partitions that separated the private rooms, there flowed the sound of youthful chatter lubricated by alcohol. We pressed the buzzer on our table and ordered crab, some sashimi, grilled mushrooms, a little abalone hot pot and a couple of ice-cold draught beers. As we waited for the food, Imai told me that he had been depressed for years after his return from Iraq. He felt as though his mission to speak up for Iraqi children had ended in fiasco. The hostile reaction in Japan was worse than the kidnapping ordeal itself, he said. 'I was only kidnapped for nine days. But during those years in Japan, sometimes I felt like I wanted to die.' He left his home town of Sapporo to study at the other end of the country, at an international university in the southern city of Oita. He kept mainly to himself. 'Even four or five years after [Iraq] some people recognized my face,' he said. 'Not so much now. I'm nearly free.' He fell silent for a bit. 'Actually I don't care,' he went on. 'This is a stressed-out society. Many people simply wanted to let off steam.'

Looking back he had no regrets. 'I became psychologically very strong and because of that I do my non-profit work.' By his fourth year of university he felt better. He travelled to Zambia with a friend who was helping to build a school. He was struck by the optimism. 'Compared to Japan I felt they had so much hope for their country. A fifth of the population is infected with HIV and the average life expectancy is just forty-six. But I sensed hope in their eyes. I came back to Japan and got on the train and everyone looked so gloomy.

Here, younger people are under a lot of pressure. I felt I should do something for young kids.'

Like Ishikawa, he had arrived via a detour, in his case selling pork and beef for a small trading company. 'Buy cheap, sell expensive,' he smirked. He quit in 2012 to devote himself full-time to mentoring troubled children. At one underprivileged high school he met a boy who had lived with three different fathers and whose mother had a multiple-personality disorder. The family was on income support and the boy sometimes worked at night to earn extra money. Imai was shocked things could be so bad for people in a country he still thought of as affluent. 'These kids don't have any self-confidence. They don't feel as though they have a future.' Secretly he wondered if they might not be right. 'The population is shrinking. Poverty among young people is rising. For people with a good education, it's invisible. But it's a big problem. Living has become too hard.'

I explained Furuichi's theory that what youngsters had lost in security they had gained in freedom. At least one survey seemed to show they had never been happier, I said. 'The future will get worse, so now is the happiest moment,' Imai replied after giving it some thought, pleased at his own logic. 'Some young people do feel like that. But it's kind of fake. Feeling happy is just for now. The future is dark.' He too worried that Japan might be living on borrowed time, slumbering on the financial cushion built up during the economic boom. How could an economy survive with so much debt, he asked? One day it had to explode, surely. 'I don't know when this bankruptcy will happen. Maybe we'll be OK for three years or five years. But ten years? I don't know.'

Imai doubted the younger generation's ability to bring about positive change. He had a sneaking regard for Hashimoto's strong convictions, though he didn't find the actual content of his ideas appealing. (Hashimoto's popularity later imploded after he made light of the use of sex slaves by Japan's army during the war.) Apathy was the default position, Imai said. 'So many of them are on Facebook or Twitter. They seem to care about the Japanese future, but do they really act for Japanese policy, to change the national situation? I cannot really see it.'

About the time we met, the anti-nuclear movement had gathered some momentum. Big crowds, including some young people, had taken to congregating outside the prime minister's office to demand an end to nuclear power. Imai doubted it would go far. 'Just a few people are moving, acting. But I don't think it's having much impact,' he said. 'I want to become effective at changing Japanese policies. That's why I am doing my non-profit work. In a few years, I would like to make suggestions to the national government.' He paused, as if digesting the implications of all he had said, looking for a way to sum it up. 'I don't know what they should call my generation,' he said finally. 'Maybe the tough generation. Certainly not the happy generation.'

# 11

# From Behind the Screen

Natsuo Kirino does not like to be called a crime writer. There is plenty of crime in her novels, but few sleuths and almost no trail of whodunit. Instead, there is sociological and psychological mining as she drills into Japan's more rancid layers in the years after the collapse of the economic bubble. There she discovers seams of poverty, violence, rage and depravity in a society that mostly sees itself as refined and orderly. Above all, she writes about how women get by in a country where they are too often treated as second-class citizens both in the home and at work. Sometimes the survival mechanisms her fictional heroines adopt are extreme.

In *Out*, a book about working-class women toiling the nightshift in a grimy boxed-lunch factory, Yayoi strangles her useless and violent husband to death. Driven to desperation she enlists three female co-workers to help her cut up, and then dispose of, the corpse. In a macabre plot development, the women soon branch out into business, helping local *yakuza* gangsters to spirit away evidence of their gangland slayings. The scene in which the women chop up Yayoi's husband reads as much like a how-to manual as a dispassionate description. Kirino spares little detail:

> Next she used her knife to cut around the hip joints. Watching the blade slip through the layers of yellow fat, she heard Yoshie mutter that it looked 'exactly like a broiler'. When she reached bone, she braced her foot on top of Kenji's leg and began sawing the femur in just the same way as one would cut through a log.

In a later novel, *Tokyo Island*, Kiyoko, a 43-year-old housewife, is washed up on an island with her husband when their cruise ship sinks.

Kiyoko adapts to hardship more easily than her hapless husband, who soon perishes. Her resourcefulness becomes more necessary when she discovers that she is the lone female on the island along with more than two dozen Japanese and Chinese men around half her age. She skilfully plays one man against another to ensure her survival and even attempts to start a religion with herself at its centre. The book was inspired by the true story of Kazuko Higa, who found herself stranded on Anatahan island in the Marianas group with nearly thirty men at the end of the Second World War. The men refused to believe the war was over and continued to live a primitive existence. Higa escaped from the island in 1950. Kirino's novel, which was later turned into a film, won critical acclaim for its exploration of group dynamics and a plot in which an ordinary woman was transformed into a sort of island goddess. 'She controls the group through sex,' Kirino told me matter-of-factly. 'So much happens, but although the leaders constantly change, in the end she survives.'

Kirino was born in 1951 in Kanazawa, the castle town where I had lived briefly in my first month in Japan. Her father was an architect and her family moved around before settling down in Tokyo when she was fourteen. She studied law and later started to write pulp romantic fiction for a mainly adolescent audience. It was not until she was forty that she won critical acclaim for one of her novels, *Rain Falling on My Face*, and started writing more serious fiction about things she considered important. Her biggest breakthrough came with *Out*, the first of her novels to be translated into English.

I met Kirino one May afternoon in 2008 in the plush surroundings of the Fiorentina, an Italian café in the lobby of Tokyo's Grand Hyatt Hotel, where large-scale works of modern art vied for attention with the beautiful people milling about. Burned once before by a foreign journalist, Kirino had brought along a female chaperone for protection, though the author of more than fifteen novels looked more than capable of looking after herself. Her face had a toughness about it. At fifty-six, she was an attractive, even beautiful, woman, though hers was not the pristine mask worn by some age-defying Japanese women. She was dressed casually in a flowery top, slacks and cork-soled shoes. Her nails were thickly painted with sparkly polish. Her voice was powerful and husky, yet of strangely low decibel.

She talked about a 'sense of pent-up retribution' driving her protagonists. 'Men and women are not on good terms in Japanese society.
They don't get along,' she said, toying with her coffee cup. 'There is
too much gender-specific role division. Men are almost like slaves in
the corporate world and Japanese women are contained within the
household. Their lives are disconnected. That is one of the sources of
this boiling rage.' Writing fiction, she explained, allowed her to
explore this deep well of anger, often unexpressed in a society that
prized smooth surface relations. 'Writers try to cluster into words the
things that lie buried in society, unconscious things. That is our duty.'

She was mindful that fiction could affect the world outside its
pages. 'Writers have to be powerful. But I also live in the real world,
and sometimes I find the power of fiction frightening. After my book
*Out* appeared – and this is scary to talk about – but I think there have
been more cases of wives killing their husbands. And there may be
people who found new ways of doing things because of what's written in my book.' Not long before we met, a case had come to court in
which Kaori Mihashi, a fashionable 32-year-old, had killed her abu-
sive husband, a Morgan Stanley employee, with a wine bottle. Like
Yayoi in Kirino's novel, she had cut him into pieces and distributed
the sections among different locations. The luxury apartment where
the murder took place was two minutes from my house.

If Kirino worried that she might have unwittingly inspired violence,
as well as depicting it, she also thought she had performed a service
by giving voice to women's rage. 'After *Out*, male readers can expect
anything from me. I think I have educated them,' she said, looking
coyly at the table. 'I was on a radio programme with a male personality
once, and during the show he wouldn't utter a single word to me.
Towards the end, he asked: "What do you think of murdering somebody?" So I said: "It's not a good thing to kill a person." And he said:
"Oh, that's good. I'm really relieved to hear that."'

Japan is often portrayed in the west as a society of powerful men and
timid, subservient women. It generally scores poorly in international
comparisons that seek to quantify equality of opportunity. According
to a 2010 global study on women's economic opportunity by the
Economist Intelligence Unit, Japan came 32nd in the world with a

score of 68.2 out of a possible 100. It was above all other Asian nations, apart from Hong Kong, but below Scandinavian countries, which scored in the high 80s, as well as the United States, at 76.7. Japan scored reasonably well in the legal and social status categories. Women's rights are, after all, protected in the post-war constitution. Article 14 outlaws discrimination based on sex and Article 24 states:

> Marriage shall be based only on the mutual consent of both sexes and it shall be maintained through mutual cooperation with the equal rights of husband and wife as a basis. With regard to choice of spouse, property rights, inheritance, choice of domicile, divorce and other matters pertaining to marriage and the family, laws shall be enacted from the standpoint of individual dignity and the essential equality of the sexes.[1]

In other categories, Japan did less well. On labour policy practice, which measured pay equality, workplace discrimination and childcare provision, it came below several developing countries, including the Philippines, Brazil and Tanzania. Even South Korea, another advanced Asian economy said to discriminate against women, did better on that measure. By contrast, Japan scored well in the 'access to finance' category, reflecting the fact that women still tend to control household income.[2] Different surveys throw up different results. In the United Nations Gender Inequality Index,[3] Japan does well, coming fourteenth in the world, below Scandinavian countries but above Britain, the United States, Canada and Australia. On the other hand, in the World Economic Forum's Global Gender Gap Index, Japan performs abysmally, ranking 98th. There it comes below such well-known bastions of feminism as Azerbaijan, Zimbabwe, Bangladesh and Brunei.

Clearly there is a good deal of subjectivity to such surveys.[4] But there are obvious ways in which Japanese women face discrimination. In business, female managers are rarer than in other rich countries, making up a lowly 1.2 per cent of senior executives in listed companies. Women don't get such good jobs as men, and earn, on average, about 60 per cent as much as they do. By law, married women are not allowed to keep their maiden name – unless, curiously, they are married to foreigners, who presumably rank even lower in the pecking order. Only about 10 per cent of Japanese legislators are women, putting Japan in 121st place out of 186 nations, and prompting a government committee to recommend mandatory quotas for female MPs.[5] Unlike Britain, Germany or India – and now South Korea, following the election of Park Geun-hye in 2012 – Japan has never had a female leader. Nor, of course, has the US. But in Japan, there are fewer role models to emulate.

Obstacles to women having what many of their western counterparts might consider a rounded life – juggling motherhood with a career – are very real. Though the traditional employment system is eroding, women hired by big companies still tend to be placed on career tracks that go precisely nowhere. It is not unusual to see women with college degrees reduced to fragrant presences in the office, bearers of green tea and objects of gossip about which colleague they will end up marrying. If women marry and have children, few take up their old job at the same company. Many firms are reluctant to let women return, particularly after a lengthy maternity break. Sometimes women themselves elect not to go back to work, although such choices are reinforced by strong social expectations about what it means to be a good wife and mother, even what it means to be happy. (In Japanese 'to become happy', *shiawase ni naru*, can be used as a synonym for 'to get married'.) The job of bringing up children is, perhaps, more respected in Japan than in some other countries, where women who don't manage to have a job as well as bring up a family are sometimes looked down upon. When my wife took our young son to Japanese kindergarten, she was touched by the fact that children were taught to thank their mothers for making their bento-box lunches, something she thought might not happen in the west. (The expectation was firmly that the mother, not the father, would have made the lunch.) Still, there are undoubtedly women in Japan who would like to work but who cannot because of a chronic lack of affordable childcare, especially for very young children.

Discrimination, like pornography, can be hard to define. But you know it when you see it. Take the example of the Japanese women's soccer team, which made history by defeating the US to win the FIFA Women's World Cup in the summer of 2011. Coming so soon after the devastating tsunami, the victory prompted national euphoria. Members of the team, nicknamed the Nadeshiko – after a pink flower, and the idealized beauty and strength of Japanese womanhood – became national celebrities. But when the victorious Nadeshiko team members set off for the 2012 London Olympics, they flew economy class. The less successful men's team was seated in business.

Japan's most neglected resource is its women. In a country with no oil, gas or precious minerals, national prosperity is almost entirely predicated on the diligence and ingenuity of its people. But social conventions have suppressed the potential of half Japan's population. Japanese women, less restrained by social convention than corporate-bound men, often strike foreigners as the more dynamic, inventive and sometimes plainly more competent half of the population. That their talents are so often sidelined strikes many as a terrible waste of national, not to mention individual, potential.

We should be wary, though, of looking only at the surface. Relations between the sexes in Japan are more nuanced than the caricature might suggest. And, as with many other areas of contemporary society, the position of women is in flux. The end of fast growth and the consequent strains at work and at home have had a profound impact on male–female relations. Richard Koo, the economist, said one of the attractions of the fast-growth period was that people didn't have to think too much. It made for smooth, if not exactly modern, relations between the sexes. 'Men concentrated on getting the job done. Someone would arrange a nice girl for them to get married to. The girl knows the guy will have job security, a steady wage increase, a nice house. So why not?' The loss of that certainty had spawned angst. 'Those guys have no idea how to date a girl or find a wife. These days the matchmakers are scared because you never know what is going to happen to this guy next, what with corporate restructuring, downsizing, outsourcing. There are a lot of men out there who never trained themselves to attract members of the opposite sex.' Women, he said, were generally not interested in men who could not provide – one reason they were marrying later. The relative shift in power had even spawned a new take on manliness and femininity. The Japanese, forever inventing new categories to describe shifting social patterns, now talked about 'grass-eating' men who were not interested in sex, and 'meat-eating' women who knew what they wanted and how to get it. *Tokyo Island*, it seemed, was not entirely fiction.

*

Noriko Hama, professor of economics at Kyoto's Doshisha University, did not fit the stereotype of a demure Japanese woman. She had forthright opinions about almost everything, often delivered with withering sarcasm in the upper-class English accent she had acquired when she lived in Britain as a child. She had a penchant for shockingly loud hair dye, often purple, and dressed in what I took to be designer clothes, thrown together in a manner that suggested they had been picked randomly from her wardrobe. We had known each other for years. Hama had never bought the argument that Japanese women played second fiddle to men. In important respects, she argued, they had been running Japan for centuries. It was a woman, the lady-in-waiting Murasaki Shikibu, who wrote Japan's – and indeed the world's – first novel, *The Tale of Genji*, in the early years of the eleventh century. Women had long been the powers behind its public figures and the bosses of its households, she said. 'Women have always had control of the purse strings and had responsibility for running everything smoothly. Japanese men have been incredibly reliant on the female of the species, not knowing where anything is, not knowing how to dress. Without women they would have to go around naked,' she told me, shooting me a look of contempt mixed with sorrow. 'There has always been a depth to Japanese women behind the silk screen. There was never that much of an idea of being the protected, pampered species put on a pedestal in the sort of "ladies are gods" culture that predominated in medieval Europe or in Victorian times. Women were deemed to be the tougher sex, tirelessly working, physically as well as mentally, taking on anything that was remotely awkward or a strain on the male intelligence.' Another look of contempt followed. I was reminded of something a well-known former geisha once told me when she described what she called the 'lady-first' culture of the west as sexist.[6]

Women were the driving force behind Japan's early industrialization after the Meiji Restoration. In the first decades of the twentieth century, 60 per cent of the industrial workforce and 80 per cent of those working in the all-important textile industry were women. They were, in the words of one historian, 'the backbone of Japan's Industrial Revolution'.[7] Today, shifting social attitudes, new economic impulses and the introduction of laws – for example equal-opportunity legislation in 1986 – were altering the landscape, Hama said. 'What's changed is that society has become more receptive towards women. That behind-the-silk-screen role was a very comfortable place to be. Women did not have to come out into the open to compete. Now that this on-stage performance has become open to women, they have started to feel that choosing to remain behind closed doors is detrimental to them. They have begun to think they need to communicate what they want and what they are thinking, and to make their positions verbally clear.' That required adjustment from both sexes. 'The virtue and talent of Japanese women used to be seen as their ability to have everything go their own way without saying a word. But that is not enough any more. They have to start making noise.'

Hama said many women would agree with Kirino that men and women moved on separate tracks. They even sometimes travelled separately since the metro had introduced women-only carriages to address the worries at the prevalence of *chikan*, or groping, in intensely crowded rush-hour trains. 'But I tend to feel that's a myth. It makes each side kind of comfortable. If you are on different tracks, your paths don't cross and it tidies the picture up. But in reality, things are not that simple. To the extent that we keep talking about things in that way, there's not a lot of room for change and progress. I don't want to pigeonhole Japanese society in that way. It is not even very challenging for men. They'll just say, "Oh yes. We're the villains of the piece. How terrible." But it doesn't actually challenge them to come up with their own ideas about how things are, or where they should go. It lets them off the hook.'

Japanese women are rebelling in powerful ways. Perhaps their most subversive act is to marry later. That has directly contributed to the low birth rate that is said by some to imperil the nation's future. Women are effectively on strike, although their participation in the labour force has edged up as a consequence of delayed marriage. But they are refusing to comply with either of the traditional roles expected of them, those of wife and mother. Until fairly recently, women who were still single at twenty-five were referred to disparagingly as 'Christmas cake', an item that plummets in value after 25 December. Now, some argued, women had turned the tables on men, holding out for partners who were financially stable, emotionally supportive and willing to help around the house. Machiko Osawa, an author and academic, said men's position had weakened relative to that of women. 'It used to be so wonderful for men in Japan. Now they're disillusioned,' she told me over lunch across the road from the grand red-brick building of Tokyo's central station. Whereas women used to fawn over the most unattractive of men with a decent job, she said, now they are much more choosy. The growing ranks of men with part-time work found it almost impossible to find a partner. 'Rather than feeling they need to do something to attract a woman, some men have just given up,' she said.

In 2008, a 25-year-old man ploughed a two-tonne truck into a crowd in Akihabara Electric Town, a gadget-crammed district of Tokyo that is a magnet to socially awkward nerds known as *otaku*. He then leapt from the vehicle and went on a stabbing spree. In all, seven people were killed and several injured. Osawa said the incident was symbolic of a growing feeling of male impotence. Before the attack, the young man had posted messages on the internet from his mobile phone, complaining he was too ugly to get a girlfriend. 'It used to be that women could not make a living without a man. Now that's changed and men have to be attractive to get a woman,' she said. For many younger Japanese, the shift in power relations meant better, more equal, relationships, she went on. Many married couples over fifty had a less-than-ideal setup. 'The husband played at making money, the wife at being a mother. It's very different from forming a real partnership.'

Yayoi Kusama, an artist who has become famous for her polka-dot-covered canvases, was also disparaging of traditional marriage. Speaking of her father's persistent affairs with geisha when she was a child growing up after the war, she wrote in her autobiography, 'The menfolk were practitioners of unconditional free sex, while the women had to sit in the shadows and bear it. Even as a child I was angered and repelled by the injustice.'[8] Kusama felt so constrained by Japanese society of the 1960s that she fled to New York. At one point in her career, she took to covering furniture in hundreds of phalluses that she had sewn herself, an act that was intended, she said, to 'obliterate' her dislike of the male organ. One photograph shows her posing naked, her back to the camera, in front of a rowing boat encrusted in penises. She called it: 'Aggregation: 1000 Boats Show'.

Old attitudes are far from extinguished. In 2003, members of Waseda University's 'Super Free' club organized gang rapes of female students after inviting them to rave parties and getting them drunk. In parliament, one MP raised a snicker when he said, 'At least gang rapists are still virile.'[9] The case did, though, provoke a strong public outcry and questioning of a legal system where rape carried a minimum sentence of two years and robbery five. Shinichiro Wada, the president of the club and the ringleader, was sentenced to fourteen years, close to the fifteen-year maximum.[10] Still, politicians sometimes found it hard to hide their Neanderthal attitudes. Hakuo Yanagisawa, the septuagenarian former health minister, referred to women between fifteen and fifty as 'baby-making machines' – and defective ones at that. Under duress, he later apologized for his remark, clarifying that what he'd meant to say was 'women whose role it is to give birth'.[11]

Changed economic and social circumstances mean many more women don't have to 'sit in the shadows and bear it' any more. As a result of becoming more selective, the percentage who remain single into their thirties has almost doubled since the 1980s. Many of the 'parasite singles' identified by Masahiro Yamada are women in their twenties, thirties or forties, living with their parents and spending their salaries on luxury goods, eating out or travelling abroad. Yamada dismissed them as 'fantasists', holding out for an elusive Prince Charming. In fact, only 4 per cent of women over forty-five remain unmarried, about half the rate of the US. One could just as easily interpret women's behaviour as a refusal to bend to social pressure by settling for marriage at any cost.

Another way in which women are asserting their independence is by divorcing. Divorces have nearly doubled since the 1990s, with about one in four marriages now ending in separation.[12] That is getting on for the same as Europe, though it is still about half the rate of the United States.[13] Research shows that Japanese women tend to initiate divorce and, unlike men, do not rush to remarry. In 2003, legislation was passed enabling women to collect back instalments of unpaid alimony. Since 2007, women who filed for divorce have been eligible for up to half of their husband's pension.[14] In 2001, the Domestic Violence Prevention Law was passed, signalling that violence within the home would no longer be treated as a family affair.

A law on the prevention of spousal violence allowed district courts to issue six-month restraining orders against the perpetrators and to evict them from the home for short periods.

The divorce rate of 45–64-year-olds rose fifteen-fold between 1960 and 2005. Since 1985, divorce among couples married more than thirty years has quadrupled. That suggests women, trapped in bad marriages by legal and social norms, are finding ways to escape. Many of the divorces take place after the husband retires and the wife discovers she can no longer stand living under the same roof with her previously absent husband. In a phrase suggesting that women are not the quietly suffering shrinking violets sometimes depicted, retired husbands are sometimes referred to as *sodai gomi*, 'big garbage', after the clapped-out appliances thrown out for collection, though the phrase can be used affectionately.

Young people, of course, get divorced too. The 'Narita divorce', named after the international airport, describes the phenomenon of post-honeymoon separations. These are said to occur when internationally minded, confident women discover that their monolingual, narrow-minded husbands can't function outside Japan. More and more women are marrying foreign men. Pico Iyer, a British-born essayist who married a Japanese woman, once told me, 'Women have everything to be gained by escaping Japan. Men are wedded in all senses to the status quo.'[15]

The fraying of the family structure might reflect growing female assertiveness, but it comes with problems. Contrary to common perceptions of a nanny state that looks after its coddled citizens from cradle to grave, Japan actually has a relatively underdeveloped social welfare system. Traditionally, care has been outsourced to families. Because of social and economic changes, those families are no longer always in a position to provide. Divorce has pushed more women into low-paid work, adding to the numbers of working poor and struggling one-parent families. According to Unesco, Japan's child poverty rate climbed to 14.9 per cent in 2012, lower than the US, but the ninth worst among thirty-five advanced OECD countries. Divorced women make up a disproportionate slice of the 20 million-strong 'precariat' – the 'precarious proletariat' without full-time employment.[16] Half of working women are stuck in part-time, low-paid jobs.[17] The proportion of Japanese single mothers who are working is the highest in the industrial world, suggesting a lower level of state support – and conceivably a stronger work ethic – than in other advanced nations.[18] The erosion of the old model, with its certainties of lifelong employment for the man and lifelong housekeeping for the woman, has brought a fluidity to male–female relations. But Kirino was less optimistic than some about the benefits of what she called 'this big societal shuffle'. Changes in the workforce might, she said, provide greater opportunity for a narrow spectrum of educated women. But for the majority, the new 'flexible' employment market would mean dead-end jobs for deadbeat pay, like the women working in her fictional lunch-box factory.

I put it to Kirino that Japanese women, certainly the more privileged ones, tended to be less constrained by social norms, more worldly, interesting and daring. They were more likely than men to speak English or to have travelled abroad. As Hama had said it was still fairly common for a man to hand over his pay cheque to his wife, who might dish him out a little 'spending money' if he was lucky. Women also appeared to be having more fun. I remembered once having lunch in Tokyo with a Chanel executive at Chateau Joel Robuchon, an expensive French restaurant. Apart from the two of us, the diners were exclusively female, all impeccably dressed and leisurely advancing from *amuse bouche* to *petits fours*. Many were sipping wine or champagne. I couldn't help picturing their overworked husbands shovelling down warmed-up pork cutlet at a desk piled with papers. 'I can't say unequivocally that Japanese women are oppressed or not oppressed,' Kirino replied after thinking about what I had said. 'In hidden places, Japanese women always had power, it's true. All Japanese men also have a tendency to suffer from *mazacon*,' she added, using the contraction of 'mother complex' to refer to the obsessive devotion men are said to harbour for their mothers. 'That is why Japanese women are seemingly rather strong . . . You talked about running the household accounts. But this means that men don't have to worry about how much to save. They are relieved of such worries. Once you get married, it is not a case of man and wife, but man and mother. Once they are married, mothers can have fun. That is what you saw in the French restaurant.'

*

Kaori Nakahara,[19] a working woman in her mid-twenties, was more privileged than most. A graduate of Hitotsubashi, one of Japan's most prestigious universities, she joined a large bank as a career-track employee. But rather than being a draw, she saw her high status as a barrier to marriage. 'Many Japanese guys hate it when the woman does better or has a better label,' she said. 'The younger career women at work are finding it very difficult to find boyfriends and future marriage prospects.' (Japanese men had told me something similar. One said, 'There's a preference for the traditional type of female. Men are not so confident in themselves these days, so they pursue women who are shorter than they are, who earn less than they do and who are less accomplished than them. There's not much of a market for over-achievers.')

Nakahara said she didn't feel discriminated against at work. In some situations, the rarity factor – in her year there were four fast-track men for every woman – could work to her advantage. She was sometimes invited to meetings she might not normally have attended simply because it was considered better to have some women present. Still, sexism persisted. One friend was admonished for asking a pertinent question in a meeting. 'You talk a lot for a woman,' her boss told her later, implying that it had been inappropriate to challenge an elder male employee in public. The primary role of many women at the office was still to look good and be subservient, she said. The reception desks at many offices and department stores are staffed with doll-like women, trained to speak in an odd falsetto and to spring to attention every time a visitor approaches. Doll-like coquettishness is generally considered an attractive feature in Japanese women. 'What they do is just take people upstairs to the meeting room and look nice and bow when someone comes in,' is how Nakahara described it. 'They have the perfect bow. That's probably what they were taught when they were recruited.'

Then there was the matter of socializing. Women were generally welcome to go out eating with their colleagues after work. But office nights out often ended with *niji kai*, after-party drinks, or *sanji kai*, after-after-party drinks. As the evening wore on, the entertainment tended to get more lewd and female colleagues dropped away, leaving the men to get on with their male bonding in hostess bars or 'soapland' massage parlours. Some women felt this tradition was detrimental to their chances of success since they missed out on the best company gossip, which flowed more easily after a night of drinking. Kumiko Shimotsubo, the human resources consultant who missed out on the promised road, called such sessions 'nomunication', an amalgam of 'communication' and *nomu*, which means to drink in Japanese.

Nakahara told the story of a young male employee at the bank. 'One day his boss took him out. The only thing he was told in advance was that they were going to one of those places with girls. Anyway, they go in and, after they were welcomed, the first thing they were told to do was to pull their pants down, underwear and everything.' The two men, both wearing business attire from the waist up, were then ushered into the exact replica of a subway carriage. There were even straps of the sort that hang from train compartments to add authenticity. The young graduate and his older boss sat opposite each other. 'Then these girls come out with school uniforms on and basically kept on touching them for an hour,' Nakahara said. The most awkward thing, her colleague later told her, was that throughout the entire experience, he was sitting within feet of his boss who was naked from the waist down. And all the time, Nakahara said, bursting out laughing, 'the boss was smiling at him'.

Many Japanese women make relatively light of such entertainment. It is not uncommon to see families go out for a stroll with their young children in the huge neon-lit red-light districts that exist in every town and city. Many of the young women who work in such places are not desperately poor, but university students seeking extra spending money. Kirino said there were fewer taboos about such things in Japan than in the US. But unlike some, who regarded the Americans as too puritanical, she was not happy about the Japanese situation at all. 'The way the sex industry exists in Japan is something that really upsets me, especially when teenage girls are exploited. Some people say: "Oh no. They love to go and work in that industry." But when I hear that, my heart is crushed. The existence of hostess bars is one of the reasons that Japanese men and women don't get along,' she said. 'You see, there are women who will perform services for men, pour their drinks, light their cigarettes. And at home, wives will cater to their husbands' needs. There is a separation of roles, of being kind to men in two different settings. So men feel that, as long as they pay, they will receive service in such places. And when they go home, they will receive service from their wives. Japan is truly a kind of men's paradise.'

# PART FIVE

# Adrift

# 12

# Asia Ex-Japan

More than six decades after the end of the Second World War and some 120 years since Japan set out on its ruinous attempt to conquer Asia, history continues to stalk Japan's relations with its neighbours and former enemies. Unlike Germany, which has dealt with its Nazi history and reconciled with the rest of Europe, Japan has never been able to put the past behind it. That is partly because it suits its neighbours to play the 'history card' by keeping the past alive. Governments in China and South Korea have become adept at switching on old hatreds when it suits them. But Japan's patchy record on facing up to its past has given them plenty of ammunition.

Many younger Japanese, with scant knowledge of what went on in the war, are bemused at the hatred still harboured by some Chinese and South Koreans towards them. Some attribute it to brainwashing by the Communist Party, but this is a less useful explanation when it comes to democratic South Korea, where it is still common to refer to the Japanese by pejorative terms such as 'dwarves'. Nor, though less spoken about, has Japan's wartime conduct been forgotten in places such as the Philippines, whose people also suffered massacres and rapes on a horrifying scale. The writer F. Sionil José once told me he had shocked his Japanese hosts – at a convention to discuss Hiroshima – by proclaiming that the Americans should have nuclear-bombed every Japanese city they could find. He was not invited again.[1]

It is true that in China, since the military crackdown on student protesters in Tiananmen Square in 1989, education has placed more emphasis on Japan's wartime atrocities, stoking a sometimes frighteningly virulent nationalism among Chinese youth. It is true too that anti-Japanese demonstrations in China can sometimes be cover for broader dissatisfaction with an authoritarian system that usually does not permit protests. Still, the common view in China is that the Japanese have never honestly repented for their wartime aggression and that Japan remains an unpredictable country in which militarism lies dangerously close to the surface.

This idea of Japan as dangerous aggressor – so far removed from the pacifist image the Japanese harbour of themselves – was not such a problem twenty or thirty years ago. Then, Japan was at the height of its economic resurgence and China was an impoverished nation only beginning to emerge from the ruinous decades of Mao Zedong's rule. Deng Xiaoping, the Chinese leader who uncorked reform in the late 1970s, took a pragmatic view towards Japan, preferring to downplay history in the interests of a more practically useful relationship. Then, the chance of conflict between a weak China and a demilitarized Japan was almost non-existent. Not so today. Now, to borrow Mao's phrase, China has 'stood up'. In 2010, as we have seen, its economy surpassed that of Japan, making China once again the strongest power in Asia. Although China continues to benefit from Japanese technology and investment, with each passing year the balance tips further in China's favour: Japan, in short, is more economically dependent on China than the other way around. With each year, too, China becomes stronger militarily. In 2012, Hu Jintao, the outgoing president, declared that China intended to become a 'maritime power', serving notice that it wanted a blue-water navy capable of projecting power in the Pacific. By most reckoning, China has already become the world's second-highest spender on its military. China's economic and military ascendancy has sparked fears in Japan, helping those on the right who have long argued the country should become more 'normal' through the restoration of its 'sovereign right' to wage war. History, in short, has become ever more pressing as the balance of economic and military power shifts within the region. For Japan, which would prefer to forget, history is an unattended corpse at the bottom of its diplomatic garden.

In 1970, Willy Brandt, chancellor of the Federal Republic of Germany, fell to his knees before a monument to victims of the Warsaw Ghetto Uprising. The gesture, apparently spontaneous, was such a convincing demonstration of German contrition that the word 'Knie-fall' entered the lexicon and Brandt went on to win the Nobel Peace Prize. Japan has never had a Willy Brandt moment. A constant refrain in Asia is that, unlike Germany, it has never properly owned up to its history – to itself or to others. Over the years, Tokyo has paid billions of dollars in lieu of war reparations and its leaders have issued innu-merable formal apologies. Rightly or wrongly, these have never been taken as sincere. In 2001, for example, Junichiro Koizumi, then prime minister, said in a typical and oft-repeated statement of regret at Japan's wartime actions, 'We conducted colonization and aggressive acts based on a mistaken national policy and caused immeasurable pain and suffering. I wish, in the light of our country's regrettable his-tory, to take this to heart, to express my deepest regret and remorse.' Such statements belie the claim, so often heard, that Japan has never apologized, though readers will judge whether it is a 'proper apology' or not.

Koizumi followed his statement of contrition, however, with a visit to Yasukuni shrine, a religious monument to Japan's war dead that is reviled in Asia as a symbol of its hated militarism. Among more than 2 million ordinary foot soldiers, Yasukuni contains the 'souls' of fourteen convicted Class-A war criminals. The Japanese like to see the shrine as their equivalent of Arlington National Cemetery, a place to show respect for those fallen in war. Many in Asia, however, regard prime ministerial visits to the shrine as the equivalent of a German chancellor laying a wreath at the tomb of Adolf Hitler. Koizumi's pil-grimage in 2001 provoked a macabre demonstration in Seoul, where twenty male protesters each chopped off a little finger. Beijing said the visit suggested Japan had not properly 'reflected' – a favoured word in this debate – on its wartime conduct. Seoul lamented that a Japanese leader would show his respect to 'war criminals who destroyed world peace and inflicted indescribable damage on neighbouring countries'.[2]

That, in a nutshell, captures the problem with Japanese apologies as seen from Beijing or Seoul. No sooner do the Japanese say sorry, goes the complaint, than someone on the right undermines it by deny-ing, or even glorifying, Japan's wartime behaviour. Part of the problem is that Japan is a democracy where people, in and out of government, are free to say what they like. Japan will never stop its wartime apologists, just as Germany cannot hope to silence its neo-Nazis. But conservatives and nationalists have tended to dominate the discourse in Japan, overshadowing the statements and actions of many Japanese who have sought to look at history more squarely. As a result, the revisionist view of history is often seen by Japan's critics as the true sentiments of its people, normally hidden but revealed after a few glasses of sake or in the company of fellow Japanese.

The rightwing has certainly kept alive the idea that Japan's was an honourable war of national defence and Asian liberation fought against western colonial aggression. Sure, the Imperial Army did terrible things, some will admit. But wasn't that the nature of war? Hadn't the Americans incinerated hundreds of thousands of civilians in Japan and didn't they go on to commit atrocities in Vietnam? Weren't the Chinese armies locked in their own civil war in the 1930s and 40s, every bit as murderous as the Japanese? And wasn't it true that, after the war, as a result of Japan's intervention, countries from Indonesia to Burma had been able to shuffle off the indignity of European colonization? Why was Japan's attempt to build an empire any more heinous than Britain's, a country that was not constantly hounded to apologize for its past excesses? In 2013, David Cameron, the UK's prime minister, expressed regret for the 1919 Amritsar massacre in which British troops opened fire on unarmed protesters, killing up to 1,000 people. But he refused to apologize, saying it would be inappropriate to say sorry for events that had taken place before he was born. The Japanese, it seemed, were being held accountable to a higher standard. Still, there were those in Japan that went further, putting a positively glorifying spin on the country's wartime record. Shintaro Ishihara, the nationalist former governor of Tokyo, once succinctly put the rightwing case to me. 'We were proud during the war and we were proud after the war. We felt the war was not just for Japanese people but was to help the countries that had been colonized by the US and Europe,' he said.[3] Forgiveness of Germany contrasted with a continued belief that Japan was congenitally evil, he added. That was both hypocritical and racist, he said.

There are several reasons why Japan has found it harder to deal with history than Germany. One is the fact that, after the war, General Douglas MacArthur, Supreme Commander for the Allied Powers, kept Emperor Hirohito on the throne. For that, Hirohito had to be absolved from all responsibility for the war on the improbable grounds that he did not know what was happening and was powerless to stop it. With US collusion, elaborate steps were taken to ensure that he was not implicated. Strict US censorship after the war made it even harder for the Japanese to assess what had gone on or come to a proper reckoning with their immediate history. Some historians still praise the decision not to try Hirohito as the foundation of Japan's post-war economic success. Without the emperor's unifying presence, it might indeed have been more difficult for a foreign occupying force to govern a defeated and demoralized Japan. But with their wartime leader exonerated, the Japanese found it harder to disinter the past. The emperor, in whose name soldiers had been sent to slaughter and be slaughtered, was still officially the nation's most revered figure. As John Dower wrote, 'If the man in whose name imperial Japan had conducted foreign and military policy for twenty years was not held accountable for the initiation of or conduct of the war, why should anyone expect ordinary people to dwell on such matters, or to think seriously about their own personal responsibility?' The Americans' exoneration of the emperor, he concluded, had turned the issue of 'war responsibility' into a joke.[4]

In post-war Germany, by contrast, Nazi leaders, including Adolf Hitler, had died or been executed. They were severed from the body politic. That made it easier for Germans to blame the now destroyed fascist regime, even though they voted for it in 1933. In Japan's case there was no such clean break with the past. Japan's militarism was closely linked with the very idea of what 'Japaneseness' had meant since the Meiji Restoration, an identity that, as we have seen, required unquestioning loyalty to a god-like emperor. (At least after the war, the emperor was relieved of his divine status.) Still, there was much that stayed the same. Bureaucrats and politicians who had served during the war continued to play a prominent role after it. That was largely a consequence of the US policies of the early 1950s when, in the name of anti-Communism, the process of purging the right was reversed. When it came to it, Washington preferred continuity with a sullied Japanese past than the dangers of unleashing a more democratic, but more unpredictable, future.

Another reason many Japanese have struggled to see themselves as aggressors is the nuclear destruction of Hiroshima and Nagasaki. Radiation washed away much of the guilt from Japan's collective memory. 'To the majority of Japanese, Hiroshima is the supreme symbol of the Pacific War,' writes Ian Buruma in *The Wages of Guilt*, his superb account of how both Japan and Germany have remembered – and forgotten – the war. 'All the suffering of the Japanese people is encapsulated in that almost sacred word: Hiroshima.'[5] If the German symbol of the war is the Holocaust – the suffering they imposed on the Jews – Japan has chosen to remember a different symbol, one that epitomizes their own suffering at the hands of others. Hiroshima has served a double function in the post-war psyche. It has obliterated the idea that the Japanese were uniquely barbaric in wartime. Whatever they did, the Americans were willing to do the same, or worse. More subtly, especially for the left, it has transformed Japan from aggressor into the sacred guardian of world peace. Hiroshima has become a global symbol. It is the pacifist people of post-war Japan, whose soldiers have not fired a shot against an enemy in more than six decades, who have been entrusted to keep the flame of peace alive.

The lingering stereotype of the Japanese in much of the world as cruel and bloodthirsty could hardly be further removed from the typical view the Japanese have of themselves. For many, their country remains uniquely peaceful and harmonious, a supposed trait sometimes attributed to the absence of a monotheistic religion. True, they might say, Japan erred once by following the aggressive example of European nations, but it dearly paid for that mistake and will never act that way again. Typical is the view of Kazuo Inamori, a legendary businessman (and subsequently Buddhist priest) who was one of the pioneers of Japan's electronics industry. When I asked him about it, he invoked Japan's abundant marine resources, plentiful rainfall and geographical isolation to explain what he saw as his country's intrinsically pacifist nature. 'We never had to conquer others with force. Conquering with force is something European countries have done repeatedly in their history. It is in their nature to be warriors. We are not like that.' Almost as an afterthought, he acknowledged Japan's less-than-pacifist tendencies in the last century. 'If you go back a hundred years, of course, Japan tried to conquer some neighbouring countries,' was how he put it. 'All in all, though, Japan has been lead-ing the world as a peaceful country.'[6]

Japan's sense of victimhood was compounded by the Tokyo War Crimes Tribunal, Asia's version of Nuremberg, held between 1946 and 1948. It is an article of faith on the Japanese right that the trial of twenty-eight so-called Class-A defendants was a kangaroo court, founded not in international law, but rather in the barely disguised desire of the victors to punish the vanquished. At Nuremberg, Britain had, in fact, argued that it would be better to dispense with the pre-tence of legality and simply hang those whom the Allies held most responsible.[7] In many ways, the Tokyo Tribunal was indeed a charade. Evidence was suppressed, not least in protecting the emperor, and some of those eventually executed were less implicated in atrocities than others never put on trial. Justice Radhabinod Pal of India, the only dissenting judge, has won lasting affection among many on the right in Japan for concluding that the trial was a 'sham' with no legal or moral authority. He also endorsed the commonly held opinion of Japanese conservatives that, as the noose of sanctions tightened around Japan, Tokyo was left with little option but to wage all-out war.

If anyone epitomized the revisionist view of Japanese history, it was Yuko Tojo, granddaughter of Hideki Tojo, the wartime leader who ordered the attack on Pearl Harbor. In 2005, I arranged to meet her in a restaurant overlooking the Imperial Palace, a good choice since more than once during our encounter she pronounced the view of the vast royal grounds at the centre of Tokyo to be 'most nourishing'. At precisely the appointed hour, a tiny woman, dressed in a green wool-len suit with gold-trimmed buttons, had come charging into the restaurant. She was wearing silver-rimmed glasses and carrying a min-iature suitcase in egg-shell blue, which she later informed me had cost her only Y500. Greeting me in the politest form of Japanese, delivered in a high-pitched voice, she bowed so low it seemed as though she were scouring the plush carpet for some lost trinket. Already small in stature, she was reduced to less than half my size by her near-ninety degree salutation.

At the time, there was much controversy surrounding her grand-father's 'soul' and its lack of suitability as a resident of Yasukuni shrine. Yasuhiro Nakasone, a former prime minister and a nationalist in his own right, had recently suggested that Tojo, along with the thir-teen other Class-A war criminals, be dis-enshrined from Yasukuni. Since there are no bodies at the shrine, an oasis of cherry trees and simple wooden structures in central Tokyo, his plan would have entailed some kind of Shinto ritual to send the fourteen unwanted ghosts packing. Yasukuni is a curious place. The 'souls' of those who died fighting for the emperor are said to reside here. Most were ordi-nary soldiers sent off to die on the battlefields. But among them are the leaders, including Tojo, who dispatched them to their fate. Curi-ously, the Koreans and Taiwanese who fought alongside as subjects of the then Japanese empire are also memorialized, often to the anguish of their hapless relatives who have, so far unsuccessfully, demanded the 'removal' of their ancestors' souls, on the grounds that they did not fight for Japan by choice. To one side of the grounds is the Yushukan museum where the 'sacred relics' of the Yasukuni deities are kept. On display is a Zero fighter aircraft; a 'human torpedo' of the sort used in naval suicide missions; and the first railway engine to steam along the Burma Railroad, the 'Death Railway' built by forced Asian labour and prisoners of war. The museum presents a deeply revisionist view of history, glossing over atrocities and glorifying the idea of sacrificing one's life for the emperor. The shrine itself is private since state Shinto was abolished after the war, but it remains, in Buruma's words, 'the holiest shrine of the militarised emperor cult'.[8]

Nakasone's suggestion to get rid of the Class-A war criminals, which he once made to me in person,[9] was a response to the bitter protests from Japan's neighbours. He hoped that the shrine could thus be rendered an acceptable place to honour Japan's war dead. For Yuko, the former prime minister had betrayed important principles of the right. 'I don't know why Nakasone keeps banging on about this, talking about Class-A war criminals all the time. Japanese people should never use the expression "war criminals",' she said. Under Japanese law, she went on, soldiers and leaders alike had committed no crime other than serving their country. Besides, even if it were desirable to remove them, it was impossible under Yasukuni's doc-trines. 'Once a soul is enshrined, you can't tear them into bits and take them from the shrine. You cannot separate the souls. They are all equal whether they are generals or rank-and-file soldiers. They are all gods.'[10] Yuko put the blame for the crisis over Yasukuni squarely on China, a country she told me – in a racist sideswipe – she associated with spitting and open-air defecation. 'Nowhere else in the world, in America or the UK, have there been complaints about the people who died. It is only China who is whipping the souls of the dead.'

Though she would have been only four or five at the war's end, Yuko had fragmentary memories of her mother taking her to visit her grandfather in the prime minister's office. Sometimes they would share quiet meals while war raged in Asia. When Tojo was in Sugamo prison awaiting trial following Japan's surrender, she recalled her brother sticking his hands through the bars to touch his grandfather. After his execution, when Yuko was a little girl, her grandfather was a hated figure, blamed for pursuing an unwinnable war. The young Yuko, who had been told by her family that her grandfather had died defending the country, had only the vaguest inkling of his reputation. She recalled, as a six-year-old, being subjected to spiteful little punishments at school. 'They used to throw stones at me and chase me around and I had no idea what the reason was.' It was not until she turned ten that she discovered what had happened to her grandfather. Whenever one particular classmate saw her, he would climb up on a chair, grip his fingers theatrically around his neck and make choking noises, shouting, 'Tojo hanged.'

Yuko's defence of her grandfather's reputation – for that had become her mission in life – was part personal and part ideological. The two mingled so closely it was hard to tell where one ended and the other began. Her starting point was that neither he, nor those he sent to war, should be seen to have died in vain. Their deaths, above all, must not have been meaningless. For that, the war they fought needed to have been honourable and their 'defence' of the nation, though they lost, somehow a necessary precondition for Japan's post-war prosperity. It was a hard argument to make, even to oneself.

Her second article of faith was that the Tokyo War Crimes Tribunal was invalid. How could the people who dropped atomic bombs on civilians in Hiroshima judge those who had participated in what she deemed a war of self-defence? 'The trial was unfair. It is unfair for the winner to make the judgement. My grandfather said himself that he had not violated international law, but he had made numerous violations against the Japanese people.' She went on, 'To deem Hideki Tojo a villain would mean the war was bad and that all the soldiers who fought in the war were bad. But their determination was respectable and they ended up protecting our lives, my life. I don't want to think of their deaths as meaningless.'

Isn't that precisely the point, I ventured. Their deaths *were* meaningless. Tojo's campaign was both idiotic and barbaric. In the name of some phoney notion of an Asia Co-Prosperity Sphere, it led to the slaughter of millions of Asians, including Japanese. Ultimately, it resulted in the near destruction of Japan itself. 'It's true that precious lives were lost and that Japan lost the war. But those soldiers fought desperately hard and stood proud,' she said, a cloud crossing her face. 'As a result Japan is enjoying peace and an affluent life. I would be sorry to say they died in vain.'

There followed a rather fractious discussion of the war in Asia in which she quibbled with my use of the word 'aggression'. 'I wish you had a deeper understanding of what happened in Manchuria,' she said, after portraying Japan's 1931 push into that region and later into China proper as a defence of land granted to Japan after its victory in the 1905 Russo-Japanese war.[11] We took to studying our food with some intensity. She dissected her fillet of lamb with admirable precision, and the frigid silence was broken only by the noise of her knife clinking against the plate. Finally she said, 'I think from the way you use the word "aggression" your stance is totally different from mine. You are looking at this from the standpoint that Japan was an invader. I say it was a defensive war. Japan did not have resources.' She meant Japan's lack of raw materials, particularly oil, and the international embargo that tightened after Japan moved into Indochina in the closing months of 1940.[12] She viewed encirclement by the so-called A, B, C, D powers – the Americans, British, Chinese and Dutch – as an attempt to deprive Japan of its lifeblood and tantamount to a declaration of war. 'This endangered the lives of 100 million people living in Japan,' she said. 'Japan had to make the difficult choice of going to war.'

We briefly touched upon the Nanjing massacre of 1937–8, which has become symbolic – along with the Bataan Death March, the slaughter of civilians in Manila in 1945, and the treatment of POWs –

of the barbarity of Japanese troops. Precisely what happened in Nanjing is a matter of fierce contention, especially between Chinese and Japanese scholars. But most historians, including many from Japan, agree that Japanese troops went on an orgy of killing and rape in the weeks after they took the city in December 1937. Estimates of how many people were massacred range from 40,000 to 300,000. Yuko said the numbers had been hugely exaggerated. She referred to work by Japanese revisionists who had sought to demonstrate that photographs of the massacre were doctored. 'Most of these were altered pictures,' she scoffed, referring to images of the Japanese bayoneting people or beheading them. 'They were wearing short sleeves in December or using guns that the Japanese army never used, the wrong-shaped swords and bayonet models that were not used then.'

By now, the politeness with which our conversation had begun had quite evaporated. 'What is your motive in interviewing me today? Is it because you and I think so differently?' Then she managed to dispel the frostiness and to retrieve an air of cordiality. She began to disinter her egg-shell blue valise and pulled out several memorabilia related to her grandfather's last days in Sugamo before he was hanged. There was a little brown box that Tojo fashioned in prison, which was presented to Yuko's elder brother on the day of the autumn equinox. An inscription on it read, 'Although the cold winds are blowing throughout the world today, do not be dismayed. The dark clouds casting Japan in shadow will clear one day, and the autumn moon will be seen again.' Then she brought out pencil stubs used by Tojo to keep the final pages of his diary and even the butt of the last cigarette he smoked. Finally, she produced a little packet from which she emptied a small clump of hair and some nail clippings – a parting gift that Tojo had prepared before a bungled suicide attempt. The relics sat there on the white tablecloth, mere inches away from the *petits fours* I had been eyeing.

There were plenty of Japanese who did not try to cover up their country's wartime history. Over the decades, many historians, teachers, lawyers and former members of the military had gone to great lengths to unearth Japan's wartime atrocities. One such was Saburo Ienaga, who spent much of his life before he died in 2002, at the age of eighty-nine, fighting lawsuits against the government to defend his right to publish school textbooks critical of the war.[13] Ienaga was a history professor who had been a schoolteacher during the war when he was expected to teach imperial myth presented as fact. That he did so filled him with shame. Right after 1945, there had been no new textbooks, so teachers were instructed by the Americans to black out passages promoting militarism or the emperor cult. I have spoken to those who remember whole pages of their textbooks hidden under a sea of black ink.

In 1946, a new book, *The Course of Our Country*, was published, the first since 1881, as Buruma points out, that started not with Japan's imperial creation myths but with the Stone Age. A new law on education stated that schools would be free to select their own textbooks, which would be published privately. Ienaga's was one of those. After the war, he wrote a series of widely used history textbooks with sections on, among other things, Japanese atrocities in Nanjing, routine use of rape by soldiers and medical experiments on human guinea pigs in Manchuria. During the years of the US occupation, in spite of heavy censorship, many Japanese wanted to understand how their society had been captured by a military establishment bent on fighting an unwinnable war. As well as his exposure of Japanese aggression, Ienaga exhibited a pacifist and leftwing leaning that was typical of many in society who entirely rejected the pre-war dogmas that had led Japan down such a disastrous path. Ienaga's politics, however, enraged the conservative education ministry, which considered him a Marxist. In a 1962 textbook, he included photographs of students being sent to the front and young girls working in armament factories with the caption, 'The destruction of people's lives'. He attributed the defeat of the Imperial Army in China to the 'democratic power of the Red armies' and referred, controversially, to the military brothels stocked by women from throughout the Japanese empire.

Ienaga was requested to rewrite dozens of items and to delete whole passages on the grounds that they were historically unproven or undermining of youthful patriotism. One examiner appointed by the ministry objected to Ienaga's use of the term 'aggression' – much as Yuko Tojo had done – to describe Japan's wartime actions. 'Aggression is a term that contains negative ethical connotations,' the examiner wrote, bemoaning its potential discouraging effect on members of the next generation. 'Therefore an expression such as "military advance" should be used.' A separate report judged that Ienaga had strayed from the proper teaching of Japanese history, whose aim should be 'to acknowledge the historical achievements of our ancestors, to raise awareness of being Japanese, and to foster a rich feeling of love for our people'. Ienaga's intention, by contrast, was to foster a disgust for imperial war and a love of Japan's new pacifist constitution – albeit one imposed by the occupying Americans. He became so frustrated with the ministry's requests that in 1965 he launched the first of three lawsuits against the government for acting unconstitutionally in curbing his free speech, a battle he was still waging into his late seventies. Though there were many legal defeats and setbacks – not to mention intimidation from rightwing thugs – in 1993, the Tokyo High Court ruled that the education ministry had overstepped its bounds by censoring his textbook.

Similar fights were still going on at the time I met Yuko Tojo. These days the battleground had shifted from publication of 'Marxist' textbooks to the attempted distribution of ones produced by revisionists presenting a whitewashed view of history. These books often contained no reference to Nanjing or treatment of the POWs. Although such textbooks were adopted by only a tiny minority of schools, their appearance was seized upon by the Chinese media, provoking widespread anger in the country.

Some Japanese teachers were alarmed about what they saw as the further encroachment of revisionist propaganda. A number of school authorities had, for instance, started demanding that teachers attending school ceremonies stand before the Japanese flag and sing the national anthem. In Tokyo, the school board had ruled that, ideally, one teacher should learn to play the *Kimigayo*, 'His Majesty's Reign', on the piano. Outside the classroom, these symbols had begun to shed their taboo status. In the 2002 soccer World Cup, co-hosted by Japan and South Korea, crowds had good-humouredly waved the flag and sung the anthem at home games. But some teachers remained intensely wary of attempts to instil – or enforce – patriotism in schools. They still regarded both the *Hinomaru* flag and *Kimigayo* anthem – with its entreaty for 'eight thousand generations' of imperial rule – as symbols of the cult that had led Japanese unthinkingly into war. Kozo Kaifu, a lawyer acting for the rebellious teachers, put it in terms that Yukichi Fukuzawa, the nineteenth-century liberal thinker who had stressed the importance of individualism, would have understood. 'Post-war education is intended to raise children not for the emperor but for themselves, so they can be the best people they can be,' he told me.

Hiroko Arai was a mild-mannered English teacher at a school in Tokyo. At fifty-nine, she was nearing retirement. One of eight siblings brought up in the intellectual ferment immediately after the war, she was among those who refused to stand. Her father had run a *sento* public bath in Fukui prefecture. As a child, Arai was taught by her parents to believe in what she called the sovereignty of the people. 'My favourite phrase is "eternal vigilance is the price of liberty",' she told me, quoting Thomas Jefferson. That meant standing up – or in her case sitting down – for what you believed in. When the *Hinomaru* flag was raised she remained resolutely stuck to her seat. As a punishment for her refusal to honour the national symbol, the school board forced Arai into early retirement with a reduced pension. She was also obliged to attend a 're-education seminar' at which, she said, she was monitored by officials who noted her every reaction on a multi-coloured form. 'During the Second World War, the *Hinomaru* flag and the *Kimigayo* became symbols of what we did,' she said of Japan's invasion of China and Southeast Asia. 'I can't show respect to these symbols.'[14]

Shy and quietly spoken, Arai had struggled with herself to carry out her protest. Japan was not the easiest society in which to be the odd one out, she said. She thought the older teachers were more rebellious than the younger ones for whom the war was more distant. Unlike the generation after the war, younger Japanese had been taught to be more obedient. She paused. 'I suppose it's the fault of us teachers,' she added, almost to herself, acknowledging her profession's role in educating generations of what she deemed quiescent Japanese. 'I didn't want to educate them to be so obedient. I wanted them to be critical of authority.' Arai was worried about the new school textbooks too. Even the old ones were bad enough, she said. Far from being masochistic, as the right claimed, they barely mentioned the suffering Japan had brought to the countries it invaded. Instead, they revelled in

Japan's own suffering. She also thought they tended to project a negative view of Asian neighbours, instilling the notion that Japan was
alone in a hostile region. One textbook, she recalled, contained the
sentence, 'Look at the map. The Korean peninsula thrusts like a dag-
ger at Japan.'

In the same year I met Yuko Tojo, the *Yomiuri* newspaper, a rightwing publication with a combined morning and evening circulation
of more than 13 million, launched a year-long investigation into
Japan's war record. The articles were reasonably probing, although
they were careful to exonerate the emperor. One of the pieces found
that Japan's leaders had treated human life across Asia with contempt,
sacrificing even Japanese soldiers as they might toss out 'a pair of
worn-out shoes'. The series was hardly revelatory for anyone with a
knowledge of the war, but for its pains the newspaper's offices were
surrounded by the black vans of ultranationalists, which blared
patriotic music and shouted menacing slogans. Tsuneo Watanabe,
octogenarian chairman of the newspaper, said he had launched the
project to counter what he deemed a lack of sincerity. 'We committed
acts of aggression in the continent and we need to study these in detail
and leave the results to posterity,' he said, speaking through a fog of
pipe smoke. Political leaders had 'failed to grasp' the need to dig into
Japan's past and squarely face up to it, he went on. 'Unless we do that,
Chinese leaders will not be able to build favourable relations with
Japan.'[15]

I discussed Japan's difficult external relations with Toshiaki Miura,
a thoughtful commentator at the left-of-centre *Asahi* newspaper and
a regular television pundit. Miura was a tall, slightly shy man with
grey hair and spectacles. There was something of the academic about
him, though he also had the jumpy quality of a good journalist waiting for the next twist in the story. In a remark that neatly summed up
Japan's international isolation, yet its keen sense of wanting a place in
the world order, he told me, 'Our psyche is very insular. But we always
see ourselves reflected in the mirror outside.' That struck me as a perfect summation of the Japanese paradox – and the root of some of its
tragic missteps. Because of its insularity, Japan's only way of understanding itself has been with reference to other nations. An obvious
benchmark in the nineteenth century had been Britain, an island

nation just like Japan and a country that had the power and status to which Japan aspired. 'Britain is much closer to the continent,' said Miura, in a commonly voiced lament about Japan's geographical – and psychological – isolation. 'One of the tragedies of Japan's position in international society is that we have no neighbours of the same size or the same level of industry. If Japan were placed in Europe, you would have Germany, Italy and England to get along with, and we could learn how to coexist with countries of the same strength, the same industrial level. But here in Asia we have a huge neighbour, China, a divided Korean peninsula, and a bunch of small states in Southeast Asia. It's very difficult to develop a diplomatic sense that we are one of many countries.'

Koizumi never stopped visiting Yasukuni, although subsequent prime ministers, including the more overtly nationalist Shinzo Abe, did refrain from doing so. In Koizumi's case, if anything, the criticism galvanized his resolve to go. He repeated his pilgrimage during each of his six years in office, the last, defiantly, on the highly charged day of 15 August, the anniversary of Japan's surrender. There was a sense of paranoia about a rising China in parts of the administration and a feeling that a stand had to be made. One diplomat, who tried to persuade the prime minister not to go, later told me about the encounter. 'Koizumi's face went completely red and he grew very angry. He said, "Don't you understand? Unless I keep visiting the shrine, China will forever bring up the issue. By continuing to go, I can put a stop to this once and for all."' One close adviser was openly fearful of a resurgent Middle Kingdom. 'We have seen nothing like this in human history, a country where massive amounts of people are geared towards profit-making and whose leaders are ready to compromise any values for an economic return,' he told me. 'It is like putting five or six Japans of the 1960s together. The level of enthusiasm for development is breathtaking.' As the US historian Kenneth Pyle wrote, Japan's post-bubble generation 'sees China not as a war victim but as a rival'.[16]

During Koizumi's period in office, relations with Beijing became the sourest in a generation. Koizumi was not once invited to China on an official visit, an extraordinary lapse of contact between what were far and away Asia's two biggest economies.[17] (Japan was then the largest and China second.) Some brushed off the costs of the diplomatic freeze, arguing that trade between Japan and China was flourishing and that officials from both countries maintained regular contact outside the public limelight. Many Japanese business leaders did not see it that way. By 2004, China had overtaken the US as Japan's most important trading partner and the business lobby began to worry that the official stand-off between the two countries would harm their interests. Toyota had already had to withdraw an advertisement in which Chinese stone lions had been depicted bowing to one of its vehicles. The commercial had provoked outrage in China's internet chatrooms which saw it as a national slur. Mori Building was forced to change the design of its 101-storey skyscraper in Shanghai because the large hole at the top of it was said to resemble the Rising Sun flag. Yotaro Kobayashi, chairman of Fuji Xerox, a company with several factories in China, publicly urged that pilgrimages to Yasukuni cease. 'Visits are rubbing against the grain of Chinese people's sentiments,' he said. For his pains, he was castigated by the ultraright as a salesman more interested in profits than in Japan's dignity. Black trucks swarmed outside his house and one day Kobayashi received an anonymous letter. The envelope contained a bullet.

China and Japan were already scrapping over gas reserves deep under the waters of the East China Sea and there were regular clashes – thankfully verbal – over fishing-boat and submarine incursions into waters administered by Japan. Long-smouldering tension escalated dramatically in 2005 when anti-Japanese demonstrations spread across China. In April, protesters in several Chinese cities targeted Japanese department stores and small businesses, hurling rocks through plate-glass windows and throwing food at Japanese restaurants and Japanese cars. In Shenzhen, up to 10,000 people surrounded the Jusco supermarket, a Japanese chain, chanting slogans and urging people to boycott Japanese goods. Young Chinese shouted insults against 'little Japs' and 'Japanese pigs'. Wen Jiabao, China's premier, said, 'The core issue in the China–Japan relationship is that Japan needs to face up to history squarely.'[20] In Japan, though, most politicians were tired of apologizing.

# 13

# Abnormal Nation

At fifty-two, Shinzo Abe was the youngest post-war prime minister and the first to be born after 1945. He was the chosen successor of Junichiro Koizumi and he came into office in September 2006, right after Koizumi had stepped down. His political heartland was Yamaguchi prefecture in western Japan. That had been the old feudal domain of Choshu, one of four that had rebelled against the *shogun* in the nineteenth-century Meiji Restoration in order to bring about a national modernization capable of repelling foreign imperialists. It was in Choshu that the concepts of a professional army and Japan's national interest had been born. These were causes close to Abe's heart. Above all, said one of his closest advisers, he sought what the Japanese call *hinkaku*, or dignity – 'to be a man worthy of respect and to build a nation worthy of respect'.[1]

Abe (pronounced Ah-bay) was a nationalist, the grandson of Nobusuke Kishi, a wartime cabinet minister and one-time economic tsar of the puppet state of Manchukuo. After the war, Kishi was arrested, but he was never convicted of war crimes, though he was accused of being responsible for the enslavement of thousands of Chinese forced labourers.[2] Kishi re-entered politics after the American 'reverse course' – which strengthened the Japanese right as Washington grew more wary of Communism – and completed his return to respectability by becoming prime minister in 1957. Three years later, he sacrificed his premiership in order to renew the unpopular US–Japan Security Treaty, whose ratification prompted massive street protests in which one woman, a 22-year-old student at Tokyo University, was killed. Nearly half a century after these events – the high-point of post-war radical expression – in September 2006, Abe, who vividly remembered sitting on his grandfather's knee as protesters surrounded the house, formed his own 'cabinet for the creation of a beautiful country'. *Beautiful Country* was the title Abe gave his book, a political manifesto in which he had argued that Japan should stop apologizing for itself, learn to appreciate its culture and stand on its own two feet. In one of his first newspaper interviews as prime minister, he told me emphatically that he would rewrite the constitution within six years.[3] 'The current constitution was written before Japan became independent after the war,' he said, referring to the period of US occupation. 'With 60 years past, there are provisions within the constitution that no longer befit the reality of the day.'[4] Among the changes he sought was a revision of the pacifist Article 9, which obliged Japan to renounce its sovereign right of war. The article, Abe said, was incompatible with the new, proactive international role he envisaged for the country. He also sought to revamp education, to make it more 'moral' with less liberal parsing of Japan's history. 'The time has come for us to step forward, with quiet pride in our hearts, to create a new country,' he told parliament in his wooden style. 'A beautiful country, Japan is a country that values culture, tradition, history and nature . . . A beautiful country, Japan is a country that is trusted, respected, and loved in the world.' Abe had obviously not been reading the Chinese press.

One of his closest foreign policy advisers, once described to me as Abe's 'brain', was Hisahiko Okazaki, an oleaginous man who had been ambassador to Saudi Arabia and Thailand and who now devoted himself to several of Japan's rightwing causes. He worked in an office hung with Japanese scrolls off Toranomon, Tiger's Gate, a busy intersection near the heart of political power at Nagatacho, Tokyo's Capitol Hill. He liked to describe himself as an intelligence officer, something still nominally illegal in Japan, and he read voraciously to keep abreast of world affairs. Okazaki had standard rightwing views. He denied the worst atrocities of the war – he said perhaps a thousand civilians had been killed in Nanjing – and still quietly fumed at the American imposition of 'victors' justice' after the war. He thought Japanese schools had been hijacked by Communist labour unions and that they taught children a peculiarly self-flagellating view of history. He wanted children to marvel at their ancient heroes, including some of their enlightened emperors. 'For the Marxists, they're all feudal, and feudal was bad,' he said.[5] Like Abe, he rejected any notion that schoolchildren should be taught more comprehensively about the war. Far from it, he said, it was time Japanese youth stopped wallowing in national guilt and learned a little pride.

Okazaki was one of those urging Abe to 'normalize' Japan by reviving its right to possess, and if necessary use, its armed forces in the service of its allies. He wanted to override what he said was a self-imposed ban on 'collective self-defence'. This meant that, although the country's defence was solely in the hands of the US, Japan was not allowed to come to America's rescue even if, say, a US ship were attacked off the Japanese coast. Shedding this restriction was necessary to balance the precipitous military rise of China, Okazaki said. 'Having a navy and an army might be a breach of the constitution. But they already exist, so the question is how to use them,' he argued, using the circular logic that pervades constitutional discussion in Japan. If Tokyo could drop its ban, the balance of power in East Asia would be altered overnight. With one stroke of a pen, Japan's battleship and supersonic jet-owning 'police force' could admit that it was actually a fully fledged fighting force. 'If you calculate the joint strengths of America and Japan, it will take the Chinese ten or twenty years to catch up,' he said.

Okazaki didn't go out of his way to disguise his resentment at America and its post-war domination of Japan. But, like many on the right, he believed Tokyo had little option but to cling more tightly to Washington. 'You know Japan's international relations only started in 1853,' he said, referring to the year of the Black Ships when America tried to force Japan open. 'Before that we were simply isolated with no international relations. For 150 years since then, apart from the fifteen years between 1930 and 1945, we were allied with either Britain or the Americans. During that time we were absolutely safe and prosperous.' So long as Japan was allied with a western power, he was saying – not left alone in its cut-throat neighbourhood with China – everything would be fine. The fifteen years from 1930 to 1945, when Japan struck out on its own, were a disastrous 'aberration', he said. It was a variation on the 'leaving Asia' theme. Japan was better off as a 'western power', or at least closely allied with one. I asked why he thought Japan and China were unable to live alone together without a foreign power to keep them apart. After all, historically their cultures had been very similar. 'I don't accept that argument. We are different countries. Your neighbour is always a competitor,' he said. 'All neighbours are like that: the Romans and the Persians, the Germans and French. Why should neighbours be friendly? Are there any examples in history?'

I had witnessed for myself just how 'abnormal' a country Japan still was a couple of years before when I went to see a contingent of Japan's Self Defence Forces. Dressed in military fatigues and wearing tin hats, they were digging ice and snow. Their mission: to produce exquisite, shimmering ice sculptures of palaces, fairy grottoes and a fifteen-foot high replica of the Parthenon. Their theatre of operations: Sapporo's world-famous Snow Festival. Carving ice sculptures was a job these men had done for decades. That told you a lot about post-war Japan. So pathologically militaristic was its society deemed to be by the Americans that, at the end of the war, it was forced to adopt a constitution for ever renouncing its right to wage war. Article 9 of a document scrambled together by young American idealists working for General Douglas MacArthur stated that: 'The Japanese people forever renounce war as a sovereign right of the nation and the threat or use of force as means of settling international disputes.' As a result, 'land, sea and air forces, as well as other war potential, will never be maintained'.

Almost as soon as the ink was dry, the Americans regretted having put Japan in its constitutional straitjacket. With the outbreak of the Korean War and the subsequent onset of the Cold War, it ill-suited Washington to have an emasculated Asian ally entirely dependent on the US for military protection. The Self Defence Forces were formed in 1950. At first, they were called the National Police Reserve. And so, the fiction of an army that was not an army gradually came into being, creating a body of men – some quarter of a million strong at its peak – that looked and felt like a military, but didn't generally behave like one. The ability to deploy this formidable force was heavily circumscribed. Only in the past decade has a series of laws been passed that, among other things, relieves tanks of their requirement to stop at traffic lights in the event that Japan comes under attack. As we saw, as recently as 1995, when the Kobe earthquake destroyed huge sections of one of Japan's biggest cities, authorities were reluctant to send in a force that, for some people at least, still retained echoes of Japan's Imperial Army. The warm reception to the massive deployment of the Self Defence Forces after the March 2011 tsunami was a revealing contrast – and may yet prove something of a turning point in public attitudes towards its own military.

One of the schemes the top brass dreamed up to improve its image – and presumably give it something to do – was to lend a hand at the Sapporo Snow Festival. From 1955, recruits from a nearby base in Hokkaido began to build the massive, yet exquisite, ice sculptures for which the festival gained fame. Over the years, the glistening creations of Japan's military grew in popularity. By 2004, the year I attended, the Sapporo festival, held in February, was attracting 2.5 million visitors. The soldiers took their duties seriously. The commanding general of the 11th Division had given the troops explicit instructions, Captain Hisashi Matsumoto told me. 'He told us we should carve spellbinding ice statues for the people,' the captain said, in a clipped voice and with no trace of irony. Matsumoto, who had joined up aged fifteen, said the nearest he had come to action in his twenty years of service was when he participated in the search for an old lady who had got lost picking mushrooms in the mountains. When he posed for a photograph in front of one of the ice sculptures, Matsumoto initially made the two-fingered peace sign beloved of Japanese when confronted with a camera. Only when he recomposed himself for a second shot did he assume a stiff-backed stance more befitting a military man.

That year, the government had ordered several hundred members of the Self Defence Forces, including some from the 11th Division, to report for duty in Iraq, where Japan was about to embark on its most controversial mission since the Second World War. Tokyo had been determined Japan should shake off some of the inhibitions – constitutional, legalistic and, after sixty years of pacifism, now socially ingrained – that had restricted its international actions throughout the post-war period. Japanese troops would go to Iraq to take part in rebuilding efforts, specifically to help fix water and electricity supplies. Part of the reasoning was tactical. Japan wanted to please its most important ally, the US, which sought a show of solidarity for its controversial war in Iraq. Part of it, though, was an effort to shake off a post-war taboo that had limited Japan's military to carving ice sculptures but had deemed its soldiers too untrustworthy to be deployed abroad.

Thus, even before Abe came to power following Koizumi's retirement, Japan had taken some important steps towards 'normalization'. Soon after al-Qaeda's attack on the US in September 2001, the Diet had passed a special law authorizing ships from the Maritime Self Defence Forces – Japan's navy by another name – to supply America's fleet in the Indian Ocean. The law restricted Japan's cooperation to refuelling and logistics, but symbolically, at least, Tokyo was providing rear support for the US-led invasion of Afghanistan. Subsequent bills passed in the summer of 2003 broadened the government's powers in case Japan's territory was invaded. Japan was also in the initial stages of installing missile-defence systems. To deploy such equipment would require overturning the restrictions on collective self-defence so disliked by Abe.[6]

Much of the Japanese public remained staunchly pacifist and wary about becoming entangled in a messy foreign adventure of Washington's making. Although the government insisted the dispatch of members of the Self Defence Forces to Iraq was not unconstitutional, those on the left opposed watering down Japan's pacifist charter. Naoto Kan, then opposition leader, denounced the dispatch as a 'gross violation of the principles of the constitution'. Only sixty years previously, he reminded parliamentarians, 'our government couldn't control the Japanese army and we did a lot of damage in China and in Asia'.

The deployment of 550 ground troops began in January 2004. It turned out to be a largely symbolic affair. The Japanese, though lightly armed, were strictly forbidden from fighting even if soldiers from allied countries came under fire. In fact, they had to be guarded by soldiers from Holland, Australia and the UK, rendering their participation, from a purely military perspective, something of a nuisance. The mission was not without its incidents. In the run-up to the dispatch, two Japanese diplomats were shot and killed in Iraq. On several occasions, mortars were lobbed into the well-fortified Japanese encampment in southern Iraq where, it was said, troops had fresh supplies of sushi flown in regularly. Yet, as the constitution dictated, there was nothing in the way of real combat. The Japanese forces did a bit of routine repair work and then left. At the end of their mission, in the summer of 2006, all 550 returned to Japan without so much as a scratch.

Even after their withdrawal from Iraq, Japanese Air Self Defence Forces stationed in Kuwait continued missions flying equipment and US and UN personnel into Iraq. I was part of the travelling press corps in April 2007 when Abe visited the Ali Al Salem airbase in Kuwait, twenty-three miles from the Iraqi border, to review his troops. Abe swept in like some feudal clan leader, his retinue marching behind a purple flag decorated with cherry blossoms, a treasured national symbol especially beloved of the right. Standing behind a makeshift podium inside an aircraft hangar, he spoke to about a hundred Japanese personnel lined up in front of a bulbous C-130 transport aircraft. 'You will be the ones who will turn the Iraqi reconstruction work into a glorious chapter in the history of Japan,' he said hopefully.[7] 'As your commander-in-chief, I want to thank you from my heart.' In my notebook, I wrote, 'Japan is forbidden by its constitution from maintaining land, sea and air forces. But no one said anything about a commander-in-chief.'

Abe's mission to further normalize Japan didn't get very far. There was little sign the public shared his urgency about the need to revamp the constitution. Those on the left, including many in the teachers' union, saw any attempt to jettison Article 9 as betrayal of post-war pacifism. One often came across small groups of earnest campaigners outside subway stations. They handed out pamphlets, often illustrated with cartoon characters, about Japan's responsibility in the vanguard of global peace. Others could see the logic of drafting a new constitution that was actually written by the Japanese themselves. What self-respecting nation had a constitution drafted by an occupying force? They differed, however, on what any new constitution would say. After sixty years of peace, pacifism – or, more correctly, aversion to the idea of Japanese dying in conflict – ran surprisingly deep among ordinary Japanese. Many felt a strong attachment to a constitution that had kept Japan safe from the tragedy of war for so long. Mariko

Hayashi, a popular essayist, summed up people's anxiousness about any attempt to change the 1946 document. 'It's like having your clothes taken off suddenly. We are used to them, and because we are used to them, we can live comfortably.'[8]

Abe pressed on with his agenda regardless. He succeeded in revising the Fundamental Law of Education, among other things, striking out a clause from the 1947 law 'on respecting the value of the individual'. Yukichi Fukuzawa, whose article of faith was the rights and responsibilities of the individual, would not have approved. Abe upgraded the Defence Agency to the Defence Ministry, a symbolic gesture that edged the country closer to normalization.[9]

Abe also got mired in the issue of so-called 'comfort women', those women who were dragooned into working in brothels used by the Japanese military throughout the empire. Many of the women, abused for years, died during the war of disease or enemy fire. In the 1980s, some Korean women who had survived took their case to Japan in search of compensation and an apology. Japan did eventually say sorry in 1993 when chief cabinet secretary Yohei Kono stated that the Japanese military had directly or indirectly been involved in the establishment of sexual 'comfort stations' and that those who worked there were in many cases 'recruited against their will, through coaxing, coercion etc'. They lived, he said, 'in misery'. Compensation was paid through a private fund though not, as the South Korean government complained, directly from the Japanese government.

Abe disliked the apology and maintained that most of the women were regular prostitutes who had gone to work in the brothels of their own free will. 'There is no evidence to prove there was coercion, nothing to support it,' he told reporters in 2007, sparking fresh anger in South Korea and disquiet in the US. Nariaki Nakayama, a lawmaker who like Abe wanted to overturn the Kono apology, said the idea of coercion impugned Japanese honour. 'Some say it is useful to compare the brothels to college cafeterias run by private companies, who recruit their own staff, procure foodstuffs and set prices,' was how he preferred to characterize what had been sexual exploitation on an industrial scale.[10]

Abe's efforts to overturn the apology and to amend the constitution ran out of time. He lasted as prime minister only eleven months, brought down by plummeting popularity and a chronic intestinal illness. His administration, out of touch with popular sentiment, became embroiled in successive scandals. Four of his cabinet ministers resigned and one committed suicide. Abe's government had also been forced to admit the loss of 50 million pension records, no joke in a nation with a rising share of elderly. The final straw came when he led his party to a humiliating defeat in Upper House elections. Two days later, in September 2007, he resigned. Few thought Japan had become more beautiful under his watch.

Yukio Hatoyama's view of a 'normal' Japan was quite different from that of Abe. A centre-left politician from the Democratic Party of Japan, Hatoyama became prime minister two years after Abe resigned – only the second leader to break the Liberal Democrats' hold on power in half a century. He felt more guilt than Abe over Japan's wartime conduct and wanted to build better relations with Asian neighbours, particularly China. For him, a 'normal' Japan was not one constitutionally unshackled to wage war but one less reliant on the US and more accepted in its own region. He had opposed prime ministerial visits to Yasukuni shrine, arguing instead for a secular memorial where Japan's war dead could be properly mourned. Yasukuni, he reminded those who had forgotten, was a fount of 'the creed used to justify Japanese wartime militarism', and spiritual resting place of those who orchestrated the war. 'For a Japanese prime minister to pay homage to war criminals who were found guilty of acts of brutality throughout Asia, some of whom bear responsibility for filling the Yasukuni shrine with war dead in the first place, should be seen as an act of profound insensitivity and arrogance towards the victims of Japan's wartime aggression,' he had said.[11]

In the weeks before his victory was sealed, Hatoyama had already alarmed officials in Washington by penning an unusual essay in the monthly journal *Voice*. More abstruse pontification than clear-eyed policy proposal, it suggested that Japan should pursue the ideal of *yuai*, or 'fraternity'. Like Abe, Hatoyama was deeply influenced by his grandfather, who had also been prime minister (1954–6) and who had adopted the word *yuai*. His grandson said it meant steering a middle course between competing ideologies. After criticizing what he called the pernicious influence of American-led 'market fundamentalism' – a philosophy that Hatoyama contended was 'void of morals' – he wrote: 'As a result of the failure of the Iraq war and the financial crisis, the era of US globalism is coming to an end and . . . we are moving away from a unipolar world led by the US towards an era of multi-polarity.' Japan, he said, was stuck between an America that was fighting to maintain its position as a dominant power and a China that was striving to become one. The upshot of Japan's delicate geographic and diplomatic position, he suggested, was that, as time went on, Japan would have to distance itself a little from the US and draw closer to Asia. 'We must not forget our identity as a nation located in Asia. I believe that the East Asian region . . . must be recognised as Japan's basic sphere of being.' Asia should work towards the goal of a single currency, he said, adding that the experience of the European Union showed how such projects could defuse territorial disputes and historical rancour. Through such means, he suggested, Japan could help in the goal of 'overcoming nationalism'. It was quite a change from Abe.

The fact that two prime ministers, serving within a couple of years of each other, could have such diametrically opposed views about what 'normalization' meant showed just how diplomatically adrift Japan still was. After all these years, it was still no nearer to solving a basic conundrum: how to reconcile its geographical reality as an Asian nation with its history as a defeated regional aggressor and a would-be power in the European imperial mould.

Hatoyama's was an interesting essay. It grappled with the trauma Japan had suffered as a consequence of its 'abandonment' of Asia in the late nineteenth century and its embrace of western Great Power logic. As Okazaki had said, Japan had done fine so long as it was allied to either Britain or America. What it had never learned was how to live comfortably in its own neighbourhood alone. For Hatoyama, to be 'normal' meant rectifying that anomaly. Japan, he said, should work towards forming an 'East Asian Community' with China and other neighbours.

There were, however, serious problems with his academic ruminations. Hatoyama had done no groundwork with either Washington or

Beijing to prepare for what amounted to a radical shift in foreign policy. Neither could be expected to have much faith in a vision of Japanese diplomacy based on his grandfather's favourite word. In public, Washington was polite. Inevitably there would be teething problems as both Tokyo and Washington adjusted to having a new party in office after half a century of almost uninterrupted Liberal Democratic rule, it said. In private, however, alarm bells were going off. In a cable dated October 2009, Kurt Campbell, US assistant secretary of state for East Asian and Pacific affairs, voiced concern at Hatoyama's recent visit to Beijing. During that trip, the Japanese prime minister had repeated his view that Japan needed to end what he deemed its 'over-dependence' on America. Those remarks 'drew surprise from the highest levels of the US government,' Campbell said. 'Imagine the Japanese response if the US government were to say publicly that it wished to devote more attention to China than to Japan,' the cable quoted him as saying. Such a posture 'would create a crisis in US–Japan relations'.[12] As Campbell said, for many years, Tokyo had been paranoid at what it called 'Japan passing'. Worse even than 'Japan bashing' – which at least meant Japan was still a country worth getting angry about – 'Japan passing' referred to the fact that Washington's attention, too, was being drawn ever more towards Beijing.

Japan's new government fumbled to put flesh on the bones of Hatoyama's vision. In the name of transparency, it began an inquiry to expose secret Cold War agreements that had allowed, among other things, American nuclear-armed warships to use Japanese ports in contravention of Japan's non-nuclear stance. Successive administrations had implausibly denied the existence of such 'secret pacts', concluded in the 1960s, even though they had long been revealed through the publication of declassified documents in the US. By acknowledging those agreements, the idea was to deal with the Japanese public more openly and honestly. For one thing, it would bring out the contradiction of Japan's reliance on a nuclear deterrent even as it clung to the charade of disavowing nuclear weapons. For some, that fiction was symbolic of a stunted democracy in which the 'happy children of Japan', in the words of artist Yoshitomo Nara, were not trusted with the whole, uncomfortable, truth.[13] They lived in a fantasy-land of happy consumerism, exquisite design and exacting hygiene standards while the blood-and-guts business of defending their nation was outsourced to the Americans. The new government also began a public review of the billions of dollars that Tokyo gave to US troops stationed in Japan, a contribution that at the height of Japan's economic power had been termed, rather condescendingly, a 'sympathy budget' – presumably sympathy for the poor state of Washington's finances.

Hatoyama's vision – and eventually his entire premiership – foundered over the issue of US bases on Okinawa, long a potent symbol of Japanese subservience to its American overlord. Okinawa, a chain of tropical islands far to the south of Japan, comprises just 0.6 per cent of the Japanese landmass, but plays host to three-quarters of US bases and more than half of the 36,000 troops stationed in Japan.[14] Many Okinawans had for years campaigned for the US to move some or all of the bases off the island, but there were few places on Japan's built-up mainland that would have them.

Okinawa was a semi-colony, incorporated into Japan only in 1879. For Tokyo, ambivalent about surrendering its territory to US bases, Okinawa was a convenient location to host foreign forces, out of sight and mostly out of mind. For hundreds of years before it was claimed by Japan, Okinawa had been the independent kingdom of the Ryukyus, with its own language and customs. It had paid tribute to China, which largely left it alone. Only when it came into closer contact with Japan was its independence threatened. In 1609, it became a vassal state of Satsuma, which was one of the Japanese fiefdoms – Choshu was another – that played a decisive role in the Meiji Restoration. After the Restoration, Tokyo formally incorporated the Ryukyus into its territory, renaming them Okinawa. Even modern-day Okinawa, the poorest prefecture in Japan, does not feel entirely Japanese. During the US occupation of the islands from 1945 until their return to Japan in 1972, some Okinawan residents complained that the Japanese knew so little about them that they asked whether they spoke English at home and used knives and forks.[15] A native sushi chef in Naha, the Okinawan capital, summed up the sense of discrimination. Referring to the quintessential symbol of what it is to be Japanese, he told me glumly, 'The people from the mainland say that

Okinawa's cherry blossoms are not real cherry blossoms. They say they're different.'

Okinawa's radicalism was born in the terrible experience of 1945, when nearly 150,000 islanders, or a quarter of the population, were killed in one of the bloodiest battles of the Second World War. Some civilians were press-ganged by the Imperial Army into committing mass suicide rather than surrendering to the Americans. Under Abe's government, the education ministry had sought to erase references in school textbooks to the enforced suicides, prompting some 100,000 Okinawans, one in ten of the population, to demonstrate against the attempted whitewash. Kenzaburo Oe, the Nobel laureate, went to court to prove the military were involved in coercing suicides, a judgment he eventually won. He told me the Japanese state was trying to spread the false idea that 'Okinawans died a beautiful and pure death for the sake of the country'.

Summing up the impact of war trauma, one senior Bush administration official said many Okinawans felt 'this should be an island of peace'. They viewed the US military bases as 'foreign transplants', he said. 'The vast majority of Okinawans think like that.'[16] Masahide Ota, a former governor of Okinawa, told me, 'The Americans occupied Okinawa during the war and they feel it is their own territory. They believe it is theirs to use as freely as they wish.'[17] Long-standing resentment had come to a head in 1995 when three American servicemen stationed on Okinawa abducted a twelve-year-old girl, sealed her mouth with duct tape and raped her. Under the principle of extraterritoriality granted by the US–Japan Status of Forces Agreement – a throwback to the unequal treaties Europeans and Americans had imposed throughout Asia – the three servicemen were exempted from Japanese law. Admiral Richard Macke, commander of the US Pacific Command, made things worse with remarks of staggering insensitivity. 'I think it was absolutely stupid,' he said of the servicemen's actions. 'For the price they paid to rent the car [in which the girl was abducted], they could have had a girl,' he said, meaning a prostitute. Not surprisingly, massive anti-US demonstrations swept Okinawa. Such was the furore that Washington decided it had no choice but to hand over the three servicemen to be tried in Japan. They were sentenced to between six-and-a-half and seven years each. In the following year, President Bill Clinton sanctioned the amendment of the Status of Forces Agreement so that, in the case of serious crimes, suspects could be handed over to Japanese authorities.

In the aftermath of the rape, the US agreed to reduce its presence on Okinawa by a fifth, amalgamating some bases and pulling back about 8,000 marines to Guam, a US territory in the Western Pacific. The Marine Corps' Futenma Air Base, dangerously situated in the middle of a dense city, was to be shifted to a more remote part of the island, with a runway jutting out into the sea. The plan to move Futenma, however, became ensnared in interminable negotiations over its environmental impact, and the noise and danger it would bring to its new location. There was also the broader question of who would pay for the redeployment. Washington wanted Tokyo to foot the bill. To make matters more complicated, this was not just a two-way discussion between Tokyo and Washington. Okinawans had their say too. With each new local election cycle, the prospect of building the new air base waxed and waned. Some senior US officials were scathing in their condemnation of a Japanese government that could allow the sentiments of a small island to obstruct the vital matter of national and international security. Not for nothing had an American ambassador once compared Okinawa to a bone stuck in the throat of the alliance.[18]

The disagreement over Okinawa reflected deeper problems in a post-war US–Japan relationship that had been tricky from the start. In one sense the alliance between victor and vanquished, what the scholar John Dower had called a 'sensuous embrace', was a miracle of twentieth-century diplomacy. The ties were mutually beneficial. Washington got a sturdy, and increasingly wealthy, ally in the Pacific. Japan snuggled under the US nuclear umbrella, releasing it from the burdens of diplomacy and the expense of self-defence. That allowed it to concentrate on the business of getting rich. Such 'free-riding' even became the name of a credo, the so-called Yoshida Doctrine, named after Shigeru Yoshida, who was prime minister for eight years after the war. 'Just as the US was once a colony of Great Britain but is now the stronger of the two,' he said, 'if Japan becomes a colony of the US it will also eventually become the stronger.'[19]

Subservience to America, however, had lasted far longer than Yoshida might have imagined. Japan had never stepped far out of line and critics had gone so far as to call it America's 'client state'.[20] Such an unequal relationship had bred resentment not only among the left, which tended to want American bases out, but also among the right. Shintaro Ishihara, the former governor of Tokyo and co-author of *The Japan that Can Say No*, a book urging greater Japanese independence, resented that his country was 'at the beck and call of the US'.[21] The view of Japan as a client state had infiltrated popular culture too. In 2005, Takashi Murakami, one of Japan's best-known modern artists, curated an exhibition of subculture in New York called *Little Boy*. The title referred to the codename for the atomic bomb dropped on Hiroshima in 1945. But Little Boy could also be shorthand for Japan's stunted development as a state and its lopsided relationship with Washington. According to the exhibition notes, Murakami sought to explore 'Japan's military and political dependence on the US; and the replacement of a traditional, hierarchical Japanese culture with a disposable consumer culture ostensibly produced for children and adolescents'. Little Boy, it said, referred to 'the infantilization of the Japanese culture and mindset', the result, in Murakami's view, 'of Japan's economic and political dependence on the west'.

Hatoyama tried to tap into this vein of dissent, with the issue of bases on Okinawa as his chosen battleground. He had recklessly promised the Okinawan people that he would scrap the plan to relocate Futenma to another part of the island and, instead, move it off Okinawa altogether. Unfortunately, his plan had not been squared with Washington, nor with his own bureaucrats in the foreign ministry who sought to undermine him by privately advising their US counterparts not to budge. He had spent months desperately seeking an alternative location on the Japanese archipelago. Unsurprisingly, it was proving difficult to find a community willing to accept noisy helicopters in their midst. Hatoyama was eventually forced to fly to Okinawa to tell angry crowds that he couldn't fulfil his pledge. A replacement for Futenma would have to be built on Okinawa after all. The decision had been 'heartbreaking', he said, but in the end he had to prioritize national security and the deterrence provided by US

Marines. His apology was not accepted. In Okinawa he was greeted by bright yellow signs that said simply 'Anger', and by jeering crowds who urged him to 'Go Home'.[22] The word on everybody's lips was 'betrayal'.

Within a few weeks of his humiliating climbdown, Hatoyama had resigned. By June 2010, he was gone. His tenure of just eight-and-a-half months was short even by the fleeting standards of Japan's prime ministers. His own view of a normal nation had been just as difficult to execute as Abe's. His grandiose vision of forming an 'East Asian Community', modelled on the European Union, had gone precisely nowhere. Of his attempt to put Japan's relations with the US on a more equal footing, he said in a tearful resignation speech, 'Someday, the time will come when Japan's peace will have to be ensured by the Japanese people themselves.'[23] That day, evidently, had not come yet.

Standing up to the US over Okinawa had done nothing to further Hatoyama's other principal policy goal of building a better relationship with China. Beijing was slow to respond to his overtures, perhaps because it had sensed, correctly, that his power base was weak in Japan. The country's merry-go-round of now-you-see-them now-you-don't prime ministers made it hard for foreign capitals to take any particular administration's proposals seriously. Hatoyama's Democratic Party lacked deep contacts in China, which had over many decades got used to doing business with the more conservative Liberal Democrats.

It was ironic that under the Democratic Party, which had held out an olive branch to Beijing, Sino–Japanese relations should actually deteriorate. The new battleground was not Yasukuni or textbooks, but something more tangible: islands.[24] Called the Senkaku by Japan and the Diaoyu[25] by China, the five uninhabited islands and three rocky outcroppings covered a total area of less than three square miles and were too small to figure on most maps. But they were a proxy for national pride and unresolved wartime animosities. They were located in the East China Sea, a little over 100 miles northeast of Taiwan and 250 miles west of Okinawa. The Chinese claimed that they had discovered the islands in ancient times and that they had appeared on Qing Dynasty (1644–1911) maps as Chinese territory. According to Beijing, the islands were war booty stolen during the

1895 Sino–Japanese War. As such, they should have been returned according to the dictates of the Potsdam Declaration of 1945, which issued the terms of Japan's surrender. This stipulated that 'Japanese territory shall be limited to the islands of Honshu, Hokkaido, Kyushu, Shikoku and such minor islands as we determine.' According to Beijing, that clearly meant Japan was supposed to give up the Senkaku/Diaoyu islands along with Taiwan, South Korea and other territory seized in war.

The Japanese argued that the San Francisco Peace Treaty of 1951, which incorporated the Potsdam Declaration, did not include the Senkaku. The reason, it said, was that the islands had not been seized in war at all but had instead been legally annexed on 14 January 1895. 'From 1885 on, our government conducted on-site surveys time and again, which confirmed that the islands were uninhabited and there were no signs of control by the Qing Empire,' Tokyo said.[26] That meant they were 'terra nullius' when Japan found them – land belonging to no one – and thus available under international law to be claimed by Japan. The upshot of the San Francisco Treaty was that the islands, rather than being 'returned' along with Taiwan, fell under US administration as part of Washington's control of Okinawa. Tokyo said Beijing had not objected at the time, although, in fairness, China was not present at San Francisco nor a signatory to the treaty. Beijing began to voice its claim, Tokyo said, only when, in the late 1960s, it was discovered there may be oil around the islands. In 1972, the US 'returned' the islands to Japan along with Okinawa over China's objections.

In subsequent years, there were periodic clashes between Japanese fishermen and those from China and Taiwan who also fished around the islands. The territory, however, remained under effective Japanese administration and Tokyo refused to concede even that there was a dispute over their ownership at all. The first intimation that the tussle over the islands was getting more serious came in September 2010 when Zhan Qixiong, a fishing boat captain from Fujian province, rammed his boat into two coastguard vessels. Some evidence later came out that he had been drunk. Zhan and his fourteen-member crew were arrested and Japan indicated that prosecutions would follow. Beijing called for their immediate unconditional release. 'We demand Japanese patrol boats refrain from so-called law-enforcement activities in waters off the Diaoyu islands,' the foreign ministry thundered.[27] Tokyo said the matter was for the courts to decide. As the stand-off worsened, Beijing retaliated by placing an informal ban on the export of 'rare earths', vital to Japan's electronics industry. Within days, Japan buckled, releasing the crew and the captain. It was a humiliating climbdown.

Yoichi Funabashi, the former editor of the left-leaning *Asahi* newspaper, who considered himself a friend of China, called the incident the 'Senkaku shock'. It was worse, he said, than the 'Nixon shock' of 1971 when Richard Nixon, the US president, normalized relations with China behind Japan's back. In an open letter entitled 'Japan–China Relations Stand at Ground Zero', he wrote that Japan's half-hearted actions, including its decision not to prosecute the Chinese captain, revealed its weakness. 'One cannot help but concede that Japan is either still clumsy in its diplomatic efforts or simply a poor fighter. In comparison, the various measures taken by the Chinese government to apply pressure on Japan can only be described as a diplomatic "shock and awe" campaign.' The clash, he wrote, exposed the fantasy of trying to forge 'a mutually beneficial relationship based on common strategic interests', the official policy between the two countries since an aborted rapprochement in 2006. Instead, Japan would have to cut its losses and discard its naïve dreams of normalizing relations with Beijing. The relationship would be in constant danger of rolling completely out of control, he argued. 'If China continues to act as it has, we Japanese will be prepared to engage in a long, long struggle.'[28] Funabashi's was a pessimistic analysis. Normalizing relations with China, he implied, was – at least for the foreseeable future – a lost cause.

In their different ways, both Abe and Hatoyama had sought to make Japan a more normal nation. Abe had wanted Japan to throw off its war guilt and its pacifist constitution and become again a 'beautiful country' that could hold its head high in the international community. He resented what America had done to Japan at the end of the war, but saw little alternative to maintaining a strong alliance with its powerful western ally. Hatoyama's normalization had been more subtle, though ultimately more confused. He had attempted to 'triangulate' the relationship with the US and China, drawing slightly away from Washington in order to be friendlier with Beijing. It didn't work. The deep historical rift with China could not be fixed with a little diplomatic repositioning. Japan was still isolated in Asia. Diplomatically, it remained lost, a prisoner of its geography and of its history.

# PART SIX

# After the Tsunami

# 14

# Fukushima Fallout

It looked like any other provincial Japanese town. There was the Shiga Hair Salon, with its red, white and blue barber's pole, offering cuts and 'iron perms'. Next door was the Watanabe Cake Shop, doing business since 1990 and housed in a two-storey mock Tudor building. Outside the nearby Jokokuji temple, a tiny granite stone Buddha figurine stood at the entrance, dressed in a weather-worn pink ceremonial shawl. The traffic lights clicked on and off, from red to orange to green and back again. Korean pop music erupted from unseen speakers, breaking what had been a fetid silence. The only thing missing in this town of Odaka, located less than ten miles north of the Fukushima Daiichi Nuclear Plant, was people.

Odaka was evacuated the day after the tsunami of 11 March 2011 set off the worst nuclear crisis since Chernobyl. In those frightening, confusing days, all 12,800 residents were told to leave, just some of the 150,000 people evacuated from the towns around the plant during the triple nuclear meltdown. So haphazard were the arrangements in what is usually one of the world's most ordered societies that many people left without realizing there had been a nuclear accident at all. Some fled with nothing but the clothes they were wearing. They left valuables and medical records, as well as the pets they were forbidden from taking. 'We didn't know there was a hydrogen explosion at the plant, so we couldn't guess why we had to evacuate,' one Odaka resident later told a parliamentary inquiry.[1]

After the massive explosion on the afternoon of 12 March, which blew apart the reactor's steel and concrete building but mercifully left its core intact, the radius of the evacuation zone was doubled to twelve miles. In subsequent days, those just outside the exclusion zone were told to remain indoors for safety. Some must have wondered quite how safe they really were given that American sailors on board the USS *Ronald Reagan* had pulled back 200 miles for fear of radiation.

Odaka had been a ghost town ever since the evacuation. Almost everyone had left, although a few did defy the official order, saying they'd prefer to be radiated than live in some miserable school gymnasium or crowded shelter. Other families sneaked back into town to check on their homes and abandoned pets. For months, packs of mud-splattered dogs were said to have roamed the streets in search of food. When I visited in 2012, a year after the tsunami, the vegetation on the side of the tarmac road was unkempt and weedy. Only when you saw it did you realize just how immaculately tended was the rest of Japan. Inside the display room of an auto-parts shop, wild grasses and bushy plants had pushed up through cracks in the floor. A school baseball field was overgrown and a telephone line sagged under the weight of more than two dozen midnight-black crows that had massed there to caw into the heavy summer air. (Someone from a coastal town further north had told me that, in the days before the earthquake, dozens of crows had mysteriously gathered. When the earthquake struck, but before the tsunami arrived, the crows vanished, never to be seen again.) In some side streets of Odaka, a couple of houses had collapsed from the force of the earthquake, their tile roofs crumpled on the ground like heaps of bones. More than two miles from the ocean, Odaka was spared the full rage of the tsunami. But even here, there were signs of water damage.

The 'dead zone' around the nuclear plant was quietly surreal. Volunteers had planted rows of yellow sunflowers after scientists suggested hopefully that the plants might be able to draw radioactive contaminants from the soil. Just outside a roadside checkpoint, manned by sweating police officers in heavy blue uniforms, sat a lone vending machine, the sort you might see on any street corner in this consumer wonderland. Behind the glass screen were rows of hot drinks in little plastic bottles, cardboard cartons or half-sized cans: Georgia Black Coffee, Georgia Emerald Mountain Blend, Espresso Blux and several types of Hot Green Tea. Below them were cold drinks: Coca Cola, Lohas Natural Mineral Water, Grape Fanta,

Aquarius Sports Drink and Aloe Vera White Grape Juice. The machine was just outside the exclusion zone in supposedly 'safe Japan'. But it sat within feet of 'contaminated Japan', where radiation levels were considered too high for human habitation. Who would buy a drink from a machine in the shadow of Fukushima? For now, it was a moot point. The company had placed a discreet white sign on the glass: 'Sales suspended'.

Iitate, another nearby town, lay well outside the exclusion zone. It had, though, been designated a 'hot spot', an area where radiation had settled in high quantities like an invisible mist. Although it sat twenty-five miles from Fukushima Daiichi, Iitate was one of six places where traces of plutonium had been detected in the soil. Now it was practically deserted, save for the orange-jacketed men who patrolled the empty houses. The world was rightly impressed with the order and discipline of ordinary Japanese in the tsunami's aftermath. There were, as some surprised TV anchors from foreign media noted, no recorded acts of looting. This was not New Orleans. Yet crime was not entirely absent either. Someone living a few miles from Fukushima Daiichi told officials, 'It is such a disappointment every time we are briefly allowed to return home only to find out that we have been robbed again.'[2]

The lights of Iitate's old people's home were still on. When the town was evacuated, authorities judged it would be too traumatic to move the elderly residents. Besides, they would almost certainly die years before the effects of any radiation poisoning showed up. As the young fled Iitate, the elderly were lining up to get in. So scarce are places for retirement homes in Japan there was now a waiting list of a hundred or so people hoping to move to the Iitate facility. Unlike the young or those with families, they were willing to spend their remaining years in the eerie calmness of the dead zone.

In recent months, groups of men wearing futuristic protective cloth-ing and white masks had been scraping off the topsoil from gardens, and blasting the walls with high-pressure water hoses. They were try-ing to clear the area of radiation. In a nearby field, industrial-thickness bags of soil lay neatly stacked, each bearing a little ticket: 4.5 µSv/h, 7.32 µSv/h, 7.67 µSv/h. The runic inscription indicated how many microsieverts of radiation the soil was emitting. The bags were labelled *kari kari kari okiba* – 'temporary, temporary, temporary storage'. These makeshift piles were no permanent fix. Locals doubted much good would come of all this hosing, scraping and bagging. With each new rainfall, radiation levels shot up again as fresh contamination was washed in from the surrounding hills. A woman who worked in the retirement home by day now commuted to work from a town many miles away. Asked if she would one day bring her young children back to live in Iitate, she slowly shook her head.

By my own crude reckoning, radiation levels did seem to have dropped. When I came to this same place, in the summer of 2011, my dosimeter was as if possessed, going off every twenty seconds. 'Beep ... beep ... beep ... beep.' Now, in March 2012, it was practically silent. On that trip the previous summer, I had come across Yosuke Saito, a 34-year-old trucking-company worker, on a deserted street. It had been a shock to see another living person. It was Obon, the festival of the dead, and he had returned to his abandoned home to light incense for his ancestors. In Iitate, only the very old and the ghosts of the dead lingered on.

The triple meltdown at Fukushima Daiichi was the worst nuclear accident in a quarter of a century. Like Chernobyl in 1986 it was rated 'seven', the highest level on the International Atomic Energy Agency scale. Three Mile Island, a partial nuclear meltdown at a plant in Pennsylvania in 1979, was a 'five'. The catastrophe at Fukushima, a sprawling site of six nuclear reactors overlooking the ocean, had an impact all over the world. It shook some governments' faith in the safety, even the viability, of nuclear power. Within weeks of the accident, Angela Merkel, the German chancellor, said her country would phase out all nuclear power within a decade.[3] The Japanese establishment had long ago hitched the country's economic fortunes to the nuclear wagon despite the fact that Japan was the only country to have suffered nuclear destruction. Now, even here, cracks began to emerge in the long-held consensus.

The accident exposed in a flash – quite literally – some of the worst traits of 'old Japan', with its elitist and secretive bureaucratic culture. That culture had served Japan reasonably well in the post-war years when it was driving economic catch-up. But it was deeply flawed.

According to a withering parliamentary inquiry, Fukushima was not a natural disaster at all, but a 'profoundly manmade' catastrophe, the result of 'wilful negligence'. The inquiry, led by Kiyoshi Kurokawa, a medical doctor who had once been president of the Science Council of Japan, found that the regulators, the government and the Fukushima operator had all 'betrayed the nation's right to safety from nuclear accidents'. It was quite a different story from the one told by Tokyo Electric Power Company (Tepco), the private company that ran Fukushima. It had blamed the cascading crisis on a millennial freak of nature, a tsunami of such force it had been impossible to predict or counteract.

The parliamentary commission strongly disagreed. The accident had been foreseeable, its 641-page report concluded. There was plenty of evidence to suggest that tsunamis of the height of 11 March had struck Japan before. Tepco had chosen to ignore it. Its negligence, the inquiry said, was the result of systematic collusion between Tepco and the agencies that were supposed to be regulating it. Both sacrificed safety in their blind enthusiasm for nuclear power and their arrogant faith in Japanese technology. Because they had not planned for disaster, when it struck they were woefully unprepared. Video footage shot inside the plant in the days after the disaster shows scenes of desperate confusion. After two explosions, the site manager begs his superiors for supplies and reinforcements. 'The site is in shock,' he says. 'We're doing what we can but morale is slipping.'[4]

At first, it had seemed that the plant would survive the assault of nature. When the ground started heaving violently at 2.46 p.m. on 11 March, the three reactors in operation did what they were supposed to do. They shut down.[5] Neutron-absorbing control rods sprang from the floor, halting nuclear fission. Power to the plant had been cut off, but there were back-up generators to keep emergency systems running. Yet, when the violent shaking stopped, there was much worse to follow. The complex had been built on the coast between the ocean and the surrounding hills. All that stood between the nuclear plant and the massive tsunami that was now barrelling towards it was a nineteen-foot sea wall. When the full force of the wave arrived some fifty minutes later it was forty-six feet high.

Once the wave had breached the sea defences, water rushed towards the plant, sweeping cars and debris before it. The wave flooded the plant's back-up diesel generators – housed, of all places, in the basement of the turbine buildings between the plant and the ocean – plunging the complex into darkness. The core cooling system quickly stopped. Attempts to get the power back on were haphazard to say the least. Tepco tried to get a generator truck to the site, but when it eventually arrived its plugs did not match the plant's sockets. The biggest nuclear operator in Japan was like an ill-prepared traveller who had forgotten to pack an adaptor. Within a few hours, a back-up condenser that had been keeping things going at reactor Number One failed. Now there was nothing to prevent the uranium fuel rods heating the water to boiling point, producing a build-up of steam and an eventual explosion of radioactive gas. Pressure did indeed build up in the ensuing hours to twice the allowable threshold, forcing Tepco's panicked officials to make an agonizing decision. To prevent a full-fledged explosion and large radiation leak, they would have to engineer a smaller leak themselves, by venting radioactive steam into the atmosphere. Even that wasn't straightforward. The valves had jammed and technicians, armed only with flashlights, spent hours fumbling around in the dark trying to open them by hand.

The venting finally started at 10 a.m. on Saturday, the morning after the tsunami. It was a last-ditch gamble, but it proved inadequate. Hydrogen began seeping into the air creating a combustible gas. At 3.36 p.m. there was an almighty explosion. Millions, including me, watched on television as the building holding the nuclear reactor tore apart, flinging debris into the air. For a while no one knew whether the core had survived the blast. It had, but now two other reactors were in difficulty. By Monday, technicians were venting radioactive steam from all three problem reactors and pumping seawater into the cores to cool them down. That was a desperate measure that meant the reactors could never be used again. Still it wasn't enough. Late on Monday morning, two days after the first explosion, an even bigger blast ripped through reactor Number Three. Problems had now spread to a storage tank containing 'spent' uranium fuel. Spent or not, without circulating water, the rods began to get critically hot. By Tuesday morning a fire had broken out in a storage pool. Meanwhile fuel rods in reactor Number Three had melted, and there was a third explosion, releasing radiation at 10,000 times normal levels.

As the crisis escalated out of control, Tepco pulled out many of the 800 technicians working at the plant. That left just a few dozen essential staff – the so-called 'Fukushima 50' – battling to contain the worst civil nuclear catastrophe in Japan's history. There was later speculation that Tepco's management had discussed abandoning the plant altogether. In those dark hours, the government secretly considered contingency plans to evacuate Tokyo, the world's biggest metropolis.[6] However, Kurokawa's parliamentary inquiry, critical in almost all other respects, found no evidence that Tepco had ever intended to pull out everyone from Fukushima Daiichi.

Whether it had or not, by the following day, 300 operatives were back at their station. They were working in the grimmest of conditions, snatching a few hours of sleep on lead-lined floors and sharing meagre rations of tinned food. At one point, managers apologetically asked workers to lend the plant money so it could dispatch a team to buy water, food and fuel.[7] Normally, workers were not permitted to receive a radiation dose of more than 100 millisieverts in any five-year period. At that level, cancer risks are believed to rise. In a desperate effort to keep the crisis-containment effort on track, the limit was temporarily raised to 250 millisieverts, five times the level permitted for US nuclear industry workers.[8] Management made an announcement over loudspeakers asking workers to 'please understand' they were being exposed to levels of radiation far above normal.[9]

Efforts to bring the situation under control became almost farcical. Military helicopters scooped up water from the sea and dropped it into the hole created by one of the explosions. Most of the water scattered in the wind. Fire engines brought to Fukushima from around the country doused the reactors with their tiny hoses. When radioactive water from the deluge started leaking into the sea, Tepco's highly trained technicians sought to plug the cracks – using newspapers and nappy-like absorbent cloth.[10] As the weeks went by, the plant lurched from one crisis to the next. In April, Tepco dumped 10,000 tonnes of contaminated water from plant storage tanks into the sea to make room for even more highly contaminated water.

Only by December, nine months after the initial explosion, was the plant finally put into 'cold shutdown', a condition of relative security. Even then, there were concerns about the precarious situation of one of the fuel storage pools, which some experts feared could collapse if there were another earthquake. That, they said, could lead to an even bigger escape of radiation than in March. It went without saying that the gutted and seawater-deluged Fukushima plant could never be used again. Decommissioning was expected to take decades and cost billions, even tens of billions, of dollars. In Japanese, Fukushima meant 'Blessed Island'. There was little blessed about it now.

The parliamentary inquiry reserved its harshest criticism for what has come to be known as the 'nuclear village', the network of business, bureaucrats and regulators that runs Japan's nuclear industry. The country started producing nuclear power in the mid-1960s, but the government drastically accelerated the programme after the 1970s oil shocks, which exposed its glaring dependence on foreign energy. Japan's colonial disasters of the 1930s and 40s were, at least in part, inspired by the notion of grabbing its own resources in a Japanese version of Nazi Germany's *Lebensraum*. After the war, Yasuhiro Nakasone, who went on to become prime minister in the mid-1980s, was an early champion of nuclear power. In August 1945, as a young naval officer, he had witnessed from a distance the mushroom cloud over Hiroshima. 'At that moment I sensed that the next age was the nuclear age,' he wrote later.[11] Nuclear power could not only solve Japan's energy problems, it would also allow Japan to study the technological mysteries behind nuclear weapons. The *Asahi* newspaper's Yoichi Funabashi, who became chairman of the Rebuild Japan Initiative Foundation after the tsunami, said, 'One of the most shocking experiences in Japan's post-war history was China's nuclear test of 1964. It was the same year as the Tokyo Olympics and some people tended to interpret this as a deliberate attempt to belittle Japan by demonstrating China's new power.' Funabashi said that some politicians had wanted Japan to go nuclear in response. The next best thing was to preserve some 'ambiguity' by developing the technology behind the nuclear bomb, including the reprocessing of uranium and plutonium.[12]

In the 1970s, the stewards of Japan's nuclear ramp-up embarked on their mission with the zeal that had characterized the nation's post-war recovery. They started by buying British and American reactors, but rapidly set about transferring know-how to Japan itself. Sites were chosen for nuclear plants, mostly in poorer, less populated regions, such as Japan's northeast coast, where lavish government subsidies were hard to resist. By the time the March 2011 tsunami crippled the Fukushima plant, no less than 30 per cent of Japan's electricity was being produced by nuclear power. There were even plans to build fourteen more reactors and raise nuclear power's contribution to a full half of the national electricity supply by 2030.

Once nuclear power became a national imperative, it was almost an article of faith that it be safe. How else to justify building fifty-four nuclear reactors, roughly one in ten of the world's total, in the most seismically unstable country on earth? That imperative bred a culture of denial, arrogance and cover-up that was breathtaking. The Nuclear and Industrial Safety Agency, the body that was supposed to be regulating the operators, was part of the trade ministry, Japan's most ardent cheerleader for nuclear technology. It was like putting the National Rifle Association in charge of gun control. Academics were funded by the nuclear industry, as was the media via expensive advertising campaigns. Parliament insisted that school textbooks downplayed any reference to nuclear accidents, such as Chernobyl. Many plants built public relations buildings-cum-amusement parks, bearing logos such as smiling uranium atoms. In one Atomic Disneyland, visited by Norimitsu Onishi of the *New York Times*, Lewis Carroll's Alice was drafted in to make the case for nuclear safety. 'It's terrible, just terrible,' said the White Rabbit in one exhibit. 'We're running out of energy, Alice.' When a robotic Dodo explained there was a clean, safe and renewable alternative called nuclear power, Alice was delighted. 'You could say that it's optimal for resource-poor Japan,' she cooed, presumably before disappearing down a rabbit hole.[13]

The nuclear industry also had deeply suspect labour policies, making it a microcosm of the two-tiered labour market that had taken hold since the bubble burst. Much of the dangerous work was done by contract workers, paid less and exposed to higher levels of radiation than regular employees. In the case of Fukushima Daiichi, nearly 90 per cent of workers in the year to March 2010 were employed by contractors, subcontractors and sub-subcontractors. The 'nuclear gypsies', who roamed from plant to plant, were brought in to clean up radiation during regular maintenance shutdowns. Often they used nothing more sophisticated than mops and rags. They were drawn from the ranks of underemployed construction workers, local farmers, itinerant labourers and homeless people, some of them hired by *yakuza* gangsters.[14] Even after the meltdown, Tepco continued to employ hundreds of contract workers. Day labourers were lured back with offers of up to $1,000 day. Two subcontracted workers were hospitalized after stepping in radioactive water. Many others were exposed to far higher doses of radiation than normally permissible. Katsunobu Onda, author of *Tepco: The Dark Empire*, claimed that over the years, tens of thousands of contract workers had received unsafe levels of radiation.[15]

So pervasive was the 'safety myth' that many nuclear plant operators never broached the subject of evacuation with local residents living in the shadow of power stations. To do so would have meant admitting the possibility of an accident. Journalists who wrote about radiation leaks were ridiculed for not understanding the science. After an earthquake in Niigata in 2006, a giant plume of black smoke rose out of the Kashiwazaki nuclear complex. (Firemen couldn't put out the blaze because – surprise, surprise – water pipes had been ruptured by the earthquake.) But journalists were told not to be alarmist. People living around the plant would apparently be exposed to one-millionth of the radiation experienced during a round-trip flight from Tokyo to New York. Like the owners of the *Titanic* who did not install sufficient lifeboats because they believed the ship could never sink, the operators of Fukushima did not have enough buses on hand to evacuate staff at the time of the tsunami. Regulators, concluded Kurokawa's inquiry, had been 'captured'. Far from pushing operators to improve safety, they helped them skirt the rules.

Evidence that nuclear regulation was a sham had been hidden in plain sight for years. A series of accidents and cover-ups demonstrated clearly that the industry habitually took short cuts and then lied about it. In 1995, there was a cover-up over the extent of an accident in the Monju fast-breeder reactor. Four years later, two poorly trained workers at the Tokaimura reactor died of organ failure due to acute radiation sickness after mixing uranium in buckets. In 2002, Tepco admitted that it had been faking safety data relating to cracks in its nuclear plants for two decades. The subsequent regulatory 'crack-down', rather than punishing Tepco, seemed more intent on helping it extend the use of ageing plants. At the time of the accident, Fukush-ima had been running for forty years. One investigative reporter described the ageing and worn-out network of pipes inside the plant as being like 'the veins of a monster' waiting to burst.[16] In 2004, four workers were killed and seven injured at a plant in Mihama when superheated steam gushed out of a broken pipe. In July 2007, an earthquake measuring 6.8 on the Richter scale jolted the enormous Kashiwazaki-Kariwa nuclear complex, the biggest in the world. It was later revealed that the plant had not been built to withstand any-thing like that magnitude of quake. To make matters worse, it may have inadvertently been built directly on top of an active faultline.

It should have come as little surprise, then, that the response to the emergency at Fukushima also lacked transparency. Tepco consistently denied there had been a meltdown and industry sympathizers blamed the foreign media for reckless scaremongering when they used the 'M' word. But there *had* been a meltdown. Tepco later admitted that fuel rods in three reactors had melted into little clumps of uranium, a meltdown even under the narrowest of definitions. Tapes reveal offi-cials had been fully aware of the possibility just days into the disaster. An announcement over loudspeakers stated, 'The fuel has been exposed for some time now, so there is a possibility of a meltdown. Repeat, there is a possibility of a fuel meltdown.'[17] Tepco also prevari-cated about injecting seawater into the reactors, possibly because to do so would mean scrapping billions of dollars of equipment for good. Masao Yoshida, the plant operator, bravely took matters into his own hands by injecting seawater anyway. Not everyone was so decisive. In the days after the accident, Masataka Shimizu, Tepco's president, disappeared for days. He was hiding in his office while the catastrophe unfolded.

The most interesting part of the voluminous parliamentary report came on its first page. In his 'Message from the Chairman', Kurokawa blamed the disaster not on particular individuals – although the report made clear some people had been terribly at fault – but rather on Japan's entire culture. 'This was a disaster "Made in Japan",' he said. 'Its fundamental causes are to be found in the ingrained conventions of Japanese culture: our reflexive obedience; our reluctance to question authority; our devotion to "sticking with the programme"; our groupism and our insularity.'

Kurokawa's list of supposed 'cultural faults' was a sort of anti-*Nihonjinron*, the study of 'Japanese essence' whose treatises still have dedicated sections in some bookstores. While most *Nihonjinron* authors made a fetish of what they claimed were the country's uniquely superior traits – the elevation of the group above the individual, of feeling above logic and of tacit understanding above spoken words – Kurokawa turned the discipline on its head. The national characteristics of which the Japanese were so proud, he suggested, were in fact fatal flaws. 'Had other Japanese been in the shoes of those who bear responsibility for this accident, the result may well have been the same,' he concluded. That was because the 'mindset' that supported the catastrophic decisions around Fukushima 'can be found across Japan'.

Kurokawa's sweeping cultural pronouncement invited obvious rejoinders. One was that, by blaming society as a whole, he had cleverly let individuals off the hook. If one were minded, one could even draw parallels with the collective assessment of Japan's wartime responsibility: everybody was guilty, and no one was guilty. Gerry Curtis, an expert on Japan at Columbia University, was one of many to take exception to Kurokawa's conclusions. 'One searches in vain through these pages for anyone to blame,' he wrote in a stinging editorial.[18] 'To pin the blame on culture is the ultimate cop-out.' Individuals matter, Curtis said. Tepco's president had made the situation worse by being hopelessly uncommunicative. Yoshida, the heroic plant manager who had defied orders by flooding the reactors with seawater, possibly saved the day. He was anything but a yes-man blindly following orders in the interests of groupism or 'sticking with the programme'. The culture of collusion inside the 'nuclear village' was hardly unique to Japan, Curtis continued. Hadn't there been pretty much the same collusion in the US between bankers and their regulators, who turned a blind eye as some of the country's biggest financial institutions led the nation towards the brink of financial ruin? If Japanese culture put the interests of the organization above the interests of the public, Curtis concluded, 'then we are all Japanese'.

If one takes the view that culture is immutable, Kurokawa's cultural explanations were, indeed, next to useless. To view culture as fixed and unchangeable borders on geographical and racial determinism. But Kurokawa may have been trying to say something quite different. Few who have lived in Japan would deny they recognize some of the national traits he identified – a tendency to look inwards, to defer to authority, to play down the importance of the individual. No serious observer of Japan, however, would pretend this was the whole story. In a thousand ways, Japanese people, individually and collectively, are constantly challenging and subverting such norms. The characteristics Kurokawa outlined, then, were not so much a description of 'culture'. They were a critique of Japan's post-war institutions and norms. If that is what he meant by culture, the implication was that it could be changed.

Kurokawa said the same organizational features that helped Japan engineer its post-war miracle had become the worst traits of the 'nuclear village'. Elite bureaucratic planning, corralling state funds into favoured projects and limited consultation with the electorate had all been elements of post-war success. But they contained the seeds of catastrophe. The guardians of the country's nuclear industry felt as though they were on a national mission to ramp up nuclear power at any cost. That made them 'an unstoppable force, immune to scrutiny by civil society', Kurokawa wrote. Such accepted norms could and should be questioned, he implied. That was the very opposite of cultural determinism. 'We should reflect on our responsibility as individuals in a democratic society,' he said of the collective failure at Fukushima. That meant strengthening what he called 'civil society'. Viewed in this light, Kurokawa's remarks were not a case of letting people off the hook. They were a call to individual and collective action.

Before the tsunami, Japan had been one of the most nuclear-dependent economies on earth. After the tsunami, everything was different. By May 2012, fourteen months after the triple meltdown, not a single nuclear plant was left operating. For a few months, until one plant at Oi in western Japan juddered back to life, the country was entirely nuclear-free for the first time in half a century. The first thing to note about this dramatic shift in energy policy is this: the lights stayed on. Japan did not shut up shop. From the first months after the tsunami knocked out substantial amounts of nuclear power, Japan learned to live with less electricity. Car manufacturers staggered production across a seven-day week so they did not all suck power from the grid at the same time. Toyota made cars from Wednesday to Sunday. In the cities, offices set air-conditioner thermostats at higher temperatures. Buildings closed earlier, depriving salarymen of hours of late-night overtime. In the summer of 2011, even press conferences at Tepco, one of the world's largest power generators, took place with the lights off and the windows open to let in the breeze. Whenever a bullet train thundered along the nearby elevated track, the sound drowned out much of what was being said.[19] By that stage, few people were listening to Tepco anyway.

For many Japanese, saving energy became fashionable. There was widespread questioning of the nation's previous addiction to its super-electrified existence. Tokyo's ranks of brightly lit vending machines were dimmed, by order of the governor, to a modest glow. Even the emperor and empress, according to palace spokesmen, were doing their bit by using candlelight at night.[20] Conservation had an immediate impact. In the summer of 2011, even with temperatures rising past ninety degrees, peak electricity usage fell by almost a quarter from the previous summer. Some thought the costs to Japan were too high. 'Everywhere living standards have degraded,' complained Yukio Okamoto, a former career diplomat, sweat pouring down his face in his stuffy office. Just as the terrorist attacks of 9/11 had marked a turning point in US history, he said, so Japan would never be the same after 3/11. 'The shortage of electricity will become a trait of civil and industrial society.'[21] Okamoto wasn't just talking about personal discomfort. Like many, he feared that unstable electricity supply and higher prices could be the final straw for Japanese industry.[22] Companies were, he said, already battling against a disastrously strong yen, high corporate taxes, unrealistic carbon emissions targets and inflexible labour laws. Japanese manufacturers were being destroyed by Korean rivals that benefited from a cheap currency and tariff-free access to foreign markets thanks to free trade agreements that protectionist Japan had been unable to sign. If you added higher electricity prices to the mix, he wondered how on earth Japanese manufacturers would survive at all.

There were other costs. Conserving energy could achieve only so much. To compensate for the loss of nuclear power, Japan had to import more oil and liquefied natural gas. That pushed up $CO_2$ emissions. The swelling energy bill also zapped Japan's trade surplus, pushing the country into deficit for the first time in three decades.[23] Although Japan still had a current account surplus, thanks to financial returns on its huge investments abroad, many worried that a permanently higher energy bill could endanger even that. If the country were to move sharply into deficit, economists questioned its ability to maintain its astronomical public debt. Yoshito Sengoku, a senior politician, had no doubt about what it would mean for Japan. He compared abandoning nuclear power to 'group suicide'.[24]

Many industrialists agreed. They said replacing nuclear power with renewable energy was a fantasy. 'Can we close down nuclear power? My answer is no,' said Minoru Makihara, former chairman of Mitsubishi Corporation. 'Somewhere in the mix, nuclear power has to come into play.'[25] Nobuyuki Idei, who once ran Sony, was of similar mind. 'Nuclear power is one of the most important technologies for the future,' he said. 'We shouldn't give it up.'[26] Even Kazuo Inamori, legendary founder of a company that pioneered the Japanese manufacture of solar panels, thought alternative energy was too unstable. Until ways were found of storing vast amounts of energy collected when the sun was shining or the wind was blowing, he said, Japan would be foolish to ditch nuclear power.[27]

Advocates argued that nuclear power was not only cleaner and more stable, it was also cheaper. Before the tsunami, nuclear power was said to cost Y5–7 a kilowatt hour against Y11 for wind power, Y12–20 for geothermal and Y47 for solar. After the tsunami, critics of nuclear power took a harder look at the numbers. The supposed cost of nuclear generation, they said, didn't take into account the hidden costs, such as the subsidies – little more than bribes – paid to local communities where nuclear plants were built, or the cost of disposing of spent fuel. Even leaving aside the billions of dollars that would be needed to clean up after Fukushima, Kenichi Oshima, an energy specialist at Ritsumeikan University, calculated that nuclear energy actually cost Y12.23/kWh. That made it more expensive than either thermal power or hydropower.[28] No less a figure than Jeff Immelt, chief executive of General Electric, one of the pioneers of civil nuclear power and the company that helped build the Fukushima Daiichi plant, argued that the economics of nuclear power were crumbling. Discovery of huge amounts of shale gas in the US and elsewhere had turned energy costs upside down, making electricity produced from gas-fired power stations much cheaper. That was happening just as, in the aftermath of Fukushima, demands for higher safety standards would inevitably raise the cost of nuclear power. 'They're finding more gas all the time. It's just hard to justify nuclear,' Immelt said. 'Gas is so cheap and at some point, really, economics rule.' In the future, he said, 'some combination of gas, and either wind or solar . . . that's where most countries around the world are going'.[29]

Taro Kono, one of the few Liberal Democrat MPs who had been a long-time opponent of nuclear power, argued the 'nuclear village' deliberately stunted the development of renewable energy. In 2000, he said, supporters of nuclear power stymied a bill to introduce a 'feed-in tariff' that would have guaranteed a competitive price to alternative-energy producers. It took the Fukushima disaster to persuade the government to set a generous feed-in tariff, obliging electricity companies to buy unlimited quantities of renewable energy from independent generators.[30]

About 8–9 per cent of Japan's electricity comes from renewable sources, most of it from hydro, with only about 1 per cent from wind and solar. That compares with about 25 per cent in Germany, which has incentivized renewable energy much more aggressively. In theory, a feed-in tariff could change Japan's incentives too, though advocates of renewable power said the new law was too narrow in scope. Kono, speaking from his dimly lit, energy-saving office, said Japan had the world's third-highest geothermal potential and its sixth-largest tract of ocean, a boon for offshore wind power. Once a pioneer in solar power, he fumed, Japan had almost deliberately thrown away its lead.

Masayoshi Son, the founder of telecommunications company Soft-bank and one of Japan's boldest entrepreneurs, quickly threw his weight behind renewable energy. His company said it would build at least ten large-scale solar-power plants to form an 'Eastern Japan Solar Belt'. Son reckoned that, if he could persuade regulators to make a fifth of unused farmland available for solar-power stations, he could generate as much power as Tepco itself.[31] 'We are going to spread natural energy throughout Japan,' he told an audience at the launch in Kyoto of his first solar project, which duly opened in July 2012.[32] Son hoped he could galvanize others to act. Even Lawson, a convenience store operator with no experience of electricity generation, said it would install solar power in 2,000 of its outlets. It would sell spare capacity to the grid.[33] The new mood was captured by Hiroshi Mikitani, the internet entrepreneur, who registered his anti-nuclear credentials by resigning from Keidanren, the powerful business lobby. Explaining his decision to quit – his resignation was sent out on Twitter, no less – Mikitani said Keidanren was blindly pro-nuclear. His own company Rakuten, an online shopping mall, had been able to cut electricity usage by 35 per cent through simple measures, he said. He was sceptical about the dire warnings that the country could not survive without nuclear energy.[34]

Most strikingly, popular opinion turned sharply against nuclear power. Opinion polls, though erratic, showed that at least half of people were in favour of the eventual elimination of nuclear power altogether, with just a quarter saying it should remain.[35] Anti-nuclear sentiment was slow-burning. In the first months after the Fukushima disaster, it was noticeable that protests halfway round the world in Germany had been much bigger than those in Japan. But as time went on, the numbers of anti-nuclear protesters began to swell. By the summer of 2012, regular demonstrations outside the prime minister's office attracted tens of thousands of people.[36] In July, Kenzaburo Oe, a Nobel laureate who had written about the after-effects of the nuclear bomb in his essay *Hiroshima Notes*, gave an anti-nuclear address. The crowd in Yoyogi Park was the biggest since mass protests in 1960 against the renewal of the US–Japan Security Treaty. Organizers claimed 170,000 people came to the 'Sayonara Nukes' protest and even police conceded that 75,000 people had attended.[37] NHK, the official broadcaster, still ready to ply the official line, barely covered an event within walking distance of its headquarters.[38]

Crowds were motivated by fear of radiation as well as by outrage at the arrogance and incompetence behind the disaster. Anger had also been stoked by a cynical display that showed the 'nuclear village' had lost none of its deceitfulness. In an effort to restart a nuclear plant in Kyushu, the local operator had sought to rig 'town-hall meetings' by flooding them with pro-nuclear messages from seemingly ordinary members of the public. When the subterfuge was discovered, the public outcry ensured the plant remained shut down indefinitely. Although some communities around nuclear plants had become addicted to subsidies, local sentiment swung against the industry. That was especially true in towns and villages that were near a plant, but too far away to benefit from state transfers. Local politicians began to tap into the anti-nuclear sentiment, making it harder for the central government to orchestrate the firing up of idle plants. 'I'm not buying this claim that we have to have nuclear power because there's not enough electricity,' said Toru Hashimoto, the populist Osaka mayor. 'There's generally more than enough.'[39]

Naoto Kan, the prime minister who had contemplated evacuating 30 million people from Tokyo – an act that would have 'come to within one inch of the end of this nation' – led the anti-nuclear charge.[40] As 2011 wore on, sensing the end of his own premiership, he decided to take the nuclear industry down with him. He launched a wholesale review of national energy policy that opened the possibility of abandoning nuclear power altogether. It was clear where Kan stood. 'Our nation should aim to become a society that can manage without nuclear power,' he said. Kan ordered a series of 'stress tests' designed to ascertain whether nuclear reactors could survive extreme situations. Tepco was nationalized. Plans were set in motion to abolish the Nuclear and Industrial Safety Agency, the regulator that had been found so badly wanting. The new regulator would be prised away from the pro-nuclear trade ministry, and housed instead in the ministry of environment. There was talk of ending the power industry's stranglehold on generation and transmission, a monopolistic set-up that had allowed it to charge some of the steepest electricity prices in the world. Kan's anti-nuclear fervour outlasted him. In September 2012, against the opposition of industry, the government adopted the formal policy of phasing out all nuclear power by 2040.

*

Driving much of the debate was fear of radiation. The Japanese, victims of two nuclear bombs, harboured a special loathing for its
invisible dread. The Godzilla films, which started in the 1950s, were a
depiction of the monstrous power let loose by nuclear explosions.
After the crisis at Fukushima, which hurled radiation into the atmosphere and pumped it into the oceans, the public quickly learned a
whole new radioactive nomenclature of millisieverts, Becquerels and
caesium. Bottled water disappeared virtually overnight from super-
markets after the government announced that levels of iodine-131, a
radioisotope, in Tokyo's water supply was double the recommended
limit for infants. In April, small fish, called sand lance, caught in
waters south of Fukushima, were discovered to contain 526 Becquerels of caesium per kilogramme, above the legal limit of 500. In
subsequent months many varieties of fish, vegetables and rice were
found with higher than normal levels of radiation. Cows from ranches
around Japan had been fed with rice straw from contaminated areas,
leading to a panic about beef. Even two minke whales caught off the
coast of Hokkaido showed traces of radioactive caesium, though fish-
eries officials pronounced them safe to eat.[41] The government warned
parents not to feed milk from contaminated areas to young infants.
When, fifteen months later, a seventy-foot dock from Japan washed
up in Oregon it too was tested for radiation. It was part of more than
1 million tonnes of debris expected to float to America's Pacific coast.

About eighteen months after the accident, scientists from the
Ryukyus University in Okinawa discovered that butterflies around
Fukushima had become mutated with dented eyes and stunted wings.
Another study, however, released at around the same time showed
that the levels of radiation in humans living around Fukushima were
extremely low.[42] Inundated with such contradictory information, people had little idea about what was safe and what was not, or what
reasonable precautions they should take. Some meticulously avoided
buying fish, vegetables or meat from anywhere near Fukushima.
Others took precisely the opposite approach, purchasing only from
those areas as a show of solidarity with struggling farmers.

In trying to gauge the possible long-term health effects of Fukushima the only real comparison was with Chernobyl. Since the
accident at the Ukrainian plant a quarter of a century ago, some

6,000 cases of thyroid cancer, almost exclusively in children under sixteen, had been discovered. So far, only around twenty cases are thought to have been fatal. A study by researchers from Stanford University concluded that additional cases of cancer as a result of the Fukushima accident could be as low as fifteen or as high as 1,300. Its best guess was 130 deaths.[43] Some scientists, however, argued that, far from seeking to cover up the real dangers of radiation, Japanese authorities actually over-reacted, exacerbating the situation by sowing panic. Robert Gale, a haematologist and a veteran of Chernobyl, went so far as to suggest that, given what he insisted were relatively low levels of contamination from Fukushima, the fear of radiation might be worse than the radiation itself.[44] As many as 600 deaths of elderly patients, for example, were designated as 'disaster related', a consequence of hurried evacuation from the Fukushima area.[45] Shunichi Yamashita of the Fukushima Medical University also suggested low-level exposure to radiation posed little health risk. He became a hate figure. Internet commentators compared Yamashita to the Auschwitz doctor Josef Mengele. In truth, Yamashita, whose own mother had survived the atomic bomb dropped on Nagasaki, was taking a brave stand by sticking to what the data were telling him.[46]

There was also great anger at revelations that some evacuees may have actually been sent into high-radiation zones because the government had not revealed information about changing wind patterns. Officials were slow to release information about 'hot spot' areas such as Iitate, which was not evacuated for more than two months after the triple meltdown at Fukushima. Some hot spots were discovered as far away as Tokyo, on the edge of school baseball fields or in piles of composted leaves. Polls in the months after the accident showed that up to four-fifths of Japanese mistrusted the information on radiation that the government was providing. A common accusation was that the authorities were seeking to play down contamination risks because of the massive compensation payments that might ensue. News programmes took to broadcasting live radiation maps like weather reports.

Public anger at the lack of credible information occasionally bubbled over, challenging the common notion that the Japanese were passive and apolitical. If they felt wronged, they could also be obstinate and pugnacious. A few months after the disaster, a group of protesters travelled from Fukushima to Tokyo, where they rallied outside the ministry of education and technology. Their anger had been roused by fear for their children. The local authority had decided, arbitrarily in the protesters' view, to raise the radiation limit at which schools in Fukushima were considered safe to open. After the noisy demonstration in which parents held up placards and shouted slogans, the ministry backed down, reversing radiation limits to their previously lower levels.[47]

When one reporter working for a foreign newspaper went to Fukushima to report on radiation levels in schools, she was handed a letter by Tomoko Hatsuzawa, a mother of two. Addressed to 'people in the United States and around the world,' it started:

> I am so sorry for the uranium and plutonium that Japan has released into the environment. The fallout from Fukushima has already circled the world many times, reaching Hawaii, Alaska, and even New York. We live 60 kilometers from the plant and our homes have been contaminated beyond levels seen at Chernobyl. The cesium-137 they are finding in the soil will be here for 30 years. But the government will not help us. They tell us to stay put. They tell our kids to put on masks and hats and keep going to school.
>
> This summer, our children won't be able to go swimming. They won't be able to play outside. They can't eat Fukushima's delicious peaches. They can't even eat the rice that the Fukushima farmers are making. They can't go visit Fukushima's beautiful rivers, mountains and lakes. This makes me sad. This fills me with so much regret.[48]

The letter, with its mixture of lyrical regret and protest, concluded by asking foreigners to put pressure on the Japanese government to take action.

Not that Fukushima's residents couldn't put pressure on by themselves. In one town hall meeting, the audience harangued government officials sent from Tokyo. 'Answer the question. Don't we have rights?' they shouted from the floor as the bureaucrats mouthed platitudes.

When the harried officials eventually concluded the meeting and made for the exit, they were chased down the corridor by townspeople waving bottles of their children's urine, which they demanded be tested for radiation. The meeting ended in disarray with the mandarins surrounded – one suspects for the first and only time in their careers – by protesters chanting, 'I implore you take this urine.'[49]

# 15
## Citizens

The government was not trusted to do the right thing about radiation. But then it was no longer really trusted full stop. The performance of Japan's leaders after the tsunami only soured the public further on a political system in which it had already lost faith. It reinforced the idea, which had been bubbling under the surface for some time, that Japanese people were more competent and reliable than their leaders and that the answers to many of the country's problems might best be solved outside the political sphere.

Indeed, there had been little belief in the nation's leaders for most of the period since the bubble burst in 1990. Since then, the ruling party had mostly persevered with its well-honed brand of money politics absent one key ingredient: money. With fast growth a thing of the past, patronage politics was not as easy as it had once been. Trust in bureaucrats, once regarded as the almost infallible guardians of the economic miracle, had also been badly shaken. Too many had shown themselves to be both dishonest and incompetent, an unappealing combination with which people were rapidly losing patience. There had been a brief resurgence of enthusiasm for government, among some at least, during the five-and-a-half years that Junichiro Koizumi was running the show with his rare brand of aplomb and conviction politics. His supporters felt that he had reinvigorated the country, bringing both political and economic momentum and the promise of radical change. But apart from that interlude – exciting for some, destructive for others – most politicians had come and gone almost unnoticed.

In 2009, however, something radically new had happened. Or at least that's how it had seemed. After half a century of the Liberal

Democrats, the centre-left Democratic Party of Japan, a relatively young political grouping led by Yukio Hatoyama, was elected into office. A harbinger of change had come in a mayoral election that summer in Chiba, a rather unprepossessing suburb of Tokyo, when an opposition candidate won on a deliberately gauche ticket of 'young, inexperienced in politics, and without money'. In the subsequent general election of August 2009, the Democratic Party benefited from the public's evident cynicism with politics-as-usual by romping home to victory. True, the vote had been more about kicking out the old Liberal Democratic Party, which had sleepwalked through power ever since Koizumi had left office. There wasn't necessarily much faith that a new set of politicians could do any better. After all, some of the Democratic Party's leading members were defectors from the ruling party. Like the party that had governed for so long, the Democratic Party contained a hodgepodge of social conservatives and liberals, fiscal hawks and free-spenders, free-marketeers and socialists, nationalists and internationalists.

There was, therefore, not a great deal of public excitement at what, on the face of it, looked like a dramatic political shift. On the night of the election, one foreign television crew was dispatched to the streets of Tokyo to film the celebrations that must surely accompany the end of a half-century of political hegemony. They came back empty-handed: no crowds massed outside the party headquarters, no car horns blared, no fountain was splashed in. Noriko Hama of Doshisha University said the electorate had voted, not out of wide-eyed innocence, but more in the spirit of a calculated gamble. Another friend, remembering the genuine excitement that had led to the election of Barack Obama as US president in 2008, said the Japanese people had opted for 'change they don't believe in and a leader they are not all that crazy about'.

Still, on the surface, the Democratic Party did hold out the promise of something new. It had long modelled itself on Britain's New Labour and had several years before started issuing detailed manifestoes outlining its political creed, a departure in a country where voting had traditionally tended to be more about personal connections than policy preferences. Hatoyama, known as the 'alien' for his slightly otherworldly demeanour, almost looked surprised to be leading the country. Such was his lack of triumphalism that, if you had watched his election night victory speech with the sound on mute, you might have thought he had lost. Yet his government had an ambitious agenda. Hatoyama said he wanted to bring policymaking into the public sphere as Koizumi had sought to do, by taming the faceless bureaucrats who had pulled the levers from behind the scenes for so long. His party would rid Japan of the sleazy money-politics that had dominated for decades, initiating instead an era of competent, technocratic rule. It would promote family-friendly policies, and he promised to double child allowance to Y26,000 a month, around $300 at the time, to help boost household spending and reverse the declining birth rate. It would tilt the balance in favour of the consumer and away from big business, particularly the mammoth exporters around which the economy had revolved for decades. It would seek to mend ties with Asian neighbours and develop a foreign policy that went beyond being America's poodle in the Pacific.

Some political analysts thought that, even if the new government faltered, its victory could perhaps be the start of a healthier two-party system. As in western democracies, the hope was that the electorate would get to choose between competing ideologies. No longer would there be a single party whose rival factions hammered out policy and divvied up the jobs behind closed doors. Rather, there would be two parties that set out clearly defined, alternative visions, allowing voters to choose between, say, a Japan with higher taxes and more social welfare, or one with a leaner state and more room for the free market. It is too early to tell whether the 2009 election marked the beginning of such a two-party system. Both main parties remained ideologically ill defined. Gerald Curtis of Columbia University considered Japan was ill suited to a US type of politics where people tended to pin their allegiance to a political colour. 'Japanese society isn't divided. There aren't fundamental differences or deep cleavages like race or religion,' he said. 'In a sense the difference is, "Do you want to buy a Nissan or a Toyota?"'[1] It was hard to sustain a politics of strong ideological conviction in such an environment.

We can, though, already make a judgement about the Democratic Party's three ensuing years in office. They were a missed opportunity. The public had voted for a new style of politics. What it got was more revolving-door prime ministers and half-implemented policies. (The Democrats, for example, had to water down their child allowance pledge when the economy contracted sharply after the Lehman shock.) As we saw, Hatoyama lasted barely nine months, brought down largely because of his failure to make good his promise on Okinawan bases. His successor, Naoto Kan, a former patent lawyer, fared no better. It was his misfortune to have been in office on 11 March when the earthquake and tsunami struck, although his government was already on the ropes by then. Kan's administration initially won some praise for quickly dispatching 100,000 Self Defence Forces to help the rescue operation, but as the Fukushima nuclear disaster unfolded, trust in his administration evaporated as rapidly as water from the pools containing spent nuclear rods. Kan was blamed for poor communication and, perhaps unfairly given the incompetence of Tepco, for mishandling relations between the cabinet and the plant operator. Later there were complaints that the government was too slow to build temporary housing, though it had managed to put up 27,200 units within ten weeks of the disaster.[2] More broadly, the public couldn't understand government infighting at a time of national emergency. In June 2011, when 100,000 people were still stranded at evacuation centres and before the critical situation at Fukushima had been brought properly under control, parliamentarians occupied themselves with preparing a vote of no confidence against Kan. The inability of the political class to rally during a national crisis was symbolized just a few days after the tsunami when Sadakazu Tanigaki, the opposition leader, rejected an offer to join an emergency cabinet as deputy prime minister.[3]

Sometimes politicians seemed to occupy a different planet. Nine days into his job as reconstruction minister – a post that was meant to coordinate rebuilding efforts – Ryu Matsumoto resigned after being caught on video berating a governor of one of the devastated prefectures. The governor's 'crime' was to have turned up for a meeting a few minutes late. Matsumoto jabbed his finger at the poor man, thousands of whose citizens had been swept away by the tsunami, telling him such a breach of etiquette was unacceptable. His supreme insensitivity summed up for many all that was wrong with a ruling elite that had lost touch with reality. Six months after waves crashed into the northeast coast, Kan's government too had crumpled.

The Democratic Party's third and final prime minister was Yoshi-hiko Noda, a man who hardly inspired the highest expectations by likening his role as leader of Japan to that of a bus driver. To be fair, Noda did get a few things done. His government passed supplemen-tary budgets, bringing to more than $200 billion the amount set aside to rebuild Tohoku. It also began tentative talks, very controversial among protectionist lobby groups at home, on joining the Trans Pacific Partnership, a high-level free trade agreement of which the US is a prospective member. Just as potentially far-reaching was the pas-sage of legislation to double sales tax by 2015 in what some saw as the first serious attempt to tackle the debt problem in years. In his typically earthy language, Noda had warned that European-style defaults of the type seen in Greece were 'not a fire on the other side of the river'. Still, raising taxes was hardly a vote-winner. Even some economists thought it was premature, more likely to tip the economy into yet another recession than to repair the nation's financial health. Passage of the bill was secured by a promise to hold an early general election, which went ahead at the end of 2012. The Democratic Party duly lost, handing back power to the Liberal Democrats after only three years in the wilderness. Noda's bus had careered over the precipice.

It was not only the Democratic Party that had disappointed. A deeper dissatisfaction had set in with the political class in general. The national response to the tsunami seemed to crystallize an idea that had been forming for decades. 'Each individual Japanese showed extraordinary strength, but as a collective unit I think we've been in a mess,' Toshiaki Miura, the commentator at the *Asahi* newspaper, told me. A country we often think of as strong collectively but weak indi-vidually had shown itself to be the exact reverse, he said. Japan, it turned out, was a nation of strong individuals and a weak state. I thought of what my friend Shijuro Ogata had often told me. 'Japan is a country of good soldiers but poor commanders.' Sawako Shirahase, a sociologist at Tokyo University, had arrived at a similar conclusion.

'It's very strange,' she said of the carousel of forgettable prime ministers. 'Japanese society used to be characterized as very top down. But we have learned that we can survive without a leader.'

There were multiple ways in which Japanese people were learning how to 'live without a leader' or, to put it another way, to organize themselves. You could call it the slow, but steady, formation of a civil society in a country whose people had a reputation, not entirely undeserved, for being passive and too respectful of hierarchy. It was also recognition of real changes. Japan Inc no longer looked after people as it once had. More Japanese were in casual work with no lifetime job prospects. More were living on the margins of a society that had regarded itself as uniquely egalitarian among advanced nations. Hama said that even the language had changed. She pointed to Hatoyama's inauguration speech back in 2009 when he had referred to the electorate as *shimin*, or 'citizens', in the style of the French Revolution, not the word that was usually used – *kokumin*, in her translation, 'people who belong to their country', or *shain*, 'people who belong to the company'. Citizens belonged to no one. Civil society was, she said, slowly 'emerging from the ranks of subjects and salarymen'.

In many walks of life, there were signs of people taking matters a little more into their own hands. One was the volunteer sector. Progress since the Kobe earthquake of 1995 – the so-called 'Year One of the Volunteer Age' – was palpable. In January 1995, more than a million volunteers had rushed spontaneously to the stricken city to help. The upsurge in popular support took the country by surprise. Volunteers were widely praised for their show of civic responsibility and most were warmly welcomed in Kobe itself. Many of them, though, were not properly organized. A few who arrived at the earthquake zone without food or any idea of where they might sleep were characterized as *meiwaku borantia*, 'nuisance volunteers'.[4] Kobe marked the stirrings of a new spirit of social solidarity and collective action, but for the most part it was amateurish. By the time of Japan's next huge disaster in 2011 it was very different. On the eve of the tsunami, there were at least 40,000[5] registered non-profit organizations in the country. The sector was more professional, better financed and better coordinated. Some of the volunteer organizations had financial backing from big business through widespread 'corporate responsibility' programmes. When disaster struck, volunteers were rapidly dispatched to the stricken coast to distribute food, medical care and counselling. Private businesses sent thousands of their own employees, both as humanitarian volunteers and as logistical help to get factories up and running again. Manufacturing supply chains were restored, sometimes at almost miraculous speed, over the ensuing weeks and months.

The government made efforts to coordinate these groups, within days of the disaster appointing a well-known former activist, Kiyomi Tsujimoto, co-founder of the Peace Boat group, as prime ministerial aide in charge of disaster volunteering. Her appointment won praise, though in practice her role wasn't always clear. In the worst affected parts of the country, it was common to hear the government bureaucracy roundly lambasted while volunteers were praised. Typical was the comment of Shigemitsu Hatakeyama, an oyster fisherman nearly drowned by the tsunami in the town of Kesennuma in Miyagi prefecture. 'Since the earthquake, I haven't got a single thing from the government,' he told me contemptuously. 'It was the volunteers who gave us food.' It was volunteers, too, he said, who had provided him with concrete advice about how to restart his devastated oyster business. He planned to build tourist accommodation and to set up a little restaurant where visitors could enjoy his Miyagi oysters fresh out of the sea. Others talked of the friends they had made among volunteers who had streamed to Tohoku, whether to refurbish buildings, sort through debris or salvage waterlogged possessions. An academic who has studied the Japanese voluntary sector concluded that, in the years since Kobe, it had 'reached a new kind of professionalism, organisation, social legitimacy and institutionalisation'.[6]

Keiko Kiyama, secretary-general of Japan Emergency NGOs, which had operated in the former Yugoslavia, Afghanistan, Iraq and Pakistan, and which organized volunteers to Tohoku, agreed there had been a lot of improvement since Kobe. But Japan's volunteer sector, she told me, still hadn't caught up with its counterparts in the US and Europe. 'Even now, I feel that civil society is not strong enough. I feel that we Japanese are fine working individually or in a small group, but we are not strong on organizational management. We need to be able to kill small differences for the bigger objective. We are not so good at coming to one big idea.' Kiyama didn't think the government knew how to handle the upsurge in volunteers. Bureaucracy was sometimes stifling, she said, and government departments were reluctant to let go. They found it hard to deal with proposals outside their immediate bureaucratic experience, such as those coming from volunteer groups that wanted to provide badly needed psychological counselling to disaster victims. An official from Give2Asia, a volunteer group, told me a story that seemed to back up Kiyama's impression of a rules-bound bureaucracy jealously guarding its turf. Some groups had been told that, for the sake of fairness, they had to distribute exactly the same items to all recipients. 'They had to provide 70,000 of every item, the exact same brand and everything,' the Give2Asia official said. 'We heard of one group that brought 197 bananas [to an evacuation centre], but there were 199 people so they refused to take the shipment – because there wasn't enough for everyone.'[7]

Such obstacles aside, Miura of the *Asahi* said that something had definitely changed. For months after the tsunami, one of his friends, a law school graduate, volunteered to go to Tohoku every weekend, travelling north under his own steam, taking supplies and helping local communities. 'It's now quite natural for the best and brightest people to think that way and do volunteer work. This is very, very new,' Miura said. I too was impressed by the number of volunteers I saw in Tohoku, not only in the days immediately following the tsunami, but for months after. Driving through devastated coastal towns, one frequently came across a school baseball team from Hiroshima or a clutch of salarymen from Mitsubishi, digging out an inundated rice field or carefully sorting through photograph albums salvaged from flooded houses. The Self Defence Forces were everywhere too, searching for the bodies of the dead and bringing food for the living. In one town, they had set up a mobile communal bath in a car park under a military green tarpaulin, so that tsunami survivors could enjoy their all-important bathing ritual. 'I do kind of believe that a new spirit and new ideas are emerging in many parts of society,' Miura said of the changes he detected after the tsunami. 'This crisis I believe has sown the seeds of new thinking. Although we have not yet come up with any new ideology or new types of leaders, people have begun to think differently.'

It would be rash to claim that a single event, even one as traumatic as the March 2011 tsunami, could change society overnight. More likely, it illuminated changes that had been going on for many years. Certainly, as Japan has adjusted to much slower levels of economic growth, there were many ways in which individuals and groups of individuals had sought to become more actively engaged. I had seen, for example, how small towns and villages, for example in Oita prefecture in southern Kyushu, had come together to look after their old people. They organized a roster of home visits and put on activities, such as calligraphy or local history classes, for the older members of their community. The creation of a vibrant civil society was partly a matter of changing customs and partly a matter of legislation, said Jeff Kingston, a long-time scholar of Japan. In his book *Japan's Quiet Transformation*, he documented the way in which laws, and with them attitudes, had been slowly shifting, extending and invigorating what he characterized as a 'stunted' civil society. 'Ordinary citizens are demanding a more democratic society marked by more transparent governance, more public participation and oversight, and greater accountability based on the rule of law.'[8]

One area of significant progress, he said, had been information, the public's right to know. Since the 1990s, there had been an accelerating push for government disclosure. Pressure for transparency had gone all the way back to at least the 1960s, when citizens' groups demanded, mostly unsuccessfully, information about pesticide use, food additives and pharmaceutical side effects. In 1985, families of the more than 520 people who had died in the country's deadliest air crash were driven to use the US Freedom of Information Act to find out what had happened, exposing the inadequacy of Japan's own laws. Grassroots groups eventually forced local prefectural governments to enact information disclosure ordinances. By 1996, the year after Kobe, all forty-seven prefectures had passed such legislation. Citizens were quick to use their new-found powers to expose wrongdoing, including bureaucrats' fake travel expense claims and improbably large entertainment allowances. In one case, officials had claimed dozens of journeys on a bullet train line that was not even in operation.

The courts became more supportive of citizens' demands for the right to know. In 2001, after years of pressure, a national information disclosure bill was finally enacted. Kingston said that public scepticism over the Fukushima nuclear disaster showed how far things had come. People were in no mood to be fobbed off by bland official assurances or pre-cooked 'town hall meetings'. They would not accept, as they once might have done, government sleights of hand, such as the attempt to render school playgrounds 'safe' by the dishonest manoeuvre of simply raising the limit of acceptable levels of radiation. Nor would they tolerate a government that they judged to have been dishonest and incompetent in its handling of the disaster. In the end, such public pressure toppled the government and yielded an independent parliamentary inquiry into the nuclear crisis. There were public hearings with archived testimony and widespread dissemination of findings over the internet, including the release (eventually) of video tapes showing scenes inside the reactors as the nuclear crisis was unfolding. 'Despite some shortcomings, it marked a milestone in transparency,' Kingston said.[9]

There were many other examples of a more active citizenry. Some, such as the installation of lay judges in criminal trials, were the initiative of the government. Others, such as opposition to the introduction of a state identification system, were the result of citizens pushing back against what they considered an overbearing state. Launched in 2002, the Juki Net proposed to collect a database of every citizen, listing their name, age, sex, date of birth, place of residency, together with an eleven-digit identification number. Given the ordered nature of Japanese society and the well-established family registry, dating back to at least 1872, one might not have expected the Juki Net to have provoked much alarm. Citizens groups, however, reacted furiously, pursuing no fewer than thirty-five lawsuits against the scheme. Yoshiaki Takashi, a retired trading company employee, spoke for many when he told me, 'The government has given a number to human beings as if we were animals or industrial products. I am furious at the men who want to know my private data when they have no business with such things.'[10]

During the tsunami, citizen journalists had also blazed a trail. Not only had they used new media to spread information about what was going on, many had done reporting shunned by the more established media. Newspapers had pulled their reporters out of areas contaminated with radiation en masse, but freelance journalists moved in to fill the gap. Reports from foreign media or experts that contradicted the official line were quickly translated and disseminated over the internet. Some journalists streamed press conferences live, bypassing the mainstream media, which often gave an anodyne account of proceedings. An academic study into the impact of social media during the disaster found 'evidence that the social media activities of these rogue journalists/translators emboldened and empowered other reporters to pose more challenging questions'.[11]

Toshiki Senoue, my photographer friend, spent weeks on end in the no-go zone around Fukushima, documenting what had happened to the abandoned towns and villages in the shadow of the nuclear plant. He had found a trail into the exclusion zone, away from the strictly controlled checkpoints, that enabled him to enter and leave the area undetected. He took photographs and detailed notes and planned to publish a book so that people would know what had gone on inside a nuclear disaster zone that was officially out of bounds to the media. On one occasion he was detained by police and warned it was illegal for him to be in the area. Toshiki was having none of it. 'The government is not going to tell me where I can and cannot go in my own country,' he told me. By this time, at least, he had got hold of a Geiger counter.

# 16

# After the Tsunami

Seizaburo Sato, who went on to be a carpenter and a volunteer fire-man, was born in Iwate prefecture in 1929. He remembered learning as a teenager how to fight with a sharpened bamboo stick in case the Americans invaded. Towards the end of the war, US planes would fly low over the fields, strafing them with bullets. All he could do was hide. Once, he remembered, he squatted behind a tiny trunk as a plane roared above him. When Japan surrendered, the planes came back. This time they dropped barrels containing clothes and medicine. There was no transport in those days, Sato said, so he never got to the barrels in time. They always seemed to land on some distant hillside. 'We'd lost the war, so there were food shortages and no jobs,' he recalled of those years after defeat. 'Back then they needed carpenters, wall plasterers. Those people could get work.'[1] Sato's parents sent him away on an apprenticeship to Sendai, then, as now, the 'capital' of the north. He stayed for four years, receiving no salary, just pocket money – enough to buy the occasional movie ticket. In Sendai, the American soldiers used to thunder by in trucks. Once he went to a baseball match to see them play. 'That's when I drank my first Coca Cola.' He was terrified of girls in those days. Besides, it wasn't thought proper to talk to them in public. The only ones he could relax around were the 'shampoo girls' who worked in the barber shops. In his early twenties, he moved back to his home town in Iwate prefecture, where he learned how to make *shoji* screens and doors. He was getting paid now and he dreamed of buying a bicycle, a radio or even a watch. 'My parents told me there's this girl. Why don't you marry her?' There were fewer 'love matches' in those days with many marriages cemented by go-betweens. Sato did as he was told. He moved with his new bride

to the fishing town where her relatives went back eighteen generations. The name of the town was Ofunato.

The first time I met Sato was a week after the tsunami. I had spotted
an old man in a white hard hat picking through the rubble of what
was once his home. Unlike many of the buildings, which had crumpled into unrecognizable mounds, Sato's house was just about
standing. It had a roof and a frame, though no walls to speak of.
Everything that had once been inside had been pushed outside by the
force of the water. Even the tatami matting, almost the sacred essence
of a Japanese home, was spewed all over the mud. A white sedan car
sat in what must have been his living room. Or perhaps it was just
outside. In the indescribable wreckage and detritus of Ofunato it was
hard to tell.

I clambered down a steep embankment to find out what the old
man was doing. He appeared to be bagging up little mementos, any
small item he could salvage from the salt and the mud. The thing that
struck me most was his sense of purpose. Everything was so wrecked
and mangled and waterlogged, there seemed little point to his activity.
It was like trying to tidy up a municipal rubbish dump. But Sato had
somehow summoned the will to go about his task. 'Gambarimasu,' he
said, when I asked him what he was doing, employing the ubiquitous
Japanese word. 'We must struggle on.'

Sato was eighty-two years old. Aside from his hard hat, which gave
him an almost comic appearance, he was wearing a bluish wind-
breaker and purple rubber boots. He was blind in one eye, the result
of a construction accident forty years before. It didn't seem to have
inconvenienced him unduly. He had gone on to be a volunteer fireman. One of the items he had salvaged from the wreckage was his
peaked fireman's cap. He removed his hard hat, put the cap on and
saluted. It was full of water, which trickled down his face, even as he
kept his pose. Sato's living room smelled of seawater. I gingerly
stepped over the threshold and onto the debris-strewn floor. I was still
wearing my shoes, an affront in normal times. These were not normal
times, though, and Sato, too, was wearing his boots. He pointed to a
solid-looking shrine of gold and black lacquer that he had built for his
mother, who had died the previous year. It was a treasured item, and

miraculously the only piece of furniture in the house that had survived the onrush of the sea.

I returned to Ofunato twice after that initial encounter to find out how Sato was getting on. The first time was in August 2011, five months later. He was standing in the street, bent over something, with a drill in his hand. It turned out he was making a screen door. Better than buying one, he said. He was wearing a yellow towel around his head to soak up the sweat. He had on shorts, a short-sleeve shirt and scruffy leather shoes with the backs trodden down so that he might slip in and out of them more easily. Sato had moved with his wife and daughter into a little house at the top of the steep embankment, a stone's throw from the destroyed house where I had first met him. All the debris had been removed. The government paid the rent on his new home, he said. He could live there for two years. It smelled of freshly laid tatami. The old tatami flooring, drenched in seawater, had been thrown out. With the help of a few neighbours, Sato had somehow managed to drag the heavy *butsudan* shrine, the one built for his mother, up the embankment and into his new home. It was a bulky item and it overwhelmed its new, smaller surroundings. 'Only two people in this area managed to save their *butsudan*,' he said. On the wall hung a picture of the Showa emperor, Hirohito, and a certificate of thirty years' service as a volunteer fireman.

Sato took me to his allotment in the hills above the town. He rode up the steep path every day on his little Honda CD Benly. (Benly, or *benri*, means 'convenient' in Japanese.) It was a large piece of land and on it he grew an amazing variety of plants and vegetables – persimmon, *daikon* radishes, tomatoes, onions, *shiso* plants, cucumbers, peppers, *mikan* oranges, potatoes, aubergines, *edamame*, soybean pods and corn. He had put up netting to keep the crows away and a wind-catcher in the shape of a Japanese plane with a Rising Sun flag. A scarecrow in one corner was dressed in a crash helmet rather like the one Sato had been wearing five months before.

I came again the following summer. It was June 2012 and Sato was still going strong. He had just laid a floor in a nearby house. When I arrived, he was pottering around his tool shed. I had never once seen him sit still. Sato had featured in a magazine article that I'd written and he had kept a copy in a special wooden box with the magazine's cover – a picture of devastation – glued to the lid.² 'It's my tsunami treasure,' he said, carefully taking the magazine out and flicking through the pages. Ofunato, Sato said, was less badly damaged than Rikuzentakata in the next valley. 'They've got nothing. Here in Ofunato we are able to eat rice and we have temporary housing,' he said. 'After the war, people picked up tin from the rubble to build their houses. These days people complain if they don't have heating or air-conditioning.' He snorted at how soft Japan had become.

Ofunato had indeed begun to stir slowly back to life, as Sato said. Most of the seafront area was still bare land, though all the rubble had been cleared away. A little set back from the water, a 'temporary high street' had been erected, an area of prefabricated buildings on a couple of 'streets' on raised wooden decking. There were shops selling electronics, cosmetics, books, CDs and cakes. There was the Chou-Chou Apparel Shop – what self-respecting high street, even a temporary one, could be without? – and a beer and *gyoza* fried dumpling restaurant. I had come to see one particular establishment: Hy's Café. It was run by Hiromi Shimodate and Yasuko Kimura, the two women I had spotted, all that time ago, walking like refugees along the railway tracks after the tsunami. The original Hy's Café had been destroyed, but here it was again, resurrected.

On that day by the twisted railway tracks, the two women had been sifting the wreckage. Hundreds of yards from where her café had once stood, Shimodate had found a tiny sieve. After I'd left, they discovered more items in the rubble. There were parfait glasses, miraculously intact, and a frying pan good enough to use. There was an espresso machine and an electric ice shaver to make *kakigori*, a dessert, though both were broken beyond repair. They found wooden furniture shredded by the force of the water and some steel chairs still intact. 'They were perfectly fine,' Shimodate said. 'I put them to one side for the next day, but when I went back for them they were gone.'

The new Hy's was cosy. There was a blackboard with a chalked menu. The noodle salad came recommended. I ordered a 'French press coffee'. It seemed surreal to be sitting there drinking it with the women I'd seen picking through the rubble on that bleak, freezing day. Shimodate had moved into temporary housing, a compact prefab. Before that, she had been staying with her older brother who runs Shimodate

Auto Body Shop, but the house had begun to lean at a worrying angle after a series of aftershocks. These rumbled on for months and, with each new tremor, the house tilted a little further. Shimodate decided it was best to move. She started volunteering. She helped distribute care packages sent from other parts of Japan. She had an actress friend in Tokyo who had collected clothes from her acquaintances and sent them to Ofunato. Soon the fishermen's wives were parading around in outfits worn by Tokyo's fashionable thespians. More than anything, Shimodate said, everyone wanted to eat fresh fish again. Some months after the tsunami, they were overjoyed to see the lights from the squid boats flashing in the bay at night. 'But we felt guilty about eating things from the sea. All those people had died because of the sea. Everybody felt it would be better to wait the hundred days,' she said, referring to the Buddhist period of mourning.

The name of Hy's Café was taken from the first initial of each of their names, Hiromi and Yasuko. Shimodate had worried that people would have neither the will nor the money to eat out, but the little restaurant had been doing brisk business since it had reopened a few months before. Both women were in good spirits. 'We probably looked really poor that day you saw us walking along in the cold, looking at the ground,' said Kimura. Now, without her facemask, she looked like a different person, pretty and nicely dressed. A tiny pink teddy bear hung from her phone strap.

Ofunato had got back on its feet quicker than some of the other towns along the coast. Rikuzentakata, which was more severely damaged, hadn't yet been able to build a temporary high street, Kimura said. Even so, Ofunato's population had shrunk since the tsunami, if only slightly. People had drifted away looking for work in Sendai, the centre of what had become a 'reconstruction boom', or in Tokyo. The two didn't know where they were supposed to live once they moved out of temporary housing. There was discussion about building homes in the hills, but nothing had been decided. 'There's not much suitable land to build houses higher up,' Shimodate said. 'They could flatten the mountain and build apartments, but I think it would be hard to persuade people to move. So the city itself may have to be rebuilt here,' she added, by which she meant exactly where it had always been. 'They may have to bring in soil to make it higher.' Up and down the coast, the land had sunk by up to five feet, making it more dangerous than ever before to live by the water. Even if suitable land could be found, Shimodate didn't know if she could afford to build a new house. Some people were still paying mortgages on homes that had been washed out to sea.

On the wall of the café was a concert poster. The star act was a rap band by the name of Deftech, the support a local band called Lawblow. The concert would be held that July. Lawblow had made a video of their song 'Ie ni kaerou', 'Let's go home'. It featured ordinary people from Ofunato walking through the debris-strewn streets, but singing of their wish to start again. It was pure schmaltz but, when people heard the song, they cried, Kimura said. A couple of customers came into the café, two young women who fancied an evening out. They ordered a glass of draught beer each, and a Caesar salad, fried potatoes and a portion of edamame to share. Shimodate went off to prepare it. The coffee, she said as she vanished into the kitchen, was on the house.

There were signs in Ofunato of a community coming together, building something that resembled a town from the rubble and the vacant lots. But Ofunato was far from normal. Someone told me that one of the town's taxi drivers continued to wait outside the train station even though the small building had been entirely washed away. The story reminded me of Hachiko, the dog who waited for his master outside Shibuya station each evening. One day the master died and so did not appear. Undeterred, Hachiko returned to the station the next evening to wait. Every evening for nine years the dog went back to wait until it too eventually died. I couldn't help but think of Ofunato's loyal taxi driver in the same terms, waiting for non-existent passengers to disembark from a non-existent train.

In the year or so since Kazuyoshi Sasaki showed me around the gutted interior of the Capital Hotel a lot had changed. For starters, Sasaki had become a city councillor, elected overwhelmingly with 1,400 votes. The Capital Hotel still stood empty. But there were plans to build a new one in a different location sixty feet above sea level. Construction was due to begin in August, with funding of several hundred million yen provided by the government. Yoshimori Oyama, the manager of the old hotel, said it would be about half the size of the original.

It was due to be finished in the spring of 2013. Oyama had wanted to rebuild the hotel on its original site. It had been designed to withstand a tsunami, he said, and the wave had indeed crashed through leaving the basic structure intact. He argued his case, but others disagreed. Hotel guests, they said, would be nervous sleeping by the water. They would prefer the safety of somewhat higher ground.

The flat valley floor where Rikuzentakata once stood had been cleared of debris. Where the wreckage had been, thin grasses had sprung up, reclaiming the land for nature. I arrived on a cool summer's evening and from a vantage point just above the flat, empty valley I heard birds twittering and the sounds of children playing baseball. About a dozen structures remained of what had been a town of 23,000 inhabitants. Even they were gutted. The people who once lived here were in temporary housing, or with friends and relatives in the hills around. Some had left altogether, perhaps never to return. More than 1,900 had died. A few cars crawled along the valley floor, tracing the roads that formed the grid of a town half-remembered. Beyond was the sea, flat as a pale blue mirror. It was hard to imagine it boiling up to devour the buildings and the people. There was still a smell of pine in the air from the densely forested hills around, though the 70,000 pines by the seashore had gone. I was standing near a stone pillar, a few feet tall, engraved with the date 3/11. The small municipal monument marked the highest point the water had reached. Like the ancient stone markers scattered along the coast, it stood as a warning to future generations.

Boats were everything for many people in Rikuzentakata. On 11 March, after the earth had stopped shaking and when the water in the bay started stirring up in muddy pools – a signal that a tsunami was coming – many fishermen rushed to their vessels. Sixty-year-old Shuichi Kanno was one of them. Despite his daughter's objections he headed not for the hills, but for the water. 'Without a boat, I can't think about my life,' he said. He decided to save the biggest of the three vessels he owned by sailing it out into the incoming tsunami, a survival technique fishermen had learned over generations. 'I wasn't at all afraid. My only thought was to protect my boat. That's what we did in the Chile earthquake too,' he said, referring to the 1960 tsunami that had swamped Rikuzentakata after an earthquake halfway around the world.

For those who lost their boats, life had been hard. Government compensation had been slow and insufficient, said Sachiko Kanno, Shuichi's 62-year-old wife. 'There's no money and there's no ship-building companies to make them anyway. It may take years and we'll all be grey by then.' Kanno was a tough, bright-eyed woman. Clothes pegs were hanging, ready for use, from her apron, which she wore over a housedress and tracksuit bottoms. 'Those without boats are collecting seaweed. It's famous in these parts. Or they're working on construction sites, or in the rice fields. Some of them aren't doing anything at all.' Now it was *uni* season, she said, when fishermen gathered the prized sea urchin that fetched high prices around Japan. They used poles, several metres long and fitted with mirrors, to hunt for the spiky creatures on the ocean floor. But many of the poles had been washed away and an argument had broken out among union members. Some were saying it was unfair to let those with poles fish while those without could not. There had been a meeting about it to thrash out a compromise.

That morning I met Councillor Sasaki. He took me back to the Fumonji temple, where the remains of unidentified bodies were being kept in wooden boxes wrapped in muslin cloth. Just twenty-three boxes remained compared with nearly 300 when I was here before. The others had been identified from their DNA and claimed by relatives. There was one new box. That April, there had been a typhoon. It washed a body up on the beach more than a year after the tsunami had claimed it. 'We're 95 per cent sure we know who it is,' Sasaki said. 'Now we just need the DNA evidence.' The body washed ashore had been wearing the remnants of a Capital Hotel uniform. Sasaki said it must be one of his colleagues, missing since the day of the tsunami. 'We escaped by bus, but she went by car to take her mother to the evacuation centre.' He gulped and fell silent. 'We feel that she's come back to us,' he said eventually.

Offerings sent by people from around Japan had been placed on rows of shelves by the altar: cans of sports drinks, jelly sweets, marsh-mallows, Hokkaido biscuits. The priest, in a blue cassock and purple bib, pointed out the temple roof beam, made with a single piece of wood twelve *ken* in length, or about eighty feet. 'You can't find a piece of wood this long any more,' he said. 'It must have taken a year to prepare a piece of wood like this.' The temple was founded in the thirteenth century, but was rebuilt away from the coast in the early sixteenth century, presumably after a tsunami. In an alcove, among Buddhist deities, was a statue of a ferocious-looking, half-naked demon, sword in one hand and some kind of sling-shot in the other. The scowling figure was riding a wave, which reared up behind it in the form of a halo. 'It's called a *nami kiri fudo*, a wave-killing god,' the priest said. 'From ancient times this temple has offered protection against tsunamis.'

The god's powers had not been sufficient in 2011. Unlike Ofunato, which was slowly creeping back towards the water, Rikuzentakata had been so destroyed it might never be rebuilt in its former location, people said. The whole town, which in the 2010 census had a population of 23,302 inhabitants, could end up being shunted away from the coast towards the hills. That was assuming people stayed at all. Sasaki worried that, unless businesses restarted soon, there would be little choice but to drift away in search of work. The number of registered residents had already fallen to 19,000 and was shrinking with each passing month. As in Ofunato, there were plans to put up a temporary shopping street, but the location had not yet been decided. Reconstruction money was pouring in from Tokyo – Sasaki said the town's budget had increased seven-fold – but there were too few people to deal with it. About one-third of the town's 300 government officials had been killed in the tsunami, leaving a deficit of knowledge and expertise. There were plans to build a sea wall, twice as high as the one knocked down, and Sasaki was betting that people would eventually move back into the town proper. 'Right now people have to live on the higher ground, but after a while they'll move back to the coast because they love and respect the sea,' he said. 'They know that one day they'll get hit again by a tsunami, but they just can't help it. That's their culture.'

Some rebuilding had already started. Sasaki took me to a house-raising ceremony on the outskirts of town to celebrate the completion of a municipal canteen. The money had been donated by people from Zushi, a city in Kanagawa prefecture outside Tokyo. Representatives of Zushi were here. Carpenters in their traditional *jika-tabi* boots were milling around. At one end of the field was the frame of a new barn-sized building. At the other, marquee tents had been erected and volunteers were cooking yaki soba noodles and cabbage. There were giant bottles of sake lined up ready to drink. Children were being taught to pound *mochi* rice cakes in a giant wooden mortar. With each swing of the enormous pestle, the crowd shouted out encouragement. On the offbeat, an old lady sloshed water into the mortar with her bare hands, removing them just before the heavy pestle came thundering down again. Inside the frame of the newly constructed house sat a little 'god-shelf' with offerings of rice, rice cakes, a pineapple, bananas, an apple the size of a bowling ball, a bottle of sake and a bream, which was considered a lucky fish.[3] On the roof, carpenters were hurriedly nailing the final pieces of plywood into place. The atmosphere was how I imagined an Amish barn-raising.

After some speeches, more jokey than solemn, a priest entered the house wearing a purple cloak and a tall black hat known as an *eboshi*. He pulled a scroll from a quiver at his side, unfurled it and began reading in a half chant, half sing-song voice. It was an almost other-worldly sound, like someone blowing through a conch shell. The words themselves were surprisingly prosaic. He named the construction company, thanked the carpenters and listed the food that would be served at the canteen. Imagine a priest chanting 'pork cutlets, rice with fish, and soba noodles' to the rhythm of the Lord's Prayer. Parents hushed their children, telling them to show respect. The priest ended with a noise like a screeching police siren, the sound becoming higher and louder and then lower and softer until it finally faded away altogether. 'We hope to have many more ceremonies like this,' Sasaki said when it was over. 'It's a sign that we're making progress.'

I wanted to see the *ippon matsu*, the solitary 270-year-old pine that had survived the tsunami. I had spotted it from a distance, a slender, solitary symbol of survival set against the backdrop of the ocean. Now we drove up close. It stood by the side of a little stone bridge. The tree had a long, spindly trunk, with a cluster of branches at the very top. It stood more than eighty feet tall, though it was leaning slightly towards one side. The bottom half of the trunk had been wrapped in a protective green material, like a bandage. Across the road, towards the water, was a long wan-coloured municipal building, collapsed at one end, like a brontosaurus with its neck resting on the ground. A tourist was standing beneath the tree, gazing upwards. It turned out she had been in Kobe in 1995 when that city was crushed by an earthquake. 'It's a miracle, isn't it?' she said, shaking her head. 'Out of 70,000 trees, this is the only one that survived.' Sasaki said the news, in reality, was not so good. Technically speaking, the tree was dead. After the tsunami, the townspeople had covered its trunk to protect it from snow and insects. They had dug a large trench around it and installed a foundation to prevent encroaching seawater from poisoning the roots. But the land had sunk so far, its roots had been inundated by the ocean all the same. The tree had been examined by arboreal experts from around the country. Normally it should have flowered in May, Sasaki said, but no flowers had appeared. 'Even after all this effort, the experts pronounced it dead.'

Experts from the Tsukuba Research Institute had subsequently taken away several cones and had managed to nurture eighteen saplings from the seeds. Sasaki had wavered over what should be done about the lone pine itself. His inclination was that the town should forget about the dead tree and focus their efforts on the living. But the solitary pine had become a symbol of the town's resilience, as well as a tourist attraction. The mayor, Futoshi Toba, had been swayed. 'As a symbol of reconstruction the lone pine offers emotional support to the people of this city,' he had said.[4]

The officials of Rikuzentakata had hit upon a plan. They were already raising donations towards the Y150 million – nearly $2 million at the time – that would be needed to put it into action. An official Facebook page entitled 'Ganbapeshi Rikuzentakata' ('Hang in there, Rikuzentakata') had been established to help collect funds.[5] The idea, Sasaki explained, was to send the tree to Kyoto to be preserved 'like a dried flower'. The trunk would be chopped into nine sections. Each would be hollowed out and treated. A carbon spine would be inserted and the trunk reassembled as it once was. The branches themselves were trickier. The plan was to create realistic replicas, made of high-grade plastic, modelled on the originals. The hope, said Sasaki, was to have the tree back in its present position by March 2013, to take its place as a memorial for the second anniversary of the tsunami.[6] As I listened to Sasaki, I thought about the meaning of the tree, with its plastic branches and newfangled carbon innards fitted by craftsmen from the ancient city of Kyoto. The 'miracle pine', I thought, would be old, yet new; dead, but preserved. It would be artifice presented as reality. It would have beaten the odds. It would be different from what it once was, yet somehow the same. It would, it occured to me in that moment, be a fitting symbol of Japan.

# Afterword

Not long after the earthquake and tsunami of 2011, John Dower, the great scholar of post-war Japan, wondered whether the shock of the tragedy might stir change, whether something new might be 'cracked open' or 'set in motion', as he put it. For years, people had speculated about what it would take to get Japan moving again. This was, after all, a country whose history – at least on the surface – seemed to be characterized by long periods of stasis followed by bursts of trans-formative activity.[1] It has become a cliché of Japanese scholarship that big external shocks have produced decisive changes in direction. The threat of being colonized in the nineteenth century led Japan to jetti-son feudalism almost overnight in the Meiji Restoration of 1868. Defeat in the Second World War caused it to pursue 'greatness' by economic, rather than military, means.

In recent years, there have been two events seemingly momentous enough to catalyse radical change. The first has been the rise of China, the biggest shift in global power in a hundred years and one intensely relevant to Japan, an island neighbour that broke so decisively with the Middle Kingdom in the nineteenth century and fought it so ferociously in the twentieth. The second is the impact of the post-1990 economic crisis, starting with the collapse of the bubble and culminating in a lengthy period of deflation and loss of economic vigour. Both shocks have been compared to the Black Ships, whose menacing presence triggered a political revolution in the nineteenth century. Both, it is true, have had a profound impact, provoking deep changes in Japan's social and economic fabric. But neither China's rise nor Japan's decline has triggered a decisive shift in direction on anything like the scale that occurred after 1868 or 1945.

What about the tsunami, asked Dower? Might it prise open the 'space' in which Japan could try something new? His question reminded me of what a senior finance ministry official had once told me a decade before. Over lunch at a little French bistro in Tokyo, he had quite taken me aback when he announced breezily, 'What Japan needs is a really good earthquake.' That would not only trigger a construction boom, he explained in remarks clearly calculated to shock me, but, more important, it would invoke the sort of can-do spirit Japan had exhibited after the war, a spirit dulled by affluence and complacency. Natural shocks had, after all, caused big national reassessments in the past, though these had not always been for the better. The Great Kanto earthquake of 1923, which flattened Tokyo and killed some 140,000 people, helped crystallize a lurch towards totalitarianism. Just a week after the earthquake, the Taisho emperor issued an imperial rescript stating that, though there had been much progress 'in science and human wisdom', this had been accompanied by 'frivolous and extravagant habits'. (The earthquake had destroyed much of the vast Yoshiwara pleasure quarters in the eastern part of the city.) The disaster, he intimated, was some sort of divine punishment. Yet brighter things came out of the 1923 disaster too. Tokyo was reconstructed as a modern city with underground trains and department stores, cafés, theatres and parks. Dower talks of a flourishing of popular society that, momentarily at least, brought with it a 'real sense of being part of the world'. Tokyo Modern, as he called it, had 'gas stations, movie theatres, dance halls'. Then twenty years later, 'it was all destroyed in the air raids, and it became a vanished city'.[2]

That sense of foreboding – and possibility – was there in the weeks and months after the great tsunami of 2011. There were those who thought the catastrophe would tip Japan over the edge by delivering a final psychological blow after years of creeping pessimism. There were others, conversely, who felt the tragedy might shake Japan from its sleepwalk and produce what Dower called 'a kind of clarity'. He wondered, for instance, whether the tsunami-engulfed coastline of Tohoku might be rebuilt in 'future-looking ways' (it was not), or whether the nuclear catastrophe might mobilize a grassroots opposition movement and force a reassessment of energy policy. There has indeed been an upsurge of anti-nuclear sentiment that has forced the government, as Dower predicted, to reassess its energy strategy. Most of the country's nuclear power plants stand idle. The old power monopolies have been broken up with the separation of generation and distribution businesses. At least a modicum of competition has been introduced to the residential electricity market. The setting of a generous 'feed-in tariff', which encourages companies to produce alternative energy and sell it to the grid, has sparked some imaginative thinking. Marubeni, a mammoth trading house, is the latest business to take the bait, in 2013 announcing plans to investigate geothermal reserves in a Hokkaido national park. Japanese scientists have also announced what could conceivably be an important breakthrough in the energy field – the extraction of methane gas from huge, frozen undersea deposits known as 'fire ice'. Though this technology is still in its infant stage, Ryo Minami, an energy official, compared it to the discovery of shale gas, the extraction of which has revolutionized US energy prospects.[3]

Yet, for the most part, during the time I took to write this book, it would be hard to have claimed that Japan had seized the moment. The authorities cleaned up the debris with admirable efficiency, but then seemed lost for inspiration as to what to do next. Economically things got, if anything, worse. Businesses accelerated their investment abroad and the economy contracted. The absence of nuclear power threatened both an energy and a balance-of-payments crisis. Japan needed to spend increasing amounts of foreign reserves on importing oil and gas. Public debt piled higher. Politics seemed as depressingly out of touch as ever. Japan was resilient, but all at sea.

Then, something curious happened. A few months after I finished the first draft of the book in the autumn of 2012, a palpable sense of optimism, or at least of heightened expectation, returned to Japan. The cause of the excitement came from perhaps the most unlikely source imaginable: the re-election of one Shinzo Abe. Abe's first term as leader, which lasted less than a year, had, after all, been an unmitigated disaster, a catalogue of pratfalls from a man whose nationalistic and sometimes reactionary convictions were out of step with the broad electorate. Why on earth would his re-election in 2012 – he took office on 26 December, like some belated Christmas present – provoke anything other than a dreadful sense of *déjà vu*? The answer was that, in contrast to Abe Mark I, who had exhibited a fondness for revisionist causes but profound lack of interest in matters economic, Abe Mark II came armed with an economic blunderbuss. It was called 'Abenomics'.

In simple terms, Abenomics was a wildly ambitious – some called it wildly reckless – experiment in psychology. The idea was to do whatever it took to banish fifteen years of deflation. It wasn't quite the Meiji Restoration, but it marked a dramatic about-turn in policy. Abe had been persuaded that Japan's economy would never regain its vigour unless it broke free of its deflationary trap. He announced that, if he were re-elected prime minister, he would set a 2 per cent inflation target and oblige the Bank of Japan to hit it. That would mean installing a governor at the central bank who believed deflation was Public Enemy Number One and that the bank possessed the firepower to vanquish it. Both would be novelties.

Abe's message was simple and bold. Indeed, many criticized it for being simplistic and dangerous. They argued that Japan's problems were deeply structural, not amenable to solution simply by running the printing presses. Yet it was precisely the boldness – almost the recklessness – of Abenomics that was so invigorating. After years of hesitant policymaking, here was a leader willing to bet the ranch on a single objective: that of returning the economy to inflation. Whatever you thought of his nationalist convictions, Abe was able, in the words of one commentator, to 'change the political weather'.[4]

As discussed in earlier chapters, an extended period of deflation can sap an economy of its 'animal spirits'. In the long run, it is also likely to be unsustainable. That is because, when prices are falling, old debts grow bigger as a proportion of a shrinking pie. Tax revenues fall with each notch down in activity. As a result, Japan's public debt has ballooned, reaching more than 230 per cent of output in gross terms. Because interest rates are low, debt can be serviced fairly painlessly. Yet all the while the debt grows bigger. Japan has spent years in a sort of stable deflationary equilibrium, the economic equivalent of a cryogenic state, but at some point it needs to get some inflationary blood coursing through its veins again.

If Abenomics goes to plan – and there are certainly substantial risks that it will not – Japan will slide gently from a deflationary equilibrium to a mildly inflationary one. Suppose it achieved Abe's inflation target of 2 per cent, and could somehow muster annual growth of another 1.5 per cent. That would mean a fairly healthy nominal growth rate of 3.5 per cent. If company profits, wages and taxes rose too, then everything – including the public debt – would start to look better. 'We need to say goodbye to a shrinking economy,' was how Abe put it.[5] Sure, Japan would still be left with big structural problems – how to finance pensions and healthcare with a declining workforce, how to raise productivity, how to compete internationally. But it would be out of its deflationary trap, and in a much more positive place.

Abenomics came in three flavours: monetary expansion, fiscal expansion and structural reform. Abe called them three arrows, a reference to Motonari Mori, a sixteenth-century *daimyo* lord who had told his three sons they would be stronger if they worked as a team. It was easy to break the shaft of one arrow, the *daimyo* had explained, but nearly impossible to snap three shafts bound together. Abe let loose his first arrow almost immediately: a spending package worth roughly $110 billion at the time, or 2 per cent of gross domestic product. The money would be spent mainly on infrastructure, including repair and construction of earthquake-proof roads, bridges and tunnels. Unshakeable bridges, not bridges to nowhere. The second arrow was the appointment of a new central bank governor to carry out radical monetary expansion. Even before he had picked his man, markets had stirred to life in anticipation. The yen started falling, and shares on the long-depressed stock market began to rise on the expectation that both a weak currency and inflation (which would restore pricing power) would be good for business.

The man Abe installed at the Bank of Japan was Haruhiko Kuroda, a finance ministry veteran who had long been scathing about the bank's impotence in the face of deflation. An international figure and fluent English-speaker, Kuroda was head of the Asian Development Bank, a regional institution bankrolled by Japan. He had the right balance of gravitas and sense of mischief to oversee the change, which meant telling proud officials at the central bank that they had been getting everything wrong for years. At Kuroda's first board meeting, the bank agreed to a volte face. It would double the monetary base – the notes, coins and electronic money in circulation – to around 55 per cent of GDP by the end of 2014, more than twice the level prevailing in the US and Europe. To achieve this, the bank would massively step up the amount of government bonds it bought. The idea was that, with no more government paper left to buy, Japan's banks, pension funds and insurance companies would be forced to put their money into riskier assets such as property and shares. Alternatively, they could invest abroad, which would weaken the yen. In fact, a weaker yen was very much part of the plan, although international etiquette meant Japanese officials had to pretend otherwise. Yet, for the most part, international institutions such as the Group of 20 and the International Monetary Fund welcomed Japan's new policy. Even Washington was on board. Better to have a Japan returned to some sort of economic health, the world seemed to be saying, than to worry too much about its depreciating currency. My own paper, the *Financial Times*, pronounced the new measures 'perhaps the boldest ever experiment by the central bank of an important country'. The headline to the main story read simply, 'Japan Starts Monetary Revolution'.

By May 2013, six months after the idea of Abenomics first took hold, Japan's broad stock market had risen 65 per cent, its steepest rally in decades. It went on to rise yet further, but lost some of those gains in a rocky June when markets and commentators alike began to lose their nerve in the ability of Abe's plan to turn the economy around. Still, the yen, which had been as strong as Y77, to the dollar, fell to about Y100, a collapse that made Japan's exports immensely more competitive. The central bank, confident of reaching its inflation target, raised its growth forecast for 2013 to a pretty respectable 2.9 per cent. Despite the market wobble, investors who had bought the Abenomics story were cashing in. One told me jokingly that he ended all his emails, 'All hail to Abe'.[6]

Naturally, Abenomics had many sceptics. Some said the new policy would simply peter out. Deflation, they argued, was a structural problem born of poor demographics and lack of demand. Seeking to beat it by printing endless money would prove useless. Nor was Abenomics new, they argued. It was simply a tired rerun of the borrow-and-spend policies that had failed so miserably in the 1990s. Why should stimulus work any better now? Abe had an answer for this, alluding to the fact that previous stimulus packages and been stop-and-start affairs. 'True, we have shot these arrows before, but only timidly, and incrementally,' he said, returning to his favourite metaphor. 'In my plan, the three arrows are being shot strong, fast and all at the same time.'[7]

Economists are nothing if not argumentative. Others trained in the dismal science feared not that Abenomics would fail, but that it might work too well. Instead of creating inflation, they worried it would cause hyperinflation. Even one of its supporters compared the reflationary exercise to pulling a brick with a piece of elastic. First, the brick wouldn't budge; then it might jolt forward uncontrollably.[8] One of the concerns was that, as inflation returned, the value of savings would be eroded and money would pour abroad. If the outflow were large, it could deprive the government of the funds it needed to feed its deficit habit. That would oblige it to borrow abroad, or print yet more money until the yen was entirely debased. In the meantime, the government would find it harder to pay the interest on the public debt. One of the virtues of deflation was that the government could borrow at super-low interest rates. If rates began to rise, servicing the debt would become harder. There was also concern about commercial banks that had stuffed their balance sheets with government bonds. If interest rates rose along with inflationary expectations then the value of those holdings would drop,[9] potentially threatening the banks' solvency. Escaping deflation, in the words of Takatoshi Ito, an academic economist, meant treading 'a narrow path'. Not a few economists predict Abenomics will end in disaster.

There was also the question of how inflation would affect ordinary Japanese. Rising prices would hardly be a good thing if wages didn't go up too. Deflation had helped preserve living standards. Inflation could erode them. In April McDonald's announced that it intended to increase the price of its burgers by 25 per cent. There was to be no commensurate rise in its employees' wages. Abe asked Japanese businesses to help his reflationary project by paying workers more. Many were unmoved, though some did respond. Lawson, the chain of convenience stores, raised salaries for most of its staff by 3 per cent from April 2013, though its boss, Takeshi Niinami, was a hardly neutral member of one of Abe's economic panels. Toyota, whose business had roared back to health after a few rough years, paid its workers an average bonus of Y2.05 million (about $21,000 at the time), the highest in five years. Still, such rises would need to become widespread if workers were not to feel poorer as the result of inflation.

Critics also objected that flooding the country with money ignored fundamental economic problems. How would cranking the printing presses, they asked, encourage more women to work, make the country more open to immigration or businesses more innovative? Abe had an answer – of sorts. His third arrow was structural reform, or deregulation aimed at creating more competition. In addition to energy deregulation, Abe proposed to free up rules governing commercial farms as well as hospitals and nursing homes. He revived the idea of special economic zones where taxes could be lower and some government regulations waived. He even began to talk about the need to get more women into the workforce and proposed a new law compelling companies to promote at least one woman to executive level. 'Women are Japan's most underused resource,' he said, echoing what foreigners had been telling Japan for years.[10]

There was much scepticism about Abe's third arrow, which sounded to many like empty rhetoric and a recycling of old ideas. Still Abe surprised many by committing Japan to join the Trans-Pacific Partnership, a sophisticated trade agreement that the US was hatching with several Asian states. Among the alphabet soup of trade pacts, the TPP was meant to stand out. For one thing, it did not include China, no doubt a big plus for the hawkish Abe. For another, it aimed to set rules governing intellectual property, non-tariff barriers, state-owned companies and public tenders. It was supposed to be the Rolls-Royce of trade agreements. Japan's cosseted farmers reacted to the idea as might be expected: with horror. But proponents argued that the TPP would force Japanese businesses to raise productivity, vital to counteract the effects of a declining workforce. 'This is Japan's last chance,' Masaaki Kanno, an economist, said somewhat dramatically.[11]

For his part, Abe told parliament, 'The future of Japan's economic growth depends on us having the willpower and the courage to sail without hesitation onto the rough seas of global competition.' It was the old debate about what it meant to be an island: inward-looking and defensive, or open and buccaneering. Abe appeared to be arguing for the latter. In reality, some Japanese business leaders had beaten him to the punch. In 2012, Japanese companies spent a whopping $113 billion acquiring foreign businesses, second only to the US and far more than China, whose companies spent $63 billion, or the UK, at $56 billion.[12] One company alone, Softbank, a telecoms giant run by Masayoshi Son, one of Japan's most swashbuckling entrepreneurs, was proposing to pay some $20 billion for a controlling stake in Sprint Nextel, the third-largest US mobile operator. Japanese companies, often with government backing, were pouring billions into emerging Asian markets, including China, Indonesia, India and Myanmar. Japan's days of fast growth were behind it, but the country was located in the world's most dynamic region. Japanese business was not about to stand idly by.

Abe's promise to restore economic vigour had not been his only selling point. Voters were also looking for someone who could stand up against China. Changed international circumstances had transformed Abe's nationalism from a negative to a positive in many voters' eyes. For months before his re-election, Sino-Japanese relations had been darkening over the issue of the Senkaku, the five uninhabited islands in the East China Sea known as the Diaoyu in China. Tokyo regarded the islands, incorporated into its territory in 1895, as indisputably Japanese. Beijing said they had been Chinese since ancient times and were stolen. In the summer of 2012, Shintaro Ishihara, the octogenarian rightwinger, in what proved to be his last significant act as Tokyo governor, began to raise private donations to buy three of the islands and develop them. His aim was doubtless to provoke China and to prod his own government into taking a stand. He succeeded on both counts.

'If Ishihara's plans are acted upon, then it will result in an extremely grave crisis between Japan and China,' Japan's ambassador to Beijing warned in unscripted remarks that were to get him sacked.[13] The official line was that the transfer of ownership made no difference since the islands were indisputably Japanese. Still, in the interests of avoiding friction, the Japanese government decided to scupper Ishihara's plans by buying the islands itself. That way it could leave them undeveloped – and, it thought, take the sting out of the dispute with China. It was a spectacularly clumsy piece of diplomacy. From Beijing's perspective, Japan had 'nationalized' the islands and thrown down the gauntlet.

On the day Tokyo purchased the islands for a little over $20 million in September 2012, all hell broke loose. The worst anti-Japanese demonstrations since the war erupted in fifty-seven cities across China, where tens of thousands of protesters took to the streets, torching Japanese factories and ransacking Japanese shops. In Xi'an, the ancient capital, now a sprawling city of 8 million people, protesters lost their fear of China's internal security forces when they overturned police cars of Japanese make. One Chinese man, Li Jianli, caught driving a white Toyota Corolla, was hauled out of his car and nearly beaten to death with a bicycle lock.[14] In Chengdu, where several thousand marched, one banner chillingly proclaimed: 'Even if China is covered with graves, we must kill all Japanese'.[15]

This was the background to Abe's re-election. Many Japanese voters were wary of Abe's revisionist tendencies and social conservatism. Yet there was a growing nervousness about China's intentions that made the election of a strongman more palatable. Abe came to power saying he would strengthen Japan's military, and even suggesting he might station Japanese troops on the Senkaku. He would not only stand up to China but also to South Korea and Russia, the other nations with which Japan has emotive territorial disputes dating back to the Second World War.[16] His re-election coincided with a once-in-a-decade political transition in China. Xi Jinping, the new Chinese president, was in no mood to appear soft either. In the waters around the Senkaku, there were now almost daily stand-offs between coastguard ships from China and Japan. Activists from both sides tried to plant flags on the remote islands. On 10 January 2013, two weeks into Abe's premiership, Chinese and Japanese fighter aircraft tangled over the Senkaku. A few days later, the *PLA Daily* reported that the General Staff Department had ordered all units to prepare for battle, in what may have been the first such order since China fought Vietnam in 1979.[17] The following month, Tokyo accused the Chinese navy of aiming its weapons at a Japanese warship, an action that involves locking a fire-control radar onto its target. If the Japanese ship had assumed it was under attack, it could have fired back, potentially provoking an armed clash. (Beijing said it had used only normal surveillance radar.) Japan's defence minister, Itsunori Onodera, called it 'extremely abnormal behaviour'.[18] One small mistake, he implied, could lead to war.

Increasing brinkmanship over the islands was doubly dangerous since the US was bound by the US–Japan Security Treaty to come to Japan's aid if Japan were attacked. To Beijing's anger, Washington confirmed that the Senkaku islands were covered by the treaty, although many policymakers privately doubted that the US would risk American lives to defend a few uninhabited rocks.[19] In short, the Senkaku islands, about which the world had scarcely heard a few months before, were now among the planet's most dangerous flashpoints. Surin Pitsuwan, secretary-general of the ten-member Association of Southeast Asian Nations, called them 'Asia's Palestine'.[20] The world has a bad record when it comes to accommodating rising powers. One academic calculates that since 1500 in eleven out of fifteen cases when a rising power rose to challenge a ruling power the upshot has been war.[21] In this case, the rising power was China and the ruling power the US. But Japan was Washington's representative in the Pacific – and it carried plenty of historical baggage of its own.

As prime minister, Abe asserted Japan's determination to defend what it regarded as its undisputable territory. 'No nation should underestimate the firmness of our resolve. No one should ever doubt the robustness of the Japan–US Alliance,' he said.[22] As the economy gave signs of flickering into life, and his approval ratings rose above 70 per cent, he began to show his nationalist colours. In April, he sent a cypress tree as an offering to Yasukuni shrine along with several members of his cabinet. Altogether, a record 168 Diet members prayed at the shrine for Japan's war dead. When I interviewed him years before, he had said, 'Yasukuni shrine is in Japan, and it is ridiculous to suggest that the prime minister can't step on a particular spot on his own soil. When they [Beijing] realize there is no room for negotiation, they will stop complaining.'[23]

Back in office, Abe raised doubts about Japan's 1995 apology for its wartime atrocities. Using the same logic as Yuko Tojo, granddaughter of the wartime prime minister, who died in 2013, he questioned the use of the word 'invasion' to describe Japan's occupation of much of

Asia in the 1930s and 40s.[24] He also stepped up his plans to revise the pacifist constitution. His approach was to change Article 96, the one that dealt with the procedure for amending the constitution itself. Instead of the requirement of a two-thirds majority of both houses, followed by a referendum, he proposed a simple majority. 'It's been over sixty years since its enactment and its contents have become obsolete,' he said.[25] Japan had not revised a single word of its constitution since 1947 compared to Germany, which had amended its charter fully fifty-eight times since 1949. Among the changes Abe sought were to restore the emperor's role as 'head of state', rather than mere symbol, and to re-establish Japan's 'sovereign right' to wage war. Six decades of pacifism notwithstanding, an editorial in the *China Daily* cast Japan as an unrepentant militaristic nation, liable to go on the rampage if its constitutional shackles were removed.[26] The Abe administration provided much grist to the mill. It launched the largest naval vessel Japan has built since the war, nominally a destroyer, but an aircraft carrier in all but name. Abe began to make appearances perched defiantly atop military equipment. Taro Aso, the deputy prime minister whose revisionist convictions were similar to those of his boss, casually suggested that Japan had a few tricks to learn from Nazi Germany. 'We should proceed quietly,' he said of plans to revise the constitution. 'One day people realized that the Weimar constitution had changed into the Nazi constitution. Why don't we learn from that approach?' Those remarks, incredibly, did not lead to his dismissal, but rather to the excruciatingly embarrassing clarification that 'The Abe administration does not perceive Nazi Germany in a positive light.'[27] No wonder that, around the same time, Paul Kennedy, a prominent academic who in the late 1980s had written in epochal terms about Japan's precipitous rise, concluded unflatteringly that Japan was 'still bewildered by the outside world [and] cramped by its past'.[28]

In Japan, too, many were alarmed by Abe's revisionism and his hankering after backward-looking traditional values. Kiichi Fujiwara, professor of international politics at Tokyo University, said he was terrified by plans to tinker with constitutional provisions protecting equality and the rights of the individual. Abe's proposals, he said, were not so much a revision as a 'dismantling' of constitutional safe-guards.[29] Most opposition centred on the threat to pacifist Article 9. 'If that goes, everything else will follow,' said Noriko Hama of Dosh-isha University. 'Who cares if it was written by Americans,' she added of the constitution's origins during the US occupation period. 'It's a fundamentally decent document. The constitution is there to protect the people from power. Abe's version is that people should have a responsibility towards the state, not the other way around.'[30]

Opposition to constitutional revision has eroded somewhat since the 1990s when surveys suggested two-thirds of Japanese objected. Still, in 2013, Pew, the international polling organization, found that 56 per cent of Japanese opposed amending the constitution.[31] If the issue of revision is ever put to the public – as it must be if the constitu-tion is to be altered – most Japanese academics say the proposition would be roundly rejected. Even Abe admitted he didn't have the numbers. In the summer of 2013, not for the first time, the idea of constitutional revision was quietly shelved. Such deep-rooted support for a progressive and uniquely pacifist document belies the idea that Japan stands on the brink of some sort of nationalist revival.

We can't pretend to unravel the causes and effects of history with any accuracy. Yet in the case of Abenomics, a bold attempt to reflate the economy, it may not be too farfetched to look for a catalyst in the twin shocks dealt by the 2011 tsunami and a more assertive China. In retrospect, the earthquake and tsunami do seem to have shaken Japan psychologically. Ishihara had echoed the Taisho emperor by declaring the catastrophe to be divine retribution. Although his remarks caused outrage and he uncharacteristically apologized, he may have hit a nerve. Perhaps what he called 'egoism' had dulled the Japanese senses after all. Perhaps, its leaders had been kidding themselves for years, imagining that Japan could somehow stumble on as usual. The tsu-nami brought with it a sense of crisis. In its wake, the economy shrank and Japanese businesses worried about locating their factories on an archipelago susceptible to natural disasters and chronically depend-ent on foreign energy. Hadn't one politician compared shutting down the nuclear reactors to 'group suicide'? Yet that was exactly what had been done. Now a nation that had built its post-war prosperity on exports was running chronic trade deficits. Soon its future might be mortgaged to foreigners. Even if there were no immediate crisis, could Japan afford more years of genteel decline? Yoichi Funabashi, my friend at the *Asahi*, thought not. Northeast Asia was 'a jungle', he said. If Japan were weak, it would not survive.[32]

That's where China came in. Beijing's uncompromising stance over the Senkaku had convinced Abe more than ever that Japan needed to huddle closer to the US. That was one of the reasons he had agreed to join the Trans-Pacific Partnership. He wanted a seat at the table where international rules were being debated. If Japan were to be taken seriously, it would have to arrest its economic decline. The idea of *fukoku kyohei*, 'rich country, strong army', went back to the Meiji Restoration, where it became the rallying cry of Japan's modernization.[33] Without a strong economy, how could Japan hope to fulfil Abe's election pledge of spending more on defence? More fundamentally, how could it expect to be taken seriously in the world, to command the respect and status it had been so desperately seeking for 150 years?

Abe had made the link crystal clear during his 2013 visit to Washington to see Barack Obama when he had declared Japan would never be a 'second-tier country'. He gave a speech, entitled 'Japan is Back', in which he time and again made the connection between economic muscle and national security. 'Japan must stay strong, strong first in its economy, and strong also in its national defence,' he declared. 'I will bring back a strong Japan, strong enough to do even more good for the betterment of the world.'[34]

Abenomics, then, was made in both Beijing and Tohoku. Yet it was not entirely a product of external or natural shocks. Contrary to common perception, Japan has not stood still in the twenty years since its bubble burst. Successive governments experimented with a multitude of policies, conventional and otherwise, to get the economy moving again. That they didn't always work attests partly to their own failings and partly to the severity of the shock that the country suffered in 1990 when its property and equity bubbles collapsed. Japan's labour market has since been turned upside down, not always comfortably so, especially for the young shut out of the job-for-life system. But the changes have allowed companies to adjust their wage bill downwards without causing mass unemployment. The relationship between men and women has changed too as the certainties of the pre-bubble years have given way to more complex dynamics in more straitened times. So has the relationship between young and old, as traditional ideas are challenged and as economic realities bring the generations into conflict. Even politics have been remade. The rudiments of a two-party system have been set down, though the Liberal Democrats are now decisively back in power. Post-Koizumi, the urban electorate has more sway and political parties, which can no longer count on the loyalty of large blocks of voters, are obliged to spell out their platforms. These days they actually write manifestoes.

For all the talk of isolation, Japan's companies are now more global than ever. The Toyota you're driving is as likely to have been built in Tupelo, Mississippi as in Nagoya, Japan. There are some 1.2 million Japanese living abroad – some 140,000 in China alone – altogether twice the number in 1990 when Japan was supposedly at the height of its international influence. Likewise, for all the justified criticism about how closed Japan can be, there are more than 2 million foreign residents living in Japan today, nearly twice the level of twenty years ago.[35]

As if to underline Japan's continued relevance, in September 2013 the International Olympic Committee selected Tokyo as the host of the 2020 Summer Olympics ahead of Madrid and Istanbul. Tales of Japan's never-ending problems and continuing leaks at the Fukushima plant notwithstanding, the committee judged Tokyo the safest bet, rich and stable enough to host the Games with ease. In Japan, the decision was greeted by some as a vote of confidence in the country's efforts to overcome years of stagnation and revive its fortunes.

Though we have got used to the idea of Japan's inexorable economic decline, it remains quite comfortably the third-largest economy in the world, the size of the combined economies of Britain and France and three times the size of India's. It is the richest economy of any size in Asia, its citizens, on average, eight times wealthier than the Chinese.[36] For all its many problems, Japan remains the pre-eminent example of a non-western country catching up with advanced living standards.[37] It seems a safe assumption that, whether Abenomics works or not, Japan will remain one of the world's top five economies for several decades to come.

Just as in the 1980s, when Japan was wrongly assumed to be on the verge of economic supremacy, so in 2013 it has been prematurely written off. Two 'lost decades' and its manifold problems notwithstanding, reports of Japan's demise are exaggerated.

Hong Kong, September 2013

# Notes

FOREWORD

1. Pico Iyer, 'Now is the Season for Japan', *New York Times*, 22 March 2012.
2. Interview with author, Boston, May 2011.
3. Quoted by Kenneth Pyle, *Japan Rising*, pp. 320–21.
4. Yoshio Sugimoto, *An Introduction to Japanese Society* (2nd edn), p. 13.
5. Iyer, 'Now is the Season for Japan'.
6. Interview with Masakazu Yamazaki, 'Live Life to the Full, Knowing that it is Fleeting', *Asahi* newspaper, 14 March 2012.


1. TSUNAMI

1. Joshua Hammer, *Yokohama Burning*, p. 62.
2. 'The Genius of Japanese Civilization', *The Atlantic Monthly*, vol. 76, no. 456 (October 1895), pp. 449–58.
3. Hammer, *Yokohama Burning*, p. 64.
4. Kenneth Change, 'Quake Moves Japan Closer to US and Alters Earth's Spin', *New York Times*, 13 March 2011.
5. Ibid.
6. Remarks to author, Rikuzentakata, June 2012.
7. European Space Agency, 9 August 2011, http://www.esa.int/esaEO/SEMV87 JTPQG_index_2.html
8. Story recounted to author by Hirotoshi Oikawa, resident of Rikuzentakata, in August 2011.
9. Interview with author, Rikuzentakata, August 2011.
10. Robert Mendick and Andrew Gilligan, *Sunday Telegraph*, 20 March 2011.
11. Michael Wines, 'Japanese Town Still Hopes as Reality Intrudes', *New York Times*, 22 March 2011.

12. From an account by Kazuyoshi Sasaki, related to author, Rikuzentakata, August 2011.
13. Interview with author, Rikuzentakata, August 2011.
14. Carl Hoffman, 'Lessons from Japan', *Popular Mechanics*, 1 August 2011.
15. Gordon Fairclough, 'Hope of the Lone Pine', *Wall Street Journal*, 9 July 2011.


## 2. BENDING ADVERSITY

1. 'Japanese Emperor: I am Praying for the Nation', *Korea Herald*, 17 March 2011.
2. Report by Rebuild Japan Initiative Foundation, quoted in Martin Fackler, 'Evacuation of Tokyo Was Considered after Disaster', *International Herald Tribune*, 29 February 2012.
3. Ibid.
4. Tyler Brule, 'Tokyo with the Dimmer Switch On', *Financial Times*, 19 March 2011.
5. Hiroshi Fuse, 'Saga Over Using Firewood from Tsunami-hit Area in Kyoto Bonfire Shows Cultural Gap', *Mainichi Daily News*, 20 August 2011.


## 3. SHIMAGUNI

1. Interview with author, Los Angeles, January 2009.
2. Jared Diamond, *Guns, Germs, and Steel*, see pp. 426–49.
3. Story related to the author by Pico Iyer, a biographer of the Dalai Lama, Nara, March 2012.
4. In some ways, it could be argued that Japanese culture is less able to absorb foreign influence than other cultures. As Donald Keene points out, English speakers use the word 'robot' with, almost certainly, no knowledge that it was derived from the Czech. But in Japanese, written in the katakana script reserved for imported words, it is for ever preserved as an alien word. See Donald Keene, *Seeds in the Heart*, p. 10.
5. Yoshihiko Noda, prime minister from September 2011 to December 2012, loved to lower expectations with self-deprecatory remarks.
6. Author's observation during visit to Hiroshima Peace Memorial Museum, 2006. In another moment of stress, a young kamikaze pilot, foreshadowing Japan's defeat in war, compared his country, and perhaps himself, to a 'carp on the cutting board'. The pilot, Hachiro Sasaki, died at the age of

twenty-two on a kamikaze mission. Quoted in Emiko Ohnuki-Tierney, *Kamikaze Diaries: Reflections of Japanese Student Soldiers.*

7. Joji Mori, *Nihonjin – Karanashi-Tamago no Jigazo* ('Japanese – Self-portrait of a Shell-less Egg'), 1977, Kodansha Gendai Shinsho.

8. 'Nippon: Japan Since 1945', BBC documentary (conceived and written by Peter Pagnamenta), 1990.

9. See Karel van Wolferen, *The Enigma of Japanese Power*, p. 348.

10. David Pilling, '. . . And Now for Somewhere Completely Different', *Financial Times*, 15 February 2008.

11. Pico Iyer, 'Now is the Season for Japan', *New York Times*, 22 March 2012.

12. Alan Macfarlane, *Japan Through the Looking Glass*, p. 197.

13. Interview with author, Kyoto, September 2003.

14. Macfarlane, *Japan Through the Looking Glass*, p. 220.

15. Gavan McCormack, *Client State: Japan in the American Embrace*, p. 8.

16. John Dower, *Embracing Defeat*, pp. 278–9.

17. McCormack, *Client State*, p. 13.

18. Diamond, *Guns, Germs and Steel*, pp. 426–49.

19. Jeff Kingston, Temple University, remarks to author, Tokyo, July 2007.

20. Andrew Gordon, *A Modern History of Japan*, p. 65.

21. Yoshio Sugimoto, *An Introduction to Japanese Society* (2nd edn), p. 62.

22. 'Japanese Author Murakami Wins Jerusalem Prize', Agence France Presse, 16 February 2009.

23. Telephone interview with author, January 2008.

## 4. LEAVING ASIA

1. Description of Christianity in an edict of 1825 issued by the Tokugawa *bakufu*, cited in Marius Jansen, *The Making of Modern Japan*, p. 266.

2. Gavan McCormack, *Client State: Japan in the American Embrace*.

3. Ian Buruma, *Inventing Japan: From Empire to Economic Miracle*, p. xi.

4. Kenneth Pyle, *Japan Rising: The Resurgence of Japanese Power and Purpose*, p. 107.

5. Interview with author, Seattle, April 2011.

6. Interview with author, Tokyo, October 2011.

7. George Sansom, *A History of Japan to 1334*, pp. 14–15.

8. Ibid., p. 63.

9. Ibid., pp. 51–9.

10. Donald Keene, *The Japanese Discovery of Europe, 1720–1830*, p. 27.

11. Andrew Gordon, *A Modern History of Japan*, p. 3.

12. Ibid., p. 19.

13. Not counting the seven years from 1945 when it was directly controlled by the US Siam, modern-day Thailand, also escaped colonization.

14. Jansen, *Modern Japan*, p. 64.

15. Ibid., p. 92.

16. George Feifer, *Breaking Open Japan*, p. 61.

17. Jansen, *Modern Japan*, p. 277.

18. Keene, *1720–1830*, p. 16.

19. Ibid., pp. 147–52.

20. Buruma, *Inventing Japan*, p. 6.

21. Cited by Keene, *1720–1830*, p. 21.

22. The *eta* today are known as *burakumin*. Until recently, they were still discriminated against and respectable families would sometimes hire private detectives to ensure that their offspring did not unwittingly marry into an untouchable bloodline.

23. Quoted in Keene, *Japanese Discovery of Europe*, p. 22.

24. Ronald P. Toby, *State and Diplomacy in Early Modern Japan*, p. 225.

25. Jansen, *Modern Japan*, p. 205.

26. Yukichi Fukuzawa, *The Autobiography of Yukichi Fukuzawa* (trans. Eiichi Kiyooka), p. v.

27. Ibid., p. 86.

28. Description by the magistrate of Uraga, cited by Feifer in *Breaking Open Japan*, p. 5.

29. Fukuzawa, *Autobiography*, p. 109.

30. Ibid., p. 91.

31. Feifer, *Breaking Open Japan*, p. 4.

32. Pyle, *Japan Rising*, p. 78.

33. Ibid., p. 75.

34. Ibid., p. 78.

35. Interview with author, Boston, May 2011.

36. Fukuzawa, *Autobiography*, p. 335.

37. Kakuzo Okakura, *The Book of Tea*.

38. Buruma, *Inventing Japan*, p. 31.

39. Quoted in Kenneth Pyle, *The Making of Modern Japan*, p. 87.

40. Quoted by John Dower, *Embracing Defeat*, p. 21.

41. For a detailed discussion of the various estimates of war casualties see John Dower, *War Without Mercy: Race & Power in the Pacific War*, pp. 293–301.

42. Pyle, *Making of Modern Japan*, p. 143.

43. Cited by Jonathan Bailey, *Great Power Strategy in Asia: Empire, Culture and Trade, 1905–2005*, p. 128.

44. Ibid.
45. Justin Wintle, *Perfect Hostage: Aung San Suu Kyi, Burma and the Generals*, p. 104.
46. Buruma, *Inventing Japan*, pp. 46–7.
47. Quoted in Gordon, *A Modern History*, p. 132.
48. Pyle, *Making of Modern Japan*, p. 164.
49. Gordon, *A Modern History*, p. 170.
50. Pyle, *Making of Modern Japan*, p. 187.
51. Ibid., p. 178.
52. Quoted in Donald Keene, *So Lovely a Country Will Never Perish: Wartime Diaries of Japanese Writers*, pp. 16–17.
53. Translated by Keene, *So Lovely*.

## 5. THE MAGIC TEAPOT

1. Recollection to author, Tokyo, April 2011.
2. Shijuro Ogata was deputy governor for international relations, formerly one rank below the full-fledged deputy governor.
3. Shijuro Ogata, unpublished memoirs in English, based on *Harukanaru Showa* (The Distant Showa Years), published by the *Asahi* newspaper, 2005.
4. Remark to author, Tokyo, July 2002.
5. John Dower, *Embracing Defeat*, p. 45.
6. For a superb analysis of how propaganda shaped American views of the Japanese and vice versa see John Dower, *War Without Mercy: Race & Power in the Pacific War*.
7. 'Nippon: Japan Since 1945', BBC documentary (conceived and written by Peter Pagnamenta), 1990.
8. *Lunch with the FT*, Paul Krugman, 26 May 2012.
9. South Korea has begun to close in on Japan when measured on a purchasing power parity basis, which takes into account the cost of living across countries.
10. Cited in Roger Buckley, *Japan Today*, p. 85.
11. *Grave of the Fireflies (Hotaru no Haka)*, 1988.
12. 'Nippon: Japan Since 1945'.
13. The Americans did provide food shipments to relieve hunger and malnutrition.
14. See Dower, *Embracing Defeat*, pp. 525–46.
15. 'Nippon: Japan Since 1945'.
16. Quoted in Buckley, *Japan Today*, p. 5.
17. 'Nippon: Japan Since 1945'.

18. Ibid.
19. Michael E. Porter et al., *Can Japan Compete?*
20. 'Nippon: Japan Since 1945'.
21. John Nathan's lovely phrase in *Sony: The Private Life*, p. 4.
22. Ibid.
23. Ibid.
24. John Nathan, 'Sony's Boldness Wasn't "Made in Japan"', *Wall Street Journal*, 11 October 1999.
25. Andrew Pollack, 'Akio Morita, co-founder of Sony and Japanese Business Leader, Dies at 78', *New York Times*, 4 October 1999.
26. Masahiro Yamada, comments to author, Tokyo, February 2005.
27. 'Nippon: Japan Since 1945'.
28. James Abegglen, *21st Century Japanese Management*, p. 15.
29. 'Nippon: Japan Since 1945'.
30. Boston Consulting Group press release, 4 May 2007.
31. See for example Gavan McCormack, *The Emptiness of Japanese Affluence*.
32. That was partly to distract attention from the political turmoil as Japan's left fought against the right over the US–Japan security alliance and other social issues.
33. Buckley, *Japan Today*, p. 73.
34. In truth, as many countries have found, the catch-up phase of development is much easier than when economies reach maturity.
35. Bill Emmott, *The Sun Also Sets*, p. 5.
36. 'Nippon: Japan Since 1945'.
37. Ibid.
38. Kenneth Pyle, *The Making of Modern Japan*, p. 271.
39. Email exchange with author, August 2012.
40. Stephen Miller, 'He Chronicled the Rise of "Japan Inc" and its Distinct Brand of Capitalism', *Wall Street Journal*, 12 May 2007.
41. Cited by Emmott, *Sun Also Sets*, p. 8.

## 6. AFTER THE FALL

1. For newspaper accounts of Mrs Inoue and her remarkable ceramic toad, see David Ibison, 'What Happened to the Gifted Toad?', *Financial Times*, 30 September 2002; and Steve Burrell, 'How a Lucky Toad Spawned a Bank Scam', *Australian Financial Review*, 19 August 1991.
2. http://www.savills.co.uk/_news/newsitem.aspx?intSitePageId=72418&intNewsSitePageId=116038-0&intNewsMonth=10&intNewsYear=2011

3. Bill Emmott, *The Sun Also Sets*, p. 120.
4. Correspondence with Clyde Prestowitz.
5. In the eighteen years to 2008, all the extra spending combined amounted to around 28 per cent of GDP. Markus Bruckner and Anita Tuladhar, 'Public Investment as a Fiscal Stimulus: Evidence from Japan's Regional Spending During the 1990s', International Monetary Fund (IMF) Working Paper, April 2010.
6. Richard Lloyd Parry, 'Found in Translation', *The Times*, 22 January 2005.
7. Haruki Murakami, *After the Quake*, p. 116.
8. Interview with author, Tokyo, June 2003.
9. David Pilling, 'Doomsday and After', *Financial Times*, 19 March 2005.
10. Interview with author, Tokyo, January 2003.

## 7. JAPAN AS NUMBER THREE

1. Calculation provided by Masaaki Kanno of JP Morgan, Tokyo. The 1995 Nikkei average was 17,355.34. By June 2012, it had fallen to 8,638.08. To find out how much Y100,000 would be worth in today's purchasing terms, one needs to apply a value of the GDP deflator, which measures inflation (or deflation) over time. Kanno suggests using the GDP private consumption deflator, which makes Y100,000 in 1995 worth Y112,000 today. If a broader measure of the GDP deflator is used, it would be worth Y122,000.
2. Akio Mikuni quoted by David Pilling in 'Heads Down', *Financial Times*, 17 May 2003.
3. Martin Wolf, 'Japan on the Brink', *Financial Times*, 14 November 2001.
4. Telephone conversation with author, 2011.
5. Measured in purchasing power parity terms, which takes into account the cost of goods in different countries.
6. A value not adjusted for inflation (or deflation).
7. Calculations based on figures from the International Monetary Fund, World Economic Outlook Database, April 2012.
8. Figures provided by Masaaki Kanno of JP Morgan, Tokyo.
9. In purchasing power parity terms, China's economy had been bigger than Japan's for many years before 2010.
10. According to the 'Urban Land Price Index' published by the Japan Real Estate Institute, national average land prices in March 2011 were 62 per cent below their 1991 peak, with commercial land down 76 per cent and residential land down 48 per cent.

11. Teizo Taya, special counsellor to Daiwa Institute of Research and a former Bank of Japan board member, estimated that total outstanding loans shrank from Y600 trillion in 1995 to Y400 trillion a decade later.
12. Interview with author and Michiyo Nakamoto, a *Financial Times* colleague, Tokyo, March 2012.
13. Nicholas Eberstadt, 'Demography and Japan's Future', in Clay Chandler et al. (eds.), *Reimagining Japan: The Quest for a Future that Works*, pp. 82–7.
14. Jesper Koll, director of equity research at JP Morgan. Even with their high yen, many Japanese find cities such as London and Singapore very expensive, yet offering lower-quality goods and services.
15. International Monetary Fund, World Economic Outlook Database, April 2012.
16. If we want to compare average real per capita annual growth rates since 2002, Switzerland grew at 1 per cent, Germany at 1.3, Brazil at 2.7 and China at 9.8.
17. Organisation for Economic Co-operation and Development, 'Harmonised Unemployment Rates', March 2012.
18. Organisation for Economic Co-operation and Development, 'Divided We Stand: Why Inequality Keeps Rising', 2011.
19. Ibid.
20. Yoshio Sugimoto, *An Introduction to Japanese Society* (2nd edn), p. 57.
21. Peter Hessler, 'All Due Respect, an American Reporter Takes on the Yakuza', *The New Yorker*, 12 January 2012.
22. European Institute for Crime Prevention and Control, International Statistics on Crime and Justice, 2010.
23. Given a US population of 315 million and a Japanese one of 127 million, the US prison population is proportionately ten times higher.
24. Interview with author, Tokyo, July 2011.
25. Richard Jerram, personal correspondence, January 2013.
26. Japan's net debt, which some argue is a better measure, was about half that in 2012, but still an uncomfortably high 113 per cent.
27. Gavan McCormack, *The Emptiness of Japanese Affluence*, p. xiii.
28. Botswana has very low debt and is well managed.
29. Peter Tasker, 'The Japanese Debt Disaster Movie', *Financial Times*, 27 January 2011.
30. Telephone interview with author, May 2011.
31. There are dangers in inflation too, says Ito. If, for example, prices started rising by 4 or 5 per cent a year, the government would need to pay much higher interest on its debt. The paradox is that, because of subdued economic activity and therefore rock-bottom borrowing rates, the gov-

ernment can easily manage its debt payments. That makes the Japanese government perversely wedded to low growth. To get out of that fix, it must tread what Ito calls a 'narrow path'.

32. Peter Tasker, 'How to Make Monkeys out of the Ratings Agencies', *Financial Times*, 11 August 2011.

33. Richard Koo, *The Holy Grail of Macroeconomics: Lessons from Japan's Great Recession*.

34. Martin Wolf, 'Unreformed, But Japan is Back', *Financial Times*, 7 March 2006.

35. Some economists argue that private debt should be included and is, perhaps, an even greater vulnerability and predictor of crisis than public debt. By this measure US debt rises to 250 per cent of GDP. Taking into account Japan's higher savings rate, on this measure, the US debt position is actually worse than Japan's. See a paper by Steve Clemons and Richard Vague, 'How to Predict the Next Financial Crisis', 2012.

36. 'Arigato for Nothing, Keynes-san', *Wall Street Journal Europe*, 24 May 2012.

37. Peter Tasker, 'Japan Needs a Radical to Tackle its Godzilla-size Public Debt', *Financial Times*, 28 June 2012.

38. Paul Krugman, 'Nobody Understands Debt', *New York Times*, 1 January 2012.

39. Interview with author, Tokyo, November 2006.

40. In fact, spending on benefits rose substantially because of what are called 'automatic stabilizers', including higher unemployment and social security payments when economies are in recession or growing slowly.

41. Anatole Kaletsky, 'Britain is Losing the Economic Olympics', Reuters, 25 July 2012.

42. Email correspondence, January 2013.

43. Niall Ferguson, 'Obama's Gotta Go', *Newsweek*, 19 April 2012.

44. Jon Hilsenrath, 'Fed Chief Gets Set to Apply Lessons of Japan's History', *Wall Street Journal*, 12 October 2010.

## 8. SAMURAI WITH A QUIFF

1. 'Lionheart' was also the name of his weekly newsletter which at its peak had some 2 million subscribers.

2. Gregory Anderson, 'Lionheart or Paper Tiger? A First-term Koizumi Retrospective', *Asian Perspective*, vol. 28, no. 1, 2004, pp. 149–82.

3. Hideaki Omura, a junior member of the Hashimoto faction, quoted in the *Financial Times*, 21 April 2001.

4. Interview with author, November 2003.

5. Heizo Takenaka, *The Structural Reforms of the Koizumi Cabinet*, p. 7.

6. She later proved a little too outspoken and became almost comically unpopular with the cautious bureaucrats of the foreign affairs ministry who spent all their time briefing against her. Koizumi fired her in January 2002; Japan's first female foreign minister had lasted just ten months.

7. Takenaka, *Structural Reforms*, p. 26.

8. http://www.kantei.go.jp/foreign/koizumispeech/2001/0507policyspeech_e. html, accessed 1 January 2012.

9. Interview with author, Tokyo, October 2003.

10. Interview with author, Tokyo, October 2003.

11. Takenaka, *Structural Reforms*, p. 17.

12. Recollection to author, October 2011.

13. Interview with author, Tokyo, October 2003.

14. Tim Larimer, 'Japan's Destroyer', *Time*, 17 September 2001.

15. Shares were treated as part of the banks' capital.

16. David Pilling, 'Advocate of "Hard Landing" May Join Debt Team in Japan', *Financial Times*, 3 October 2002.

17. David Pilling and Mariko Sanchanta, 'Japan Central Bank's Bad Loan Warnings Fall on Deaf Ears', *Financial Times*, 25 September 2002.

18. Gillian Tett, 'Revealing the Secrets of MoF-tan', *Financial Times*, 31 January 1998.

19. Takenaka, *Structural Reforms*, p. 76.

20. *Newsweek*, October 2002.

21. Takenaka, *Structural Reforms*, p. 87.

22. Resona's capital adequacy ratio, which measures the amount of core capital a bank has against its risk-weighted assets, fell below 4 per cent. The shortfall came about as a result of auditors' stricter interpretation of how banks should account for deferred tax assets, credits on future tax bills. In Japan, these were considered suspect since there was no guarantee banks could make future profits against which to offset those assets. See ibid., pp. 96–104.

23. Ibid., p. 109.

24. David Pilling, 'Rising Sum', *Financial Times*, 15 November 2006.

25. Adam Posen, 'Send in the Samurai', in Clay Chandler et al. (eds.), *Reimagining Japan: The Quest for a Future that Works*, p. 104.

26. Spending on public works had risen to about 6 per cent of gross domestic product in the late 1990s when the government was seeking to use stimulus measures to jolt the economy into life. By the end of Koizumi's term, this had fallen to around 3 per cent of GDP. See Peter Tasker, 'Japan

Needs a Radical to Tackle its Godzilla-size Public Debt', *Financial Times*, 28 June 2012.

27. David Pilling, 'Japan's PM Turns his Back on Big Government', *Financial Times*, 19 July 2002.

28. Interview with author, Nagano, July 2002.

29. David Pilling, 'Tokyo on Road to Normality as S&P Upgrades Debt Outlook', *Financial Times*, 24 May 2006.

30. David Pilling, 'Japan's Economy and the Koizumi Myth', *Financial Times*, 17 October 2007.

31. Interview with author, Fukuoka, January 2003.

32. David Pilling, 'Land of the Rising Inequality Coefficient', *Financial Times*, 14 March 2006.

33. Noritmitsu Onishi, 'It's a Landslide for Koizumi', *International Herald Tribune*, 12 September 2005.

34. Takenaka, *Structural Reforms*, p. 129.

35. Interview with author, Tokyo, May 2002.

36. David Pilling, 'Japan's Post Office Sell-off Could Prove Hard to Deliver', *Financial Times*, 20 April 2005.

37. David Pilling, 'Storming the Castle, Koizumi Shakes up the World's Biggest Financial Institution', *Financial Times*, 13 September 2004.

38. Patricia Maclachlan, University of Texas at Austin, in remarks to author, April 2005.

39. Julian Ryall, 'Ex-LDP Stalwart in Epic Battle', *South China Morning Post*, 8 September 2005.

40. Norimitsu Onishi, 'Koizumi Party, Backing Reforms, Wins by a Landslide', *New York Times*, 12 September 2005.

41. Ibid.

42. David Pilling, 'Koizumi Expects Speedy Passage of Postal Bills', *Financial Times*, 21 September 2005.

43. David Pilling, 'A Second Chance for Koizumi', *Financial Times*, 10 September 2005.

44. David Pilling, 'Koizumi Vindicated', *Financial Times*, 13 September 2005.

45. Interview with author, Nagano, 2006.

46. By the late 2000s, Japan's Gini coefficient was 0.329 compared with 0.345 in the UK and 0.378 in the US and an OECD average of 0.314. The higher the number, the greater the inequality, with 0 as perfect equality and 1 as absolute inequality. By contrast, Sweden has a Gini coefficient of 0.259 and Germany of 0.295, making both more egalitarian societies than Japan, although both actually saw a sharper rise in inequality than Japan in recent years. Chile, also an OECD member, has a coefficient of

0.494. See 'Divided We Stand: Why Inequality Keeps Rising', OECD, 2011.

47. Pilling, 'Land of the Rising Inequality Coefficient'.

48. Tetsushi Kajimoto, 'Income Disparities Rising in Japan', *Japan Times*, 4 January 2006.

49. Interview with author, Tokyo, March 2007.

50. Takehiko Kambayashi, '"Tide of Populism" Decried', *Washington Times*, 16 June 2006.

51. Telephone interview with author, 2011.

52. Interview with author, Tokyo, March 2007.

53. Interview with author, Kyoto, April 2011.

54. Interview with author, Hong Kong, May 2012.

## 9. LIFE AFTER GROWTH

1. David Pilling, 'Reasons to Doubt the Doomsayers', *Financial Times*, 14 March 2007.

2. In 1966, the Year of the Fire Horse, which came around once every sixty years, the fertility rate plummeted to 1.58. That was because girls born in that year were reputed to be cursed with sending their husbands to an early grave. In 1967, the fertility rate bounced back strongly.

3. Keizai Koho Center (Japanese Institute for Social and Economic Affairs), 'Japan 2011, An International Comparison'.

4. According to the United Nations, Britain had an average fertility rate of 1.82 from 2005 to 2010.

5. Official figures supplied by the Silver Human Resources Centre, Tokyo.

6. George Magnus, *The Age of Aging*, p. 35.

7. David Pilling, 'Radical Steps Needed to Unlock Japan's Labour Market', *Financial Times*, 16 January 2004.

8. 'Japan's Centenarians at Record High', BBC, 12 September 2008.

9. United Nations, 'Life Expectancy at Birth, 2005–2010'.

10. Interview with author, Tokyo, July 2011.

11. Magnus, *Age of Aging*, p. 72.

12. Ibid.

13. Masahiro Yamada, interview with author, Tokyo Gakugei University, March 2012.

14. It is worth comparing Japan's situation with Russia's, where the population fell for fifteen straight years after the break-up of the Soviet Union, though it has ticked up again since 2009. In contrast to Japan, that was the result of collapsing life expectancy. At fifty-nine, male life expectancy

in Russia is more than twenty years lower than in Japan. Clearly there is more than one route to a declining population.

15. Magnus, *Age of Aging*, p. 40.
16. Ibid., p. 42.
17. Ibid., p. 55.
18. Interview with author, Tokyo, July 2011.
19. In fact, Japanese youth are very sceptical about the pension system. The working assumption of many seems to be that it will be bankrupt by the time they retire and that they will need to make their own arrangements.
20. Magnus, *Age of Aging*, p. 70.
21. Pilling, 'Radical Steps Needed to Unlock Japan's Labour Market'.
22. Ironically, this is partly because, anxieties about the future aside, there is now a higher sense of financial stability than in the post-war years when there was a strong memory of poverty.
23. Jesper Koll of JP Morgan calculates that people over sixty-five own 75 per cent of the Y1,000 trillion in net financial wealth. That will either be spent during their lifetime or, in part, captured by the government in the form of inheritance tax. When today's youth retires its savings are likely to be far more limited.
24. The ministry of health and the ministry of education have not always seen eye to eye over pre-school education.
25. According to data from the Conference Board, from 1995 to 2011, Japan's output per hour rose 1.71 per cent annually compared with 1.87 per cent for the US. Output per hour was about 60 per cent of US levels, reflecting a much more inefficient – or more liberally staffed – services sector.
26. World Bank figures. A high female participation rate in the labour force cannot be taken as an automatic proxy of economic advancement or women's rights. The 'best' performing countries in terms of female participation include China (67 per cent), Vietnam (68 per cent) and Mozambique (85 per cent).
27. Atsushi Seike of Keio University says the range of work available to Japanese women has expanded, though prejudice about a woman's supposedly warmer hands still means you will never see a female sushi chef. But women are operating bulldozers and driving trucks in what Seike calls the 'feminization of construction'.
28. Kathy Matsui, 'Womenomics', Goldman Sachs paper, October 2010.
29. Interview with author, Tokyo, February 2003.
30. Coco Masters, 'Japan to Immigrants: Thanks But You Can Go Home Now', *Time*, 20 April 2009.
31. Remarks to author, Tokyo, October 2011.

32. According to OECD numbers, which are meant to be roughly comparable across nations, Japan's youth unemployment rate in 2012 of 8.0 per
cent compared favourably with almost all other advanced nations. By
comparison, the US number was 17.3 per cent, the UK 20.0 per cent and
Spain an extraordinary 46.4 per cent, OECD iLibrary, 'Employment and
Labour Markets: Key Tables: 2. Youth Unemployment Rate'.
33. Estimate from Jesper Koll, director of equity research at JP Morgan.
34. Ibid.
35. Conversation with author, Tokyo, March 2012.
36. Jonathan Soble, 'In Search of Salvation', *Financial Times*, 5 January
2012.
37. Ibid.
38. Kaoru Yosano, interview with author, Tokyo, April 2006.
39. Soble, 'In Search of Salvation'.
40. Christian Oliver, 'Samsung Poised to Overtake Rival HP in Sales', *Financial Times*, 29 January 2010. Note that the decline of Japan's electronics
industry has become so commonplace that Samsung's extraordinary
profit compared with that of its Japanese peers did not even strike the
headline writer as worthy of note.
41. Michiyo Nakamoto, 'Scrutinising Stringer', *Financial Times*, 22 June
2006.
42. Yasuchika Hasegawa, 'Toward a Lasting Recovery', in Clay Chandler et al.
(eds.), *Reimagining Japan: The Quest for a Future that Works*, p. 49.
43. In fairness, the same lament could be made of the UK or even Germany.
44. Some Japanese scientists may be at a disadvantage because their papers
tend to be written in Japanese, meaning they get fewer citations.
45. Interview with author, Tokyo, July 2011.
46. Daisuke Wakabayashi, 'How Japan Lost its Electronics Crown', *Wall
Street Journal*, 15 August 2012.
47. Masayoshi Son, 'Beyond Nuts and Bolts', in Clay Chandler et al. (eds.),
*Reimagining Japan: The Quest for a Future that Works*, pp. 57–8.
48. Figures supplied by Dealogic.
49. Norihiro Kato, 'Japan and the Ancient Art of Shrugging', *New York
Times*, 21 August 2010.
50. On a purchasing power parity basis, which takes into account the cost of
goods across countries, China had overtaken Japan many years before.
51. It blipped up again in 2006 before beginning a steady, if so far gradual,
descent in 2007.
52. The UN Human Development Index is, as it happens, a fairly simple
combination of per capita income, life expectancy and education/literacy.

53. Per capita income measured on a purchasing power parity basis. In dollar terms, it has a per capita income of less than $2,000.

54. Natsumi Iwasaki, 'What Would Drucker Do?' in Clay Chandler et al. (eds.), *Reimagining Japan: The Quest for a Future that Works*, pp. 133–7.

55. Stephen Miller, James Abegglen Obituary, *Wall Street Journal*, 12 May 2007.

## 10. THE PROMISED ROAD

1. Interview with author, Tokyo, January 2003.

2. *Yutori* is also applied to education, meaning a system that places less emphasis on rote-learning and a crammed curriculum and more on critical thinking. Many older Japanese see the adoption of '*yutori* education' as one reason for falling standards and continued economic difficulties.

3. Masahiro Yamada, 'The Young and the Hopeless', in Clay Chandler et al. (eds.), *Reimagining Japan: A Quest for a Future that Works*, pp. 176–80.

4. Ibid.

5. The survey was produced by the Japan Productivity Center.

6. Interview with author, Tokyo, July 2004.

7. 'Held Hostage to Public Opinion', *New Zealand Herald*, 1 May 2004.

8. Yoshio Sugimoto, 'Class and Work in Cultural Capitalism: Japanese Trends', *The Asia-Pacific Journal*, 40-1-10, 4 October 2010.

9. Camel Cigarettes, cited in Jeff Kingston, *Japan's Quiet Transformation: Social Change and Civil Society in the Twenty-first Century*, p. 38.

10. Mure Dickie, 'Osaka Mayor Has Old Guard Running Scared', *Financial Times*, 19 May 2012.

11. Eric Johnston, 'Hashimoto Admits Affair, Doesn't Deny "Cosplay"', *Japan Times*, 20 July 2012.

## 11. FROM BEHIND THE SCREEN

1. These two articles were written by Beate Sirota Gordon, a translator for the administration of General Douglas MacArthur, Supreme Commander for the Allied Powers. She later said that it was vital to institutionalize women's rights, since traditionally women had been 'treated like chattel; they were property to be bought and sold on a whim'.

2. 'Women's Economic Opportunity: A new global index and ranking', Economist Intelligence Unit, 2010.

3. The Gender Inequality Index (2011) seeks to measure women's disadvantage in the areas of reproductive health, empowerment and labour practice. The empowerment sub-category measures women's representation in parliament and access to secondary and higher education. The labour element is measured by women's participation in the workforce, which may not adequately take into account the type of work performed.

4. The authors of the Gender Inequality Index report, for example, are careful to mention the limitations of the index, pointing out that much data is difficult to collect and that it makes no attempt to measure gender-based violence, participation in decision-making or even asset ownership.

5. Mariko Sanchanta, 'Japan Weighs Female Quotas in Politics', *Wall Street Journal*, 24 June 2011.

6. Mineko Iwasaki, interview with author, Kyoto, September 2003.

7. Gail Lee Bernstein, quoted by Kenneth Pyle, *The Making of Modern Japan*, pp. 152–3.

8. Yayoi Kusama, *Infinity Net: The Autobiography of Yayoi Kusama*, p. 112.

9. Mari Yamaguchi, 'Japanese Rape Scandal Puts Spotlight on Club', *Los Angeles Times*, 14 September 2003.

10. Yumi Wijers-Hasegawa, 'Gang Rape Ringleader Gets 14 Years', *Japan Times*, 3 November 2004.

11. William Pesek, 'A Failure to Innovate', *Bloomberg News*, 13 February 2007.

12. The rate went from 1.28 per 1,000 in 1990 to 2.27 in 2001. It has since fallen back to around 2.0. That compares with 3.6 in the US. Interestingly, Japan had a very high divorce rate in the late nineteenth century. This then fell consistently until 1964 when, along with rapid industrialization, it started to rise again.

13. Jeff Kingston, *Contemporary Japan*, pp. 67–70.

14. Ibid., pp. 69–74.

15. Remark to author, Nara, March 2012. In fact, more Japanese men marry foreign women, though such marriages often involve men in rural parts of Japan finding brides from poorer Southeast Asian countries.

16. Machiko Osawa and Jeff Kingston, 'Japan Has to Address the "Precariat"', *Financial Times*, 1 July 2010.

17. Yoshio Sugimoto, 'Class and Work in Cultural Capitalism: Japanese Trends', *The Asia-Pacific Journal*, 40-1-10, 4 October 2010.

18. Kingston, *Contemporary Japan*, p. 71.

19. Not her real name. A few minor details have been changed.

## 12. ASIA EX-JAPAN

1. Remarks to author, Manila, December 2012.
2. 'Beijing and Seoul Denounce Visit', *International Herald Tribune*, 14 August 2001.
3. Interview with author, Tokyo, July 2002.
4. John Dower, *Embracing Defeat*, p. 28.
5. Ian Buruma, *The Wages of Guilt*, p. 92.
6. Interview with author, Tokyo, July 2012.
7. Buruma, *Wages of Guilt*, p. 143.
8. Ibid., p. 64.
9. Interview with author, Tokyo, November 2003.
10. In Japanese the word she used for god was *kami*, which could be translated as 'spirit'. It can be used as much for the gods that are said to inhabit the rivers and trees as for the spirits of soldiers who died serving the emperor.
11. After its defeat of Russia in 1905, Japan took over the administration of the South Manchurian Railway, which gave it a foothold in Manchuria. Its influence spread after the Russian Revolution of 1917. In 1931, in what has become known as the Mukden Incident, the Japanese military staged an attack on the railway as a pretext for invading all of Manchuria. It went on to establish the puppet state of Manchukuo under Puyi, the 'last emperor' of China's Qing Dynasty.
12. Kenneth Pyle, *The Making of Modern Japan*, p. 201. The fact that Vichy France allowed Japan to occupy its colonial possessions in Indochina because of Japan's alliance with Nazi Germany rather undermines the argument of Japan as liberator. The French continued to administer the area, the rough equivalent of modern Cambodia, Laos and Vietnam, under Japanese military occupation.
13. For a detailed account of Saburo Ienaga, see Buruma, *Wages of Guilt*, pp. 189–201.
14. Remarks to author, August 2004. In 2006, a Tokyo court ruled that it was unconstitutional to oblige teachers to stand in front of the national flag or sing the national anthem. But subsequent rulings by the Supreme Court quashed similar cases, saying it was not illegal to require teachers to stand. See David Pilling, 'Japanese Teachers Freed from Singing National Anthem', *Financial Times*, 22 September 2006.
15. Interview with author, Tokyo, December 2006.
16. Kenneth Pyle, *Japan Rising*, p. 373.
17. Koizumi did attend the inaugural Boao Forum, intended to become a sort of Chinese Davos, in April 2002.

20. Hugh Williamson and Ray Marcelo, 'United Nations Warns on Asian Tensions', *Financial Times*, 12 April 2005.


## 13. ABNORMAL NATION

1. *Kokka no Hinkaku* or 'Dignity of a Nation' was the title of Masahiko Fujiwara's 2005 book.
2. John Dower, *Embracing Defeat*, p. 454.
3. David Pilling, 'Abe to Work Towards New Japanese Constitution', *Financial Times*, 31 October 2006.
4. David Pilling, 'To Befit the Reality', *Financial Times*, 1 November 2006.
5. Interview with author, Tokyo, August 2006.
6. Japanese military officials explained that if, say, North Korea launched a missile, Japan would need to shoot it down before it knew for sure whether it was headed for Japan or another country. If the missile turned out to have been headed for the US, then, by shooting it down, Tokyo would have engaged in collective self-defence. If, on the other hand, it waited until it was sure the missile was going to land on Japan, it might then be too late to attempt to shoot it down at all.
7. David Pilling, 'Abe Assumes Command of "Pacifist" Forces', *Financial Times*, 1 May 2007.
8. Interview with author, Tokyo, March 2004.
9. Gavan McCormack, *Client State: Japan in the American Embrace*, p. 198.
10. Norimitsu Onishi, 'Abe Rejects Japan's Files on War Sex', *New York Times*, 2 March 2007.
11. Yukio Hatoyama, 'The Wrong Memorial', *Financial Times*, 13 August 2001.
12. Martin Fackler, 'Cables Show US Concern on Japan's Readiness for Disaster', *New York Times*, 4 May 2011. The cables in question were leaked by Wikileaks.
13. Interview with author, Tokyo, July 2006.
14. Troop numbers have gradually dwindled from about 50,000 when Koizumi was in office.
15. Steve Rabson, *Okinawa: Cold War Island*, p. 79.
16. Interview with author, Naha, Okinawa, January 2006.
17. Interview with author, Tokyo, January 2006.
18. Edwin Reischauer, former US ambassador to Japan. Recounted in Yoichi Funabashi, *Alliance Adrift*, p. 129.
19. Quoted in Kenneth Pyle, *The Making of Modern Japan*, p. 233.

20. See McCormack, *Client State*.
21. Shintaro Ishihara co-wrote the book in 1989 with Sony co-founder Akio Morita, arguing that Japan should be more than a mere 'yes man' to the US.
22. Martin Fackler, 'Japanese Leader Gives in to US on Okinawa Base', *New York Times*, 24 May 2010.
23. Martin Fackler, 'US Relations Played Major Role in Downfall of Japanese Prime Minister', *New York Times*, 3 June 2010.
24. Japan had other territorial disputes with both Russia and South Korea. In both cases, the situation was the reverse of that with China. Japan claimed what it called the Northern Territories, but these had been administered by Russia, which called them the Southern Kuriles, since the end of the war. It also claimed what it called Takeshima island, which was administered by South Korea as Dokdo.
25. Taipei, which also claimed the islands as part of Taiwan, called them Daioyutai.
26. Quoted by Han-Yi Shaw, 'The Inconvenient Truth Behind the Diaoyu/Senkaku Islands', http://kristof.blogs.nytimes.com/2012/09/19/the-inconvenient-truth-behind-the-diaoyusenkaku-islands
27. Mure Dickie and Kathrin Hille, 'Japan's Arrest of Captain Angers Beijing', *Financial Times*, 8 September 2010.
28. Yoichi Funabashi, 'Japan–China Relations Stand at Ground Zero', *Asahi* newspaper, 9 October 2010.

## 14. FUKUSHIMA FALLOUT

1. The Official Report of The Fukushima Nuclear Accident Independent Investigation Commission, Survey of the Evacuees (Appendices).
2. Ibid.
3. Gerrit Wiessmann, 'Germany to Scrap Nuclear Power by 2022', *Financial Times*, 30 May 2011.
4. Hiroko Tabuchi, 'A Window into Chaos of Fukushima', *International Herald Tribune*, 11 August 2012.
5. Some of the following description is taken from Jonathan Soble and Mure Dickie, 'How Fukushima Failed', *Financial Times*, 7 May 2011.
6. Martin Fackler, 'Evacuation of Tokyo Was Considered After Disaster', *International Herald Tribune*, 29 February 2012. In practice the evacuation of such a massive city would take weeks or months, rendering such an exercise, to all practical purposes, impossible.
7. Tabuchi, 'A Window into Chaos of Fukushima'.

8. Evan Osnos, 'The Fallout: Letter from Fukushima', *New Yorker*, 17 October 2011.

9. Tabuchi, 'A Window into Chaos of Fukushima'.

10. Soble and Dickie, 'How Fukushima Failed'.

11. Norimitsu Onishi, 'Safety Myth Left Japan Ripe for Nuclear Crisis', *New York Times*, 24 June 2011.

12. Interview with author, Tokyo, August 2011.

13. Onishi, 'Safety Myth Left Japan Ripe for Nuclear Crisis'.

14. Hiroko Tabuchi, 'Braving Heat and Radiation for Temp Job', *New York Times*, 10 April 2011. Also see, Jake Adelstein, 'How the Yakuza Went Nuclear', *Daily Telegraph*, 21 February 2012.

15. Interview with author, Tokyo, March 2012.

16. Onda Katsunobu, interview with author, Tokyo, March 2012.

17. Tabuchi, 'A Window into Chaos of Fukushima'.

18. Gerald Curtis, 'Stop Blaming Fukushima on Japan's Culture', *Financial Times*, 10 July 2012.

19. Account by Jonathan Soble, *Financial Times* correspondent, Tokyo.

20. Peter Landers, 'Japan Snaps Back with Less Power', *Wall Street Journal*, 29 July 2011.

21. Interview with author, Tokyo, June 2011.

22. Tepco announced its intention to raise electricity prices in Tokyo and the surrounding area to compensate for the cost of compensation and the nuclear clear-up.

23. Ben McLannahan, 'Japan Deficit Rises to Record in January', *Financial Times*, 21 February 2012.

24. Martin Fackler, 'Japanese Leaders, Pressed by Public, Fret as Nuclear Shutdown Nears', *New York Times*, 5 May 2012.

25. Interview with author, Tokyo, August 2011.

26. Interview with author, Tokyo, March 2012.

27. Interview with author, Tokyo, July 2012.

28. Andrew Dewitt et al., 'Fukushima and the Political Economy of Power Policy in Japan', in Jeff Kingston (ed.), *Natural Disaster and Nuclear Crisis in Japan*, pp. 156–71.

29. Rebecca Bream, 'GE Chief Warns on Nuclear Prospects', *Financial Times*, 3 August 2012.

30. At Y42 per kilowatt hour for solar, the tariff was twice that set by Germany and three times that of China.

31. Mariko Yasu, 'Softbank's CEO Wants a Solar-powered Japan', *BloombergBusinessweek*, 23 June 2011.

32. Mari Iwata, 'Renewable Hopes in Japan Fall Short', *Wall Street Journal*, 3 July 2012.

33. Kaneshima Hironori, 'Feed-in Tariff Energy System Gets Under Way', *The Daily Yomiuri*, 3 July 2012.

34. Landers, 'Japan Snaps Back with Less Power'.

35. Jonathan Soble, 'Japan to Phase Out Nuclear Power', *Financial Times*, 14 September 2012.

36. Inevitably, police and organizers' estimates of crowd sizes differed greatly.

37. 'Japan's Anti-Nuclear Protests', *The Economist*, 21 July 2012.

38. Correspondence with Jeff Kingston.

39. Landers, 'Japan Snaps Back with Less Power'.

40. Kyung Lah, 'Former Japanese Leader: "I Felt Fear" During Nuclear Crisis', CNN.com, 28 May 2012.

41. 'Nuclear Leaks Hit Marine Life', *Metro*, 17 June 2011.

42. 'Butterfly Mutations Found Near Fukushima', Associated Press, 16 August 2012.

43. Hiroko Tabuchi, 'Japan: Estimate of Cancer Toll', *New York Times*, 18 July 2012. Original study: John E. Ten Hoeve and Mark Z. Jacobson, 'Worldwide Health Effects of the Fukushima Daiichi Nuclear Accident', DOI 10.1039/c2ee22019a www.rsc/org/ees

44. Pico Iyer, 'Heroes of the Hot Zone', *Vanity Fair*, 1 January 2012.

45. Hiroko Tabuchi, 'Inquiry Sees Chaos in Evacuations After Japan Tsunami', *New York Times*, 23 July 2012.

46. Mure Dickie, 'A Strange Kind of Homecoming', *Financial Times*, 10 March 2012.

47. Osnos, 'The Fallout: Letter from Fukushima'.

48. Translated by Hiroko Tabuchi, http://www.zerohedge.com/article/letter-fukushima-mother

49. David Pilling, 'Japanese People Make Mandarins Feel Nuclear Heat', *Financial Times*, 31 July 2011.

## 15. CITIZENS

1. Gerald Curtis, talk at the Foreign Correspondents' Club of Japan, Tokyo, September 2005.

2. Jeff Kingston, 'The Politics of Disaster, Nuclear Crisis and Recovery', in Jeff Kingston (ed.), *Natural Disaster and Nuclear Crisis in Japan*, p. 192.

3. Ibid., pp. 188–9.

4. Simon Avenell, 'From Kobe to Tohoku' in Kingston (ed.), *Natural Disaster*, p. 60.

5. Figure provided by Kiyomi Tsujimoto.
6. Avenell, 'From Kobe to Tohoku', p. 54.
7. Telephone interview, February 2012.
8. Jeff Kingston, *Japan's Quiet Transformation: Social Change and Civil Society in the Twenty-first Century*, p. 3.
9. Email correspondence, August 2012.
10. Remarks to author, Tokyo, June 2005.
11. David H. Slater, Nishimura Keiko and Love Kindstrand, 'Social Media in Disaster Japan', in Kingston (ed.), *Natural Disaster*, pp. 94–108.

## 16. AFTER THE TSUNAMI

1. Related to author, Ofunato, June 2012.
2. David Pilling, 'Japan: The Aftermath', *Financial Times*, 25 March 2011.
3. The word for sea bream, *tai*, is contained in the word *omedetai*, which means 'congratulations'. For that reason it is considered to bring good fortune.
4. '"Miracle Pine" Preservation Plan Questioned Over Y150m Cost', *Japan Times*, 23 July 2012.
5. When I checked in September 2012, it had 7,584 'Likes'.
6. In July 2013, the preserved tree, its scaffolding removed, was lit up with an LED display. The plan was to leave it illuminated for an entire year, *Asahi* newspaper, 29 June 2013.

## AFTERWORD

1. John Dower and other scholars have long argued that this view is too simplistic. Of the classic example of stasis followed by rapid change, Dower told me, 'The challenge was to revise the view that Japan, prior to the Meiji Restoration, had been this stagnant society, this dark feudalistic society. Then, so the story goes, you come to this Meiji miracle and they are transformed. Of course, what we see now is this terrific dynamism going on in all aspects of [Tokugawa] society and that becomes the baseline for understanding why Japan was able to move so fast after Meiji.'
2. Interview with author, Boston, May 2011.
3. Jonathan Soble, 'Japan Warms to "Fire Ice" Potential', *Financial Times*, 12 March 2013.
4. Remarks to author by Lionel Barber, editor of the *Financial Times*, Jakarta, March 2013.

5. Ben McLannahan, 'Abe Takes First Step on Road to Recovery', *Financial Times*, 11 January 2013.

6. Telephone interview with Peter Tasker, Arcus Investments, April 2013.

7. Shinzo Abe, address to Center for Strategic and International Studies (CSIS), Washington DC, 22 February 2013.

8. Martin Wolf, 'The Risky Task of Relaunching Japan', *Financial Times*, 5 March 2013.

9. Bond prices fall when interest rates rise and vice versa.

10. Jonathan Soble, 'Abe Pushes for More Women in Senior Roles', *Financial Times*, 19 April 2013.

11. Telephone interview, April 2013.

12. Dealogic, 'Global Cross-border M&A Volume by Acquirer Nationality, 2012'.

13. Mure Dickie, 'Tokyo Warned Over Plans to Buy Islands', *Financial Times*, 6 June 2012.

14. Amy Qin and Edward Wong, 'Smashed Skull Serves as Grim Symbol of Seething Patriotism', *New York Times*, 10 October 2012.

15. 'A Squall in the East China Sea', *Financial Times* Editorial, 21 August 2012.

16. In fact, as prime minister, Abe went on to open negotiations with Moscow over four disputed islands.

17. John Garnaut, 'Xi's War Drums', *Foreign Policy*, May/June 2013.

18. Jonathan Soble and Kathrin Hille, 'Abe Blasts China over Maritime Incident', *Financial Times*, 6 February 2013.

19. 'Panetta Tells China That Senkakus Under US–Japan Security Treaty', *Asahi* newspaper, 21 September 2012.

20. Ben Bland, 'Asean Chief Warns on South China Sea Spats', *Financial Times*, 28 November 2012.

21. Graham Allison, Director of the Belfer Center for Science and International Affairs at Harvard University, in 'Thucydides's Trap Has Been Sprung in the Pacific', *Financial Times*, 21 August 2012.

22. Address to CSIS, Washington DC, 22 February 2013.

23. David Pilling, 'The Son Also Rises', *Financial Times*, 15 September 2006.

24. Toko Sekiguchi, 'Japanese Prime Minister Stokes Wartime Passions', *Wall Street Journal*, 25 April 2013.

25. Yuka Hayashi, 'Abe Seeks to Rewrite Pacifist Charter', *Wall Street Journal*, 25 April 2013.

26. Ibid.

27. Gideon Rachman, 'A Gaffe-prone Japan is a Danger to Peace in Asia', *Financial Times*, 12 August 2013.

28. Paul Kennedy, 'The Great Powers, Then and Now', *International Herald Tribune*, 13 August 2013.
29. Remarks to author, Tokyo, July 2013.
30. Remarks to author, Tokyo, July 2013.
31. Pew Research Center, 'Global Attitudes Project', 11 July 2013.
32. Interview with author, Tokyo, March 2012.
33. Kenneth Pyle, *The Making of Modern Japan*, p. 99.
34. Address to CSIS, Washington DC, 22 February 2013.
35. Keizai Koho Center (Japanese Institute for Social and Economic Affairs), 'Japan 2013, An International Comparison'.
36. International Monetary Fund, *World Outlook Economic Database*, April 2013. Even on a purchasing power parity basis, which adjusts for prices across nations, the Japanese are on average four times richer than their Chinese counterparts.
37. City-states such as Singapore and Qatar, both richer than Japan in per capita terms, are too small to provide meaningful comparisons. South Korea and Taiwan have both successfully emulated Japan's economic development, but neither has quite caught up with Japanese living standards, and both face demographic problems every bit as severe as those of Japan. Other fast-growing economies in Asia, Latin America and Africa are still leagues behind Japan's economic and industrial prowess.

# Select Bibliography

Abegglen, James, *21st Century Japanese Management: New Systems, Lasting Values* (New York: Palgrave Macmillan, 2006)

Adelstein, Jake, *Tokyo Vice: An American Reporter on the Police Beat in Japan* (New York, Toronto: Random House, 2009)

Bailey, Jonathan, *Great Power Strategy in Asia: Empire, Culture and Trade, 1905–2005* (London: Routledge, 2006)

Benedict, Ruth, *The Chrysanthemum and the Sword: Patterns of Japanese Culture* (paperback edition, Boston: Houghton Mifflin, 1989)

Bestor, Theodore, *Tsukiji: The Fish Market at the Center of the World* (Berkeley, Los Angeles, London: University of California Press, 2004)

Bix, Herbert, *Hirohito and the Making of Modern Japan* (paperback edition, New York: Perennial, 2001)

Buckley, Roger, *Japan Today* (third edition, Cambridge, UK: Cambridge University Press, 1999)

Buruma, Ian, *Inventing Japan: From Empire to Economic Miracle* (paperback edition, London: Orion Books, 2005)

— *The Wages of Guilt: Memories of War in Germany and Japan* (paperback edition, London: Orion Books, 2002)

— *A Japanese Mirror: Heroes and Villains of Japanese Culture* (London: Jonathan Cape, 1984)

Chambers, Veronica, *Kickboxing Geishas: How Modern Women are Changing their Nation* (New York: Free Press, 2007)

Chandler, Clay et al. (eds.), *Reimagining Japan: The Quest for a Future that Works* (San Francisco: VIZ Media, 2011)

Chiba, Kazuo, *Please! Just Let Me Finish . . . : A Posthumous Collection of the Writings of Kazuo Chiba* (Tokyo: Japan Echo, 2005)

Chomin, Nakae, *A Discourse by Three Drunkards on Government* (translated by Nobuko Tsukui, eighth edition, Boston, MA: Weatherhill, 2010)

Clancey, Gregory, *Earthquake Nation: The Cultural Politics of Japanese*

*Seismicity, 1868–1930* (Berkeley and Los Angeles, CA: University of California Press, 2006)

Curtis, Gerald, *The Logic of Japanese Politics: Leaders, Institutions, and the Limits of Change* (New York: Columbia University Press, 1999)

Dale, Peter, *The Myth of Japanese Uniqueness* (paperback edition, London: Routledge, 1995)

Daly, Herman, *Beyond Growth: The Economics of Sustainable Development* (paperback edition, Boston: Beacon Press, 1996)

Diamond, Jared, *Guns, Germs, and Steel: The Fates of Human Societies* (New York, London: W. W. Norton, 2005)

Dower, John, *Cultures of War: Pearl Harbor, Hiroshima, 9/11, Iraq* (New York: W. W. Norton, 2010)

—, *Embracing Defeat: Japan in the Wake of World War II* (paperback edition, New York, London: W. W. Norton, 2000)

—, *War Without Mercy: Race & Power in the Pacific War* (paperback edition, New York: Pantheon Books, 1986)

Emmott, Bill, *The Sun Also Sets: The Limits of Japan's Economic Power* (New York: Simon & Schuster, 1989)

Feifer, George, *Breaking Open Japan: Commodore Perry, Lord Abe, and American Imperialism in 1853* (New York: HarperCollins, 2006)

Fingleton, Eamon, *In Praise of Hard Industries: Why Manufacturing, Not Information Technology, Is Key to Future Prosperity* (Boston, New York: Houghton Mifflin, 1999)

—, *Blindside: Why Japan is Still on Track to Overtake the US by the Year 2000* (London: Simon & Schuster, 1995)

Fujiwara, Masahiko, *Kokka no Hinkaku [The Dignity of a Nation]*(Japanese edition, Tokyo: Shinchosha, 2005)

Fukuzawa, Yukichi, *The Autobiography of Yukichi Fukuzawa* (translated by Eiichi Kiyooka, paperback edition, New York: Columbia University Press, 1966)

Funabashi, Yoichi, *Alliance Adrift* (paperback edition, New York: Council on Foreign Relations, 1999)

Gluck, Carol, *Japan's Modern Myths: Ideology in the Late Meiji Period* (Princeton, NJ: Princeton University Press, 1985)

Gordon, Andrew, *A Modern History of Japan: From Tokugawa to the Present* (second edition, New York, Oxford: Oxford University Press, 2009)

Hammer, Joshua, *Yokohama Burning: The Deadly 1923 Earthquake and Fire that Helped Forge the Path to World War II* (paperback edition, New York: Simon & Schuster, 2006)

Hearn, Lafcadio, *Japan: An Attempt at Interpretation* (paperback edition, New York: Cosimo, 2005)

Hersey, John, *Hiroshima* (paperback edition, London: Penguin Books, 1946)

Hodson, Peregrine, *A Circle Round the Sun: A Foreigner in Japan* (London: Heinemann, 1992)

Huang, Joseph, *The Enigma of Japan* (paperback edition, London: Minerva Press, 1996)

Jansen, Marius, *The Making of Modern Japan* (Cambridge, MA, London: Harvard University Press, 2000)

Johnson, Chalmers, *Okinawa: Cold War Island* (Cardiff, CA: Japan Policy Research Institute, 1999)

—, *MITI and the Japanese Miracle: The Growth of Industrial Policy, 1925–1975* (paperback edition, fourth printing, Tokyo: Tuttle, 1992)

Kaji, Sahoko, Hama, Noriko and Rice, Jonathan, *The Xenophobe's Guide to the Japanese* (London: Oval Books, 1999)

Kaplan, David and Dubro, Alec, *Yakuza: Japan's Criminal Underworld* (paperback, Berkeley, Los Angeles: University of California Press, 1995)

Kaplan, David and Marshall, Andrew, *The Cult at the End of the World: The Terrifying Story of the Aum Doomsday Cult* (New York: Crown Publishers, 1996)

Katz, Richard, *Japanese Phoenix: The Long Road to Economic Revival* (New York, London: M. E. Sharpe, 2003)

Keene, Donald, *So Lovely a Country Will Never Perish: Wartime Diaries of Japanese Writers* (New York: Columbia University Press, 2010)

—, *A History of Japanese Literature, Volume I: Seeds in the Heart* (paperback edition, New York: Columbia University Press, 1999)

—, *The Japanese Discovery of Europe, 1720–1830* (Stanford, CA: Stanford University Press, 1969)

—, *Modern Japanese Literature* (paperback edition, New York: Grove Press, 1960)

Kelts, Roland, *Japanamerica: How Japanese Pop Culture has Invaded the US* (New York: Palgrave Macmillan, 2006)

Kerr, Alex, *Dogs and Demons: The Fall of Modern Japan* (London: Penguin Books, 2001)

Kingston, Jeff (ed.), *Natural Disaster and Nuclear Crisis in Japan: Response and Recovery after Japan's 3/11* (London, New York: Routledge, 2012)

—, *Contemporary Japan: History, Politics, and Social Change since the 1980s* (Sussex, UK: Wiley-Blackwell, 2011)

—, *Japan's Quiet Transformation: Social Change and Civil Society in the Twenty-first Century* (London, New York: RoutledgeCurzon, 2004)

Koo, Richard, *The Holy Grail of Macroeconomics: Lessons from Japan's Great Recession* (London: John Wiley and Sons, 2011)

Kusama, Yayoi, *Infinity Net: The Autobiography of Yayoi Kusama* (London: Tate Publishing, 2011)

Macfarlane, Alan, *Japan Through the Looking Glass* (London: Profile Books, 2007)

Magnus, George, *The Age of Aging: How Demographics Are Changing the Global Economy and Our World* (Singapore: John Wiley & Sons, 2009)

McCormack, Gavan, *Client State: Japan in the American Embrace* (paperback edition, London, New York: Verso, 2007)

—, *The Emptiness of Japanese Affluence* (revised edition, Armonk, NY, London: M. E. Sharpe, 2001)

Miyazaki, Manabu, *Toppamono: Outlaw. Radical. Suspect. My Life in Japan's Underworld* (Tokyo: Kotan Publishing, 2005)

Morita, Akio and Ishihara, Shintaro, *The Japan That Can Say No: Why Japan Will Be First Among Equals* (Tokyo: Kobunsha, 1989)

Morris-Suzuki, Tessa, *Re-inventing Japan: Time, Space, Nation* (paperback edition, New York: M. E. Sharpe, 1998)

Murtagh, Niall, *The Blue-eyed Salaryman: From World Traveller to a Lifer at Mitsubishi* (paperback edition, London: Profile Books, 2006)

Murakami, Haruki, *After the Quake* (New York: Alfred Knopf, 2002)

—, *Underground: The Tokyo Gas Attack and the Japanese Psyche* (paperback edition, London: Random House, 2003)

Muruyama, Masao, *Thought and Behaviour in Modern Japanese Politics* (London, Oxford, New York: Oxford University Press, 1969)

Nathan, John, *Mishima: A Biography* (paperback edition, Cambridge, MA: Da Capo Press, 2000)

—, *Sony: The Private Life* (Boston, New York: Houghton Mifflin, 1999)

Ohnuki-Tierney, Emiko, *Kamikaze Diaries: Reflections of Japanese Student Soldiers* (Chicago, London: University of Chicago Press, 2006)

Okakura, Kakuzo, *The Book of Tea* (paperback edition, London: Penguin Books, 2010)

Ota, Masahide, *Essays on Okinawa Problems* (Gushikawa City, Okinawa: Yui Shuppan, 2000)

Patrick, Hugh, *Japanese Industrialization and Its Social Consequences* (paperback edition, Berkeley, Los Angeles, London: University of California Press, 1976)

Porter, Michael et al., *Can Japan Compete?* (London: Macmillan, 2000)

Pyle, Kenneth, *Japan Rising: The Resurgence of Japanese Power and Purpose* (New York: Century Foundation, 2007)

—, *The Making of Modern Japan* (second edition, Lexington, MA, Toronto: D. C. Heath, 1996)

Sadler, A. L., *The Ten Foot Square Hut and Tales of the Heike* (North Clarendon, VT: Tuttle Publishing, 1972)

Sansom, George, *A History of Japan to 1334* (paperback edition, ninth printing, Boston, Ruthland, Vermont, Tokyo: Tuttle Publishing, 2000)

—, *A History of Japan 1334–1615* (paperback edition, ninth printing, Boston, Ruthland, Vermont, Tokyo: Tuttle Publishing, 2000)

—, *A History of Japan 1615–1867* (paperback edition, ninth printing, Boston, Ruthland, Vermont, Tokyo: Tuttle Publishing, 2000)

Seidensticker, Edward, *Tokyo from Edo to Showa: The Emergence of the World's Greatest City, 1867–1989* (paperback edition, North Clarendon, VT: Tuttle Publishing, 2010)

—, *Low City, High City: Tokyo from Edo to the Earthquake, 1867–1923* (paperback edition, London: Penguin Books, 1985)

Singer, Kurt, *Mirror, Sword and Jewel: A Study of Japanese Characteristics* (London: Croom Helm, 1973)

Smith, Patrick, *Somebody Else's Century: East and West in a Post-Western World* (New York: Pantheon Books, 2010)

—, *Japan: A Reinterpretation* (paperback edition, New York: Random House, 1998)

Sugimoto, Yoshio, *An Introduction to Japanese Society* (second edition, Port Melbourne, Australia: Cambridge University Press, 2003)

Takenaka, Heizo, *The Structural Reforms of the Koizumi Cabinet: An Insider's Account of the Economic Revival of Japan* (translated by Jillian Yorke, Tokyo: Nikkei Publishing, 2008)

Toby, Ronald, *State and Diplomacy in Early Modern Japan: Asia in the Development of the Tokugawa Bakufu* (paperback edition, Stanford, CA: Stanford University Press, 1991)

Umesao, Tadao, *Seventy-seven Keys to the Civilization of Japan* (paperback edition, Osaka: Sogensha, 1985)

Van Wolferen, Karel, *The Enigma of Japanese Power* (paperback edition, fourth printing, Vermont, Tokyo: Tuttle Publishing, 1998)

Vogel, Ezra, *Japan as Number One: Lessons for America* (paperback edition, Cambridge, MA, London: Harvard University Press, 1999)

Walker, Stephen, *Shockwave: The Countdown to Hiroshima* (London: John Murray, 2005)

West, Mark, *Law in Everyday Japan: Sex, Sumo, Suicide and Statutes* (Chicago, London: University of Chicago Press, 2005)

Whiting, Robert, *Tokyo Underworld: The Fast Times and Hard Life of an*

*American Gangster in Japan* (paperback edition, New York: Random House, 2000)

Wintle, Justin, *Perfect Hostage: Aung San Suu Kyi, Burma and the Generals* (London: Hutchinson, 2007)

Wood, Christopher, *The Bubble Economy: The Japanese Economic Collapse* (London: Sidgwick & Jackson, 1992)

Zielenziger, Michael, *Shutting Out the Sun: How Japan Created its Own Lost Generation* (paperback edition, New York: Random House, 2007)

# Glossary

**Aum Shinrikyo:** The doomsday cult led by Shoko Asahara that organized a sarin gas attack on the Tokyo subway in March 1995. The attack killed thirteen people and injured several hundred more.

**Bushido:** The 'way of the warrior', or the code of ethics attributed to the samurai.

**Choshu:** One of the four domains that rebelled against the Tokugawa shogunate in what became the Meiji Restoration. Some of Meiji's greatest intellectuals were from Choshu. Shinzo Abe, who became Japan's prime minister for a second time in 2012, has deep political roots in Choshu, modern-day Yamaguchi prefecture.

**Class-A war criminals:** Those tried at the International Military Tribunal for the Far East, also known as the Tokyo trials, for their leadership role in Japan's 'crimes against peace'. Japan accepted the findings of the tribunal, though its parliament does not recognize those convicted as criminals.

**Diet:** The Japanese parliament.

**Edo:** The name of the city where the Tokugawa shogunate lived. It gives its name to the 'feudalistic' period of rule by the Tokugawa family between 1603 and 1868. After the Meiji Restoration, which ended Tokugawa rule and established the foundations of modern Japan, the city was renamed Tokyo and became the capital.

**Fukoku Kyohei:** 'Rich country, strong army', a rallying cry of the Meiji Restoration that still resonates today.

**Fukushima:** A prefecture in northeast Japan and the name of the nuclear complex that suffered a triple meltdown after the tsunami of March 2011.

**Hikikomori:** A term referring to acute social withdrawal, especially among adolescents and young adults. Often translated as 'shut-ins'.

**Kaizen:** A term for 'continuous improvement' that encapsulated the management style, worker commitment and attention to detail that underpinned Japan's post-war economic miracle.

**Kamikaze:** The 'divine wind' – really a typhoon – that is said to have saved Japan from a Mongolian invasion led by Kublai Khan in the thirteenth century. It later gave its name to the suicide pilots sent to crash into US ships at the close of the Second World War.

**Keiretsu:** A grouping of businesses with interlocking interests and shareholdings.

**Liberal Democratic Party (LDP):** Founded in 1955, it governed Japan almost uninterrupted until it lost power to the Democratic Party of Japan (DPJ) in 2009. The LDP returned to power in December 2012 with Shinzo Abe as leader.

**Meiji Period:** Era of the reign of the Meiji emperor (1868–1912).

**Meiji Restoration:** The movement that overthrew the Tokugawa shogunate in 1868 and led to the modernization of Japan.

**Mono no aware:** The concept of fleeting beauty epitomized by the brevity of a flowering cherry blossom. Sometimes translated as 'the pathos of things', it is often said to express a unique Japanese sensibility.

**Nagatacho:** The political heartland of Tokyo.

**Nihonjinron:** The study of what it means to be Japanese. An exercise in exceptionalism, it underpins a strong Japanese sense of national identity but is often taken to fetishistic extremes.

**Ofunato:** A coastal town in Iwate prefecture, northeastern Japan, that was heavily damaged by the March 2011 tsunami.

**Rangaku:** 'Dutch learning', or study of the west, during the closed period of the Tokugawa shogunate.

**Rikuzentakata:** A coastal town in Iwate prefecture, northeastern Japan, all but destroyed by the March 2011 tsunami. Location of the *ippon matsu*, the lone pine, that has come to symbolize regional and national resilience.

**Sakoku:** Literally 'closed country'. Used to describe the period of relative isolation under the Tokugawa shogunate (1600–1868).

**SCAP:** Supreme Commander for the Allied Powers, General Douglas MacArthur's title during the US post-war occupation. The term became synonymous with the occupation administration.

**Senkaku/Diaoyu:** Islands in the East China Sea that are administered by Japan but also claimed by China.

**Setsuden:** Power saving. It became common to see 'setsuden' signs all over Japan after the power shortages that followed the Fukushima disaster.

**Shimaguni:** Literally 'island nation'.

**Shinkansen:** The name of the bullet train, which started operating between Tokyo and Osaka in 1964 to the amazement of the world.

**Shogun:** Military rulers of Japan between 1603 and 1867. The period of the shogunate is called Tokugawa after the family that held power, or the Edo period, after the city in which they lived.

**Showa Period:** Era of the reign of the Showa emperor (1926–89). During his lifetime, the Showa emperor was called Hirohito.

**Shushoku katsudo:** The mass hiring of graduates by large companies. Few who are not hired straight out of university have any chance of entering the shrinking 'lifetime employment' system.

**Taisho Period:** The period during the reign of the Taisho emperor (1912–26).

**Tepco:** Tokyo Electric Power, the electricity utility company that ran the Fukushima nuclear complex along with other nuclear plants in northern Japan.

**Tohoku:** Northeastern Japan, the area most affected by the March 2011 tsunami.

**Tokugawa Period:** The period when the Tokugawa family ruled Japan as shoguns (1600–1868).

**Yasukuni shrine:** A Shinto shrine in Tokyo built to commemorate those who died for the emperor in the Meiji Restoration of 1868. The 'souls' of more than 2 million people who have since died in war, including the Second World War, are commemorated at Yasukuni. Among those whose names are listed at Yasukuni are fourteen Class-A war criminals convicted at the Tokyo trials.

**Zaibatsu:** Business conglomerates or 'national champions' originating in early Meiji. The Americans blamed them for supporting Japan's war effort and sought to break them up after 1945, though many survived in a slightly different form.

# Acknowledgements

The cast of people who helped me with this book is Tolstoyan in scope and it would take a *War and Peace* to thank them all adequately. I arrived in Japan in late 2001 knowing practically nothing about the country and left, nearly seven years later, a trifle less ignorant. For that modicum of progress I have to thank the hundreds of people whom I met over those years, either in formal interviews or more informal encounters. Since the tsunami of March 2011, I have interviewed dozens more people during multiple trips back to Japan for the specific purpose of writing this book. It would be impossible to thank by name everyone who contributed, but to all those, mentioned and unmentioned in these pages, I do thank you.

We should begin at the beginning. Mitsuko Matsutani and Nobuko Juji are the twin pillars of the *Financial Times* office in Tokyo. It would be hard to find two more graceful, yet sturdy, pillars anywhere. They helped me track down dozens upon dozens of interviewees, both famous and obscure. Mitsuko, in particular, developed a technique to bludgeon even the most reluctant into submission, no easy task given the delicacies of the Japanese language. Both too supported my life in Tokyo in innumerable ways. It goes without saying that I owe you sushi – and plenty more besides.

Thank you, too, to the two families with whom I stayed on month-long homestays as I sought to improve my Japanese. To the Nishida family in Kanazawa, especially Junko and Hiroshi, I am grateful for your generous introduction to Japan's many delights, from tea ceremony to late-night ramen. Kanazawa will always be my favourite Japanese city. Thank you, too, to Masaya and Yoshie Shin in Inukai, a village in Kyushu, who opened up their home not only to me but also to students from all over Asia. It was in your lovely house that I studied for my final *ikkyu* Japanese language exam and, much later, started to write this book.

I'd also like to thank my Japanese teachers, Koichi Shimoie in Kanazawa, and Hiroshi Goto and Akiko Koyama in Tokyo, from whom I
learned so much, not only about grammar and characters but also about
Japan itself. Many journalists turn to taxi drivers when they want to take
the pulse of a nation. I turned to you.

At the *Financial Times* I must especially thank Lionel Barber, our brilliant and dynamic editor, who has supported me for fifteen years and
who gave his blessing to this project. I am fortunate indeed to have
worked for such a fine news organization for so many years. Much of the
material in this book, particularly the part dealing with the Junichiro
Koizumi years, was originally researched for the *FT*.

I would also like to thank Richard Lambert and John Thornhill, who
as then *FT* editor and Asia editor respectively, had the courage all those
years ago to send a Japanese novice out to Tokyo to see what he could
turn up. John Plender talked to me at length about Japan before I set off
and some of the themes we discussed back then feature prominently in
this book. Going back further still, I must warmly acknowledge the late
Dick Hall, a humanist and a pioneering Africa hand who encouraged me
to join the *FT*, as well as Michael Holman, the paper's former Africa editor, and Michael Thompson-Noel, a great *FT* travel editor of years past.
All of you placed mysterious trust in me as a writer long before anyone
else saw any potential.

In Tokyo, I must thank Gillian Tett, my formidable predecessor, who
was never less than generous with her contacts and advice. In the *FT*
bureau, special mention must go to Michiyo Nakamoto, a fount of
knowledge and wisdom, and to colleagues past and present, Ken Hijino,
Bethan Hutton, David Ibison, Atsuko Imai, Louise Lucas, Ben McLannahan, Bayan Rahman, Gwen Robinson, Mariko Sanchanta, Jonathan
Soble and Lindsay Whipp. I learned much from all of you. Thanks, too,
to Mure Dickie, my excellent successor in Tokyo and one of the nicest
kendo masters you're ever likely to meet.

In Hong Kong, I'd like especially to thank Demetri Sevastopulo, who
knows more than I ever will about Japan but who has always encouraged
me in my efforts to learn. In running our *FT* news operation day-to-day,
he also helped create a little space for me to think about a book amid the
daily torrent of work. Patricia Wong, my assistant at the *FT*, has ensured
my life runs as smoothly as possible. Without her I would have missed
planes and probably left this manuscript in the back of a taxi. Also at the

*FT*, Geoff Dyer and Henny Sender have given me a valuable perspective on Japan from angles I might not otherwise have considered.

I'd like to thank the many people who read individual chapters of this book or, indeed, the whole thing. Their comments have proved invaluable. Kenneth Pyle, the marvellous historian of Japan, graciously went over what must have seemed to him like an undergraduate's fumbling attempt to explain, in a single chapter, a period stretching from 1600 to 1945. Misako Kaji, a close Japanese friend, went over several chapters with the sort of scrupulousness perhaps only she can muster. If there's a comma out of place, you have my sincerest apologies.

Shijuro Ogata read the chapter on Japan's post-war economic recovery, which includes a section from his autobiography. He has always been one of my favourite people to talk to in Tokyo. An iconoclast and internationalist, in his way he is a disciple of Yukichi Fukuzawa, the great nineteenth-century liberal thinker. I am fortunate, too, to have got to know his even more famous wife (his words, not mine), Sadako Ogata, the former UN High Commissioner for Refugees. Gerry Curtis, the brilliant scholar of Japanese politics, made comments on the Koizumi chapter and has been incredibly generous with his time and keen observations over many years.

Jonathan Soble, Mure Dickie and Kae Hada looked at some or all of the tsunami and post-tsunami chapters. Thank you for your help and support. Jennifer Zhu Scott, a friend in Hong Kong, read several of the chapters and made useful comments. Rahul Jacob looked at an early chapter and was so kind about what I'd written I was minded to carry on. Barney Jopson, a former colleague in Tokyo, read the whole manuscript with his usual precision and sensitivity. I hope he has forgiven me for recommending he return to London to become our accountancy correspondent. (He has since escaped to New York.)

For the economics chapters I was fortunate to have the matchless Martin Wolf, the *FT*'s ferociously intelligent chief economics commentator, review my work. I sent my efforts off to him with more than a little trepidation. I'd also like to thank Keith Fray, our head of statistics at the *FT*, who provided me with much of the data. Jesper Koll, who describes himself as Japan's last optimist, Masaaki Kanno at JP Morgan, and Kiichi Murashima at Citigroup all read chapters and have helped my understanding of Japan's economy over the years. So, through their tireless tutorials, have Paul Sheard, now chief economist at Standard & Poor's,

Peter Tasker, a man of savage intelligence and rapier wit at Arcus Investments, and Teizo Taya, a wise man at the Daiwa Institute. Richard Jerram, now at the Bank of Singapore, has performed a similar role. Clyde Prestowitz, a Japan expert with whom I have had many stimulating conversations, read the chapter on Japan's post-war economic recovery and made important suggestions.

Speaking of the economy, I am most grateful to many people at the Bank of Japan, who have spent untold hours with me over the years explaining the intricacies of monetary policy, deflation and structural reform. They include current governor Haruhiko Kuroda, previous governor Masaaki Shirakawa, Hiroshi Nakaso, now deputy governor, and two former BoJ executives, Eiji Hirano and Akinari Horii. Of the current and former officials at the Ministry of Finance, I'd particularly like to thank Yo Takeuchi, whose humour and insights are so refreshing, Masaki Omura, who helped me to get to know Osaka, and Masato Miyazaki. I'd also like to thank Takatoshi Ito at Tokyo University and Heizo Takenaka, who have always been most helpful.

Above all, when it came to reading chapters and making suggestions, I must thank Jeff Kingston, who read practically every word of the manuscript and who provided a detailed and most generous critique. I have shamelessly tapped his encyclopaedic knowledge of Japan and his huge network of contacts. I thank him for his wisdom, but most of all for his friendship and encouragement. His wife, Machiko Osawa, has also been very thoughtful, particularly in helping me to interpret social trends. She once travelled several hundred miles by bullet train for the express purpose of talking to me.

In the 'above all' category, I must thank Toshiki Senoue, a great friend and fearless photo-journalist. Toshiki travelled with me to the devastated northeast coast right after the tsunami and on two subsequent trips. He acted as driver, photographer, fixer and even chef on the occasions when food, or time, were scarce. I will for ever be enormously grateful – though I still never brought you that Geiger counter. Toshiki also generously allowed me to use his wonderful photographs of Ofunato and Rikuzentakata for this book. Thanks too to Hikari Ohta and Ega Hiroshi, who helped me penetrate the thick Tohoku accent and, more importantly, provided great companionship during those trips up north.

Those who have helped me in other ways are far too numerous to mention. I could not forgive myself, however, if I did not single out a few.

Yoichi Funabashi, one of the great Japanese journalists of his era, has treated me to numerous lunches but, more importantly, to his incomparable experience and insights. Noriko Hama has been scattering me with provocative ideas about Japan for years. Sahoko Kaji generously gave me permission to quote from one of her many lengthy emails to me. Yukio Okamoto, whom I first met in London, has been extremely open with his time and penetrating analysis. Ippei Takeda, the chief executive of Nichicon, has taught me much about Japanese business and treated me to some of the most splendid food imaginable in Kyoto's fine restaurants. Akira Chiba has been a reliable sounding board on Japanese culture and attitudes.

Karel van Wolferen has always been extremely helpful in chatting over complex issues and never anything but kind about my journalistic endeavours. His book, *The Enigma of Japanese Power*, remains a work of startling originality and deep penetration. Although I don't know them well, my hero John Dower, and Donald Keene, a peerless scholar of Japanese literature, spent several hours with me discussing some of the themes of this book. The late James Abegglen, a pioneer in the field of understanding how Japanese business worked, was always helpful and encouraging. Patrick Smith, an author and academic with extensive knowledge of Japan, has always been most helpful.

I am very grateful, too, to Yasuo Takebe and Junzo Matoba, who helped me enormously in exploring the political roots of Shinzo Abe. Tomohiko Taniguchi, Hiroshi Suzuki and Noriyuki Shikata have been diligent and informative over the years. Takao Toshikawa, a man from whom Japan's politicians can keep few secrets, was always willing to share his hard-won knowledge. Kaoru Yosano, a former economics and fiscal policy minister, and Yuriko Koike, who became well known as environment minister, have always made time for me.

I am also especially indebted to Peter Pagnamenta, who kindly dispatched a box to Hong Kong containing a treasure trove of material from his wonderful BBC series on Japan's post-war rise, 'Nippon'. The fascinating interviews contained therein proved invaluable for my chapter 'The Magic Teapot'.

In Tokyo, I was blessed with many accomplices. David d'Heilly is a dear friend and as steeped in Japanese culture as a *daikon* radish in broth. He and his wife, Shizu Yuasa, helped me hugely with research and interpretation. Shizu found obscure and colourful historical snippets, including the origins of the 70,000 pines in Rikuzentakata that form the opening of this book.

I have also been blessed with other close friends, including Reiko Yamaguchi, who was bold enough to transform a chance encounter at a bus stop into a close and lasting friendship. Kazuto Iida has been a friend ever since he studied with my late father in London in the 1980s. Stephen and Kimiko Barber, frequent visitors to Tokyo, have provided warm words and stimulating conversation over many a fine meal. I'll never forgot one occasion when Stephen turned white as a ghost on seeing the bill.

To my editors at Penguin, Ann Godoff in the US and Simon Winder in the UK, thank you. This is my first book, and I'm sure at times it showed. Ann's forthright and insightful comments helped me tighten the structure and sharpen my thinking. Simon's close editing helped improve the writing. Above all, he instilled in me a confidence to carry on. Bela Cunha, my copy editor in London, caught several infelicities and helped me make sense of my endnotes. My agents, Felicity Bryan in London and Zoe Pagnamenta in New York, have provided valuable comments and cheered me on throughout.

None of what's here would have been possible without every one of the people mentioned above, and many more besides. While I would love to blame them for my errors and take any credit for myself, convention – and adherence to the truth – compel me to do the opposite. Whatever merit or wisdom is contained in these pages belongs to others. The faults are entirely of my own doing.

Finally, I must turn to my family. I'd like to express my deep gratitude to my mum, a source of inspiration, who selflessly supported me in the journalistic endeavours that have kept me so far from London for so long. Most of all, I would like to thank my wife, Ingrid, my most perceptive reader, my lifelong friend and the great love of my life, as well as my two wonderful (if ludicrously tall) boys, Dylan and Travis. All three set out with me on our Japanese adventure and all three have suffered my long hours and frequent absences. Along the way, we have grown up together. Without their love and support, none of this would have been possible.

# Index